T5-BAH-279

Liberalization in the Process of Economic Development

Liberalization in the Process of Economic Development

EDITED BY

Lawrence B. Krause
and Kim Kihwan

UNIVERSITY OF CALIFORNIA PRESS
Berkeley   Los Angeles   Oxford

338.9
L695

University of California Press
Berkeley and Los Angeles, California
University of California Press, Ltd.
Oxford, England
© 1991 by
The Regents of the University of California

Library of Congress Cataloging-in-Publication Data

Liberalization in the process of economic development / edited by
  Lawrence B. Krause and Kim Kihwan.
    p.   cm.
  Includes bibliographical references and index.
  ISBN 0-520-06357-0 (cloth)
  1. Economic policy.   2. Economic development.   I. Krause,
Lawrence B.   II. Kim, Kihwan.
HD87.L53   1991
338.9—dc20   90-41127
                                                                  CIP

Printed in the United States of America

1   2   3   4   5   6   7   8   9

The paper used in this publication meets the minimum requirements of American
National Standard for Information Sciences—Permanence of Paper for Printed Library
Materials, ANSI Z39.48-1984. ∞

In Memory of Kim Jae-Ik

UNIVERSITY LIBRARIES
CARNEGIE MELLON UNIVERSITY
PITTSBURGH, PA   15213-3890

CONTENTS

PREFACE

This book is dedicated to the memory of Kim Jae-Ik, a gifted economist and outstanding Korean policymaker who died at the age of forty-five in the Rangoon bombing incident of October 1983. In this tragic incident, seventeen of Korea's most able and talented policymakers lost their lives.

Kim Jae-Ik had a character and personality that left indelible impressions on all those who knew him. Some of us who had the privilege of knowing him decided to dedicate to his memory a book dealing with the subject to which he had devoted his most productive years, namely, economic development through liberalization.

All the authors in this volume knew Kim Jae-Ik personally and responded enthusiastically when asked to contribute. The truly outstanding quality of their work is a testimony to the deep admiration and affection they had for Kim Jae-Ik.

The editors would like to thank the individual scholars for their excellent contributions. They would also like to thank the Brookings Institution for allowing one of the editors to spend time there while working on this volume. Furthermore, their special thanks go to Elizabeth Phillips for her most able assistance throughout the project and to Richard Rice, who did a wonderful job typing the manuscript.

Lawrence B. Krause
Kim Kihwan

KIM JAE-IK: HIS LIFE AND CONTRIBUTIONS

Kim Kihwan

Until his tragic death in Burma in 1983, Kim Jae-Ik was one of Korea's most gifted economists and a highly influential policymaker. Few were as dedicated to the cause of economic growth and development, and fewer still had as great an impact on Korea's economic policymaking. He played a key role in steering the Korean economy out of crisis in the early 1980s and was one of the chief architects of the liberal economic reforms launched in Korea.

The youngest of nine children, Kim Jae-Ik was born on November 26, 1938, into a family that owned substantial tracts of land in South Chung-chong Province. He finished primary school in Seoul and went on to Kyonggi Middle School. During the Korean War his family's fortunes were reversed, and as a consequence the family suffered hardship and deprivation. Not only was his father killed, but three of his older brothers—one a young instructor at Seoul National University and the other two university students—disappeared during the war, presumably taken by North Korean troops. The destruction of his family relationship had a determining impact on his life. Responsible for his mother's welfare, Kim Jae-Ik took various part-time jobs to support his mother and put himself through school.

In spite of these hardships, he managed to do well academically. He passed a high school equivalency test in his junior year at Kyonggi High and went on to take the college entrance exam that earned him a place at Seoul National University, where he majored in international relations. Although it had only fifteen members, Seoul National's international relations class of 1960 boasted an extraordinary crop of students, including Suh Suk Joon, deputy prime minister and minister of economic planning, and Lee Kee Wook, vice minister of finance, both of whom were also killed in Rangoon. In addition to this network of friends, Kim Jae-Ik met another important person in his life at Seoul National University: the former Lee Soon Ja, a bright, energetic, and attractive French literature major, who later became his wife. They seemed a perfectly suited couple; he was reserved while she was outgoing. They were married in 1961.

Although Kim Jae-Ik wanted to pursue graduate studies after college, financial need forced him to take a job. After graduating from Seoul National in spring 1960, he joined the research department of the Bank of Korea, the nation's central bank. While holding a full-time job there, he continued his studies as a part-time graduate student at Seoul National University and received his master's degree in international relations in 1964. An opportunity to do graduate work on a full-time basis came in 1966, when the East-West Center in Hawaii awarded him a scholarship in its master's program in economics. Two years later, with master's degree in hand, he enrolled at Stanford and earned his master's degree in statistics in 1972 and his Ph.D. in economics the following year.

While at Stanford, Kim Jae-Ik renewed his acquaintance with an individual who would have a major influence on his later career: Professor Nam Duck-Woo of Sogang University, who at the time was taking his sabbatical at Stanford. Nam had been among the first Koreans to receive a doctorate in economics in the United States, and he played a pioneering role in introducing modern economics into the university curriculum in Korea. Kim Jae-Ik had already met Nam in his Bank of Korea days, when he assisted him on a research project dealing with Korean monetary policy.

After finishing at Stanford, Kim Jae-Ik received several job offers from international organizations and universities in the United States, but decided to return to Korea in the early fall of 1973 and serve his country.

KOREA'S ECONOMIC POLICY SHIFT IN THE 1970S

In the early 1960s, when Kim Jae-Ik was beginning his career at the Bank of Korea, the Korean economy succeeded in its first economic take-off. This was in large part owing to the adoption of an outward-looking development strategy that enabled the country to make good use of its comparative advantage in labor-intensive manufactured exports.[1] Thanks to this strategy, Korea's real GNP grew at an annual rate of 9 percent from 1962 to 1971. Despite such remarkable success, the Korean government was making a policy shift toward import substitution in the early 1970s.[2]

Why such a shift occurred can best be understood in terms of the basic changes in the external and internal environment that Korea faced at that time.[3] In 1971 the United States reduced its ground troop strength in Korea by a third. The Korean government saw this as the first step toward the eventual withdrawal of all U.S. troops from Korea. It was also around this time that Korea began to encounter growing protectionist barriers against its labor-intensive manufactured exports. What's more, the worldwide commodity boom of 1972–73 greatly inflated Korea's agricultural import prices, thereby putting great pressure on its balance of payments. In addition, the growing gap between rural and urban incomes, a consequence of rapid industrialization in the late 1960s, was becoming an important political and social problem.

In order to deal with these challenges, the government adopted a policy of accelerating the development of the heavy and chemical industries and achieving greater self-sufficiency in agricultural production. To accelerate the development of the so-called "strategic" industries, such as steel, shipbuilding, automobiles, machinery, and petrochemicals, the government extended low-interest loans and preferential tax treatment to these industries.

There is little question that these policy measures brought about an accelerated development of the heavy and chemical industries, but they did so at great cost to the country. The cheap credit and preferential tax treatment extended to strategic industries brought about inflation by stimulating growth in money supply. Furthermore, they gave rise to a serious structural imbalance in the economy. While the heavy and chemical industries suffered from excess capacity owing to overinvestment, the light industries suffered underinvestment because they were starved of funds. Because the light industries still accounted for the bulk of Korea's exports, this structural imbalance resulted in a decline in the

1. For a fuller description and analysis of the policy changes taken during this period, see Frank, Kim, and Westphal 1975, 197–200, and Hasan 1976, 54–78, 93–94. See also chap. 7, sec. 3.

2. The economic policies of this period were import-substitution policies in that domestic production replaced capital and intermediate goods that had previously been imported. For a description of these policies, see chap. 7, sec. 4.

3. For a fuller analysis of the changes in Korea's external and internal environment, see Kim Kihwan 1985, 9–11.

overall competitiveness of Korea's exports. With sluggish growth in exports came a slowing down of the nation's economic growth.

The policy of accelerating the development of the heavy and chemical industries also caused a setback in the remarkable gains in income distribution made in the 1960s. Investment in these capital-intensive industries failed to generate sufficient new employment opportunities. Furthermore, the rapid development of these industries increased the demand for skilled workers at the expense of unskilled workers, thereby driving a wedge between the wages of skilled and unskilled workers. In addition, the prices of ordinary consumer goods, on which lower-income households spent a larger proportion of their income than upper-income households, rose much faster than the overall rate of inflation.

Government efforts to achieve self-sufficiency in agricultural products, particularly in staple grains, also created problems. To be sure, the price support programs adopted to achieve self-sufficiency brought about impressive gains in yield per acre as well as in farm incomes. But in operating the program, the government incurred large budget deficits, which added to inflationary pressures. By encouraging the production of grains at a time when demand was shifting to nongrain products, the program also contributed to a rise in overall food prices.[4]

AT THE ECONOMIC PLANNING BOARD

It was precisely in solving these problems of inflation, structural imbalance, loss of export competitiveness, slowdown in economic growth, and deterioration in income distribution that Kim Jae-Ik was to make his major contributions to Korea's economic policy later on. However, at the time he returned to Korea, he could not have foreseen these problems.

The first three years after his return to Korea were a period of reorientation for Kim Jae-Ik rather than of direct involvement in policymaking. Upon returning to the Bank of Korea, he was asked on a loan-basis to serve as an economic policy analyst in the Office of the President, commonly referred to as the Blue House. In 1974 Nam Duck-Woo, with whom Kim Jae-Ik had spent so much time at Stanford, was appointed deputy prime minister and minister of economic planning. Upon assuming this position, Nam asked Kim Jae-Ik to join the Economic Planning Board (EPB).

4. See ibid., 11–15, for a fuller analysis of the effects of Korea's economic policies in the 1970s.

Established in 1961, the EPB has the responsibility of formulating the nation's economic plans and the government budget. The head of the EPB also holds the title of deputy prime minister and serves as the nation's top economic policymaker. The EPB thus coordinates and controls conflicts among the economics ministries and generally has the last word on economic policy.

Because Korea's civil servants are normally selected on the basis of a formal examination, Nam arranged for Kim Jae-Ik to enter government service through special provisions, sparingly applied, that permit non-careerists of exceptional ability to enter government service in mid career. After a year as chief secretary to Deputy Prime Minister Nam, Kim Jae-Ik was appointed deputy director general of economic planning.

In 1976 Kim Jae-Ik was promoted to the position of director general of economic planning. In this capacity, his job was basically overseeing the implementation of the policies designed to accelerate the development of the heavy and chemical industries. He soon became acutely aware of the many problems that have already been noted. Yet he was not in a position to do much about these problems, because during this period a great deal of the advice coming out of the EPB was being overruled by policymakers in the Blue House who were bent on accelerating the development of Korea's heavy and chemical industries, regardless of cost.

Nevertheless, Kim Jae-Ik managed to carry out two reforms of major significance during these years. In 1974 he made a study trip to Taiwan; where he found the electronic digital telephone switch system to be far more efficient than Korea's mechanical switching system. He felt that in the long run Korea would benefit greatly from an electronic switching system and strongly recommended its introduction. In doing so, he encountered serious opposition to a policy change for the first time in his government career. In opposing the shift to an electronic system, the local manufacturers of telecommunications equipment went so far as to question Kim Jae-Ik's personal integrity. Nevertheless, the change was made in 1980, which not only improved telephone service throughout the country but also provided Korea with an updated communications infrastructure and technology that has been vital in maintaining its competitiveness in the international markets.

The other major contribution was in public finance. In 1977 Kim persuaded Deputy Prime Minister Nam to introduce a value-added tax (VAT) in Korea. The VAT proved to be a highly productive source of revenue compared to the eight special excise taxes it replaced, such as the business activity tax, petroleum products tax, and the textile products tax. By 1979 the VAT became the largest single source of government revenue, accounting for some 25 percent of the total. Being a universal and uniform tax, the VAT does not distort resource allocation. In spite of these merits, however, this new tax met with tremendous resistance from the general public, particularly from retail merchants, who prior to this change had tended to underreport earnings.

THE 1980 ECONOMIC CRISIS

Despite the many problems caused by the shift to an import-substitution strategy in the early 1970s, fundamental changes in policy direction were not forthcoming until 1979. Toward the end of 1978, however, a cabinet reshuffle took place, providing an opportunity for Korea's policymakers to bring a new approach to tackling the nation's economic problems. In early 1979 the new deputy prime minister, Shin Hyon Hwak, asked Kim Jae-Ik and his bureau to formulate a comprehensive stabilization program that aimed at nothing less than restructuring the entire economy so as to enable the country to make full use of its potential for continued high growth.[5]

The stabilization program had four major components. To reduce excessive liquidity, the government set lower targets for growth in money supply and formulated reforms for the financial sector. To correct imbalances in the industrial sector, the government temporarily suspended all new projects in the heavy and chemical industries and made more credit available to the light manufacturing industries. The government also lifted price controls on many items in order to correct price distortions. Finally, the government took the first major steps toward liberalizing imports.

This stabilization program enjoyed some success. For example, the relaxation of price controls did lead to the normalization of prices by the end of 1979, and it put an end to artificial shortages of basic commodities caused by price controls and the practice of "dual pricing." On the whole, however, the effectiveness of the 1979 stabilization was limited by a number of external and domestic shocks. The second major oil shock

5. The best summaries in English of the objectives, rationale and contents of the policy measures taken in the stabilization program can be found in the speeches by Shin Hyon Hwack, then deputy prime minister and minister of economic planning, and by Kang Kyong Shik, then assistant minister of economic planning, both given to the Tenth Annual Meeting of the International Economic Consultative Group for Korea, June 20, 1979, Paris.

came only three months after the program was launched, and Korea's oil import bill nearly doubled in the following twelve months. The resulting strain on the nation's balance of payments made it impossible for Korean policymakers to continue with their import liberalization program. Furthermore, the worldwide recession brought about by the oil shock considerably reduced the growth of Korea's exports.

On the domestic front the assassination of President Park Chung Hee in October 1979 threw the country into political confusion. By the spring of 1980 this confusion had turned into a full-blown crisis. Violent student demonstrations and strikes by the labor unions were the order of the day. Under these conditions employers gave in easily to demands for excessively large wage hikes, and they had little reason to invest, given the great political uncertainty of the nation. To make things worse, an unusually cold, damp summer led to a disastrous harvest that year, agricultural production dropping by no less than 22 percent. As a result of these unfavorable developments, the Korean economy suffered negative growth for the first time in two decades, contracting by 5.2 percent, while inflation soared to 29 percent in consumer prices and 39 percent in wholesale prices. Korea's current account deficit ballooned to over $5.3 billion.

In May 1980, a new de facto government emerged in the form of the National Emergency Council headed by General Chun Doo Hwan. In order to meet the crisis head-on, the council brought in Kim Jae-Ik and a number of his like-minded colleagues, who were eager not only to propose measures to pull the economy out of crisis, but also suggest wide-ranging reforms to restore to the economy its rich growth potential. In July 1980 Kim Jae-Ik was appointed chairman of the Committee on Economic and Scientific Affairs of the National Emergency Council. In this capacity Kim Jae-Ik's responsibilities were twofold: to deal with urgent day-to-day economic management problems and to prepare an agenda for reform. He and his staff worked feverishly throughout the summer. Upon the inauguration of the new government of President Chun Doo Hwan in September 1980, Kim Jae-Ik was appointed senior secretary to the president for economic affairs. He served in this post until he died in Rangoon on October 9, 1983.

It was as the president's senior economic advisor that Kim Jae-Ik had the greatest influence on the nation's economic policy direction. The senior secretary to the president for economic affairs wields much more power and influence than the title may imply, because he is in constant contact with the president. Owing to this proximity to the president, the senior secretary can and often does speak in the president's name and has considerable influence on appointments to high-level economic positions. Furthermore, although the deputy prime minister is Korea's highest economic policymaker, differences of views on economic policy occasionally arise at the cabinet level that even he cannot resolve. In such cases, the senior secretary often steps in to help resolve the conflicts.

ACHIEVING PRICE STABILITY

Soon after it was established, the new government launched wide-ranging economic policy reforms based on the agenda prepared by Kim Jae-Ik and his colleagues. The agenda highlighted three main objectives: achieving price stability, restoring growth, and improving the distribution of income.[6]

The policies for achieving price stability that Kim Jae-Ik and his colleagues formulated had in turn three major thrusts. The most important was to reduce the government deficit. In the Korean context, as long as the government had a deficit, the nation's central bank had no option but to finance it through money creation. For this reason, Kim Jae-Ik worked very hard to achieve a balanced budget for the entire government sector. The essential part of this effort was reducing the subsidies to public enterprises, as well as to a number of special accounts, such as the Grain Management Fund and the National Investment Fund. The most drastic step taken by the government to achieve a balanced budget was the 1983 decision to freeze total expenditure for the following year. As a result of these efforts, the total government deficit as a percentage of GNP fell from 4.7 percent in 1981 to 1.4 percent in 1984.

The second major thrust lay in tightening monetary policy. Not only was the targeted growth in money supply reduced, but the nominal interest rate on bank deposits was raised so as to make the real interest rate positive. As a result the annual growth in money supply, broadly defined, which stood at 26.9 percent in 1980, was brought down to 15.2 percent in 1983 and 7.7 percent in 1984.

The third major thrust was to restrain the growth in wages. The government first announced a small increase in wages for the public sector and then used this announcement to limit wage increases in the private

6. See Kim Jae-Ik 1983 for his views on price stability, continued economic growth, and improved distribution of income.

sector. The banks reinforced this policy by urging private firms to reduce their debt/equity ratios if they wanted to grant wage increases higher than the rise in productivity. In this way, the annual increase in money wages was reduced sharply from over 30 percent in the late 1970s to 11 percent by 1983 and to less than 9 percent in 1984.

A discussion of Kim Jae-Ik's efforts to bring inflation under control would not be complete without mention of the land registration system. A problem that continued to plague Korean policymakers in their fight against inflation was the rampant speculation in real estate, which not only fanned inflationary psychology but diverted savings to socially unproductive investment. What made curbing such speculation difficult was the lack of a timely record of who was buying and selling property; without such a record, individuals were free to speculate in as many property deals as they could afford. The opportunity to move decisively to curb this speculation came in the summer of 1983 on the heels of a scandal in which the Myung Sung business group was found to have illegally channeled bank funds into large-scale speculation in real estate. Riding on the public outcry that ensued, Kim Jae-Ik initiated work to establish a computerized system of land registration that would promptly record all real estate transactions.

PROMOTING GROWTH THROUGH STRUCTURAL REFORMS

Kim Jae-Ik and his colleagues in government felt very strongly that the best way for Korea to maintain its growth momentum would be by achieving greater efficiency in the allocation of resources through the market. To this end, they went about liberalizing external economic policies and promoting competition in every sector of the economy internally. The heart of the liberalization of the nation's external economic policies was a preannounced schedule whereby market-opening measures would be published well in advance in order to alert businesses to prepare for market opening and make necessary adjustments. In accordance with this approach, adopted in 1981, the Korean government steadily liberalized its import regime. As late as 1979, only 68 percent of all products were allowed to enter Korea without prior import licensing. Since that time, the import-liberalization ratio has continued to rise: the ratio, which stood at 76.6 percent in 1982, rose to 84.8 percent by 1984 and 91.5 percent by 1986, and by 1988 almost all industrial products entered Korea subject only to tariffs.[7] In addition to removing nontariff

7. For a discussion of the practical significance of these figures, see chap. 7, sec. 5.

barriers in this manner, the policy reformers sought not only to reduce the average tariff rate but also to narrow tariff differentials among different items.

In the months following the assassination of President Park, Kim Jae-Ik and his colleagues were very concerned about the possibility that foreign investors in Korea might pull out of the country owing to political uncertainty and the deteriorating investment climate. They were determined to take bold steps to liberalize policy on foreign investment in order to forestall this possibility. To this end, in September 1980 the government allowed foreign investors up to a 100 percent equity share in many industries, while for the time being maintaining existing tax incentives and other benefits for foreign investors.

Kim Jae-Ik was convinced that Korea could not become an industrially advanced nation unless it undertook fundamental reforms in the financial sector. Furthermore, he had the view that Korea should someday become a new financial center of Asia, in the manner of Singapore and Hong Kong. In 1980, with these objectives in mind, he played a key role in establishing two new commercial banks in joint ventures with foreign entities.

Kim Jae-Ik knew, of course, that the first essential step to liberalize the banking sector would be to denationalize Korea's major commercial banks. He had long been waiting for an opportunity to implement reform. The opportunity finally came in the summer of 1982, when the so-called curb market scandal rocked the very foundations of the nation's financial system.[8] Capitalizing on this crisis, he succeeded in persuading the top policymakers in government to relinquish government holdings in the country's major commercial banks during the following year.

A major step that Kim Jae-Ik and his colleagues took to promote competition throughout the economy was to enact a law prohibiting monopolistic practices and collusion among firms. Thanks in large measure to their efforts, such legislation was passed in 1981, and soon there-

8. The curb market scandal of 1982 basically involved huge loans extended by an individual named Chang Young-ja to a large number of Korean companies that were caught in a liquidity crisis. What made Chang's operation highly unusual was that she received from her borrowers as collateral a large quantity of short-term "accommodation" bills far in excess of the value of the loans. She used these bills to obtain additional funds by discounting them heavily in the short-term financial market. When the bills so transacted in the market were presented for payment, it was beyond the capacity of the original issuers and the banks that had endorsed them to make good, and thus the financial crisis ensued.

after the Fair Trade Commission was established within the Economic Planning Board to enforce it.

One of Kim Jae-Ik's priorities in achieving greater efficiency in investment allocation was to phase out the practice of extending preferential access to credit and favorable taxation policy to "strategic industries." This preferential treatment was gradually replaced by equal incentives for investment, technology development, and manpower training in all industries, thereby allowing all firms and industries to compete on their own merits.

Kim Jae-Ik also attempted major reforms in the area of taxation. In 1983 he and his colleagues in government proposed significantly to reduce the highest marginal rate on both corporate and personal income taxes. They did not succeed, however, in obtaining the reductions they had hoped for. The national legislature, overly concerned about the possible shortfall in revenue, made only a small downward adjustment: the highest marginal tax rate on corporate income was reduced from 38 to 30 percent and that on personal income from 65 to 55 percent.

Kim Jae-Ik placed great importance on the promotion of science and technology as the basis on which to sustain Korea's long-term economic growth and development. His efforts to promote science and technology included lobbying for greater budgetary allocations for research and development, expanding industrial extension services by organizations such as the Small-Medium Industry Advancement Corporation, and encouraging venture capital in Korea. In addition, he played a key role in launching the Science and Technology Promotion Council, a powerful body consisting of high-level government officials and business and academic leaders, which meets quarterly to review the nation's progress in the field of science and technology under the chairmanship of the nation's president.

IMPROVING INCOME DISTRIBUTION: MACRO-MICRO APPROACH

Kim Jae-Ik believed that any governmental efforts to improve income distribution should center around the expansion of employment opportunities through continued high growth with price stability. He reasoned that in a competitive economy, the expansion of employment opportunities with a low level of inflation is bound to bring about a steady increase in the real wages of workers and income.

Critical as these macroeconomic policy efforts were, Kim Jae-Ik believed that they should be supplemented with a number of microeconomic programs. In his thinking, the most crucial element in this approach was increasing access to education for all groups in society. He often cited the experience of many industrialized countries showing that enlarging educational opportunities is the surest way of guaranteeing equitable income distribution in the long run, while increasing the supply of skilled and technical manpower in the short run.

Because of this belief in the value of education, in 1978 Kim Jae-Ik spearheaded efforts to raise the ceiling on the number of students entering university each year. Thanks to this effort, university enrollment rose from some 330,000 in 1979 to 870,000 in 1984. In addition, he exerted all his influence to increase government expenditure on education and vocational training. In part owing to his efforts, public expenditure on education as a percentage of the total government budget rose from 17 percent in 1980 to 19 percent in 1984.

Another important element in the microeconomic approach to improving income distribution favored by Kim Jae-Ik was increasing the supply of housing units within the reach of low-income families. To this end, he succeeded in persuading the Seoul city government to develop a large tract of land where small, cheap housing units could be built. Kim Jae-Ik also believed that expanding public services and facilities would go a long way toward improving the welfare of low-income groups. For this reason, he was a strong advocate of expanding Seoul's subway system as well as of building more parks and recreational facilities in Seoul and other urban areas.

The approach to improving income distribution espoused by Kim Jae-Ik and his like-minded colleagues has apparently worked well. From 1980 to 1984 the percentage of national income held by the lower 40 percent of Korean households rose from 16.1 to 18.9 percent, while that accounted for by the upper 20 percent declined from 45.4 to 42.3 percent,[9] leading many foreign scholars and international organizations, including the World Bank, to point out that Korea's record with regard to income distribution is second only to that of Taiwan.

KIM JAE-IK THE POLICYMAKER

How was Kim Jae-Ik able to bring about so many economic policy reforms despite his relatively short career in government? The answer lies in his deep understanding of how government works and his outstanding personal qualities. The greatest obstacle to policy changes in any

9. See Suh 1985, 22.

country is the resistance change itself always encounters. The status quo has its defenders, especially among those who administer or benefit from existing regulations. Thus when an external event occurs that demands a policy response—a crisis of some sort—an opportunity is created to improve policy. Kim Jae-Ik understood this very well and capitalized upon such moments to promote policy changes that he had previously determined to be desirable. He also recognized that the public had to be willing to accept policy change. In order to increase public understanding of the merits of market-oriented solutions to economic and social problems, he organized many educational efforts in the form of public seminars, workshops, and television programs.

Kim Jae-Ik also had a remarkable combination of personal characteristics that made him effective in a governmental setting; he was an easy person to agree with. He was genuinely modest and soft-spoken, but that did not keep others from recognizing that he had a brilliant mind. He could persuasively and persistently argue for his positions. He knew how to marshal facts, figures, and logic for his case for the purpose of convincing others rather than overwhelming them.

Kim Jae-Ik was appreciated and trusted by his superiors and subordinates alike. He rarely claimed credit for his policy innovations. He enjoyed the full confidence and trust of even the highest public officials. He had a considerable case of workaholism, and he expected that of his staff; yet his enthusiasm for work was so infectious that subordinates became extremely loyal to him. He responded in kind by furthering their careers and promoting their welfare.

Finally, Kim Jae-Ik had deep philosophical convictions and a vision of the future of his country. He never doubted the superiority of the market over government fiat. To him, the market was not only more efficient in resource allocation but in the long run most conducive to the advancement of democracy. Furthermore, he believed that with liberal economic reforms and efficient management, Korea could one day emerge as a world-class industrial power. These beliefs and visions gave him tremendous strength and confidence. At all times he was serene, and to the end he was an optimist.

REFERENCES

Frank, Charles R., Jr., Kim Kwang-Suk, and Larry E. Westphal. 1975. *South Korea*. Vol. 7 of *Foreign Trade Regimes and Economic Development*. New York: National Bureau of Economic Research.

Hasan, Parvez. 1976. *Korea: Problems and Issues in a Rapidly Growing Economy.* Baltimore: Johns Hopkins University for the World Bank.

Kang Kyong Shik. 1979. "Korea's Recent Economic Policy Adjustments and Requirement for Foreign Capital." In *Report on the Tenth Annual Meeting of the International Economic Consultative Group for Korea.* In Korean. Seoul: Economic Planning Board.

Kim Jae-Ik. 1983. "The Korean Economy: Current Reforms and Future Prospects." Speech to the Annual Conference of the Hong Kong Management Association. Hong Kong, October 3.

Kim Kihwan. 1985. *The Korean Economy: Past Performance, Current Reforms, and Future Prospects.* Seoul: Korea Development Institute.

Korea, Republic of. Economic Planning Board. 1986. *The Sixth Five-Year Economic and Social Development Plan.* In Korean. Seoul: Economic Planning Board.

Shin Hyon Hwack. 1979. "New Challenges and Opportunities for the Korean Economy." In *Report on the Tenth Annual Meeting of the International Economic Consultative Group for Korea.* In Korean. Seoul: Economic Planning Board.

Suh Song-Mok. 1985. "Economic Growth and Change in Income Distribution: The Korean Case." Working Paper no. 8508. Seoul: Korean Development Institute.

Introduction

Lawrence B. Krause

The story of development is one that mixes economics and politics. Economic development so profoundly changes a society that political change must be involved on both sides of the equation—that is, as a cause of economic development and also as a result of it. Many economists and other social scientists thus view economic development as part of a process of overall modernization; some, however, argue that growth initiated and controlled from abroad does not lead to the modernization of a society. Such a case could exist in theory; in reality, however, whenever a country has managed to raise per capita income for an extended period of time, significant societal change has taken place.

No matter how abruptly change may occur, the evolution of a society reflects its previous history. Thus the story of development is different in every country. There are similarities among countries (the science of development is aimed at discerning these similarities), but unique elements always mark the development experience in a given country.

The story of development is also one of a swinging pendulum. Pressures force public policy in one direction to a point of exaggeration, followed by a reaction in the opposite direction. Upon achieving political independence, most developing countries found Adam Smith's invisible hand wanting and the lure of free markets not very appealing. Laissez-faire did not satisfy the desire of Third World governments to be active and do something to speed development.

In the early literature of economic development, economists viewed the state as a solitary, benevolent actor behaving solely in the societal interest. The state was seen as being able to obtain needed information, and then, with that knowledge and the policy instruments available to it, to intervene in an optimal way to correct any market failure and capture positive externalities. It would thereby in theory not only promote rapid development but also achieve distributive justice. With this in mind, policies were instituted to control the primary sector (mainly agriculture), to create and structure an industrial sector, to interfere with the trade and payments regime to provide needed incentives and distribute resources according to a plan, to constrain the labor market to make it conform to a desired wage structure, and to mold the capital market to allocate resources according to a distribution selected by policymakers.

However, the pendulum was pushed too far. The view of the state as a benevolent actor was dissipated by the reality of governmental actions that often did more harm than good. Government failure became more serious than market failure. Government bureaucrats were often forced to make business decisions with even less information than was available to the private sector. Politicians and bureaucrats turned out to be motivated by personal ambition and desires that did not necessarily lead to public good. And government power was manipulated by private agents to benefit particular groups, often at the expense of the general welfare. The policy of liberalization was devised to counter and correct these exaggerations.

Liberalization, by which we mean a policy shift toward market or marketlike devices, is a reaction to excessive intrusion of governments into national economies. The pressure to liberalize may arise because of widespread government failures (for example, it has been suggested that agricultural liberalization in China following the death of Mao grew out of a spectacular crop failure in the province of Anhui), or it may come from the fear of potential government failures in the future, despite generally good results in the past (such is reported to be the case in Singapore). If as economies grow and become more complex, the role of government remains large or even expands, then significant problems can be anticipated. Liberalization is a way of avoiding these problems, or at least of depoliticizing them.

Liberalization is itself a policy of government, and therefore the political setting in which it takes place must be part of the analysis. Rarely is the promise of significant economic gain sufficient to bring about a fundamental change of policy. Policy change occurs as a result of a crisis. If the status quo cannot be maintained, then change will be contemplated. If the situation is very difficult, then a change of policy direction has a chance of being considered.

What kind of government is best suited to bring about liberalization? The evidence is by no means clear on this issue. It has been noted that some of the most successful liberalization programs have been undertaken either by authoritarian governments or by ones whose quality of democracy falls far short of Western ideals. Some have even suggested that a regime that does not have to seek approval from an electorate has greater freedom to make difficult decisions and take actions involving short-term losses in order to obtain long-term benefits. Experience indicates, however, that many authoritarian regimes do not take liberalizing measures or introduce economic reforms of any sort. Indeed, some of the most market-distorting policies are followed by "populist" authoritarian governments in Latin America. Furthermore, under the right conditions, democratic governments can introduce liberalization—New Zealand is the most recent example. What appears to be the case is that in order to devise and make effective a program of liberalization, a government must be able to command a consensus within the society, and this can be achieved under several different political forms.

While a liberalization program may need a crisis to trigger it, not all crises lead to desirable policy adjustments—some just debilitate. The job of the analyst is to discern which elements promote effective policy adjustment and which simply retard it. This is a task that cannot be done by one academic discipline, but rather requires inputs from many branches of social science. One observation that seems to be a common feature of most crises is that a workable policy strategy for adjustment cannot be devised in the country after a crisis has begun, especially by the policymakers who are responsible for crisis management. Either the alternative policy direction must long have been under discussion within the country, or major elements in the plan must be suggested from the outside. Often both occur. Thus it is difficult for historians to unravel the story, to document the date when "reform" began, and to give proper identification to its origin.

LIBERALIZATION IN THE PROCESS OF ECONOMIC DEVELOPMENT

This volume systematically explores the theory and practice of liberalization as it has been applied in a number of developing countries. The experiences of the East Asian newly industrializing countries (NICs)—and especially South Korea—have been given the most attention, as is appropriate in a volume dedicated to the memory of Kim Jae-Ik.

The volume takes the perspective of economics, since all of the authors are professional economists. This means that it is economic issues that are selected for analysis and primarily economic forces and instruments that are turned to for explanations. While economics is tremendously important in studying the Asian NICs, it is not the whole story of modernization. Some fascinating political issues, including the role of the military, are obviously worthy of intensive study, but are not addressed here. For example why should a currency devaluation (just another price to an economist) initiate a military coup in Thailand? While intrigued by the question, we do not believe that we are properly prepared to find an answer. Economists believe in comparative advantage, and we have limited ourselves to our expertise. Obviously not everything can be done in one volume. We leave it to our colleagues in political science to answer these questions.

Industrial Development and Liberalization

In chapter 1, Anne O. Krueger describes a simple model of economic development that captures the essence of countries that, like the Asian NICs, have a high ratio of labor to land (natural resources). Traditional trade theory suggests that such countries have a comparative advantage in labor-intensive industries. The model traces an efficient development path whereby the country is transformed from one producing primarily agricultural products and providing a meager standard of living to one specializing in the production of industrial goods.

The model has two sectors, agriculture and industry, many commodities, and three factors of production—land, which is utilized only in agriculture; capital, which is employed only in industry; and labor, which is employed in both sectors. As capital is accumulated and devoted to its most profit-maximizing use (labor-intensive products), labor is rapidly drawn away from agriculture. The process continues until full employment is reached and labor productivity rises in agriculture. By now the country has not only replaced imports of labor-intensive goods, but is also exporting them. When the point of full employment is reached, wages are driven up, and capital will be diverted to more capital-intensive industries. The process continues as capital is accumulated, with production becoming more capital-intensive and comparative advantage shifting in that direction as well. If capital accumulation is faster in the country than in other industrial countries, it will begin to catch up with them both in the product composition of its production and exports and in its standard of living.

If the government should interfere with this process and distort the goods, labor, and/or capital market, then the capital/output ratio will rise prematurely and economic growth will suffer. Experience suggests that the most distorting interference comes in the trade and payments regime, especially if the exchange rate is kept in an overvalued disequilibrium. Liberalization reverses these distortions. While theory has little to say concerning many questions surrounding liberalization, experience has shown that liberalization of the trade regime and correction of an over valued exchange rate can have surprisingly good economic results.

Toward a Model of Development

In chapter 2, Gustav Ranis adds political elements to the theorizing concerning the development process and thereby supplements the Krueger model. He also shifts the emphasis from the accumulation of capital (in the Krueger model) to capturing and utilizing science and technology in its manifold applications. As a result, an underlying question is posed: What accounts for the relatively greater success of East Asian NICs such as Taiwan and South Korea when compared to Latin American countries such as Colombia and Mexico?

The Ranis model identifies the crucial points in the evolutionary process of development where governmental policies can be particularly important in determining subsequent outcomes. Though four stages of growth are identified (S_0-S_3), the model does not depend upon the stages following one another in a mechanistic way. The model suggests that six instruments of policy are of particular importance in setting the policy framework: the interest rate, the growth of the money supply, the foreign exchange rate, levels of tariffs and other trade barriers, tax and subsidy rates, and the wage rate. Typical profiles are drawn of the use of these instruments in each substage.

A significant difference exists between the initial (predevelopment, or S_0) conditions in typical East Asian NICs and the Latin American LDCs (less developed countries). The East Asian NICs (and Japan) all had heavy population pressure relative to usable land, a relatively small size, a good human-resource base, and a shortage of natural resources. They are termed natural-resource-poor (NRP). The Latin American LDCs, by comparison, are natural-resource-rich (NRR). In terms of economic structure and the like, the NRP and NRR countries are similar at point S_0, in that most production is of primary products, though the NRR achieve a higher standard of living out of it.

Transition growth begins in S_1 as both groups start to import capital goods in order to produce consumer goods, rather than just importing the final manufactured goods. To encourage this shift, governments employ various protective devices designed to create incentives to support a new industrial class. Human resources are developed during this subphase to make factory workers productive and to train entrepreneurs. While protective trade policies lead to windfall profits and create many inefficiencies in the industrial sector, the traditional primary producing sector is discriminated against during this subphase. At this point, both the NRP and the NRR follow essentially the same policies, but in practice the East Asian countries neglected agriculture somewhat less and maintained somewhat lower levels of protection than did the Latin American countries. Subphase one comes to an end when domestic production more or less completely replaces imports of manufactured consumer products.

The policy choice made at the beginning of S_2 is critical for subsequent development. Essentially, the choice is between promoting secondary import substitution, that is, replacing imported capital or producer goods with domestic production (usually done by NRR), and promoting the export of domestically manufactured consumer products (generally the route of NRP). This latter choice is called primary export substitution, since previously exported primary products are now replaced by consumer manufactures. Primary export substitution was chosen by the East Asian NICs—in the early 1960s in Taiwan and Korea—and exports as a share of gross domestic product increased dramatically.

The package of policy instruments used to promote primary export substitution generally includes monetary and fiscal measures to reduce inflation and provide resources to the government through explicit taxation, the reduction of protection, the adoption of a more realistic exchange rate, and the avoidance of both artificial increases in industrial wages and depression of the internal terms of trade for agriculturalists. These policies may be supplemented by export-promoting measures such as the creation of export-processing zones and rebates of import tariffs on exports. This can be considered the start of liberalization.

For the NRP the beginning of S_3 is marked by the sustained rise of the wage rate of unskilled workers, signifying full utilization of the labor force. (During the previous subphase there is an accelerated shift of labor from agriculture to nonagricultural employment, and underemployment is reduced on a massive scale.) In order to stay competitive, producers shift to more skilled labor and technologically intensive products and methods of production. The output from this upscaled manufacturing sector is simultaneously sold in the domestic market and exported. Typically food and other natural resources are imported in increasing amounts as economic growth outpaces the limited natural-resource base. Taiwan and Korea entered this phase between the mid and late 1970s.

The NRR countries, having chosen secondary import substitution at the end of S_1, remain on a different and less successful path of development than the NRP. It may well be that the existence of the natural resources themselves is the most influential factor in determining this outcome. The purpose of S_1 is to create profits in industry and revenues for the government at the expense of agriculture and the primary exporting sector. If the sector being squeezed is rich, then the process can continue for quite some time. Clearly the existence or absence of natural-resource rents is critical in the linkages between politicoeconomic developments and the policy outcomes they generate. It would appear that the more resources there are to waste, the longer the wastage will go on.

Public Finance for Developing Countries
In chapter 3, Assar Lindbeck traces the evolution of thinking about the budget in market-oriented developing countries. Originally considered just the main tool for mobilizing and allocating resources, the budget has become an instrument for promoting efficiency in the economy. Earlier policy thinking was defective mainly because it failed to take into account the nature of the political system and the administrative capabilities of the bureaucracy of the country for which it was designed. Successful policy may be less dependent on theoretical sophistication than on effective and honest implementation.

The government, through its budget expenditure, has to achieve certain tasks that it alone is qualified to perform. These include supplying public (collective) goods such as the legal system and protection of the environment and making infrastructural investment in human and physical capital. Furthermore, the government may want to help develop market-oriented institutions and should utilize policy instruments that are market conforming. In order to make these policies successful, macroeconomic stabilization must also be achieved.

Compared to industrial countries, the level of tax revenues in developing countries is generally low to moderate. However, serious problems exist in tax collection, which may reflect the difficulty of dealing with many small firms, the lack of administrative capability on the part of tax collectors, and possibly a low level of country identification and loyalty. Thus, as massive cheating may be taking place, improving tax collection may be the most productive form of tax reform.

However, questions do also arise concerning tax structure. While theoretical advances have been made in describing an optimal tax, they provide little guidance for policy in a real world setting. Rather, developing countries are well advised to stick to a simple, nondistorting structure of taxes (a uniform commodity tax is a good base), which may include an income tax, tariffs, and some subsidies. The less selective the tax, the less will be the political lobbying and corruption.

The process of liberalization will change public finances, but the net effect is ambiguous. While collection of tariff revenues may be reduced, expenditures on subsidies and the like will also be less. The transition to a fully liberalized system merits careful attention.

Attention is also given to the issue of equity in the economy, as the budget is often used as an instrument of income redistribution. While greater income equality (particularly raising the status of the poorest members of society) is recognized as an appropriate goal of policy, great caution is counseled. The best approach to income equality may be through additional increases in economic efficiency—especially if it includes the reaching of full employment, an outward-oriented industrial policy, and geographic dispersion of economic activity.

The Role of Medium-Term Plans in Development

Over the years, "plans" have become standard fare in developing (and many industrial) countries. In chapter 4, Chen Sun recognizes that since all of the major factors determining development can be subjected to government policy, they can therefore be included in government planning and incorporated into a comprehensive development plan. Development plans are of various lengths and kinds, but generally include a survey of current economic conditions, a statement of proposed government expenditures, a forecast of likely developments in the private sector, some macroeconomic projections, and a review of government policy. The objectives of planning are to encourage fast economic growth both in the aggregate and on a per capita basis, high utilization of the labor force, stable prices, improved income distribution, and a manageable balance-of-payments position. While these objectives are laudable, a question remains as to whether development planning promotes them or not—especially since some of the objectives are in conflict with each other. In the main, analysts are skeptical of the efficacy of comprehensive development planning, and planning advocates have generally been disappointed in their accomplishments. Whether the unsatisfactory outcomes are the result of poor planning or bad execution is a matter of contention.

Planning to promote growth can attempt to increase either the labor force or labor productivity, or do a bit of both. In practice, while some attempts are made to mobilize the labor force, most effort is directed at improving labor productivity by promoting domestic savings (and thereby permitting more domestic investment), attracting foreign investment, increasing education, encouraging research and development expenditures, and improving sociocultural conditions in general.

In most developing countries the government takes a direct hand in increasing national savings. Unfortunately, these efforts have usually been disappointing, especially when the losses of state-owned enterprises are recognized. In general, less than 25 percent of government expenditures in LDCs (about 3 to 4 percent of GDP) have been for economic development—so the amount of savings being mobilized is rather small, even when the budget is balanced. Furthermore, high taxes may be counterproductive for savings of the private sector, and moreover, the lack of technical progress in many LDCs because of a lack of incentive depresses both domestic savings and domestic investment. In recognition of this, less attention is now being given to just increasing investment as a route to faster growth.

One critical question that governments must face is how to allocate investment between social infrastructure (with long-term benefits) and productive investment (with immediate returns). In the earlier stages of development, the government may use direct methods to make this allocation; however, after some liberalization occurs, more indirect methods are used in order to gain some guidance from the market.

Because education is critical for improving labor productivity, but the lead times are quite long, much attention in development planning is addressed to it. Again, the allocative decision as between general and vocational education, and broad-based knowledge and higher technical skills, is very difficult to make, but a necessary part of development planning.

Further trade-offs may appear between such things as stability and equity or stability and growth. The choice appears in this form because when resources are not available for implementing development plans, the temptation is to go forward anyway, knowing that inflation is likely to result. Some of the disappointment in development planning is certainly the result of plans implemented without adequate resources.

Ironically, development planning grew out of Keynesian economics, with its emphasis on demand management. Successful development planning, however, occurs only when supply capability is enhanced. Thus true development planning can only occur with a medium-term time horizon.

Adjustment to External Shocks

In chapter 5, Parvez Hasan examines the experiences of developing countries in response to external shocks—both positive and negative. During the 1970s and early 1980s, the world economy was marked by numerous sudden changes: the end of the Bretton Woods monetary system, oil price increases and decreases, rises and falls of real interest rates, and significant fluctuations in the prices of raw materials. An external change (such as a change in terms of trade, losses or openings of markets, immigration of workers, or a financial disturbance) can be considered a shock if it is long-lasting (that is, not reversed within a year or two) and large relative to both GNP and export earnings.

Following a major shock, there is often a second shock, which may either offset or reinforce the first one. For example, after the first oil shock in 1973–74, an offsetting shock occurred for oil-importing developing countries—negative real interest rates were made available on international borrowings, opportunities were created for workers to go abroad and earn large incomes in OPEC countries, and concessionary assistance was increased. After the second oil shock in 1979–80, however, the secondary shock was reinforcing—real interest rates rose sharply, a deep worldwide recession occurred, and credit availability from foreign banks dried up. These secondary shocks make measuring shocks quite difficult.

In order to overcome a negative external shock, a country must adjust. It must reduce national expenditures to compensate for the loss of national income, and it must switch expenditures from foreign to domestic resources to correct the balance of payments. Given the need for time to bring about a proper adjustment, foreign borrowing is an option that can be usefully employed, provided that a country has not already used up its borrowing capacity. However, foreign borrowing should not be used merely to postpone adjustment and should be invested in assets that can provide a flow of goods and services that can service the foreign debt. A reasonable time horizon for adjusting to a true external shock might be from five to seven years. During that time, a country must expand its capacity to export and its capacity to replace imports. It is likely that in order to do this, domestic prices relative to the rest of the world will have to be adjusted—probably through an exchange-rate devaluation—and domestic savings must be raised relative to domestic investment—probably through an improvement in the fiscal position of the government. Furthermore, an improvement in the allocation of investment resources is almost essential—that is, the incremental capital/output ratio and, if possible, import elasticity with respect to income should be reduced.

A review of ten oil-importing developing countries (that is, countries that experienced negative oil shocks) for the period 1974–84 indicates a wide variety of experiences: great difficulties were encountered, and among the most seriously affected countries only Korea managed to sustain overall economic growth rates close to previous levels while avoiding a major debt problem. Five of the ten countries failed to make an adjustment during this period, with Turkey only turning around (but then with a vengeance) in 1980.

Five oil-exporting countries that experienced positive shocks in the 1974–84 period are also examined in chapter 5. A positive shock increases both resource availability and borrowing capacity. Whether the positive shocks of the period gave lasting help on balance to these countries is an open question; they clearly had a downside to them. In most countries, waste increased, corruption flourished, and consumption expanded tremendously. Several went into excessive foreign debt. In fact, only Indonesia avoided a serious debt problem. The contrast between Indonesia and Egypt is marked, with Indonesia performing much better, even in the execution of similar types of programs. The better Indonesian experience seems to be the result of better use of pricing signals (the exchange rate was kept closer to equilibrium and domestic pricing of energy was more realistic), lower public sector subsidies, larger government savings, and a quicker response to the reversal of oil prices.

A number of lessons can be deduced from these experiences, not the least of which is that a shift from an inward- to an outward-oriented approach is robust strategy, regardless of whether a country is subject to positive or negative shocks. Second, the ability to adjust to external shocks depends primarily on the quality of macroeconomic management—relying on market signals, selectivity in public sector intervention, fiscal discipline, and quick reaction, as well as maintaining an outward orientation—all seem to be important. Third, it appears that countries should put more emphasis on the quality of their investments rather than just concentrating on increasing the quantity. Fourth, a country's ability to adjust to a shock seems to bear little relationship to the size of the shock. Fifth, preexisting external debts are a major constraint to adjustment, and extreme swings in the real interest rate make adjustment quite difficult. Sixth, a negative shock can be a blessing in disguise if, as in the case of Turkey, adjustments that have long been required are finally made politically feasible. Finally, shocks by their very nature cannot be predicted, but the uncertainty created by external shocks can be better managed if countries treat shocks symmetrically, rather than assuming that positive shocks will last forever and negative shocks will quickly be reversed.

Export Liberalization

In chapter 6, Juergen Donges and Ulrich Hiemenz analyze the theory of export liberalization and the adoption of an outward-oriented trade regime; they also examine the experience of countries attempting the transformation. Arguments against adopting an outward orientation include concerns over excessively high adjustment costs in countries that have long had import-substitution (IS) policies, fear of social upheavals in response to the necessary adjustments, and a belief that foreign-exchange shortages will necessarily occur, forcing a reversal of liberalization, and a return to IS.

A distinction needs to be drawn between activist governments that choose to intervene intensively in their economies and governments that distort prices through IS policies. Many governments give up IS and become outward-oriented, but remain interventionists. To make interventionism compatible with outward orientation, incentives to industrialize and the like must be consistent with an optimal allocation of resources—that is, relative prices must not be distorted. Export incentives should be no greater than necessary to offset export discrimination, and no sectoral preferences should be introduced. While it is possible to promote exports beyond what would occur in a distortion-free environment, the danger from this distortion is much greater in an IS regime, where budget constraint, which often limits export subsidies, is lacking.

The way to adopt an outward orientation is to expose the domestic economy to international competition for the purpose of improving allocative efficiency, capturing economies of scale, managing risk through export diversification, and accelerating technological innovation and the formation of human capital. Two tasks that need to be undertaken are the substitution of price signals for administrative controls and the adjustment of domestic relative prices so that they conform to relative prices internationally.

The need and desire for outward orientation grows out of the inadequacies of the IS regime. Even protective tariffs of the infant industry type disadvantage the unprotected sector, including export industries. Efforts to avoid and evade restrictions force governments increasingly to use more distorting devices. When easy IS is completed, the economy is saddled with a complex network of controls. Balance-of-payments difficulties, resulting in part from overvalued exchange rates, bring pressures for capital controls and foreign borrowing. The extension of controls to the capital market is most serious, since an efficient capital market is essential in order for resources to be allocated properly. Often these controls lead to an excessive use of capital (too little use of labor), especially if real wages themselves are elevated by artificial means.

When there are multiple distortions in an economy, theory demands liberalization in all major markets. Theory would also suggest that the liberalization be instantaneous in every market. In the absence of constraints, abrupt liberalization would be best, since it would cause a rapid adjustment, could be in place before political opposition was mobilized against it, and would reduce uncertainty (inasmuch as the policy would become credible quite rapidly).

Unfortunately, concerns over adjustment costs and political disruption may make this unfeasible. The first tasks therefore are to remove the obstacles to export expansion that result from trade policies and to effect a real devaluation of the currency. Since there are risks and unknowns in export expansion, greater reliance should be placed on import liberalization rather than on export subsidies. Also, a rational exchange-rate policy may require frequent changes, which because of their impact on domestic prices will require strict stabilization policies. This will be made easier if the capital market is deregulated so that funds can be properly allocated to promote sectoral shifts of resources.

Many analysts (including some other authors in this volume) prefer to delay capital market liberalization. The case can be made, however, that the difficulties some countries encountered in liberalizing capital markets were the result of inconsistent domestic policies rather than of liberalization per se.

What keeps liberalization from occurring is often not a lack of knowledge of what to do but an absence of political will to do it. Liberalization redistributes benefits from import-competing industries, organized labor, and the government bureaucracy in favor of consumers, unorganized labor, export industries, and agriculture. The potential losers may well have more political power than the potential gainers, and the change is thus likely to be thwarted.

The evidence indicates that countries that chose outward orientation during the 1960s and 1970s have performed spectacularly well. Their exports grew twice as fast as world trade, and that growth can be attributed to trade and trade-related policies. Exports have been the major force promoting growth in these countries and have also led directly to creation of employment. There have been two generations of outward-oriented NICs, and the threat of the markets of developed countries becoming clogged, thus inhibiting latecomers, has not materialized. The fear of a glut in markets results from a fallacy of composition, in that demand as well as supply is created. Indeed, trade among NICs themselves provides an expanding market opportunity. However, as growth is a supply phenomenon, there must be world demand for the products of the NICs in order for the outward-oriented strategy to work. Fear of protectionism is thus well-founded.

Import Restriction and Liberalization

In chapter 7 Wontack Hong uses the experience of Korea to examine import restraints and their liberalization in the context of an economy that is promoting exports. Economic theory strongly supports the proposition that as restrictive devices, quotas are much worse than tariffs, and, moreover, that rather than using tariffs, governments should use general taxes and subsidies to achieve desired goals. Nevertheless, developing countries invariably enforce trade restrictions, and usually use import quotas quite extensively. Why the disparity between theory and reality? Apparently domestic political forces that benefit from protection cannot be constrained during the process of development, and policymakers remain convinced that infant industry protection is superior to other devices for promoting development and maximizing foreign sales from existing export industries.

The analytical framework designed to examine import restraints recognizes that an export-promotion regime is superior to a generalized import-substitution regime because it promotes the upgrading of human resources and production technology, is better at achieving economies of scale, is less likely to be abused because of external pressures, is better at relieving foreign-exchange constraints, and captures the static efficiency gain of larger trade and the induced growth benefit from larger savings propensities. However, given that import restraints are inevitable, serious welfare loss will be avoided if the biases created in favor of certain products and industries conform to a country's comparative advantage.

The use of tariffs puts a country in a second-best world, but if policies are adopted that offset the distortions created, little efficiency loss need occur. However, offsetting policies will be required as long as the tariffs are maintained—even as growth raises the production possibility frontier. Protection of a monopolistic export industry may even increase the share of exports out of total sales by permitting the firm to practice price discrimination, but at the expense of the welfare of domestic consumers.

If, however, policies (such as allocating credit to industries in which there is no comparative advantage) reinforce the distortion of protective tariffs, significant costs will be incurred, and an immiserizing structural adjustment will result.

Korea in the 1950s had a heavy bias toward import substitution and badly distorted markets. In 1961 a multifaceted program to move the country toward export promotion was begun. Since import protection is equivalent to a tax on exports, it was clear that export promotion could not be launched while maintaining drastic import restrictions. Thus a tariff exemption was given to products used in export production and the general level of quantitative restrictions was lifted. A real and symbolic change occurred when the system was altered from one in which it was presumed that an import was not allowed unless specifically approved to one in which it was presumed that an import was allowed unless expressly prohibited.

Between 1967 and 1978 very little progress was made in liberalizing Korea's import restrictions. However, during this period remarkable progress was made in expanding exports, because the surviving import restrictions were maintained in such a way as not to inhibit exports. Korea shifted from being a tiny exporter of primary goods to being a significant exporter of manufactured consumer goods, and the growth of the Korean economy was phenomenal. Even though there had only been a minimum degree of import liberalization, the export-promotion measures more than offset the import-substitution bias. Indeed, tariff protection may even have promoted growth, since tariff receipts made up 40 percent of government revenue, and a growing government surplus was important for increasing the national savings rate.

Beginning in the mid 1970s, Korea began to promote domestic production of intermediate and investment goods, not only for the purpose of being self-sufficient, but also to create new export industries. As part of the effort, imports of competing goods were newly restricted—even when they were to go into export production. By the end of the 1970s, Korea's export basket had shifted considerably to include heavy and chemical industry products, and imports of such products were sharply reduced (as a share of total imports). As this was done at a time when Korea had no comparative advantage in such products, however, the cost was considerable. It led to very high capital intensity in production of both exports and import-replacements, greatly raising total production costs. As a result, the growth rate of exports declined and the rate of growth of the entire economy also ebbed.

By 1978 it was recognized that extensive import liberalization was necessary to improve efficiency. A small effort was mounted in that year, but the bureaucracy remained very skeptical. The only products to be covered were ones not currently produced in Korea and for which no plans existed to start domestic production. This effort was halted by the economic difficulties of 1980, restarted in 1981, turned off again in 1982 in the face of a deteriorating balance-of-payments position, and finally started again in 1983—this time with a firm schedule that looked forward to complete liberalization. As theory suggested, quotas were removed first, even if it required a temporary increase in tariffs to ease the adjustment.

From the perspective of political economy, it might be concluded that since consumers have little organized political muscle, the products of direct importance to them are likely to be highly protected in the early stages of development, at significant expense to their welfare. In later stages of development, however, a large number of intermediate and investment goods producers emerge. They sell substantial portions of their products to domestic industries. These buyers, or so-called end-users, are better organized than consumers in general to mobilize a concerted effort against the protection accorded to the producers of intermediate and investment goods. Domination by sellers and uncontested protection rents tend to disappear in these sectors, since there finally exists an equally powerful group who stand to benefit by eliminating import restrictions. Then the chances of liberalizing consumer products improve, as the interests of the newer producers are aligned with those of consumers. In fact, in Korea consumer items were among the first to be liberalized and consumer welfare was quickly improved. Subsequently liberalization has gone forward on schedule.

It appears that when industries are promoted for the purpose of exporting, the harmful effects of protecting other import-competing industries are eliminated with the passage of time. However, if import-substituting industries are the focus of promotion, significant costs occur and can rise over time. Also, although comprehensive import liberalization is not a condition for high-growth performance in the initial stages of development, it becomes necessary in the later stages of growth.

Agriculture in the Liberalization Process

In chapter 8, D. Gale Johnson discusses the special case of agriculture. To be effective, liberalization of agriculture must include permitting market forces to determine how agricultural products are produced, as well as how they are traded at the border. Significantly, governments distort agricultural prices to force them below world levels as well as to raise them above those levels. It is the poorest countries that tend to force farm prices down, thinking that it will help the industrial sector, but thereby failing to capture some of agriculture's important contributions to the development process. As countries become richer, the share of agriculture in the economy declines, setting the stage for import protection.

While agriculture has always been treated differently from manufactured goods, the rationale for, and desirability of, agricultural free trade is in fact no different. Nevertheless, agricultural protectionism has had a long history. Before 1940 import restrictions were generally low to moderate, except in Japan, where rice was heavily protected even in the 1920s and 1930s. Since the formation of the European Community (EC), however, agricultural protection has been rising in Europe and also sharply in Japan and Korea.

Statistical analysis suggests that protection against agricultural imports is likely to be higher the greater a country's per capita income, the fewer its exports of agricultural products, and the smaller agriculture's share in the economy is. These findings support a political explanation for protection pursued by organized pressure groups.

Concern for food security is often presented as a rationale for agricultural protectionism, and it is apparently widely accepted in Japan. However, it is clearly a self-serving argument pushed by those wanting high levels of protection, who exaggerate concerns over possible supply interruptions. Self-sufficiency in food production does not provide food security if the inputs into the food production process must be imported, as is the case in Japan.

There has been little success in liberalizing trade in agricultural products because the United States undermined such efforts in the General Agreement on Tariffs and Trade (GATT) in the 1950s and the European Community has been staunchly opposed since then. However because of the escalating costs of agricultural programs for both the EC and the United States, and the recognition of their failure in supporting farm incomes, there is more hope for the Uruguay round of GATT negotiations in the 1980s.

Liberalization of agricultural products is unlikely to really hurt the income level of farm families (except during a transition period) because farm incomes are determined by the educational level of rural peoples, the per capita income levels outside agriculture, and the accessibility of rural people to nonfarm employment. If agriculture were liberalized, world prices would tend to rise, helping agricultural producers, and there would also be significant efficiency gains from reallocating resources in the EC, Japan, and also Korea, where per capita income could rise by at least 7 percent.

Financial Repression and Liberalization

In chapter 9, Yung Chul Park tackles the difficult subject of liberalization of domestic financial markets. From almost all perspectives, financial liberalization is more difficult and more complex than trade liberalization, and in fact all efforts in developing countries to achieve comprehensive financial liberalization have failed. Whether the failures have been owing to inherent incompatibilities, external events, inappropriate macroeconomic policies, or inauspicious original conditions cannot be sorted out. Any of the above would be sufficient to cause failure. Chapter 9, however, is devoted primarily to examining the intriguing question of whether there are inherent incompatibilities, and if so, how they might be approached and understood.

At the outset it must be recognized that banks are different from other businesses. Society has a strong interest in having a well-working payments system and in sustaining confidence in its money. Since banks create money as well as being intermediate between savers and borrowers, they are agents of society—that is, the financial system has characteristics of a public good. In recognition of this, governments have provided deposit insurance and lender-of-last-resort facilities for commercial banks. Given the existence of these government guarantees, the market will not judge the soundness of banks based on the banks' own behavior, and knowing this, bank management may not behave in a responsible manner. In other words, a classic moral hazard problem is necessarily created, which even in the best of circumstances will require extensive government regulation.

In developing countries the banking system is usually the only available capital market—indeed the absence of a nonbank capital market is, by definition, underdevelopment. Thus, banks perform the critical function of allocating resources among industries. Governments simply will not leave this critical function to the market—which they often distrust in general. Thus the government may choose to run the banks themselves, control bank management, or insist on loan allocation according to policy design, or all of the above. Though regulation is greater in LDCs, even in developed countries banks are heavily regulated.

Just because the government must be involved in bank regulation is no guarantee that it will do it well; indeed, all too often it is done badly. Interest-rate ceilings are usually enforced—often below inflation rates. Consequently, obtaining a bank loan constitutes a windfall, excess demand is created, favoritism and corruption flourish, and the financial system is repressed. Existing banks are protected from new entrants, both domestic and foreign. Private savers and unfavored borrowers are forced into an unofficial, or kerb, market at sharply higher interest rates, carrying huge risks, and efficient capital allocation is lost. If financial repression can be corrected, there are significant gains to be made. Thus there is reason enough to desire financial liberalization.

History demonstrates that a well-working financial system can make a major contribution to economic development, and that economic growth can help improve financial institutions. Recognition of this in developed countries has spurred financial deregulation there, and this has helped sustain financial liberalization in LDCs.

Monetary reform can be considered the first stage of financial liberalization and is often very successful in promoting development. It involves the curtailing of excess creation of money, establishing positive real rates of interest (especially to borrowers), and cracking down on some of the abuses in the allocation of bank credit. Monetary reform can be very successful in promoting development, as it has been in countries such as Korea.

The next step to complete financial liberalization has never been successfully mastered in developing countries, with the failures in the
Southern Cone of Latin America being the most notable. There, financial liberalization complicated macroeconomic management by creating
incentives for destabilizing behavior, failed to mobilize savings despite
high real interest rates to depositors, did not lead to the establishment
of a competitive structure in financial markets, did not produce efficiency gains as credit allocation was distorted, and acted to dry up long-
term finance.

Failure in finance has at times brought down the entire liberalization
effort. It is now conventional wisdom that undisciplined financial liberalization will not succeed. Analysis indicates that the moral hazard problem is an insuperable barrier to complete financial liberalization, particularly in the absence of stringent prudential regulation. Banks will
take excessive risks, and then try to manage nonperforming loans by of-
fering ever-higher real interest rates to depositors in a desperate attempt to stay afloat. Such a race necessarily ends in disaster. In this competition, the adventurous banker will drive out the responsible banker
and then bring down the system. Furthermore, if at the time of deregulation banks are saddled with a portfolio of nonperforming loans (as a
result of previous government policy lending), then they will begin in a
weak profit position, and this will encourage speculative behavior from
the start. Also, close association between banks and large nonfinancial
business groups is difficult, if not impossible, to prevent, since it is only
in such groups (or individuals behind such groups) that there exists a
large enough pool of investable assets to operate a bank. Consequently,
the temptation for self-dealing and other banking abuses is overwhelming. Finally, rapid deregulation does not provide enough time for bankers to adequately learn their trade. It appears that there is a cruel trade-
off between obtaining efficiency gains and safeguarding the safety and
integrity of the financial system.

Recognizing that at least some financial liberalization is desirable
along with liberalization in other markets, there are still questions about
the optimal path and phasing of the effort. Theory gives little guidance.
A case can be made for immediate and simultaneous liberalization, but
that appears neither feasible nor desirable because of externalities, market imperfections, and political constraints. Thus a stages approach to
both trade and financial liberalization is inevitable. To sustain credibility,
the liberalization effort needs to be preannounced and adhered to. It
would appear that current account liberalization (trade and nonfinan-

cial services) should precede liberalization of capital flows, since asset markets adjust faster than commodity markets and commodities therefore need a head start. Current account liberalization should also precede domestic financial liberalization. Actually some liberalization should begin simultaneously on all fronts, but they may proceed at different speeds. Of course, there is a dilemma in dealing with the second best, in that we can never be completely sure that welfare is promoted by removing one distortion while others are preserved. It may be that some things must be taken on faith or no change is possible.

Certain reform proposals do seem to follow from the analysis. First, safeguards need to be instituted to prevent close linkages from being formed between large financial intermediaries and large nonfinancial business groups. Second, it is wise to try to separate the monetary and intermediary functions of banks, possibly by creating several categories of deposit liabilities, each with different reserve requirements. Finally, it is desirable to develop nonbank financial intermediaries less subject to stringent government control.

Monetary Stabilization in LDCs

In chapter 10, Ronald I. McKinnon takes up the issue of stabilization in relation to liberalization and then draws some implications concerning the desirability of international capital flows during the process of liberalization. Like Park in chapter 9, he draws lessons from both Chile and Korea.

It is clear that without stabilization, liberalization cannot succeed. In the absence of stabilization, inflation rates will be both high and variable, and this uncertainty will translate into real interest-rate and exchange-rate uncertainty and undermine the possibility of a successful trade and/or domestic financial liberalization. Thus stabilization may be a prerequisite for liberalization, or at a minimum require simultaneous accomplishment. Complicating the task of stabilization and liberalization is the fact that in trying to cope with inflation uncertainty several critical prices in the economy may have been indexed to actual inflation experience.

The first element in stabilization is correction of the government's fiscal imbalance, because inflationary monetary growth cannot be curtailed without doing so. After this is accomplished, real interest rates can be made positive for depositors, borrowers, and financial intermediaries. Financial repression can be ended and liberalization of trade and finance begun.

A crucial decision must, however, be made as to where to set the real interest rate. In Korea the real interest rate was pegged below the market clearing rate, and credit allocation was required. This choice runs the risks of impropriety and of inefficiency in the allocation of credit. Alternatively, if the real interest rate is permitted to rise high enough to clear the market, as was done in Chile, several difficulties may follow. The economy may be faced with adverse risk selection and improper risktaking by the banking system. Furthermore, excessively large flows of capital may be attracted from abroad, which could lead to the appreciation of the currency or loss of monetary control and ultimately a rekindling of inflation. Both of these problems are worsened by the moral hazards resulting from guarantees by both domestic and foreign governments.

Overborrowing from abroad by countries during or following successful stabilization and liberalization programs is a result in part of a market imperfection. International banks, following herdlike instincts, rush to add new foreign assets to their portfolios without properly evaluating the risks. Regulatory restrictions on international lending by commercial banks plus elimination of government guarantees could solve this problem and permit the re-creation of an international market for long-term debt and equity paper of developing countries.

CROSS-CUTTING ISSUES

Several of the themes in this book appear in more than one chapter and in different contexts and various perspectives. In order to gain greater insight, four of them have been selected for further discussion. The first arises from the attempt to design a blueprint for liberalization that has some hope for success. This requires the intermingling of the substance of a liberalization program with the tactics of how to bring it about. If it is to occur at all, the decision to liberalize is likely to be made in the midst of a crisis. At first glance this seems peculiar, as it raises two related dilemmas: a crisis requires immediate action, but the benefits of liberalization occur only in the medium and long run; similarly, a crisis generally grows out of a problem of demand management, but the solution liberalization offers is improved supply capability. The resolving of these dilemmas may possibly be found in the discussion in chapter 10 of a stabilization program. A stabilization program is directed at demand management, and the results may occur immediately. Stabilization alone often appears as "all pain, no gain," but if it is presented as the first step in a larger program of liberalization, a light is kindled at the end of the tunnel, and the whole effort can be made more politically appealing. The threat of the crisis can be used to form a political consensus between groups who find their position being undermined and those dissatisfied with the previous distribution of benefits.

The second issue relates to the allocative decisions that must be made in the process of liberalization and that often arise in the context of development planning. Despite the fact that liberalization itself is designed to let the market do more of the allocating, certain allocative decisions will still be required of the government because they involve things the state has a comparative advantage in supplying (such as education). The policymakers in a liberalized regime must be able to interpret market signals in order to guide their decisions. For example, if a country is soon to enter a phase of development beyond producing and exporting labor-intensive manufactured products (subphase three in chapter 2), human capital must be developed in time to be available when needed. Unfortunately, the market is notoriously poor in providing signals for its needs more than five years in the future. This is where policymakers can turn to the experiences of other countries for guidance. While industrial history does not exactly repeat itself, examination of other more advanced countries can give useful hints. This was the approach of MITI in Japan and of MTI in Korea—both with good results. Comprehensive economic planning may be neither possible nor desirable, but some systematic thought about the future is essential.

The third issue concerns the timing and phasing of a liberalization program and leads to several different views in this volume. Theory can provide some insight, but not an answer to the twin questions of what to do first and how fast to do it. The arguments for a comprehensive and an immediate liberalization program are mainly found in chapter 6, where Donges and Hiemenz contend that the only real assurance that a liberalization program will be welfare-promoting is to remove all distortions completely and simultaneously; the credibility of a program (which is essential for its success) is only assured when everything is in place, for only then are the politicians fully committed to it. These writers further argue that the length of time needed for the economy to adjust to the program is minimized, and the likelihood of consistent policies is maximized, if all elements in the liberalization program are present.

The arguments for a phased and gradual program rest on both theoretical and practical considerations, and seem to be supported by actual experience. The adjustment costs involved in a program of liberalization can be huge, and a society's tolerance can be overwhelmed if too much is attempted at one time. (How much educational reform will French students accept in one gulp?) If the program is phased in on an anticipated schedule, then adjustment costs can be reduced and disruption contained.

Most authors agree that trade liberalization should come before financial liberalization. However, since monetary reform is part of stabilization policy, and stabilization policy should be the first step toward liberalization, it can be argued that trade and financial liberalization should be started together, but at different speeds. Theory does recognize that different markets adjust at different speeds and that asset markets adjust much faster than commodity markets, so that there is justification for placing trade liberalization on a faster track than financial liberalization. It is also probably true that financial managers have a great deal to unlearn about how to operate profitably under liberalization (even partial liberalization), since it is so different from accepted behavior under government control. It may take some time for bankers to learn how to be responsible. Nonfinancial firms must also adjust, but this merely involves paying more attention to business, and less to rent-seeking—which is an easier adjustment.

Within trade liberalization, there is little theoretical guidance as to what should come first, the export or the import side. The important requirement is to get relative prices set correctly, and this might require simultaneous liberalization. However, the Korean experience suggests that import liberalization can lag behind export promotion quite considerably without excessive costs, though there are dangers involved. Eventually external pressures will appear to force the pace of import liberalization if it is seen as lagging too far behind export promotion. For some countries external pressures for liberalization may be highly desirable as a way to keep the process going, but for others they may be counterproductive. To avoid the latter case, a country is well advised to have an announced (and adhered to) program for import liberalization that will satisfy its trading partners.

Within financial liberalization, the argument has been made, domestic financial markets should be liberalized before international capital flows. This is the experience of Chile as interpreted in chapter 10. A theoretical argument can also be constructed in support of this proposition by noting the disproportionate size of investable assets in the world at large as compared to a single country, and the difficulty of getting efficient price-clearing when institutions change in such circumstances. However, a counterargument can be made that as long as markets are separated artificially, an incentive remains to circumvent the restrictions, which will drain energies and misdirect resources. Given the history of the Southern Cone of Latin America, however, it is likely to be some time before a developing country tries anything other than a step-by-step, gradual liberalization of financial markets.

The final issue that needs to be discussed concerns the dependence that a country develops on the rest of the world as a result of liberalization. Of course, dependence is just interdependence viewed from one side, but when a country is small, it is understandable that it should feel unable to influence the actions of others, but be concerned about being influenced by them.

The first question a country must ask itself is whether the risk of exposure is worth taking. The answer, from analysis and experience, is overwhelmingly yes. De-linking is immensely expensive, unnecessary, and probably impossible. The next question, in abstract terms, is how a country can take out insurance against an external disturbance when no company or market exists to write such a policy. The solution to this problem is risk management. This can partly be done through diversification (by both product and market), and also by improving adjustment capability (reducing the time needed to recognize a new situation and then to react to it). Finally, a country should make use of any external leverage that it may have, make alliances with other like-minded countries, and work within the international community to keep disturbances from occurring. Experience has clearly shown that those countries operating in an outward fashion have coped better than inward-oriented countries in times of external shock.

CONCLUSIONS

At the beginning of this introduction, it was recognized that development is the story of a swinging pendulum. Is it possible that the pendulum could swing too far toward liberalization? The question is worth asking, even if only hypothetically. The pendulum will have swung too far if, in the atmosphere in which they must operate, free markets do not provide the best signal for adjustment within a country.

If, for instance, the international trade regime were characterized by mercantilism on the part of all major players, then a pure free-market approach might not be desirable for any country. To maintain its bargaining position in such a situation, the government would have to accept the necessary role of moderating market outcomes. In the field of finance, if the market is unable or unwilling to properly evaluate financial intermediaries, there will be an important role for stringent prudential regulations by government. Finally, the pendulum will have swung too far with respect to certain markets if enterprises become too large to be controlled by the market, or distort other (such as financial) markets. Then again the government will be called upon to moderate the situation for the good of society. The implication of all this is that liberalization does not mean that there is no role for government. Rather, it implies that the role of government should conform to both the circumstances within the country and the existing external environment.

ONE

Industrial Development and Liberalization

Anne O. Krueger

In the past four decades analysts have learned a great deal about the development process, not just from theoretical models but also from the experience of developing countries as they have sought more rapid growth and higher living standards for their people. Among these experiences, none has contained more lessons than that of Korea.

Until the dramatic turnaround in Korean policies starting in the early 1960s, few believed that sustained real growth rates of 10 percent or more were attainable. Fewer still believed that a poor developing country, with about 88 percent of its exports in primary commodities, could within a short period of time become a competitive force to be reckoned with by producers in developed countries. And it was entirely unthinkable that Korea might ultimately even challenge Japan.

A number of factors joined to bring about the dramatic Korean transformation. Analysts may disagree on the relative importance and contribution of some of these factors, but all observers would agree that the wisdom, judgment, and pragmatism (not to mention the willingness to contemplate and implement bold strategies) of Korean policymakers was an essential ingredient without which the miracle could not have been achieved. Kim Jae-Ik was one of the foremost of these policymakers. It is to honor his memory that this chapter is therefore devoted to an effort to place the Korean experience with industrialization and liberalization in analytical context, and to attempt to synthesize some of the lessons of that experience that are relevant for other countries.

I am indebted to Larry Krause and Nam Chong Hyun for helpful comments on an earlier draft of this paper.

The first section of the chapter sets up a basic model of an efficient development path against which policy alternatives can be evaluated. The model, partly inspired by the Korean experience, was developed earlier (Krueger 1977) and is summarized here. The second section then examines how policies may affect growth, resource allocation, and the efficiency with which resources are used in light of the model. It identifies the types of policies that are likely to prove inimical to sustained growth as well as the sorts of policies that are conducive to it according to the theory. A key question is how the shift from growth-inhibiting to growth-enhancing policies can best be accomplished. Much of the process of shifting is, in fact, the process of liberalization, and theory cannot provide much of a guide to it. The reasons for this, and the Korean experience, are the subject of section 3. A fourth and final section then sets forth some hypotheses about the interaction between liberalization policies and industrial development in the course of economic growth.

1. THE DEVELOPMENT PROCESS

The basic model of the development process used here is a two-sector, multicommodity, three-factor model of an efficient development path. It combines the Lewis notion of development with a model of industrial development founded in traditional Heckscher-Ohlin trade theory. With Arthur Lewis (Lewis 1954), the process of efficient development is regarded as that of transforming the country's economic activity from being largely rural and agricultural to being largely industrial and more urban.[1] For ease of exposition, *agricultural* and *rural* are used synonymously throughout, as are *industrial* and *urban,* although in principle (and sometimes in practice) there is no reason why workers cannot change from working in agriculture to working in industry without moving to an urban area.

In this section, focus is on the way development would proceed with an efficient allocation of resources, which is assumed to take place. In

---

1. To assert that this transformation occurs in the development process does not imply anything about a causal mechanism or that development happens as industry grows. Indeed, for most now-developed countries, growth was spurred by rapidly rising productivity in agriculture that freed resources that could then be used elsewhere. Many policymakers in developing countries have learned to their sorrow that a stagnant agricultural economy is inconsistent with rapid growth of nonagricultural activity.

section 2, the model is used to investigate the effects of distortions, either policy-induced or exogenous. In an important sense, the removal of distortions is the process of liberalization.

For simplicity, output of the agricultural sector is assumed to be produced with labor and land.[2] Output of the industrial sector is produced with capital and labor. Thus, although there are three factors of production, capital and land are each specific to a particular sector and labor is the mobile factor of production.[3] All savings is allocated to capital accumulation, and labor is allocated between agricultural and industrial activities so as to equate the wage between the two sectors.[4]

There are any number, n, of possible industrial products, all of which are assumed to be tradable on world markets. Their relative border, or international, prices are therefore given through international trade. Because of this, all producers of tradables face perfectly elastic demand curves and there can be no monopoly profits.

In contrast to the assumption that there are many commodities produced by the industrial sector, agricultural output is assumed to consist of a single homogeneous commodity. When a high proportion of the total labor force is employed in agriculture, it follows that the economy-wide wage is effectively determined by the agricultural wage. At early stages of development, this is typically the case, and hence the economy-wide wage can be thought of as being initially determined in the agricultural sector.

Given international prices for industrial goods and the rural wage, the determination of what industrial commodities will be produced under an efficient allocation of resources is straightforward. Under the usual Heckscher-Ohlin assumptions (including constant returns to scale, diminishing marginal product of each factor, and so on) the many industries within the industrial sector can be uniquely ranked from

2. This assumption simplifies exposition and assists in understanding the essential features of the model. As will be seen when we discuss the Korean experience, however, the fact that agriculture employs capital does not significantly alter the interpretation of the model. At the end of this section, the roles of factors not formally included in the model— human capital, entrepreneurship, and technology—are considered.

3. Jones (1971) developed the basic two-commodity, three-factor model of trade from which the present development model is derived.

4. It would not significantly affect the model if it required an urban wage higher than the rural (either by some multiple, m, greater than unity or by a constant amount) to induce labor to migrate. That would accord somewhat better with observed behavior and would also provide a "source" of growth additional to those contained in the model.

most to least labor-intensive. That is, the profit-maximizing or cost-minimizing labor-capital ratio in each industry can be ascertained and the ranking of industries by factor intensity will be the same for all wage-rental ratios.

Under these circumstances, where capital will earn the highest return will depend on the relative price of labor in the country: for the lowest-wage countries (presumably those with the lowest marginal productivity of labor in agriculture, which is the same thing as the highest man/land ratios if all land is of equal quality), at the early stages of development an efficient allocation of resources will imply that the country will produce the most labor-intensive industrial goods, using very labor-intensive methods.

As additional savings permits an expansion of the industrial sector, capital will continue to be allocated to the most labor-intensive industries, and labor will migrate from rural areas to work with the capital. Should the agricultural wage remain constant in the face of this migration (the pure Lewis case), factor-proportions in the industry will remain unchanged as the industry expands in proportion to the rate of increase of capital. If, however, outmigration from agriculture is rapid enough (and/or productivity increases in agriculture outstrip population growth) so that the rural wage rises, capital-intensity will increase in existing industries.

If the real wage keeps rising (at constant relative world prices), there will come a point where it will be economically efficient for the next more capital-intensive industries to begin operation and for the most labor-intensive industries to close down. In the simplest version of the model, there are thus two discrete stages of industrial development: a stage during which the country's manufactured output is specialized in the existing industry mix and, with capital accumulation, the industry expands, but possibly becomes more capital-intensive; and a stage at which the industrial composition of output is shifting toward more capital-intensive activities. During this stage, the real wage would remain constant and continuing capital accumulation would imply a Rybczynski-like shifting of resources toward the more capital-intensive industry and a contraction of the older, more labor-intensive industries. In reality, of course, the existence of sunk costs in existing factories and transport costs (so that c.i.f. and f.o.b. prices differ, thus conferring a margin of natural protection that permits some change in domestic price) implies that the process will not be as discontinuous as a strict interpretation of the model would suggest.

Among the properties of this model in its simplest form, two are of particular interest for interpreting Korean development. First, there may be large differences in initial conditions among developing countries. Some may be land-rich, and thus have relatively high wages and a comparative advantage in somewhat more capital-intensive goods even at early stages of development. Others, which are land-poor, may have very low wages for a considerable period of their development.[5] There may thus be rich developing countries (Argentina), poor developing countries (Korea in the 1950s), rich developed countries (the United States) and poor developed countries (Japan). To be sure, rich-poor and developed-developing are both continua, and any cut-off point between them would be somewhat arbitrary. Nonetheless, in this framework there are at least two dimensions to consider in assessing a country's development strategy.

Second, the model has some interesting implications for the evolution of the pattern of trade, especially for a country that embarks on rapid development from a highly labor-abundant initial situation, as did Korea. This may be regarded as the economics of catch-up, or of growth sufficiently more rapid than that of the rest of the world so that the country is "overtaking" countries initially higher up the capital-intensity scale. On one hand, any catching-up country will experience rising industrial and falling (because of assumed positive marginal product of labor with no technical change) agricultural output. Thus, such a country would gradually shift from being a net exporter of agricultural output to being a net importer. On the other hand, it should also be noted that the determination of which goods are produced within the industrial sector is independent of whether they are imported or exported. Indeed, in this model of development, one would expect that new industries as they developed would at first be import-substitutes, but as their output expanded they would become exportables, and then later contract yet again and become import-competing before their costs became so high as to make them uneconomic. Nonetheless the relative special-

5. If the model were amended to take into account the possibility of population growth, it is conceivable that in some countries population growth might be so rapid that the land/ labor ratio was declining and that comparative advantage was shifting toward more labor-intensive commodities. Such an outcome would, of course, imply falling real wages and would thus constitute negative development, or retrogression. A more plausible hypothesis emanating from the model is that countries experiencing rapid population growth will be likely to experience a much more gradual shift of comparative advantage, and a much slower rate of increase of real wages, than would countries with much lower rates of population growth.

ization implied by the model does suggest that countries will tend to be net exporters of a significant portion of their industrial outputs.

Further implications, especially with regard to the effects of policy-imposed distortions and the benefits of liberalization, can be drawn. Before turning to them, however, consideration should be given to some important factors omitted from the model. These are human capital, entrepreneurship, and technology.[6] Although their formal incorporation into the model is well beyond the scope of this chapter, each has been sufficiently important in development, and especially in the Korean experience, to merit attention as to how they relate to the model.

The importance of the accumulation of human capital is by now widely understood. It is clearly an essential and important component of the growth process. More highly educated and trained labor can be incorporated into development models in a variety of ways: one can regard more educated workers as representing more efficiency units of labor than do less educated workers; one can regard human capital as a separate factor of production; one can model human and physical capital formation as two alternative uses of savings with rates of return to each augmenting income streams of the capital owners (see Kenen 1965 for an interesting model of this type). The first view is readily incorporated into the model presented above: incomes would rise not only as workers moved to industrial activities and the real wage rose, but also because the effective supply of labor increased. In this view, the model's implications are entirely unchanged, although the rate at which a country might "catch up" might be slower the more rapid the rate of human capital accumulation.

The second interpretation would require adding a third factor of production to either or both of the two sectors. Incorporating human capital as a specific factor like physical capital used in industrial activities would not significantly alter the model unless some commodities were more intensive in the use of human capital per unit of output than were others. If, as seems plausible, this latter is the appropriate interpretation, the straightforward ranking of industries by labor intensity is no longer possible. While a more complex ranking can be technically derived, its intuitive interpretation is no longer as clear. Clearly, for labor-abundant, low-wage countries, one would anticipate that industrial expansion would occur first in industries that were unskilled labor-intensive relative to their use of either physical or human capital.

6. There are also some more "technical assumptions," such as the nonexistence of home goods, that can be relaxed. See Krueger 1977 for an exposition.

Based on the experience of rapidly developing countries, one might conjecture that "catch-up" would first proceed in the more physical-capital-intensive industries, leaving industries with high human-capital inputs to a later stage of development. But careful scrutiny of the results that might arise from formal derivation of such models of empirical analysis is beyond the scope of this essay. To ignore the role of human-capital formation in the formal model, however, should not be interpreted to imply that it is not important in the development process.

Consideration of entrepreneurship presents many of the same challenges as does human capital. If some activities are more entrepreneurially intensive than others, and entrepreneurship is another factor of production, any ranking of industries would entail the same difficulties as does human capital. Worse yet, consideration of how a "supply of entrepreneurship" changes over time would represent a formidable task. A more promising alternative appears to be to regard entrepreneurship as something needed in fixed amounts in each economic activity, with some participants in the labor force choosing to become entrepreneurs rather than workers. If entrepreneurial "experience" or "human capital" is gained on the job (perhaps as a function of prior education and training) then the supply of entrepreneurship would grow with development (both as more persons became entrepreneurs and as those involved in entrepreneurial activities gained experience).

If each activity has one "entrepreneur," whose function is to organize factors of production, deciding what to produce, how to produce it, and accepting risk, then analysis is somewhat more straightforward. As long as entrepreneurship is associated with each activity, the basic growth model sketched above is unaffected. If "more entrepreneurship," in either quantity or quality terms, is associated with capital-intensive activities than with labor-intensive ones, the "catch-up" process would have yet one more factor contributing to growth. In fact, entrepreneurship was very important in Korea. However, its role seems to have been largely in the liberalization process, as will be discussed below.

There is, finally, technology. In a formal sense, technical change can be represented in any model as an outward shift in the output possibilities attainable with given inputs. In fact, however, for most developing countries, technical know-how (perhaps not unlike complex machinery and equipment) cannot be acquired and profitably used without the education and training of enough members of the labor force to master it. In an important sense, therefore, the acquisition of technological know-how can be regarded as a form of physical capital formation, highly complementary to human capital formation.

2. RELEVANCE OF THE MODEL FOR ECONOMIC POLICY

As set forth, the model indicates the properties of an efficient resource allocation, but has no policy implication as to how that allocation might be achieved. In principle, it could be attained by central planning or by well-functioning markets. In practice, most developing countries have sizable private industrial sectors,[7] although many have also established a number of state-owned manufacturing enterprises. However as will be discussed in section 2.1, the activities undertaken by those enterprises bear no resemblance to the pattern of industrial activity suggested by the model.

2.1. Optimal and Actual Policy

To attain economically efficient resource allocation through private markets, optimal trade policy in the context of the model of section 1 would consist of a free-trade regime unless there were monopoly power in trade. This would permit relative prices in world markets to be reflected to domestic producers. If there were domestic market failures of any sort (see section 2.2 below), optimal policy would be to correct them at the source, by, for instance intervening in domestic markets. Since market failures typically occur when there are significant uncapturable externalities, public goods, or major indivisibilities or economies to scale, governmental economic policy would largely be addressed to correcting these, either by appropriate tax-subsidy policy or by direct provision of the externality-generating, large-scale, indivisible projects. These are usually collectively termed infrastructure, and efficient provision of those services—communications, transportation, etc.—is essential to economic growth.

Within the industrial sector, however, profit-maximizing firms would be expected to choose the appropriate mix of outputs when confronted with prices of tradables, labor, and capital services that appropriately reflected their opportunity costs (in terms of agricultural production for labor and of alternative industrial activities in the case of capital).

7. Almost all have predominantly private agricultural sectors; focus here is on the analysis of industrial liberalization and growth as it is relevant for understanding the Korean experience. In many countries today, agricultural liberalization may well be a necessary first step for development. See section 2.3.1.

Beyond this, the model offers little guidance as to what optimal economic policy should be, but provides considerable insight as to inappropriate policies. In practice, in the early years of conscious development effort after World War II, policymakers deliberately adopted policies designed to achieve results almost the opposite of those that would emanate from the two-sector, three-factor trade model developed in section 1. They typically used direct controls to influence resource allocation, especially among industrial activities, toward "import-substitution." Simultaneously, the relative prices—real exchange rates, exportables relative to importables, wage rates, and capital services—that confronted private producers systematically discriminated against exports.

Some government economic activities were the deliberate choice of policymakers. The establishment of state-owned enterprises (SOEs) to perform particular manufacturing functions, especially those regarded as capital-intensive and requiring large initial investments that the private sector was thought unwilling to undertake, was often one such deliberate choice. Often, these investments were defended on "infant industry" grounds, as it was initially believed that these industries would eventually become competitive.

As a logical corollary of these choices, curbs were placed on many aspects of private-sector activity: licensing of investments, required permissions for expansion, price controls where it was believed that there was monopoly power, and so on. These controls extended to agriculture via pricing policy intended to keep food cheap for urban workers and via government marketing agencies that had monopolies on the purchase of agricultural outputs and supplies of agricultural inputs. They also extended to labor markets, as minimum wage legislation, social insurance provisions, training and housing requirements for workers, and guarantees against layoffs all raised the cost of hiring labor. Likewise, the banking and financial system was heavily regulated, with the intent being to channel "low-cost credit" into those lines of economic activity deemed compatible with rapid growth. As a consequence, interest rates paid by those producers with access to credit were well below those reflecting the opportunity cost of capital, and were often negative in real terms. In most of these cases, motives for intervention centered on a belief in market failure. Establishment of SOEs was undertaken on infant industry or indivisibility grounds. Agricultural marketing boards were intended to prevent "monopolistic exploitation" of small peasants; labor markets were regulated in the belief that individual employers had considerable monopsony power with respect to their labor forces, and so on. Credit rationing was used to "direct" investment to those industries deemed to be "high priority" for development; they were usually capital-intensive, and often loss-making, despite high walls of protection through tariffs or quantitative restrictions.

There were many unanticipated consequences of these policies. Inflationary pressures were often considerably greater than expected; with domestic price levels rising more rapidly than international prices, governments adhered to fixed nominal exchange rates, which therefore represented increasing overvaluation in real terms. Reluctance to devalue was based partly on the notion that export earnings of developing countries could not grow ("elasticity pessimism") and partly on the idea that increasing the price of foreign exchange would make capital goods more expensive and thereby discourage investment.

Foreign-exchange earnings (which originated almost exclusively in nongovernmental activities) almost always fell short of expectations—usually growing less rapidly than national income, and often declining as real exchange rates appreciated. Demand for foreign exchange, associated with the heavy investment requirements of capital-intensive industries and with overvalued exchange rates, grew much more rapidly. Balance-of-payments crises were the almost universal consequence of these phenomena. Typical responses included "too little too late" devaluations, combined with stringent exchange controls and reliance upon import licensing to restrain demand for imports.

As is only too well known, the consequent impetus to "import substitution" went far beyond anything that might have been defended on infant industry grounds, or that might have been intended under the initial policy design. Policies were often internally conflicting, and results were often very different from, if not opposite to, those intended. Strict rationing of imports of intermediate goods and raw materials often gave domestic producers determinate output levels and shares of the domestic market. With import prohibitions prevailing—rationalized on the ground that domestic production already existed—foreign competition could not provide a spur, and capital/output ratios rose sharply. Economies that had initially been dependent on the international market for consumption and investment goods became instead dependent for employment and output, as factories could not produce the consumer and capital goods without imported raw materials and intermediate goods.

The disincentives for hiring labor associated with labor legislation and the relative cheapness of capital for those with access to it combined to yield powerful incentives for using capital-intensive techniques of production. Consequently, industrial employment grew much more slowly than industrial output, as much new investment was allocated to labor-saving, rather than output-expanding, investments. Moreover, this cost structure obscured the social profitability of producing more labor-intensive goods and thus contributed to a resource allocation very different from that suggested by the model of section 1.

Each of these policies had direct costs in terms of inefficiency and forgone growth, as will be discussed in greater detail in section 2.3. However, they also interacted in ways that magnified their impact—overvalued exchange rates further reduced returns to agricultural producers; their supply response further shrank export earnings and induced policymakers to further restrict imports on balance-of-payments grounds; that, in turn, provided yet further discrimination against agriculture, and so on.

The combined effect of these policy inefficiencies cumulated over time, and in country after country growth rates fell despite increases in savings rates. In early thinking about development, emphasis had been placed almost exclusively on resource accumulation as a means of attaining economic growth. A major lesson arising from experience with the types of policies described above has been that attaining economic efficiency is at least as important as resource accumulation. Moreover, economic inefficiency can result not only from "market failure," as was recognized earlier, but also from "government failure." The analysis of economic policy and liberalization in developing countries therefore has several parts. First, a framework is required for analysis of "market failure" and "government failure"; that is the topic of section 2.2. Next, there is analysis of how "government failure" may impede growth, the topic of section 2.3. Finally, there is analysis of the ways in which liberalization, or the removal of controls that inhibit economic activity, may affect growth, which is covered in section 2.4.

2.2. *Interactions of Policies and Growth*

For purposes of analyzing policy, it is useful to distinguish between policy impacts on resource accumulation and policy impacts on resource allocation—although clearly there are a large number of policies that affect both simultaneously. An efficient resource allocation is characterized by equalities between: (1) the domestic marginal rate of transformation (DMRT) and international marginal rate of transformation (IMRT) in production, (2) The DMRT and the domestic marginal rate of substitution (DMRS) in consumption, and (3) the marginal rate of substitution between factors of production in all uses. For resource accumulation, necessary conditions would include the real return to investment at least being reflected to savers.

Bhagwati (1971) classified departures from efficient markets (distortions) as being of two types: exogenous and policy-induced. For present purposes, exogenous distortions can be regarded as "market failures," while "policy-induced distortions" can be regarded as instances of "government failure." Distortions are defined as phenomena that result in failure of the optimality equalities to hold. Examples of government failure distortions would include the imposition of tariffs when a country has no monopoly power in trade (thereby breaking the equality between IMRT and DMRT), effective minimum wage legislation that results in a higher wage in the formal sector of the economy than in the informal (so that the marginal rate of substitution between labor and capital differs between the two sectors), and tax structures that drive a wedge between factor or goods payments as perceived by the two sides of the market, to name just a few.

Market failure distortions are those that are independent of policy. These might include the existence of externalities in production or consumption uncorrected by appropriate taxes or subsidies, monopoly power in trade (which is a case of externality as viewed from a national perspective) under a regime of free trade, economies to scale under laissez-faire, or the absence of well-functioning markets (as is often thought to be the case with financial markets or labor markets in developing countries).[8]

For purposes of analyzing policy, it is evident that there are four ways in which policy can affect growth, either positively or negatively. Positively, inherent market failures can be corrected so that either (1) resource allocation or (2) resource accumulation decisions more correctly reflect the relevant trade-offs. The converse would, of course, be if government intervention in fact moved the trade-offs as reflected

8. Interesting questions arise as to when an observed "exogenous" distortion is really a distortion and when the information costs of attaining an outcome that would clearly be superior under certainty become so high as to make the observed outcome optimal. One example arises in the literature on tenancy, sharecropping, and interconnected factor markets. It was long thought that tenancy and sharecropping clearly provided an inappropriate set of incentives for factor use. However, once it was recognized that the landlord could not monitor the effort of the tenant or sharecropper, it became evident that arrangements such as tenancy and sharecropping, with the landlord also becoming a moneylender, might well be optimal. See Bell and Srinivasan 1985.

to decision makers even further away from their true relations. Negatively, "government failure" can cause trade-offs as perceived by private agents to diverge from social opportunity costs between (3) present and future consumption (resource accumulation) and/or (4) production and consumption activities. The positive side of these policies would be liberalization of one or more markets.

Policies of the first type might include government introduction of agricultural research institutions, provision of mass vaccination programs, and provision of elementary education opportunities. To be sure, these activities could be so inefficiently undertaken as to yield a negative real rate of return, in which case the intervention would lead away from, rather than toward, an efficient allocation of resources. Generally, however, the evidence suggests that rates of return on these activities are high.

Many observers believe that financial markets are undeveloped in most developing countries and that the absence of appropriate financial instruments is a strong disincentive to additional savings. If this is so, an example of the second kind of positive government action would be policies designed to create a framework for more efficient financial intermediation. Creating a legal framework for financial markets, or otherwise encouraging their more efficient functioning, would then permit increased resource accumulation. There might, of course, be some degree of market failure, and yet the policies intended to remedy it (such as credit rationing) might lead to a worse outcome than the original market imperfection; this would be an instance of a negative government action of the second type.

The third kind of policy action would be of the opposite type: governmental regulations that provide a disincentive for savings, such as interest rate ceilings, are a good case in point. Savers confronted with low or negative real returns would save less, thereby reducing the rate of resource accumulation.

Policies of the fourth kind would include the imposition of tariffs or quotas on imports (in the absence of monopoly power in trade), minimum-wage legislation that resulted in substantial unemployment and induced firms to use more capital-intensive techniques and less labor than they otherwise would, and controls on producer prices of particular agricultural commodities.

Although each of the examples cited above would probably have its primary impact either on resource accumulation or on resource allocation, many policy-induced distortions directly affect both accumulation and utilization; policy changes that improve resource allocation, either by improving functioning of markets or by mitigating the impact of existing policies, probably also affect rates of resource accumulation. Thus, interest-rate ceilings probably affect not only the willingness of individuals to save, but also the behavior of financial intermediaries and borrowers: either financial intermediaries charge market rates of interest for their loans and reap rents that themselves become a source of distortions, as large numbers of those intermediaries compete for deposits, or ceilings are also imposed on interest rates that may be charged to borrowers with consequent misallocation of scarce resources. Moreover, insofar as economic efficiency increases, it is reflected in higher real rates of return to investment (and higher payments to other factors of production) and thus in higher growth.

2.3. Impact of Government Failures on Efficiency and Growth

As already mentioned, active government intervention was based largely on the belief that private market failure was all-pervasive. Once begun, however, there were a number of unintended policy outcomes, many of which led to further interventions. Often policies were far different than those that might originally have been anticipated. For example, "foreign-exchange shortage" led to import restrictions far more severe and protective than those envisaged under the aegis of infant industry protection.

Moreover, activist governments, and especially direct controls, led to the creation of many valuable property rights that were allocated by government officials. Import licenses, investment licenses, permissions to expand capacity, sales of commodities at controlled prices, subsidies on inputs such as fertilizer, and agricultural credit all were highly valuable to the recipient. Administration of these allocations was costly, both in terms of the drain on scarce administrative and bureaucratic talent, and in terms of the resources then devoted to attempting to capture licenses and permissions. Certainly, the implicit assumption underlying the rationale for government intervention in the case of market failure was that these interventions were costless. But, on the contrary, they were often very expensive.

Although governments have intervened and "failed" in many fields of economic activity—for example, energy pricing, transport charges, and pricing and delivery of communications—there are several broad areas in which intervention has had overriding macroeconomic effects on efficiency and growth. They are: agriculture, industry, the trade and payments regime, the labor market, and capital markets.[9] These are areas of intervention that have been most frequently encountered in developing countries, and that have had demonstrably harmful effects on growth rates in many instances. For present purposes, the discussion will be confined to the negative effects on growth and resource allocation of intervention in these five areas, in line with the model of growth presented in section 1.

2.3.1. Intervention in Agriculture.   A strict interpretation of the model presented in section 1 would suggest that the role of agriculture in growth is severalfold: (1) to generate savings enough to permit capital accumulation in the industrial sector; (2) to provide a highly elastic source of labor to the urban sector; and (3) although the model does not explicitly derive a trade balance, it is apparent that at early stages of growth, imports of manufactures would greatly exceed exports, and that these would be financed by exports of agricultural commodities. In the growth process, incomes accruing to those employed in agriculture would rise as the land/man ratio rose with outmigration, although in a more complete model of the agricultural sector, investment in agriculture, technical change, and other productivity-raising activities would also raise incomes.

In reality, of course, agricultural growth has yet other functions. It became well understood in the marketed-surplus discussion of the 1950s and the 1960s[10] that growth of agricultural output is a prerequisite for development at its early stages, and that policies that provide sufficient disincentives to agricultural production can effectively thwart growth prospects. In addition to the savings, labor supply, and foreign-exchange earning functions identified by the model, there are other reasons for this. First, such a very high fraction of population and output originate

9. There is another important area that is neglected here: that of provision of government services along the lines suggested at the beginning of this section. Infrastructure, health, education, research, communications, transport, and other services are usually government-provided and financed, and represent instances where market failure should be corrected. The unreliable delivery and high resource cost of some of these services, the pricing of their outputs and the techniques used for financing them are sources of inefficiency in some developing countries. Certainly in Korea efficient provision and expansion of these services have been very important in permitting rapid growth. The focus in this chapter is elsewhere, however, because the process of liberalization is essentially that of removing "government failure." It can be argued that one of the high costs of focusing on controls and regulation of private economic activity was the consequent diversion of efforts away from these essential governmental functions.

10. For a review of the literature, see Hayami and Ruttan, 1985, chap. 2.

in agriculture at the early stages of development that failure to generate any increase in agricultural output effectively implies no growth. Second, the model abstracts from population growth. The fact that in most developing countries populations are growing implies that diminishing marginal product will lower rural real wages in the absence of measures that raise agricultural output (either through increasing land use or by increasing yields).[11] As if these arguments were not enough, imagine that in one way or another, the industrial labor force could grow with stagnant or declining total agricultural output. Either exports would have to decline sharply with industrial growth, as urban demand for agricultural output rose, or prices of food would have to rise sharply. Neither of these outcomes would be compatible with long-term growth.

Finally, it is inconceivable that there could be sustained growth of the industrial labor force with declining food production at early stages of development; it has already been pointed out that agricultural products would be the exportables. With no increase in food production, and rising urban demand for food, the price of food and hence urban labor costs would surely rise, thereby choking off prospects of further industrial growth.

Some governments, usually weighing this last argument very heavily, attempted to contain industrial wage costs by legislating price controls on food commodities for urban areas.[12] Because the budgetary costs of financing these below-market prices would have been excessive, many countries instead followed policies of keeping producer prices low. Others, usually countries with specialized export crops, attempted to achieve the savings from agriculture by direct or indirect taxation (through agricultural marketing board policies and also through overvaluation of the exchange rate, which serves as an implicit tax on exports) of agricultural exports. In both instances, the result has been a shift by producers to noncontrolled (sometimes nonmarketed) crops. In extreme cases, exports and output of exportables have fallen sharply— Ghanaian cocoa may be the best known example.

It is a reasonable hypothesis that sufficient repression of the agricultural sector at early stages of development in effect foredooms any reasonably satisfactory development effort until policies toward that sector are reformed.

11. Because populations are growing, increases in agricultural output must be even more rapid if export earnings are to grow.
12. See chap. 8 below on the costs of these policies.

2.3.2. Distortions in Industry. As indicated earlier, the major stated rationales for direct intervention in the industrial sector (as contrasted with indirect intervention through the trade and payments regime, which is analyzed in section 2.2.3) were three, not necessarily consistent, beliefs: (1) the infant industry argument that some industries might prove economic in the longer run, but that owing to externalities, those incurring the initial high costs of production would be unable later to reap the returns, (2) a deep-seated suspicion of the monopoly position of private producers, and (3) the view that large-scale industrial ventures would not be undertaken by private entrepreneurs because the initial costs and risks would be too great to be acceptable. These second and third beliefs both focused on some aspects of entrepreneurship and implicitly implied that government entrepreneurship would function more efficiently than did private.

While market failure was also thought to occur because of indivisibilities and economies to scale, those phenomena presumably underlay one of the other three reasons for direct intervention.[13]

Here, attention is focused on the ways in which, in practice, government failure led to inefficient industrial growth. In some countries, governments established public sector enterprises to produce a variety of industrial commodities. Often these commodities were precisely the capital-intensive ones that are inconsistent with efficient resource allocation. Often, too, production techniques were highly capital intensive. Again in contrast to the model of section 1, most of these public enterprises were established and managed on the assumption that they would sell only in the domestic market. In many public sector enterprises, this immediately implied uneconomically small production runs, and considerable excess capacity owing to lack of domestic demand and/or sufficient foreign exchange to purchase raw materials and intermediate imports.

In part because public sector enterprises can obtain their financing from government treasuries, there appears to have been little attention to cost control, with deficits of sizable proportions financed by the

13. It should be noted that the model presented in sec. 1 is based on a very different view of the world. If the model were applied to a market economy, there could be no monopoly power, because of the assumption that prices are given on world markets. The factor-proportions explanation of trade essentially asserts that comparative advantage, at early stages of development for a land-scarce country, lies in labor-intensive commodities and not in big ticket, capital-intensive industries. Because these are different models of industrial development, their relevance can be tested only by empirical evidence, and the Korean experience presents a nice case study, to which attention turns in sec. 3 below.

government. Because public sector enterprises were seen as a potential instrument of government, politicians often loaded extra objectives on these agencies, including the imperative to employ redundant workers, to select those politically favored for posts for which other, better qualified, candidates were available, and so on. In practice, SOEs were not innovative, competitive, and entrepreneurial, but were rather genuine high-cost monopolies, unable to change their ways.

In many countries SOEs existed side by side with private sector firms. Because of suspicions of private economic activity, however, much of it was heavily regulated—especially for larger enterprises. Often regulations governed the types of economic activities that could be undertaken privately. Those private enterprises undertaking activities deemed "priority for development" were then accorded special privileges, including access to rationed credit at low or negative interest rates, import licenses for capital goods to be purchased at overvalued exchange rates, tax holidays, and other valuable, but incentive-distorting, privileges. One consequence was that these private enterprises had much the same incentive to employ capital-intensive techniques as did their SOE counterparts.

Requirements that private firms apply for various licenses and permits, meet various restrictions, provide services for their labor forces, and otherwise meet regulations can impede efficiency to a greater or lesser extent, and can slow down growth of industrial output. This result obtains because investment per unit of output rises (as it does with anything that slows down or reduces the efficiency of the process of plant construction and equipment installation) and because the composition of investment shifts toward activities with lower rates of return.

2.3.3. The Trade and Payments Regime. The model of section 1 implies that industrial growth can most rapidly be achieved through reliance on the international market. There are two reasons for this. First, capital will have a higher marginal product in the more labor-intensive industries. Second, a given savings rate will result in a greater upward shift in the demand for labor under free trade than it would in a closed, or protected, economy because investment can be more heavily concentrated in labor-intensive industries when output of those industries can be sold abroad in exchange for capital-intensive goods that would otherwise have to be produced domestically.

While direct regulation of agricultural and industrial production has had high costs in a large number of developing countries, the evidence suggests that in most situations the negative impact on growth of direct intervention was generally less than was the impact of the trade and payments regime. Moreover, once restrictive trade and payments regimes were in place (often imposed in response to immediate balance-of-payments pressures), they became subject to manipulation for a variety of purposes.

Whereas many of the regulations directly governing agricultural and industrial production were the intended consequence of belief in market failure, many of the inefficiencies associated with highly restrictive trade and payments regimes were the unintended consequence of policies undertaken for other purposes. Moreover, if there was ever a clear-cut case of government failure, it was in the trade and payments regimes: whatever the original motive for intervention, the evolutions of trade and payments regimes over time demonstrated that particular types of controls, once in place, bring into being political pressures to manipulate their uses.

The foreign-exchange market in and of itself can be more or less distorted. In practice, however, restrictive trade regimes have affected not only the foreign-exchange market, but also the market for industrial and agricultural commodities. For countries that have been able to achieve a rate of growth of agricultural output that permits a satisfactory rate of industrial growth, at least in principle, the foreign-trade regime has proved to be the instrument most governments have used to influence (both deliberately and with unintended side effects) the market for industrial output.

While there are instances of some degree of monopoly power in trade, few if any regimes intervene in ways that would be consistent with correcting an exogenous distortion. Almost all distortions have been policy-induced, although they have not all been deliberate. Many highly restrictive trade regimes have been put in place as a (distorting) policy response to an excess demand for foreign exchange and as a not-necessarily-recognized alternative to alteration of the exchange rate. The existence of an overvalued exchange rate and a highly restrictive import-licensing regime has then had pervasive consequences for both the agricultural and the industrial output in many developing countries.

Indeed, it can be argued that many of the apparent inefficiencies of the industrial sectors in developing countries have resulted from trade and payments regimes that have provided individual producers with quasi-monopoly positions, sheltering them from the international market and preventing domestic competition (partly because of the small size of the domestic market) through import and investment licensing procedures designed to prevent "excess capacity" and to accord individual firms "fair shares" of available imports of intermediate goods and raw materials.

Moreover, the highly protected domestic market has served as a sizeable disincentive for exporters, and countries with highly restrictionist trade and payments regimes have typically found the commodity composition of their exports heavily centered on raw materials in whose international price there is a significant component of rent, as new resources have been channeled almost exclusively into production for sale on the more profitable, highly protected, domestic market. (See Krueger 1984 for a fuller analysis of the costs of these trade regimes.)

2.3.4. The Labor Market.　A crucial implication of the multicommodity, two-sector, three-factor model is that a major gain from trade for developing countries derives from their ability to export "embodied labor" and to import "embodied capital." Since the competitive positions of individual firms are determined by the profitability of alternative activities, it is readily apparent that economic efficiency would obtain when firms in countries with very high labor-land ratios found it profitable to produce and export very labor-intensive commodities. This would occur when the wage rate (or wage structure, in a more general model) reflected the relative abundance of labor.

If firms in labor-abundant countries are confronted with relatively high labor costs, they will find it profitable to produce goods that are less labor-intensive, and comparative advantage would not be realized. If real wages are legislated, the outcome might even be a "reversal" of comparative advantage, with exports of more capital-intensive goods and imports of labor-intensive commodities. In such a circumstance, of course, there would either be open unemployment in the economy or there would be a wage differential between regulated activities and the rest of the economy. (See Magee 1973 for analysis of "reversal" of comparative advantage under a wage differential model and Brecher 1974 for analysis of the rigid real wage–unemployment case).

Hence, in a market economy, efficient use of the international economy to accelerate industrial growth could be thwarted by regulation of wages as much as by protection of domestic production and exchange rate overvaluation. If wages are effectively set at levels significantly above those at which a sufficient labor supply would be forthcoming from the agricultural sector, it could preclude reliance on the international market and the type of outward-oriented development implied by the model of section 1.

It has already been shown that many developing countries have attempted to regulate wages and conditions of employment. In some cases, these regulations have been largely ineffective.[14] In other cases, however, they have been enforced, at least over the "formal sector," which encompasses all sizable enterprises. Since there is a reasonable presumption that most industrial exports will be produced by firms large enough to be visible, and hence subject to these regulations, there is a presumption that highly restrictive labor legislation can preclude the development of production for export of manufactures in countries that might otherwise have had a significant comparative advantage in export of labor-intensive manufactures.

In countries with highly restrictive trade and payments regimes, regulations effectively raising real wages to levels that lead to open urban unemployment can significantly retard growth. But even with an open trading regime, the potential benefits of the international market can be choked off if wages are set significantly above levels consistent with comparative advantage.

2.3.5. Capital-Market Interventions. The frequently encountered phenomena of credit rationing, interest ceilings, and fragmented and regulated financial markets have already been mentioned. Some (see, for example, McKinnon 1973) believe that the costs of these regulations have been so high as to dwarf the effects of the four types of distortions discussed thus far.

Clearly, if capital services are artificially cheap to some producers, there will be an excess demand for them. If some investable resources are directed to recipients who would not find it profitable to pursue their activities at a realistic interest rate, there will necessarily be others who would have been able to find profitable activities at that rate but are excluded by whatever rationing mechanism supports the credit rationing. In those instances, the consequences of credit rationing will be identical to those of regulating real wages at levels inconsistent with comparative advantage, and the costs of interest ceilings and credit rationing,

14. See Carvalho and Haddad 1981 for suggestive evidence on the ineffectiveness of Brazilian minimum-wage legislation (because actual wages were well above the legislated minima) during the 1960s and early 1970s. Corbo and Sanchez 1985 provides some interesting evidence as to the effects of removal of some of the regulations governing employment in Chile.

from the viewpoint of the model set forth in section 1, will be the same as those of labor-market interventions, so the analysis need not be repeated here.

It should be pointed out, however, that the costs of "financial repression," to use McKinnon's phrase, would presumably rise over time with capital accumulation in the two-sector, multicommodity, three-factor model. This would follow simply by virtue of the fact that the costs of given divergences between rates of return to capital-starved and capital-abundant activities would become greater as the size of the capital stock increased.

3. LIBERALIZATION AND ECONOMIC GROWTH

To this point, a model of efficient outward-oriented growth has been developed, and the resultant theory of economic policy briefly sketched. That theory has two sets of implications for policy. First, it points to the importance of an open trade regime (which in turn requires a realistic exchange rate) and well-functioning factor markets as essential elements of a development policy and, by implication, assigns to the state important responsibilities for delivery of reliable infrastructural services to support relatively rapid export growth. Second, and the obverse of the first part, it suggests the kinds of costs that may result from government failures of the type described in section 2.3.

While the model provides a guide to appropriate economic policy, a key question remains. What are the implications for a policymaker desirous of achieving more rapid growth if he starts in a situation characterized by the types of interventions outlined in section 2.3. and is, in addition, constrained by the political process (perhaps because of the built-in vested interests and political pressures that surround interventions of the type described) as to the number and magnitude of reforms that can be undertaken?

3.1. Theory and Liberalization

Theory provides very little guidance in addressing this question. In the first place, the theory of the second best suggests that in general one cannot be certain that liberalization of any particular market will increase welfare in the presence of other, unremovable, distortions (given that total liberalization of all markets will lead to the very best outcome). Second, insofar as there are costs to adjustment (which would be the main analytical rationale for reducing the speed of adjustment), it is entirely an empirical question as to how sizable these might be. Furthermore, the magnitude of those costs might well differ from country to country as a function of the prior history of attempted liberalizations, the credibility of the policymakers, the initial set of policies that are in place, and the timing of the liberalization effort in relation to the cyclical phase of the international economy.

The empirical evidence, however, suggests that most market liberalizations that were sustainable have had at least some welfare-improving effects.[15] And, for purposes of the present discussion, it will be assumed that any liberalization will produce some positive benefits to the efficiency of resource allocation and to growth.[16]

The very concept of "liberalization" is associated with the removal of intervention and the shifting toward reliance on market forces to achieve objectives. Liberalization is therefore a process of removing the types of interventions detrimental to growth, described in section 2.3. Except in the sense that the theory described in sections 1 and 2.1 suggests that removal of controls may contribute to growth, theory can provide little guidance to policy for such questions as:

(1) Starting from an initial situation of multiple interventions and controls, if there is a constraint on the number of fronts on which action can simultaneously be taken, which markets should be liberalized first?

(2) Is it preferable to liberalize all markets at about the same rate, or entirely to liberalize first one market and then another?

(3) What are the costs of adjustment associated with liberalization and can these costs be reduced if, as may be unrealistic, policymakers can announce a credible and unalterable schedule of liberalization to permit more gradual adjustment?

15. Unsustainable liberalizations would include such policy actions as the removal of all quantitative restrictions on imports at a highly overvalued exchange rate, liberalizing the domestic money market while "prefixing" the exchange rate in an effort to hold down inflation, and removal of controls on capital flows in the face of repressed domestic financial markets. Because liberalizations such as these are not sustainable, an important question in these circumstances is whether the present gains from liberalization outweigh the losses associated with shifting resources twice in response to altered incentives and/or the reduction in future consumption that will necessarily finance higher present consumption levels.

16. For a discussion of the benefits that accrued to the Egyptian nominal devaluation of 1962, despite the fact that effective exchange rates hardly altered, see Hansen and Nashashibi 1975.

(4) Is there a critical minimum amount of liberalization that must be undertaken in order to be reasonably confident that the benefits will exceed any adjustment costs?

None of these questions can be answered in theory. Adjustment costs might be negligible or highly significant; they might differ from firm to firm, industry to industry, or country to country. The speed of reaction might also vary widely according to circumstances.

Hence, efforts to understand the process must rely on empirical evidence. This can be of two kinds. Efforts can be made to ascertain the structure of a particular economy, focusing on estimation of the likely magnitude of the key response parameters. There are several difficulties with this. One problem is that the types of growth-inhibiting policies described above significantly reduce the response of the economy to such changes as do occur. And, since in most instances liberalization is an event taking place outside the range of observations of past economic behavior, empirical evidence, or even inference ex ante about the likely response in a particular country, is exceptionally difficult to obtain, and professional economists can reasonably disagree as to its implications.

The second kind of evidence as to the probable magnitude of the parameters is from countries that have previously liberalized, or attempted to liberalize, one or more markets. It is in this context that the Korean experience provided a valuable laboratory in which to examine the liberalization process.

3.2. Lessons from the Korean Experience

In the 1950s the Korean economy was subject to many of the policies described in section 2.1.[17] Macroeconomic imbalances were severe, with inflation averaging 35 percent annually (and peaking at 85 percent), government budget deficits ranging around 5 percent of GNP, investment averaging around 11 percent of GNP, and domestic savings around 3 percent of GNP. Aid inflows covered much of this imbalance, and were around 10 percent of GNP in the mid to late 1950s.

The government's efforts were largely directed at containing inflationary pressures, along with postwar reconstruction. As part of the anti-inflationary policy, nominal exchange rates were held fixed for long intervals before adjustments were undertaken; these adjustments nonetheless left the exchange rate chronically overvalued. In response to chronic excess demand for foreign exchange, the government resorted

17. Unless otherwise indicated, data in this section are derived from Frank, Kim, and Westphal 1975, Kim and Roemer 1979, and Mason et al. 1980.

to multiple exchange rates, high tariffs, and quantitative restrictions on imports. Exports were consequently discriminated against, and were only 3 percent of GNP as late as 1960, when imports were 10 percent of GNP.

Again motivated largely by a desire to contain inflation, the Korean government depressed the prices of agricultural commodities, especially rice, a policy made possible by large quantities of PL 480 grain. The nominal purchase price of rice was already depressed in the mid 1950s, and it remained constant between 1956 and 1960 despite an increase of 23 percent in the wholesale price index over that period.

Import-substitution industries were developed behind high walls of protection, with average annual growth rates in excess of 15 percent in real manufacturing value-added for the last half of the 1950s in production of paper products, chemical and petroleum products, rubber products, basic metals, and metal products, including machinery and transport equipment. These compared with average annual growth rates of real manufacturing value-added of less than 10 percent for textiles and leather products, two sectors that were major sources of export growth in later decades. (Data are from Kim and Roemer 1979.)

Interest rates were kept well below inflation rates, and credit rationing prevailed; financial markets in Korea in the 1950s were therefore highly repressed and fragmented. Only in the labor market does Korean policy in the 1950s appear to have been less distortionary than that of many other developing countries. The labor market appears to have been relatively unregulated in the 1950s, as well as in the period of Korea's rapid growth (see Kim and Roemer 1979, 162).

These distortions were reflected in generally slow growth in Korea. Despite the huge inflow of aid and the end of the Korean War in 1953, which should have permitted fairly rapid growth with reconstruction, the average annual rate of growth of real GNP was only 4.1 percent, which, with flows of migrants from the north and high birth rates after the war, resulted in per capita income growth of only 1.7 percent annually for the years 1953–55.

The sequence of reforms cannot be neatly demarcated. Policy changes began in 1958, but it was not until 1964 that the features of the new policy regime were reasonably well defined and understood. Starting in 1958 there was a considerably greater adjustment in the nominal exchange rate and depreciation of the won in real terms, but it was not until 1964 that the exchange rate was unified and permitted to float to maintain a virtually constant real value. And, starting in 1957–58,

serious efforts were undertaken to achieve greater macroeconomic stability. The inflation rate as measured by the GNP deflator slowed drastically, averaging 3.8 percent annually in 1957–60 compared to a 36 percent annual average from 1953 to 1957. However, it rose again to an
average of 22 percent over the 1960–64 period, when further fiscal and
interest rate reforms were introduced. Thereafter, it remained moderate, averaging 12 percent annually over the years 1964–73.

Similarly, by the early 1960s, quantitative restrictions on imports were
almost entirely abolished insofar as they affected producers of exportables. Exporters could import any intermediate input used in production and were, in addition, the only ones eligible to receive import licenses for other commodities, mostly luxury consumer goods. It was not
until 1967, however, that the government shifted from a positive list of
eligible imports to a negative list of ineligible imports and began significantly to reduce tariffs. The import liberalization–tariff reduction process continues to this day.[18]

For agriculture, suppression of producer prices remained the order of
the day until the late 1960s, although the rate of increase of agricultural
production in the 1960s exceeded that of the 1950s, presumably because
a more realistic exchange rate and import liberalization had reduced the
extent of discrimination against agriculture. By the late 1960s, however,
it became apparent that rural farmers' incomes were not rising as rapidly as urban ones, and policies were shifted toward inducements to agriculture. In the Korean case it seems evident that liberalization of the
trade regime, and especially removal of the bias toward import substitution, spurred industrial growth, and that rapid industrial growth in turn
"spilled over" via increased demand for agricultural products (and increased demand for urban labor, which led to rural outmigration and
rapid increases in real urban wages).[19] Until the 1970s Korean agriculture benefited from liberalization chiefly through the effects of a more
realistic real exchange rate and from rising urban demand. Thereafter,
efforts to support rural incomes led to a reduction in the disparity between rural and urban incomes.[20]

18. See chap. 7 below for a fuller description of the trade liberalization process in
Korea.

19. Real wages in the urban areas rose sharply after about 1964. The nonfarm labor
force increased at an average rate of around 6 percent, and unemployment fell sharply
(from 7.8 percent in 1960 to 4.5 percent in the early 1970s). Real wages in manufacturing
more than doubled between 1965 and 1975.

20. See chap. 8 for a fuller discussion.

As to financial liberalization, it has not been fully accomplished to this date. Major reforms in 1964 greatly reduced the ability of the government to borrow or print money and closed the budget deficit. Simultaneously, ceilings on nominal interest rates were raised sharply, so that real interest rates were positive in the late 1960s. In the early 1970s, however, they were again controlled, despite a sharp increase in the inflation rate.

If one were to attempt to characterize the Korean experience in general terms, it would be that the sharpest policy reversal, and earliest liberalization, was in the trade and payments regime, and especially in removing the bias of the regime against the international market. The response of the economy to that liberalization was very rapid and far greater than had been anticipated. Although many opposed the removal of protection for domestic industry in the late 1950s, opposition appears to have been sharply reduced by the unanticipated magnitude of the success. That export earnings in dollar terms could grow by more than 35 percent annually over the fifteen-year interval following 1960 attests to the magnitude of that response. That it exceeded all expectations is evidenced not only by statements of Koreans, but by the fact that a five-year plan introduced in 1962 had to be abandoned because its goals were all achieved in the first half of its intended life.

Consistent with the model set forth in section 1, Korea's exceptionally rapid growth in the early 1960s was spurred by the growth of the industrial sector, which in turn was led by the growth of exports of labor-intensive goods. As Mason et al. (1980) point out, the leading growth sector was industry; agriculture benefited and grew largely because of the spillover of demand in the rapid-growth environment. That labor-intensive industry was where comparative advantage lay initially cannot be doubted: textile exports rose from $4.1 million in 1961 to $54.5 million in 1965; lumber and plywood from $1.2 million to $18.2 million; and metal products from $1.6 million to $17.8 million; later on electronics products also entered the list (see Krueger 1984, 101). By almost any method of measurement, the role of import substitution in growth was larger than that of export expansion in the 1950s, whereas export expansion accounted for more than twice as much of the rapid growth as did import substitution in the 1960s and 1970s. For the period 1963–73, one estimate put the contribution of export expansion to growth at 40.1 percent of total growth compared to 9.9 percent for imports.[21]

21. See Kim and Roemer 1979, table 46. Domestic demand growth "accounts" for the remainder of growth.

Interestingly, many of the new industries that arose in response to export incentives—wigs, plywood, electronics, and so on—were initially developed as export industries. To the extent that they were sold on the domestic market, it was secondary right from the start.

Another episode in Korea's remarkable experience serves as partial verification of the model. That is, in the second half of the 1970s, the government decided to undertake substantial investments in the heavy and chemical industries, which was, in effect, a reversal of the policies (which turned out to be temporary) that had served the economy so well over the preceding years. This program was decided upon based on the belief that the Korean economy had by that date progressed far enough to sustain that sort of development. However, it became evident that the Korean economy was not yet ready: as Kim Kihwan points out: "These policy changes were achieved at the cost of a high rate of inflation. . . . In addition, these changes resulted in serious imbalances in the economy. The most serious imbalances were an over-investment in heavy industries and under-investment in light industries; extensive price distortions and lack of competition due to government controls; and a rise in real wages which exceeded productivity improvement. These imbalances led to a weakening of export competitiveness, and brought about a slowdown in the overall growth in the economy" (Kim 1985, 15). Only in 1981–82 were the policymakers able to resume the outward-oriented stance of the earlier era and to return to growth. That Korea's comparative advantage did not lie in the capital-intensive heavy industries even after a decade and a half of rapid growth and rising real wages became manifestly evident.

One final point needs to be mentioned: examination of the history of policy change in Korea strongly suggests that "liberalization" was not a once-and-for-all policy action. Rather, it was a continuing process, with difficulties encountered at each step. Yet, the Korean experience since the mid 1950s strongly suggests that rapid growth was not, in any sense, assured after the initial liberalization; rather, as restrictive policies increasingly appeared to represent impediments to further growth, policymakers grappled with the problem of how to liberalize further still.

A second factor of importance in Korea was that the labor market was relatively free and therefore did not have to be liberalized. And while financial liberalization was far from complete, the reforms that were undertaken implied far smaller subsidization of successful borrowers than had earlier been the case.

4. TIMING AND SEQUENCING OF LIBERALIZATION

Given the remarkable transformation of the Korean economy, it is relatively straightforward to infer what happened there. Quite clearly the gains from liberalization were enormous, and the shift toward reliance on the international market, with accompanying liberalization of other parts of the economy, permitted a sustained rate of growth that had earlier been regarded as unattainable under any circumstances.

One question remains: what lessons does the Korean experience provide for countries whose economies are still subject to the same sorts of controls as was the Korean economy of the 1950s? On one hand, the evidence appears overwhelming that the potential gains from a major shift in policy stance could be very large. The real and more difficult question is what sorts of liberalization measures are most likely to be successful in achieving significant increases in efficiency and growth at least cost.

Some lessons seem to follow straightforwardly from the model and from the Korean experience. Attention turns first to them. Thereafter, some more conjectural hypotheses as to the liberalization process, which are not inconsistent with the Korean experience but can in no way be verified by it, are put forth in the hope that further research, perhaps involving comparative analysis, might shed light.

Turning first to those conclusions that seem fairly solidly based, the first, and probably most significant, conclusion is that liberalization of the trade and payments regime could not have succeeded had the authorities not simultaneously ensured the continuing maintenance of a realistic exchange rate.[22] Second, and closely related to the first, the Korean export drive could not have succeeded had imports, and the trade and payments regime more generally, not been liberalized. This was essential both in order to ensure that potential producers would be willing to take the risks associated with exporting (which would have appeared far less attractive had there remained a sheltered domestic market) and to ensure that exporters could efficiently obtain needed imports in order to compete with suppliers in other countries. Third, Korea's labor market was not subject to heavy regulation, which was undoubtedly a necessary condition for the early success in exporting labor-intensive goods. Had there been minimum-wage legislation and other policies that sharply increased the cost of employing labor, it is difficult to imagine

22. In this regard, it is significant that Frank, Kim, and Westphal (1975, 84–85) found that a 1 percent increase in the real reward to exporters for earning a dollar of foreign exchange induced twice the supply response when that increase emanated from the real exchange rate rather than being the result of increased export subsidies.

that Korea could have been successful, especially in the early stages of the export-oriented drive.

At the more conjectural level, other hypotheses emerge. Note in particular that Korea did not initially liberalize all markets entirely. Indeed, the outward-oriented export strategy had been in effect at least four years before there was any degree of financial liberalization and, except to exporters, imports were not entirely liberalized for an even longer period.

It is tempting to postulate that successful economic growth brings with it an increasing complexity of the economy, which it surely did in the Korean case. With that increasing complexity, a system of direct controls probably becomes more difficult to administer, and the cost of errors probably increases. This is not only because the range of particular decisions that has to be taken increases (as the number of products, intermediate goods, types of labor, etc., increases), but also because the transparency of the effects of particular controls diminishes to policymakers and the public alike. This diminishing transparency means that the regulators cannot readily know the implications of their decisions, and simultaneously that individual entrepreneurs have more opportunity for misrepresenting their situations in order to avail themselves of the profitable opportunities inherent in a system of direct controls. The consequences of these two phenomena combined are probably increasing complexity of controls and increasingly costly mistakes as growth progresses.

Because of the role of the international market as a regulator of economic behavior and the increasingly profitable opportunities that a direct-controls regime creates, it is likely that direct controls over foreign trade will become increasingly costly the further industrial development progresses. Part of the observed rapidly rising capital/output ratios in countries clinging to direct control systems may be a reflection of this phenomenon, rather than only of the rising capital intensity of new import-substitution lines.

By a similar line of reasoning, it may be that credit rationing and interest-rate ceilings do not, at early stages of development, impose very high direct costs, because of the transparency of the opportunities for very highly profitable investments. However, as the complexity of the industrial structure increases, and the contribution of capital as a factor of production rises (because there is more of it), the costs of misallocation of scarce capital may rise, while the quality of the information on which decisions as to credit allocations are based diminishes.

Using the Korean experience as a model, it seems evident that credit rationing could not have imposed too high a cost on the economy in the early 1960s. The fact is that exporting was highly profitable. Resources should have been drawn into export industries. Credit was allocated preferentially to exporters, and this simple rule probably ensured a reasonably efficient allocation of investable resources, although there were undoubtedly inefficiencies and discrimination against small firms. As development progressed, however, a sufficiently high fraction of all investment was in exportable activities, so that the simple rule probably failed to perform as well. When differentiation had to be made among exportable activities as to which were likely to yield higher rates of return, allocation rules would have resulted in larger and more costly mistakes.

Based on the Korean experience, therefore, one might tentatively conclude that liberalization and reduction of the bias of the trade regime, and especially the regime as it affects exporters, is an essential prerequisite for satisfactory industrial growth. Especially for countries with a high labor/land ratio and therefore a strong comparative advantage in very labor-intensive industries, a reasonably free labor market is also essential. Financial liberalization, while clearly important for sustaining it, may not be as necessary initially if a government starts in a situation where many markets are regulated. Sustained growth will nonetheless ultimately require liberalization of the financial markets; their liberalization remains a major challenge for Korean policymakers.

REFERENCES

Bell, Clive, and T. N. Srinivasan. 1985. "Agricultural Credit Market in Punjab: Segmentation, Rationing, and Spillover." DRD Working Paper no. 7. Mimeographed.

Bhagwati, J. N. 1971. "The Generalized Theory of Distortions and Welfare." In J. N. Bhagwati, R. W. Jones, R. A. Mundell, and J. Vanek, eds., *Trade, Balance of Payments and Growth*, 69–90. Amsterdam: North-Holland Publishing Co.

Brecher, Richard. 1974. "Minimum Wage Rates and the Pure Theory of International Trade." *Quarterly Journal of Economics* 88 (February): 98–116.

Carvalho, Jose L., and Claudio Haddad. 1981. "Foreign Trade Strategies and Employment in Brazil." In Anne O. Krueger, ed., *Trade and Employment in Developing Countries: Individual Studies*, 29–81. Chicago: University of Chicago Press.

Corbo, Vittorio, and Jose Miguel Sanchez. 1985. "Adjustments by Industrial Firms in Chile during 1974–82." In Vittorio Corbo and Jaime de Melo, eds., *Scrambling for Survival: How Firms Adjusted to the Recent Reforms in Argentina, Chile and Uruguay.* World Bank Staff Working Paper no. 764. Washington, D.C.: World Bank.

Frank, Charles R., Jr., Kim Kwang-Suk, and Larry E. Westphal. 1975. *South Korea.* Vol. 7 of *Foreign Trade Regimes and Economic Development.* New York: National Bureau of Economic Research.

Hansen, Bent, and Karim Nashashibi. 1975. *Egypt.* Vol. 4 of *Foreign Trade Regimes and Economic Development.* New York: National Bureau of Economic Research.

Hayami Yūjirō and Vernon W. Ruttan. 1985. *Agricultural Development: An International Perspective.* Baltimore: Johns Hopkins University Press.

Jones, Ronald W. 1971. "A Three-Factor Model in Theory, Trade, and History." In J. N. Bhagwati, R. W. Jones, R. A. Mundell, and J. Vanek, eds., *Trade, Balance of Payments and Growth,* 437–59. Amsterdam: North-Holland Publishing Co.

Kenen, Peter B. 1965. "Nature, Capital and Trade." *Journal of Political Economy* 73 (October): 437–60.

Kim Kihwan. 1985. *The Korean Economy: Past Performance, Current Reforms, and Future Prospects.* Seoul: Korea Development Institute.

Kim Kwang-Suk and Michael Roemer. 1979. *Growth and Structural Transformation.* Studies in the Modernization of the Republic of Korea, 1945–1975. Cambridge, Mass.: Council on East Asian Studies, Harvard University.

Krueger, Anne O. 1977. *Growth, Distortions and Patterns of Trade among Many Countries.* Essays in International Finance no. 40. Princeton: International Finance Section, Department of Economics, Princeton University.

———. 1984. "Comparative Advantage and Development Policy Twenty Years Later." In M. Syrquin, L. Taylor, and L. E. Westphal, eds., *Economic Structure and Performance,* 135–56. Orlando, Fla.: Academic Press.

Krueger, Anne O. and Baran Tuncer. 1982. "Growth of Factor Productivity in Turkish Manufacturing Industries." *Journal of Development Economics* 11 (December): 307–25.

Lewis, W. Arthur. 1954. "Economic Development with Unlimited Supplies of Labor." *Manchester School* 22 (May): 139–91.

McKinnon, Ronald. 1973. *Money and Capital in Economic Development.* Washington, D.C.: Brookings Institution.

Magee, Stephen P. 1973. "Factor Market Distortions, Production and Trade: A Survey," *Oxford Economic Papers* 25 (March): 1–43.

Mason, Edward S., Kim Mahn Je, Dwight H. Perkins, Kim Kwang Suk, and David C. Cole. 1980. *The Economic and Social Modernization of the Republic of Korea.* Cambridge, Mass.: Council on East Asian Studies, Harvard University.

Stiglitz, Joseph E. 1985. *Economics of Information and the Theory of Economic Development.* NBER Working Paper no. 1566. Cambridge, Mass: National Bureau of Economic Research.

World Bank. 1983. *World Development Report, 1983.* Washington, D.C.: World Bank.

TWO

Toward a Model of Development

Gustav Ranis

1. INTRODUCTION

There can be little doubt that future historians will view the effort at transition to modern growth by contemporary less developed countries as the major economic and political event of the late twentieth century—an event equaled only by the development of atomic energy. The effort by two-thirds of humanity to move from colonial agrarianism toward what Simon Kuznets has described as the epoch of modern economic growth is surely a monumental societal undertaking. In the so-called mature industrial countries, this process began in England with the Industrial Revolution during the last quarter of the eighteenth century. From there it spread gradually across Europe and into North America, Japan, and Russia, but stopped short of the so-called overseas territories, thus helping to create the current dichotomy between developing and industrially advanced countries.

This phenomenon of modern economic growth encompasses major structural change away from agriculture in terms of both value added and employment over time by enlisting the routinized and institutionalized exploration of science and technology in its manifold applications. It entails a most profound change in the way of life of a society as well as in the institutional environment that helps regulate economic activity. This new way of life has been deemed attractive and irresistible and seems to be the objective of most of the Third World—almost regardless of initial conditions, cultural milieu, or even ideological preference.

This chapter has benefited from very helpful comments by Larry Krause on an earlier draft.

TABLE 2.1 Average Annual Real Per Capita GDP Growth Rate
(in %)

	1950–59	*1960–69*	*1970–79*	*1980–84*
Taiwan	4.7 (1952–59)	5.9	8.1	3.9 (1980–83)
South Korea	1.3 (1953–59)	4.9	7.5	3.1
Colombia	1.7 (1951–59)	1.9	3.9	.4 (1980–82)
Mexico	3.4 (1952–59)	4.1	1.9	.1

SOURCES: Indices in United Nations, *Statistical Yearbook*, various years; Summers and Heston 1984; Taiwan, *Statistical Yearbook of the Republic of China*, various years.

Accordingly, the effort that spread geographically from England to the Continent, the United States, Canada, and Japan in the nineteenth century and to eastern Europe as well as parts of Latin America in the early twentieth century was only temporarily interrupted and was resumed with greater vigor as well as impatience in the postindependence, postwar era. The development effort we are now witnessing thus really represents the resumption of the spread of that transitional growth effort to Asia, the rest of Latin America, and parts of the Middle East, with Africa bringing up the rear.

It has, moreover, become increasingly apparent in recent years that of all the contemporary LDC transitional efforts, those of the so-called East Asian NICs, Taiwan, South Korea, Hong Kong, and Singapore, have been most successful. In addition, I believe that Japan, an unquestioned case of earlier success, had much in common, in terms of initial nineteenth-century conditions, with these contemporary East Asian situations. Furthermore, it is quite obvious that what the entire East Asian family of nations seem to have in common is relative shortage of natural resources—with the possible exception of the favorable entrepôt locations of Singapore and Hong Kong—in association with heavy population pressure on limited land, a relatively good human-resource base, and a relatively small size.

The contemporary East Asian NICs, like Japan in the late nineteenth century, may thus be labeled as belonging to a group of open dualistic economies characterized by the coexistence of a large agricultural and a small nonagricultural production sector internally and by the relative importance of international trade externally. These systems have clearly been more successful than other postwar LDCs by any criteria contrasting East Asian performance with that of Latin American countries over the postwar period (see tables 2.1 and 2.2). They have clearly done well

TABLE 2.2 Income Distribution
(Gini coefficients)

	1953	1960	1970	1980
Taiwan	.56	.44 (1959)	.29	.29 (1978)
South Korea	—	—	.39	.38 (1976)
Colombia	—	.53	.56	.52 (1982)
Mexico	—	.54	.58	.50 (1977)

SOURCES: Shail 1975; Fei, Ranis, and Kuo 1979.

on all counts, not only in terms of per capita income growth but also in terms of the generation of sufficient employment to mop up their labor surpluses by the end of the 1960s and the maintenance and even improvement of an equitable distribution of income during exceptionally rapid periods of growth.

The "why" of this success is, however, still little understood, as is the extent to which the experience is transferable to differently situated developing countries. It is not at all obvious why the initial conditions more or less shared by these five countries—their poor natural-resource endowment, the relatively high quality of their human resources, the heavy pressure of their populations on the land, and their relatively small or medium size—should all add up to a natural advantage in effecting a successful transition to modern growth.

While it is fashionable nowadays to say that success resides in "good management," that these countries somehow pursued "good" economic policies, this does not take us far. It is, as we shall see, undoubtedly true—but we must try to probe deeper and again ask ourselves, "Why?" In other words, it is clear that there must be some politicoeconomic forces at work that led to the adoption of relatively better policies in these countries than elsewhere, and that permitted them not only to perform better in general, but also to be able to adjust much more flexibly to the deterioration of the international environment during the past decade. It is my hope to relate the initial conditions cited to the issue of a conformable evolution of policy and, in so doing, to try to show both the longer-term policy direction of a society and the absence of undue oscillations in that policy to be at least to some extent endogenous. In other words, a satisfactory approach to understanding a particular model of development relevant to this type of developing country must go beyond a description of what happened and try to relate it to politicoeconomic forces within the system.

While most of the prior work on the analysis of transitional growth has focused on the discovery of statistically measurable regularities in countries' performances and production structures over time, the deviations from that average convergent pattern have usually been explained in a rather ad hoc descriptive fashion. This is certainly characteristic of the work of Chenery (1979) and Kuznets (1966) as well as of many of the descriptive analyses of the East Asian historical cases in the literature.[1] Perhaps the time has now come to try to focus on precisely why, in these few cases, a conformable evolution of policies has resulted in a more or less linear set of policy changes, whereas in the majority of LDCs there has been inconsistency and policy oscillation in spite of the profusion of advice from academics, international organizations, and so on. It is no longer sufficient to dismiss the East Asian NICs as "special cases." We must ask what, if anything, can be learned from them and see whether their experience is relevant for other developing countries, still largely marching to a different tune. This is the basic motive for attempting to explore the model of development of the natural-resource-poor LDC in this chapter.

The search for a prototypical case, of course, always runs up against the problem of each individual country's inevitable "specialness," and even within our subfamily of five natural-resource-poor countries there are obviously marked differences that could take up much of our energy and space. I have therefore decided to focus most heavily on one case, that of Taiwan, partly because it is best known to me, and partly because Singapore and Hong Kong can easily be eliminated as extremely atypical city-states. I shall, however, also make reference to both South Korea and historical Japan, while maintaining the main focus on Taiwan as a prototype for the exploration of the natural-resource-poor (NRP) development model. The contrasting example of the natural-resource-rich LDCs (NRR), as illustrated by a "typical" Latin American case, will also be useful.

Traditionally, the analysis of policy stresses its economic impact on growth, distribution, employment, labor allocation, trade patterns, and so forth in assessing its economic costs and benefits. Analysis typically does not focus on the question of why certain policies were adopted and/ or abandoned in the first place. The fundamental hypothesis of this chapter is that major development policy instruments (the interest rate, the foreign-exchange rate, the rate of monetary expansion, the rate of

1. See, among others, Galenson, ed. 1979; Fei, Ranis, and Kuo 1979; Mason et al. 1980; and Fei, Ohkawa, and Ranis 1985.

protection, the tax rate, the unskilled wage rate) must be interpreted as political instruments to achieve certain social objectives, benefiting some classes at the expense of others, and that there are usually good and sufficient reasons for certain countries pursuing what might be called "bad policies," whereas the East Asians have generally pursued "good policies." I do not, in other words, intend simply to accept superior wisdom or cultural advantages as an explanation for the different paths followed by the East Asians and the rest of the developing world in the postwar era. Moreover, I intend to demonstrate that the relative shortage or abundance of natural resources represents a key ingredient of the explanation.

Section 2 will focus on the set of initial conditions shared by the family of natural-resources-poor countries (NRPs) in contrast to the natural-resource-rich countries (NRRs) in the context of transition growth. Section 3 describes the actual evolutionary performance via different subphases of transitional growth that has been in evidence in the two types of LDCs. Section 4 focuses on the "why" of this divergence, emphasizing especially the importance of the natural-resource endowment for political economy.

2. INITIAL CONDITIONS

Postwar Taiwan, like South Korea and like Japan in the third quarter of the nineteenth century, quintessentially exemplifies the natural-resource-poor country. Not only were there no large deposits of exportable minerals or reproducible raw materials in existence, but even the amount of good arable land was limited (22 percent of the total land area in Taiwan, 25 percent in Korea, 14 percent in Japan) and the population density on that available land was high (see table 2.3). Such scarcity of basic natural resources, critical to the thesis of this chapter, is, of course, never an absolute matter. Yet at the simplest level of causation, it means that with the natural temptation to find an "easy solution" rendered inoperative by the absence of abundant natural resources to be exploited along the way, the overall success of the typical NRP country has to be explained in terms of the ability to exploit "something else," something that *is* available, namely human resources.

The successful mobilization of a system's human resources must in turn be associated with collective traits conducive to modern growth. According to Kuznets, these include secularism, egalitarianism, and nationalism. As he put it, "secularism is the concentration on life on earth

TABLE 2.3 Natural Resources

	Land/Man Ratio (acres per capita)	Forests	Minerals	Fuels	Rivers
Taiwan	0.2	Cover 55% of land area.	Not rich in minerals. Relatively abundant salt, limestone, silicone sands, dolomite, talc, low-grade graphite. Limited sulfur, pyrite, low-grade copper, gold.	Ample coking coal, bad-quality bituminous coal, some natural gas, little petroleum.	Great hydroelectric potential.
South Korea	0.2	Depleted, acute shortage, some reforestation.	Poor-quality anthracite coal, small deposits of bismuth, graphite, gold, silver, iron ore, copper. Among largest deposits of tungsten in world.	Poor-quality coal, no petroleum.	Little importance. Some hydroelectric potential.
Colombia	2.6	Valuable timber, somewhat depleted.	Iron ore, copper, salt, gold, silver, platinum, lead, mercury, world-famous emeralds, uranium.	Large coal and petroleum reserves.	Great hydroelectric potential.
Mexico	6	Cover 20% of area.	Rich deposits. Zinc, lead, silver, iron ore, mercury, sulfur, antimony molybdenum. Significant deposits of other industrial minerals.	Substantial coal deposits of limited value; large petroleum reserves.	Great hydroelectric potential; poor navigability.

that assigns priority to economic attainment. Egalitarianism means the denial of any inborn differences among human beings unless and except as they are manifested in human economic activities. . . . All this is bound by nationalism, the claim of the community of feeling grounded in a common historical past" (Kuznets 1966, 12–13).

The so-called pragmatism of the East Asian populations, which as we shall see affected their policy choices and their success, undoubtedly represents a mixture of these three elements, all of which are to some extent associated with an initially high level of literacy and other societal attainments. But the critical element is a belief in a reward system that encourages the deployment of existing human capacities. The tradition of secularism, in other words, means a preoccupation with the here and now and not with the otherworldly—contradicting the contrast between Eastern otherworldliness and Western pragmatism that one frequently finds in the literature. Egalitarianism in the Kuznets interpretation is the fundamental belief that social distinction is expected to be awarded to those who perform economic tasks with distinction. Belief in the eventual equalization of opportunity through the educational system and participation in markets on a relatively equal footing are clearly important ingredients of success in East Asia, where both competitive examination systems and equitable land-tenure systems exhibit strong elements of this egalitarian credo.

Finally, nationalism as conceived by Kuznets was very much in place in Taiwan and the other East Asian cases. What might be called "mature nationalism" is basically acquired from an awareness of one's own history and the belief that one continues to exist as a member of a group—the understanding that some public cohesion and a sharing nexus may be required, at least temporarily, putting limits on acquisitive individualism. In other words, there exists a basic feeling of concern for the larger national, more or less homogeneous, community—even though differences always exist, of course (for example, between the indigenous Taiwan population and the migrants from the mainland). The trick is to translate this sense of an essentially common heritage into behavioral rules conducive to the institution of orderly reforms that express calculated sympathy with other members of the community without endangering the underlying principles of a self-interested and acquisitive reward system. The historical Japanese case well demonstrates the point (see, e.g., Ranis 1955). Such "organic nationalism" is to be differentiated from a situation where, in the absence of these conditions, the government often seems to value an activist role almost for its own sake—for the headlines and the expectations it produces. Such manifestations of what may be called "synthetic nationalism" are often associated with the willingness of governments to take actions whose costs do not have to be faced for some time. Given national cohesion, as in East Asia, there is less need to continue to mollify competing interest groups by means of inflation and the other components of import-substituting interventionism.

In Taiwan the tradition of pragmatism and the fact that a mature nationalism already existed and did not have to be invented by the newly independent government meant that it was easier for the population to come to realize that government had important functions to perform, but should not be exclusively relied upon to dependably provide benefits over time. It does not stretch the imagination too far to see the significance of these elements in determining the nature of a system's transitional growth effort. They are clearly conducive to an increasingly market-oriented economy (the pursuit of a gradual liberalization process in various markets) or, another way of putting it, the gradual depoliticization of the economic system.

Traditional analysis of transitional growth stresses the economic impact on such factors as employment, growth, labor allocation, and trade, assessing the economic costs and benefits without much reference to arguments from political economy. Conversely, a central component of the approach of this chapter is to examine not only the policy impact of various structural changes but also the process by which they are adopted and/or abandoned within a given political milieu. As stated above, the fundamental hypothesis underlying my analysis of the natural-resource-poor economy is that major development policy instruments (interest rate, foreign-exchange rate, rate of monetary expansion, wage rate, rate of protection) must be interpreted as political instruments for promoting growth by transferring income among social groups, in other words, to "manufacture profits" for one class at the expense of another—a task initially facing every newly independent government. It is the early, if gradual, abandonment of massive interventions of this type that distinguishes the East Asian NRPs from much of the rest of the Third World.

In this context it is helpful to differentiate between "on the table," or overt, revenue- and expenditure-related government policies and "under the table," or covert and implicit, income transfers among various groups. In the context of an essentially political process, "under the table" transfers are usually sanctioned by a powerful need to solve short-run problems, with the possibility of social conflict being put off to a later point in time. The aforementioned major policy instruments are often used in this "under the table" fashion. For example, incomes are artificially transferred, say by overvalued exchange rates or by inflation, in ways very different from those of the market system, supplemented by government taxation and expenditures, used in the type of advanced economy toward which transitional growth efforts are pointed. The deployment of covert policy instruments not only touches almost everyone indirectly, as is well recognized in the literature, but also plays an important political function, as is less well recognized.

In contrast, "on the table" policies—including sectoral taxation and expenditures on education, on science and technology, on social-overhead investment, and for public enterprises, all real or alleged cases of public goods or external economies—serve to accommodate the transition process in the sense that such interventions tend to be a part of the game in even the most laissez-faire advanced economies. I intend to develop the thesis here that, while initial politicization of the economy is common to almost all LDCs, the rate, extent, and linearity of the subsequent liberalization trend of some economic systems, primarily involving a shift from "under the table" to "on the table" policy interventions, are related to the natural-resource wealth or poverty of the particular developing country. Clearly, such a shift does not necessarily mean a diminished role for government, but merely a changed role, as its direct functions may actually increase with the continued progress of liberalization even as its indirect functions diminish.

What differentiates the evolution of policy in the NRPs is the relative linearity of movement in the direction of gradual liberalization in contrast to policy oscillation elsewhere. In the NRP model we witness a more or less continuous metamorphism (albeit, of course, with fluctuations) around the trend, whereas in the typical NRR case of Latin America and Southeast Asia we encounter cycling without a clear trend.

What I would therefore like to stress here is that the NRP development type has been witness to a gradual withdrawal of political forces from various crucial markets over the almost forty years of its development experience. The underlying notion is that if a country is to perform well, as Taiwan clearly has, and to achieve not only production and structural contours similar to those of the developed countries but also the associated organizational features, it is inevitable that these political forces must gradually become less important and that implicit policy interventions must yield to the explicit type. Otherwise, LDCs are bound to continue to pay a heavy toll in terms of both policy oscillation and inferior economic performance. In that sense, the changing performance as well as the organizational features observed in the NRPs should be viewed not as mere historical accidents but as part of a broader nexus of political economy that requires explanation and is tied up with the initial conditions cited above. The same, of course, holds for the NRRs.

3. CONTRASTS IN TRANSITION GROWTH

The very notion of transitional growth presumes an evolutionary view of economic development. This metamorphic stance envisions the existence of subphases in the course of transition to Kuznetsian modern growth, with each subphase characterized by a distinct set of structural characteristics and a distinct mode of operation helpful for the analysis of postindependence performance. By this I do not mean to imply any sense of inevitability attending movements along a fixed historical pattern, only to record what can be observed as a set of evolutionary phenomena.

During the colonial or pretransition period, the East Asian NRPs (like the Latin American and Southeast Asian NRRs) routinely consumed imported factory-produced nondurable consumer goods, while exporting traditional agricultural products (in the case of Taiwan, rice and sugar). Taiwan possessed somewhat more favorable natural/geographic features than Korea in terms of climate, soil, and the potential for multiple cropping and related land-saving technology change, but both Korea and Taiwan benefited from the Japanese emphasis on such infrastructural investments as irrigation and such institutional investments as farmers' organizations.

The basic structural condition of this pretransition phase, labeled S_0 for the typical NRP, is shown in diagram 1a of figure 2.1. The agricultural sector, A, produces the domestic food supply, F, as well as traditional exports, E_a, which help to finance the import of manufactured nondurable consumer goods M_t (such as textiles) consumed by the household sectors, H.

Given this colonial heritage, the NRP, here typified by Taiwan, initiated its modern transitional growth effort during S_1 with the customary primary import-substitution pattern, as shown in diagram 2a. A portion of the traditional export earnings, E_a, is now diverted from the importation of nondurable consumer goods, M_t, to the importation of producers' goods, M_p. This permits the emergence of new import-substituting industries, I_n, producing domestic non-durable consumer goods, D_t, which gradually substitute for the previously imported M_t in the domestic market. Such a growth type, fueled by traditional exports, entails two observable import-substitution phenomena: substitution in the foreign exchange allocation sense, $M_p/(M_p + M_t)$, and substitution in the domestic market sense, $D_t/(M_t + D_t)$. Both indices can be expected to rise markedly over this period.

Moreover, foreign trade as a percentage of national income can be expected to decline during this same subphase, given the fact that the policy syndrome that accompanies it differs from the colonial pattern in that it strongly favors domestic markets by erecting various protective devices in support of a new industrial class. Given a long-run relative shortage of natural resources, a relative abundance of unskilled labor, and a good educational base, the development of human resources—entrepreneurial and managerial—appropriate for industrial production must gradually become an essential ingredient of the growth process. During subphase S_1, modern factory production for domestic markets, often with the help of foreign capital, S_f, was rapidly expanded; traditional populations were converted into modern factory workers; land-based or commercial entrepreneurs were converted into industrial entrepreneurs capable of absorbing modern science and technology; and law-and-order-oriented civil servants tended to become developmental change agents.

It is common knowledge that during this S_1 subphase all the policies of government are directed toward supporting the new industrial class. With profits taking on a windfall character not directly linked to productive efficiency, we usually encounter inefficient capital-intensive technology and output mixes, a neglect of rural industry, and an even more serious neglect of the food-producing agricultural sector. But what is especially noteworthy here is that the East Asian countries chose a relatively mild version of the syndrome; they neglected their agricultural sectors less and maintained lower levels of effective protection of their industries than is "typically" the case. Thus, while the well-known strategy combining tariffs, import licensing, overvalued exchange rates, and low interest rates conforms to the stereotype, its execution in the East Asian countries was milder and more flexible.

As is also well known, this process of primary import-substitution growth, which lasted approximately a decade in the East Asian NRPs, must inevitably come to an end. The inevitability of its termination rests

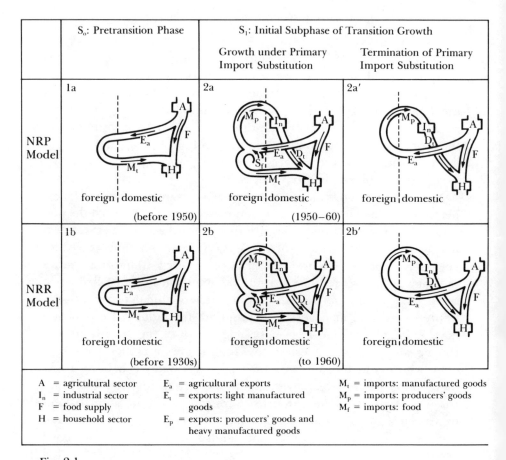

	S₀: Pretransition Phase	S₁: Initial Subphase of Transition Growth	
		Growth under Primary Import Substitution	Termination of Primary Import Substitution
NRP Model	1a foreign | domestic (before 1950)	2a foreign | domestic (1950–60)	2a' foreign | domestic
NRR Model	1b foreign | domestic (before 1930s)	2b foreign | domestic (to 1960)	2b' foreign | domestic

A = agricultural sector E_a = agricultural exports M_t = imports: manufactured goods
I_n = industrial sector E_t = exports: light manufactured goods M_p = imports: producers' goods
F = food supply M_f = imports: food
H = household sector E_p = exports: producers' goods and heavy manufactured goods

Fig. 2.1

S₂: Growth under Primary Export Substitution	S₃: Growth under Secondary Import Substitution with Secondary Export Substitution (4a) or Export Promotion (4b)
3a foreign¦domestic (1960–70)	4a foreign¦domestic (1970 on)
n/a	4b foreign ¦domestic (1960 on)

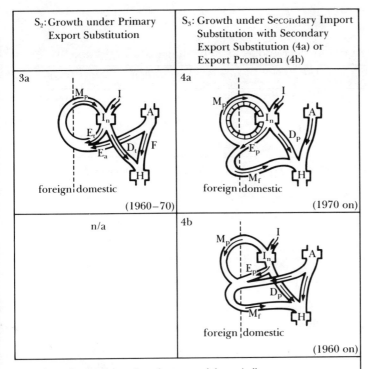

D_t = domestic manufactured goods consumed domestically
D_p = domestic producers goods consumed domestically
I = domestic investment
S_f = foreign capital

TABLE 2.4   Agricultural Exports as Percentage of Total Exports

	1950	1960	1970	1980
Taiwan	—	51.7	22.5	10.2
South Korea	82.3	51.4	16.7	8.9
Colombia	83.1	78.9	81.2	76.7
Mexico	53.5	64.1	48.8	14.2

SOURCES: Indices in United Nations Conference on Trade and Development, *Yearbook of Trade and Development Statistics*, various years; Taiwan 1982.
NOTE: Agricultural exports = SITC $0 + 1 + 2 - 2.7 - 2.8 + 4$.

TABLE 2.5   Mineral Exports as Percentage of Total Exports

	1950	1960	1970	1980
Taiwan	—	2.1	0.7	3.6
South Korea	11.2	8.3	8.3	10.5
Colombia	16.3	18.9	10.8	2.9
Mexico	38.6	24.0	21.2	71.6

SOURCES: Indices in United Nations Conference on Trade and Development, *Yearbook of Trade and Development Statistics*, various years; Taiwan 1982.
NOTE: Mineral exports = SITC $2.7 + 2.8 + 6.7 + 6.8$.

on the fact that, once "all" nondurable manufactured goods imports, M_t, have been substituted for by domestic output, D_t, any further industrialization must slow to the pace of population and per capita income change. The resource-flow picture that emerges at this point, roughly in the early 1960s, is shown in diagram 2a[1].

Difficult social decisions, such as whether to maintain the import-substitution strategy (but shift to the domestic production of previously imported producers' and durable consumer goods) or move toward the exportation of the same nondurable consumer goods previously produced for domestic markets, now had to be made. The East Asian NRPs, after some hesitation, chose the latter, and entered the S_2 subphase pictured in diagram 3a. This is termed "primary export substitution" because the basis for comparative advantage in foreign trade now gradually shifts from land to unskilled labor, with E_t exports gradually "substituting" for E_a exports. By the end of the 1960s their relative roles had, in fact, been dramatically reversed—from 90 percent land-based to 80 percent labor-based (as seen in tables 2.4–2.6)—while the trend in

TABLE 2.6 Manufactured Exports as Percentage of Total Exports

	1950	1960	1970	1980
Taiwan	—	46.2	76.8	86.2
South Korea	6.4	40.3	74.9	80.2
Colombia	0.5	1.4	8.0	19.7
Mexico	7.9	11.9	30.0	10.9

SOURCES: Indices in United Nations Conference on Trade and Development, *Yearbook of Trade and Development Statistics*, various years; Taiwan 1982.
NOTE: Manufactured exports = SITC 5 + 6 − 6.7 − 6.8 + 7 + 8.

TABLE 2.7 Export Orientation Ratio
(Exports as % of GDP)

	1950	1960	1970	1980
Taiwan	10.1	11.1	29.6	52.2
South Korea	2.1	3.3	14.3	37.7
Colombia	10.9	15.7	14.6	16.3
Mexico	17.0	10.6	8.2	22.4

SOURCES: International Monetary Fund, *Yearbook*, various years; World Bank 1981; Taiwan, *National Income of the Republic of China*, various years.

the overall trade orientation, E/GDP, increased markedly as a consequence of prodigious increases in labor-intensive industrial exports (see table 2.7).

Moreover, the rate of labor reallocation (the shift of the labor force from agricultural to nonagricultural pursuits over time) accelerated substantially during this S_2 subphase owing to a combination of rapidly increasing agricultural productivity and the expansion of labor-intensive industrial output now destined for relatively unlimited international markets. Once industrial entrepreneurial maturation, combined with the relative non-neglect of food-producing agriculture, had laid the foundation, labor-intensive export industries offered a full opportunity, really for the first time, to absorb the system's underemployed on a massive scale. This labor-based "vent for surplus" led to a pronounced increase in the rate of domestic intersectoral labor reallocation, culminating in not only a relative but an absolute decrease in the agricultural labor force, and, in the course of little more than a decade, the exhaustion of the labor-surplus condition, as indexed by nearly constant unskilled wages giving way to rapidly rising wages. This export-substitution mode, it should be noted, implies both vigorous domestic intersectoral growth and a substantial integration of the East Asian economies into the world economy. It meant a spurt in domestic agricultural/nonagricultural exchanges, as well as spectacular expansion of international trade. At the same time, in spite of considerable political and strategic uncertainties—especially in the case of Taiwan—capital inflows more than replaced the earlier infusion of concessional foreign capital.

Such a shift into export substitution must, of course, be accommodated by a shift in public policies that is difficult to achieve. Any enhanced orientation toward international markets on a competitive basis requires, first of all, a shift from an inflationary (under the table) method of taxing the landed interests on behalf of the new industrial classes to one of more explicit (on the table) taxation. It requires, moreover, a reduction in protection, the adoption and maintenance of more realistic exchange rates, interest rates closer to their shadow levels, and the continued avoidance of the temptation to artificially increase elite industrial workers' wages and depress domestic agriculture's terms of trade. The transition to export substitution in East Asia was also facilitated by such direct government actions as the establishment of export-processing zones and the rebating of import duties on raw materials destined for exports, as transitional devices.

This primary export substitution, or S_2, subphase also, of course, had its limits. Once the unskilled labor surplus has been exhausted, as it was by the early 1970s in East Asia, unskilled real wages began to rise in a sustained fashion. Competitive industrial output and exports tended to become more skilled labor-, technology-, and capital-intensive, and the subphase of secondary import and export substitution, S_3 (see diagram 4a), was gradually entered. As their skill, entrepreneurial, and technological capacities increased further, Taiwan and Korea have, in fact, since the mid 1970s moved into the production of capital goods and consumer durables, as well as the processing of raw materials for the domestic market and, almost simultaneously, for export (with the degree of simultaneity related to the importance of economies of scale in the context of the size of their domestic markets). At the same time, the slack in the system's agricultural sector in the form of sustained "Green Revolution" productivity increases had been substantially mopped up. As the agricultural sector becomes less of a leading sector and more of an appendage to the rest of the economy, the basic need for food imports in a natural-resource-poor system increasingly asserts itself. As indicated in diagram 4a, East Asia now supplies both domestic (D_p) and export markets (E_p) with producers' goods, while importing an increasing volume of food (M_f).

The per capita growth rates in Korea and Taiwan during their more than a quarter century of transitional growth have been remarkably high (see table 2.1). At least as interesting is an examination of their employment, labor share, and size distribution of income performance, which have also been outstandingly favorable by any standard. We should not, of course, be too surprised by an improvement in equity during S_3 once the labor surplus has been absorbed, wages rise, and industrial output shifts according to the product cycle in continuing response to changes in the endowment. This is in accordance with both cross-sectional evidence and the crude theorizing surrounding the inverse-U-shaped, or Kuznets curve, hypothesis (Kuznets 1955). What is of special interest, however, is that the distribution of income seems not to have worsened and even to have improved substantially during the period of most rapid early transitional growth, especially S_2 (see table 2.2), which runs counter to overall LDC experience and to the inverse-U-shaped hypothesis.

The East Asian countries under discussion provide striking cases of a remarkably strong growth performance, especially during their S_2 phases in the 1960s, combined with low and falling levels of income inequality, owing largely to initially high and rising relative shares of labor, and rapid absorption of unskilled labor hours in new rural and urban activities during the decade. The distribution of rural families' merged "agricultural incomes" also showed an improvement during the fifties and sixties, not only because of the initially favorable effects of land reform, but also because technologies were developed and promoted that rendered small farm holdings more productive over time. This was a function both of the more intensive use of land via double cropping, and of the shift to new, more labor-intensive, and higher-valued crops, such as vegetables and fruit for the domestic market and mushrooms and asparagus for the foreign market, in contrast to the more land-intensive traditional crops. Such shifts in cropping pattern were of particular benefit to the poorer (smaller) farmers, who were able to participate more than proportionately in these activities.

Turning now to the Latin American NRR case, which, of course, hides a great deal more heterogeneity within itself, the most striking characteristics are these countries' more favorable initial man/land ratios and natural-resource endowments generally, their more concentrated rural assets structure, their somewhat larger size, and their somewhat higher initial levels of wealth and income. Nevertheless, as indicated in diagram 1b, the initial colonial resource-flow pattern during S_0 in the Latin American case bears a substantial resemblance to the East Asian case (the export mainly of land-based raw materials—mostly minerals and tropical cash crops—E_a, in exchange for mainly industrial consumer goods, M_t). Essentially the same holds true for S_1, the easy import substitution subphase of transition starting in the Depression years of the 1930s (some say earlier), but focusing once more on reallocating the proceeds from the traditional natural-resource-based exports, mainly to finance new import-substituting industries producing nondurable consumer goods.

It should be noted that growth rates during the postwar primary import-substitution period were on the average as high in Mexico and Colombia as in East Asia, undoubtedly related to the higher levels of initial endowments and per capita incomes in Latin America (see table 2.1). On the other hand, the primary, or "easy," import-substitution policy package there may be judged to have been more severe, partly perhaps as a consequence of its substantially longer duration (from the 1930s to the early 1960s). One important consequence of this was a relatively much greater neglect of the food-producing agricultural subsector, reinforcing colonial policy antecedents that concentrated attention on the lucrative extractive enclaves. In short, both types of countries share an infant industry rationale that calls for the creation of a new industrial class out of the landlord or commercial elite, with the help of reasonable levels of protection and profit transfers.

The most striking difference, however, resides in the choice made at the end of S_1, the primary import-substitution subphase of transition. Faced, as were the NRPs, with a decline in the rate of industrial growth and the threat of price wars in protected domestic markets for consumer nondurables, the NRRs decided to continue with the import-substitution mode, but now focused on the manufacture of producers' and durable consumer goods—first for the domestic market and, somewhat later, for export as well (see diagram 4b).

This metamorphosis seems initially to parallel the secondary import- and export-substitution subphase recently reached by the NRP cases. But only at first blush. The most crucial difference is that the system now moves *directly* from primary import substitution into the production of the more skilled labor-, capital-, and technology-intensive products instead of *by way of* primary export substitution. Thus, not only was the protection and controls-oriented policy structure maintained, but its further deepening and strengthening was required. So, during the 1960s (after the end of primary import substitution), while the rates of effective protection declined somewhat in East Asia, they rose in most of Latin America. Interest rates generally remained at low, if not negative, real levels; the agricultural sector's terms of trade continued to be depressed; and even traditionally self-sufficient or food-exporting countries became net importers.

Moreover, given the still narrow domestic markets for the products of secondary import substitution, especially in the 1970s, the NRRs have, in fact, pushed for and achieved some sizeable increases in their nontraditional industrial exports (see table 2.6). While some of this expansion has admittedly been in the nondurable consumer goods area, particularly shoes and textiles, most of it has taken place in such higher technology, higher capital-intensity areas as automobiles, electrical machinery, chemicals, and even aircraft. In many cases it is related less to the march of dynamic comparative advantage or the product cycle than to the government's willingness to subsidize industrial exports that are by now generally recognized as the hallmark of successful development.

This industrial export phenomenon thus differs markedly from the primary export-substitution subphase encountered in East Asia, and instead entails the promotion of exports on top of a deepened import-substitution regime. It is distinguished by a difference in the composition of industrial output, by the fact that it is not preceded by a pronounced change in the overall policy package, and by the prevalence of substantial subsidies. Under it, particular industries or firms are selected for direct encouragement either via public sector tax rebates, differential interest rates, and export subsidies or via enforced private sector cross-subsidization (such as assuring companies of continued high windfall profits in protected domestic markets in exchange for compliance with rising export targets).

Both the composition of exports, as between traditional and nontraditional (see tables 2.4–2.6), and the change in the overall export orientation (see table 2.7) present a startling contrast between the NRPs and the NRRs, with the NRRs remaining much more oriented toward natural resources, fuel, and domestic markets. Also, in the NRRs the relative neglect of food-producing agriculture, already noted during S_1, is exacerbated during S_3 as protectionism deepens. As a consequence, with more and more traditional granaries empty, more of the cash crop exports proceeds, supplemented by foreign capital, must typically be devoted to food imports.

The prolongation of import substitution in this fashion, with export promotion eventually added, is evidently likely to be socially costly even if privately profitable (for obvious reasons). But the key fact is that with a favorable natural-resource base it can be "paid for," as exports and tax proceeds can continue to pay the piper, and in so doing help maintain very respectable growth rates (see table 2.1). What is less clear, however, is whether the consequences of this "skipping" of the S_2 export substitution subphase and moving directly from S_1 into S_3 are acceptable from the employment and distributional points of view.

Turning to the employment and income-distribution outcomes, the different transition paths chosen yield very different bottom lines. In the rural sector the combination of a worse distribution of land with the relative shift toward, rather than away from, traditional primary export cash crops tends to make for lower labor intensity and a higher (less favorable) agricultural income Gini. Rural nonagricultural incomes, which are more equally distributed than are agricultural incomes, constitute only 15 percent of farm family income, declining to 10 percent over time, in Colombia, in contrast to the initial 30 percent, rising to 60 percent, in Taiwan. Moreover, such rural industry and services as exist, given the maintenance of the import-substitution regime, are much more capital-intensive and contribute much less to favorable employment and distributional outcomes than they would in an NRP-type regime. Rural industry's labor share in Colombia, for example, was much lower (and falling) than was Taiwan's over virtually the entire period under discussion here. The same sources also indicate a sizeable gap in the urban labor share between the two countries. The much less favorable, and worsening, distributional outcome associated with the Latin American choice of a growth path should therefore come as no surprise.

All the statistical evidence that can be brought to bear thus indicates that the NRPs pursued a more or less linear path of policy liberalization and registered far and away the better development performance. On the other hand, in the NRRs we witness a different, less clear-cut, and more oscillatory pattern of policy or organizational choices, with market-oriented episodes displaced by the occasional return to import-substitution types of interventions, and much less successful outcomes in terms of the assessment of economic performance.

It is indeed a challenge for economists to try to move toward a better understanding of the fundamental causes of this divergent pattern. In that sense it is necessary to proceed beyond the above description of divergent growth performance (the skipping of a particular subphase in the case of the NRRs) and toward a comparative development perspective that includes the evolution of organizational and policy choices as part of the explanatory framework. A better understanding is needed as to why, in the NRP case, a more or less conformable evolution of policy resulted in the linearity of policy change, while in the NRR case we have been exposed to more or less continuous oscillation in spite of the profusion of "good advice" offered by economists and the donor community. It is to this political economy explanation of the divergence of performance that we now turn.

4. NATURAL RESOURCES AND THE POLITICAL ECONOMY OF TRANSITIONAL GROWTH

In discussing import substitution I identified six main instruments of interventionism: the interest rate, the exchange rate, the rate of monetary expansion, the rate of effective protection, the tax rate, and the unskilled wage rate. It is my basic contention that what has characterized NRP success is gradual, but consistent, adherence to liberalization in these various markets over time. This meant, in part, that interventions in period S_1 were milder than in the NRR case in the first place, and, more important, that liberalizing trends were maintained thereafter, even as the international situation deteriorated from time to time as a consequence of oil crises, recession abroad, inflation, and protectionism.

With respect to the first dimension, the policies in place in Taiwan did not differ very much from those in other developing countries during S_1—except for their relative mildness. Taiwan's policymakers set out to deploy the major macro policy instruments to achieve two main purposes: first, to promote the relatively new industrial sector through the creation of profits for domestic industrial entrepreneurs; and, second, to create revenues for the government. As noted above, these two purposes, creating profits and creating revenues, represent political acts. While both tariffs and quantitative restraints hold off foreign competition, monetary expansion, along with import licensing, low interest rates, and other direct allocations, permits windfall profits or rents to be awarded to the industrial and importing sectors, while the agricultural and exporting sectors are squeezed.

Most LDCs, in fact, view the increase in the supply of money as a way of putting purchasing power into the hands of the government so that it can accomplish certain developmental objectives. The fact that the resulting inflation may also muddy the water of relative prices by which people allocate goods and services rationally is often a not undesired outcome; it is a means of obscuring the transfer of resources that has taken place among various groups. At the individual level an expansionary monetary policy on the part of the government can be traced in part to the fact that there is an erroneous generalization by society as a whole that a plentiful supply of money has pleasant effects on individual beneficiaries, and that even those who are adversely affected get the benefits eventually. For the government it is tempting to view the creation of purchasing power through the printing press as a powerful instrument for acquiring goods and services in the market and for achieving larger resource mobilization for the system as a whole without having to seek taxation through some sort of consent by the population.

While such a move is, of course, easily tolerated when national survival is at stake, many contemporary LDCs resort to the same convenience in the absence of such an emergency. There is simply a general desire to make the tax burden less explicit and smaller, to avoid opening it to debate and/or to obscure the fact that government has this ability to create its own purchasing power. Thus, while inflation is generally symptomatic of the evasion or postponement of the assumption of some of the responsibilities by government, and is often tolerated by a narrow social consensus, this was not the case in the NRPs.

An expansionary monetary policy clearly represents a substantial convenience for a typical LDC government. It is also a welcome blessing for large-scale industrial enterprises that can borrow cheaply from the organized banking system. While these businessmen may not know the full theoretical implications of a rapidly expanding money supply, they are clearly aware of the advantages to themselves of a low interest rate combined with expansionary monetary policy. The credit rationing that results is only occasionally a problem for them—it is the medium- and small-sized companies and the farmers who are unable to borrow at these low rates. Moreover, if money creation leads to inflation, debt is made cheaper to repay. Thus the expansionary monetary policy typical of LDCs is popular with powerful segments of the business community, who expect inflation to "bail out" their borrowing. Not only is money creation and inflation a form of taxation, it is also an income-transfer mechanism whereby the purchasing power of the consuming public is transferred as windfall profits to the elite business class. It is thus a political act and an important component of the import-substitution strategy that was pursued in the typical LDC but abandoned in Taiwan and South Korea. The easiest way for the government and its favorite large-scale industrialist allies to obtain the rents basically generated on the land is through this policy combining low interest and inflation, as the central bank is typically an instrument of the government's efforts to acquire purchasing power through the monetary expansion mechanism.

In the natural-resource-rich LDC, inflation through monetary expansion is always intertwined closely with the foreign-exchange rate, as a crucial component of the import-substitution strategy. As is well known, the exchange rate is also almost universally regarded as a policy instrument rather than as an equilibrating market price regulating the level of imports and exports. In such an economy, overvaluation of the domestic currency benefits the import-substituting manufacturing class and amounts to an explicit tax on producers of export products. Here again we see the clear exercise of political power transferring windfall profits from where they exist, the rural primary-producing export sector and the consumer, to the urban manufacturing sector. Producers of import substitutes can buy imported raw materials and capital goods at artificially low prices and sell the finished products behind tariff walls at artificially high prices.

Such politically and artificially created cheapness of foreign exchange certainly makes it attractive to import at the official exchange rate, but it also generates two types of problems. First, the available foreign currency must be rationed, leading to import licensing, again a political process, and the possible use of different exchange rates for different categories of goods. Second, artificially set prices usually lead to "parallel" markets, a polite word for gray or black markets, again with certain groups having a distinct advantage over others. Usually, as domestic price inflation continues, the official exchange rate is occasionally devalued to at least partially correct for its excessive overvaluation. However, the pace of devaluation typically lags behind the domestic inflation rate; as a consequence the external purchasing power of the domestic currency is almost always higher than its internal purchasing power, as in even the crude versions of the purchasing-power parity theory. Typically again, the government is usually hesitant about the timing and scale of devaluations since it can easily be accused of aggravating preexisting domestic inflation, inasmuch as imported products immediately suffer price rises in terms of the domestic currency. Such a directly visible consequence of a political act is unpalatable, especially when price increases naturally apply to many items of mass consumption.

But, on the other hand, if the government does not devalue occasionally, domestic inflation means an increasing degree of overvaluation, which makes imports ever more attractive, and places an ever-heavier tax on land-based exports. Moreover, this hesitancy about whether or not to devalue usually strengthens the false belief that domestic inflation is mainly import-cost pushed, with the attention diverted from the fact that it was the excessive monetary expansion in the first place that fed the inflation. In this way, the government creates a complicated set of problems for itself: a controlled exchange rate hand in hand with monetary expansion, itself a function of the government's need to try to capture resources for itself and favored private groups. The complexity of the intervention policies, in terms of the administrative systems that need to be devised to replace the market and partially correct for the problems created by direct interference in the first place, then leads to the large-scale diversion of entrepreneurial resources to the pursuit of rents, well described by Anne Krueger (1974) and others.

In the attempt to carry out an import substitution strategy with the help of a substantial expansion of the money supply and an overvalued exchange rate, the extent of initial natural-resource wealth provides an important possible constraint. If the depressed profits of raw material producers discourage production, it may well be that natural resources can no longer be "squeezed" as effectively, exacerbating problems in other areas; for instance, export-product-related workers may have to be laid off, and so forth. On the other hand, if the natural-resource situation is comfortable, much more can be squeezed out, and for a much longer period of time, which can include finding new types of natural-resource-based exports (or foreign capital) to keep the process going.

What differentiates the NRP from the more typical NRR type, therefore, is that the extent of the NRP's import substitution policy regime has to be more limited—its duration shorter and its severity more restricted. We all know that primary import substitution must ultimately come to an end everywhere, especially in relatively small or medium-sized economies once domestic markets are exhausted. What is less well understood is that it is likely to end earlier, *ceteris paribus*, in situations where natural-resource endowments are poorer, since, in such cases, traditional exports are not ample enough to continue to fuel import substitution after it has reached its "natural" termination in terms of the exhaustion of domestic markets for nondurable consumer goods. Once excess capacity in textiles appeared in Taiwan in the late 1950s, the industry exerted pressure for cartelization, market sharing, even the subsidization of exports (dumping). But after some considerable filling and backing, it was recognized that the system could not "afford" this way of escaping from its cul-de-sac, any more than by shifting to a strategy of secondary import substitution.

The relative "mildness" of Taiwan's primary import-substitution subphase manifested itself in several dimensions. For one, the usual explicit discrimination against the agricultural sector, partly carried out via imposed terms-of-trade deterioration (by means of the rice/fertilizer barter system), and partly via relatively heavy taxation of land-based exports, was relatively less severe. Secondly, the customary resort to low interest rates plus an inflationary tax to shift resources "under the table" toward the new industrial urban elite was less pronounced. As early as the 1950s—during the height of the primary import-substitution subphase—the Taiwan authorities had already directed their attention to bringing inflation under control by means of interest rate reforms, along with monetary and fiscal cutbacks, as well as the timely help of foreign aid. Industrialization, in tandem with a dynamic agriculture and aided by the provisions of the land reforms of 1949–53, was already exceptionally dispersed into the rural areas. Even the level of protection (the usual combination of tariffs and quantitative restrictions) was exceptionally low, with QRs abandoned in favor of tariffs by 1958.

At the end of this relatively mild version of S_1, the prototypical East Asian NRP then shifted gradually into S_2, characterized by export orientation of the primary export-substitution type (which constituted a shift toward the exportation of the same labor-intensive nondurable consumer goods previously produced for the domestic market). In order to achieve international competitiveness in these areas, a substantial change in each of the various crucial policy areas, all in the direction of enhanced liberalization, was required. This was accomplished through the famous nineteen points of reform during the late 1950s and early 1960s, which included a further liberalization of domestic financial markets, the unification and devaluation of the exchange rate and the maintenance of more or less realistic levels thereafter, plus the maintenance of fairly restrictive monetary and, especially, fiscal policies throughout. It should be noted that the level of tariffs was not radically reduced at this time nor were international financial markets liberalized.

Taiwan, in fact, enjoyed a period of considerable price stability throughout its most rapid growth decade, the externally oriented 1960s, an experience unmatched anywhere else in the developing world. Even during the period of the pronounced worldwide inflation of the 1970s, inflation on Taiwan was only permitted to occur in short spurts, interspersed with longer periods of relative price stability. While "growth

with stability" was a slogan first popularized in the 1950s, largely in response to the dangers of mainland hyperinflation, inflation as a political
expedient continued to be rejected even during the period of the post–
oil shock 1970s, when it would have been easy to point the finger at cost-
push explanations. From the beginning, Taiwan seems to have accepted
the notion that, for the long term, sustained severe inflation is a basically
monetary phenomenon and that thus, to control it, it is necessary to
curb the growth of the money supply. This well-accepted conservative
tenet is an important distinguishing characteristic of the East Asian
model, though occasionally abandoned in the South Korean case.

It is thus, I believe, the absence of an ample natural resource endowment to help finance a Latin American style direct progression from the
easy primary to the more costly secondary import-substitution subphase
that is the key to explaining the comparative success of the Taiwan economy. Both the relative mildness of the earlier primary import-
substitution subphase and the shift from import to export substitution
before moving into the more capital- and technology-intensive output
mixes can basically be laid at the doorstep of Taiwan's natural-resource
scarcity. There was no alternative possibility of pursuing a dependable
path of employment and output generation by combining the system's
own natural resources with its abundant supplies of unskilled and semiskilled labor.[2]

In contrast, in the more typical Latin American NRR case, as the exhaustion of domestic demand forces the inevitable termination of primary import substitution, the economy moves into secondary import
substitution (durable consumer goods, capital goods, and the processing
of raw materials) skipping the labor-intensive S_2 phase. The dramatic
shift in the composition of exports in the NRP case, as well as the dramatic shift in overall export orientation, both in contrast to the NRR
case, is illustrated in tables 2.4–2.7. Put bluntly, as long as substantial
windfalls exist, as in Latin America, powerful interest groups will fight
off changes in the system as well as be in a position to buy off pressures
emanating from "outsiders," such as exporters, agriculturalists, and

2. Hong Kong and Singapore (once separated from its Malaysian agricultural sector)
clearly had even less choice. Their urban concentration and small size, coupled with unusually strong entrepreneurial capacities from the outset, meant the virtual absence of
import-substitution policies, especially in the case of Hong Kong. As Scitovsky puts it,
"among the larger countries that had a choice [sic] between alternative policies, Taiwan
and Korea were the first to recognize the gains to be had from encouraging the production
for export of those products in whose manufacture they had an advantage," i.e., primary
export substitution (Scitovsky 1985, 234).

consumers. Importers, industrialists and civil servants continue to be the beneficiaries of the policy package in S_3, and as long as the rents emanating from natural-resource-intensive exports are ample enough and can be "squeezed out" via the indirect transfer mechanisms referred to earlier, it is difficult politically to change the rules of the game. There is neither desire nor necessity to do so, and the existing strong tendencies to continue to promote growth by various "under the table" policy interventions in various markets will persist. This means that, while industrial entrepreneurs and governments continue to benefit, the burden continues to fall on consumers, who have to pay higher prices for inefficiently produced goods, as well as on the dispersed farmers who are providing agricultural output for both domestic and export destinations.

These costs are, of course, bound to be even higher as the system moves deeper into S_3 and tackles ever more capital- and skill-intensive output and export mixes. In fact, as I have pointed out, S_3 in the NRR cases usually requires an increasing subsidization of industrial exports and is thus more appropriately termed "export promotion" as distinct from the "export substitution" of S_2, which results from the more nearly neutral set of policies between import-competing and export activities in the NRP case. Export promotion can be economically sustained only as long as it can be "afforded," in other words "paid for" out of largely natural-resource-generated rents, and it can be politically sustained only as long as domestic consumers can be appealed to by way of the "synthetic" nationalism that governments usually continue to trot out at this stage, and/or as long as they remain ignorant of the additional burdens they are being asked to carry.

During S_1 essentially the same kind of policy syndrome is in place in both the NRP and NRR: an overvalued currency, import controls, and substantial increases in the money supply—except that the NRP version is milder and briefer. In this very direct sense, Taiwan's shortage of natural resources can be seen to have been a substantial advantage. With its main primary product exports, rice and sugar, reaching market limits by the late 1950s, an alternative approach became a necessity. It was soon realized, although the record of policy discussions of the late 1950s indicates a good deal of back-and-forth hesitation, that, since natural resources were limited, the economy had to turn to its abundant labor supply for the new engine of growth. The shift to a human-resource base became a necessity. The exchange rate, which had been overvalued during import substitution, was now consistently undervalued, contributing

to the emergence of the frequent export surpluses of the sixties and seventies and assuring all the actors that the government was indeed serious about its refusal to relapse into import-substitution-type policies
even when threatened by external business cycles and other shocks.[3]

With respect to the level and method of taxation, it is, of course, possible to mobilize resources without taxation by consent. When a government incurs a budget deficit, increases the money supply, and permits
price inflation, these are part and parcel of the mechanism for covert
forms of taxation; they avoid the necessity of assessing, negotiating, de-
bating, and imposing a system of taxes. While such a system of ambiguous, non-negotiated burden sharing in the development effort is usually
tolerated when national survival is at stake, it is surprising that contemporary LDCs continue to resort to it in the normal course of their transitional growth effort. Clearly there exists an unwillingness to make the
tax burden too explicit, too open to debate, or to abandon the sheer convenience of the government creating its own purchasing power and directing precisely how it should be allocated. In fact, the inflationary process described is generally symptomatic of the desire to postpone "on
the table" responsibilities, which require much more of a social consensus as to who ought to pay the taxes and who ought to benefit from development expenditures.

In the early stages of import-substitution growth, it is usually tariffs
that are imposed, partly for protective, partly for revenue reasons, and
they constitute most of the existing tax yield. This is partly because of
the convenient point specificity of their method of collection. There
thus exists a commonality of interest between governments requiring
revenue and infant manufacturers requiring protection—both provided
via the use of high tariff walls as a crucial component of the import-
substitution policy package. The adoption of this tariff wall, of course,
also represents an income-transfer mechanism in that the consuming
public must pay for the inefficiency of the infant manufacturers as they
face higher prices for previously imported consumer goods. Thus income is transferred by political force, in the form of windfall profits,
from consumers to urban industrialists. Since the now domestically
produced items have traditionally been scarce and expensive, many

3. On the other hand, it also led to the perhaps premature exportation of capital from
Taiwan and the accumulation of foreign-exchange reserves beyond the needs of a rapidly
growing economy. There was probably also a military security motivation behind the accumulation of foreign-exchange reserves in the wake of the U.S. recognition of the People's
Republic of China and Taiwan's increased political isolation.

TABLE 2.8 Tax Rate
(% of GDP)

	1950	1960	1970	1980
Taiwan	11 (1952)	11	14	17 (1979)
South Korea	6 (1953)	10	16	18
Colombia	3	4	9 (1972)	10
Mexico	8	7	9	13 (1975)

SOURCES: International Monetary Fund, *Yearbook*, various years; World Bank 1981; Taiwan, *National Income of the Republic of China*, various years.

consumers may not even be aware that this scarcity and the likely deterioration of quality that accompanies it are created by political force.

An income tax system was established in Taiwan in 1955; by 1961 the government's fiscal deficits had been brought under control. By 1964 there was a budgetary surplus and the emphasis had shifted to fiscal restraint, including the generation of surpluses over many years as an anti-inflationary device. Here again we see the need, because of the natural-resource shortage, to shift taxes from a land base to a human-capital and, later, physical-capital base.

Thus, previously referred to monetary reforms (raising interest rates and moving toward greater central bank autonomy) and these fiscal reforms (legislation shifting from land-based taxes to income taxes on the rest of the system) represent major evolutionary steps in the NRP-type country—all part of the gradual depoliticization of the economy as income transfers and resource reallocations, once hidden, are gradually discontinued and become subject to "on the table" public scrutiny. The displacement of the habit of printing money cannot, of course, be accomplished overnight. The typical LDC government's ability to raise taxes is limited, and there will be an increased tendency to reduce import duties—not only to help with import liberalization, but also because urban consumers increasingly come to realize that they have been paying for the inefficiency of domestic industries. But only as liberalization in the first stage makes it possible to experience a substantial increase in the GNP growth rate is a government likely to be in a position to close the budget deficit by raising other taxes and effecting the shift from agricultural to nonagricultural levies previously referred to. A shift in the composition of taxes, in other words, is likely to have to be associated with an increase in the overall level of taxes (see tables 2.8–2.10). Finally, the increased revenues place the government in a position to increase its other developmental functions via increased expenditures

TABLE 2.9   Composition of Taxes
(Customs duties as % of total taxes)

	1950	1960	1970	1980
Taiwan	26 (1952)	23	28	24
South Korea	17 (1953)	21	13	12
Colombia	18	27	19 (1972)	18
Mexico	34	31	20	11

SOURCES: International Monetary Fund, *Yearbook*, various years; World
Bank 1981; Taiwan, *National Income of the Republic of China*, various years.

TABLE 2.10   Real Effective Exchange Rates
(1975 = 100)

	1965	1970	1980
Taiwan	—	96.17	95.50
South Korea	98.18	73.00	94.84
Colombia	79.71	81.20	81.73

SOURCES: International Monetary Fund, *Yearbook*, various
years; World Bank 1981; Taiwan, *National Income of the
Republic of China*, various years.

on such things as science, technology, agricultural research, education,
overheads, and so forth.

In a broader context, the existence, and persistence, of substantial
economic rents leads, as we have already seen, to artificial support of urban areas and neglect of agriculture and rural industries. Politically, economically, and technologically sensitive cities represent the usual base of
modernization, which includes the capacity to produce inputs for agriculture incorporating modern science and technology. However, the acceleration of these linkages through government expenditures is likely
to be reserved for a later stage of any liberalization. The excessive costs
of too-early or forced urbanization, so typical of the NRR case, were
avoided in the NRP case. The need for a food-producing agricultural
revolution as precursor to or, better, companion of an industrial revolution, in a balanced growth context, has been amply demonstrated in the
NRP case; they generally permitted their agricultural sectors to fulfill
their historical mission en route to becoming an appendage to the
system. In chapter 8 D. Gale Johnson observes the tendency of the NRPs
to subsidize their agricultural sectors at a later stage. But this is *after* they
have permitted this sector to fulfill its historical mission, essential to the
success of the system's development effort in the first place. Apparently

TABLE 2.11 Public Expenditure on Education
(% of GNP)

	1972	1981
Taiwan	3.5	4.5 (includes science and culture)
South Korea	3.0	3.4
Colombia	2.9	2.9
Mexico	2.0	3.8

SOURCES: United Nations, *National Accounts Statistics*, various years; Taiwan, *Statistical Data Book*, 1985; UNESCO, *Statistical Yearbook*, various years.

in this area, as well as in the fields of social security, welfare legislation, and so on, the successful NRPs also become subject to "rich man's" diseases.

In the NRR, by contrast, we witness more of an implicit assumption (somewhat modified in recent years) that there is no need to have an agricultural revolution, and that the agricultural sector can be discriminated against from the outset by means of the covert policies of government intervention, as we have already seen, as well as by the more overt biases in allocating human and physical infrastructure. It is very difficult to move toward a market-oriented approach and liberalization as long as rent-seeking political forces deny farmers the purchasing power that rightly belongs to them.

The requirement of balanced rural growth to propel the economy forward also carries with it the need for a more participatory or "open" education system, focused on primary education in the rural areas rather than higher education for the urban elite. In fact, it may be helpful to take a brief synoptic look at contrasting educational policy and expenditure patterns in the NRR and NRP cases. Table 2.11 indicates that the NRP governments generally spend somewhat more on education than the NRRs, even though they undoubtedly start with somewhat higher levels of human capital in place at the outset.[4] But what is certainly as significant is the much greater emphasis on ensuring a broadly based primary and secondary education structure over time in the NRP cases (see table 2.12). This is reflected both in public-sector expenditure allocations and, more subtly, in the much greater access to talent via competitive examinations at every level. There can be little doubt that the necessity of relying more on one's wits—or, if one prefers, less on the ability to "afford" education as an elite consumption good—is reflected

4. Adult literacy rates, however, were not markedly different in the 1950s.

TABLE 2.12   Public Expenditure on Education by Level
(% of funds allocated)

	Primary		Secondary		Higher	
	1972	1981	1972	1981	1972	1981
Taiwan (1968)	37.5	41.0	44.4	40.3	18.1	18.7
South Korea	65.4	69.1	26.5	19.4	8.0	11.5
Colombia	53.8	48.6	23.7	27.6	22.5	23.8
Mexico	56.2	46.2	22.8	21.9 (1982)	21.0	32.0 (1982)

SOURCES: United Nations, *National Accounts Statistics,* various years; Taiwan, *Statistical Data Book,* 1985; UNESCO, *Statistical Yearbook,* various years.

in both the educational policies and expenditure patterns under observation in the NRPs.

Since newly independent governments normally face demands for spending that easily exceed available revenue, as well as for imports in excess of export earnings, other means must be found to deal with deficits. This holds for NRRs as well as NRPs. In East Asia in the 1950s the inflow of foreign aid, mainly from the United States, was helpful in that context, as was the inflow of private foreign capital in the 1960s and 1970s. While concessional capital inflows played an important historical role in both filling governments' budget gaps and helping to combat inflation, it is wrong to assume that foreign capital has been of overriding importance in financing overall capital accumulation during the past three decades in the NRP cases, as is sometimes asserted. Even if this may seem to hold for South Korea, foreign capital amounted to only 7 percent of cumulative investment in Taiwan, the most successful LDC, over that period (see table 2.13). The NRRs have received as much, if not more, foreign capital (measured either on a per capita basis or as a percentage of the total investment fund), so it can hardly be said that the relatively greater success of the NRPs is owing to the greater generosity of foreign friends and investors.

More generally, while aid was admittedly qualitatively important at particular points in time in helping, say the Taiwan government, to accept and bind up the wounds of policy change, the quantitative role of foreign aid, not dominant throughout, declined steadily after the mid 1950s, and was completely phased out by the early 1960s.[5] It seems

5. In fact, there are some who claim that the announcement of an impending aid phaseout a few years down the road was helpful in concentrating policymakers' minds and getting reforms adopted.

TABLE 2.13 Share of Foreign Capital
Inflow in Total Investment
(cumulative)

	%	Years
Taiwan	7.4	1956–83
South Korea	22.2	1953–83
Colombia	14.5	1956–82
Mexico	20.3	1960–82

SOURCES: International Monetary Fund, *International Financial Statistics*, various years; Taiwan, *Statistical Data Book*, various years.

generally true for the East Asians, certainly including historical Japan, and with only Korea as something of a deviant,[6] that, with the exception of emergencies such as earthquakes, floods, or droughts, foreign aid in the sense of open-ended, long-range resource transfers to help growth is not really needed. Where it can be very helpful is in particular timely infusions, or what may be called the temporary "ballooning" of aid, in relation to major policy changes that governments may be ready to undertake.[7]

With respect to the official attitude toward private capital, both direct foreign investment and, later, commercial bank or portfolio investments, we may again note the role of "synthetic nationalism," under which foreign intrusions into the domestic market are often resented. Not needing to "create" a nationalist spirit and national self-confidence at the outset also meant a greater willingness by the early 1960s to accept private foreign capital and foreign companies in substantial quantities in Taiwan.[8] This early evolution away from synthetic nationalism moved the system in the direction of a greater integration of its financial markets with those of the rest of the world, even if the full liberalization of the capital market was clearly postponed and is only now under full consideration.

We can thus also observe a gradual depoliticization of long-term capital movements via the replacement of politically negotiated foreign aid by the inflow of private foreign investment induced by the market, as

6. The precise reasons for this deviation, related inter alia to Korea's less full agricultural mobilization, are spelled out in Ranis and Fei 1975.

7. This is similar to the view expressed in Scott 1979.

8. See Ranis and Chi 1985. All this may be somewhat complicated by the fact that part of the motivation may also have been to put in place a tripcord mechanism in the event of an attack from the mainland.

foreign investors sought to combine their capital and technology with the abundant labor supplies of Taiwan. The fact that foreign investment increased substantially in spite of the shift of diplomatic recognition from Taiwan to the People's Republic of China in the 1970s is a powerful indicator of the gradual integration of the East Asian economies into world markets. Increased levels of foreign investment over time, as comparative advantage changed rapidly, can be viewed not simply as a means of attracting capital or providing employment for the surplus labor population, but also as a vehicle for transferring technologies that could then be adapted to Taiwan's own requirements. But full integration into international capital markets, short- or long-term, was delayed. Such a reduction of capital controls and the accompanying increase in competitive pressure for industry and banking, likely to facilitate a more rapid transfer and adaptation of technology, is only now being fully considered.

The final important policy parameter for consideration is, of course, the wage rate, or more precisely, the extent of intervention in the unskilled nonagricultural labor market. As we have seen, the initial land/labor ratios differ markedly in the NRR and NRP cases, presumably leading to higher equilibrium levels of real wages in the former. But what is of special interest to us here is the extent to which governments intervene, especially in urban labor markets, and the politicoeconomic reasons for doing so. It is well recognized, for example, that unionism and minimum-wage legislation had much greater strength in the NRR than in the NRP cases. Unionism is, in fact, a phenomenon that may be said to be primarily political, stemming from governments' efforts to establish a political base and demonstrate a sense of strength among urban workers. It is thus very much related, on the one hand, to the existence or nonexistence of an initial "organic nationalism" (the need to create cohesion among the citizens of a society) as well as, on the other hand, to the existence or nonexistence of natural resources to pay for what might be considered elite benefits accruing to a small minority of the laboring class. While the wages, benefits, and prestige of the usually 5–10 percent of the industrial working class that may be termed "organized" can indeed be raised by direct intervention, the impact on that class as a whole is likely to be negative. As long as a "labor surplus" condition exists—definable in terms of relatively unskilled workers—unions' ability to raise real wages, like the effect of minimum-wage legislation, depends almost entirely on government actions and support. However, no one can successfully "legislate" against the endowment; such measures are capable only of raising real wages for an elite subgroup of workers at the expense of wage incomes for the majority—even if union and government pronouncements invariably pretend to argue the case for the entire working class.

"Premature" (before the unskilled labor supply is absorbed) urban-rural wage differentials can, of course, be a serious handicap for societies potentially in a position to export labor-intensive manufactured goods to world markets. They are bound to induce the wrong choice of technology and the wrong choice in the direction of technology change. Thus, a minority, perhaps as few as 10 percent of the workers in the nonagricultural sector, may effectively deprive their nonunionized colleagues of employment opportunities and deny the country the comparative advantage of lower labor costs in competitive markets. In the presence of natural-resource-generated rents, it is possible for a bilateral oligopoly of industrialists and elite workers to divide up these rents in a bilateral bargain. In the absence of such rents, a labor-surplus country clearly faces a choice between high wages for a minority and unemployment for the majority, and is likely to find it politically difficult to maintain a favored position for the few under those circumstances. It is this difference, and not simply the presence of a "repressive" set of governments, which led to the virtual absence of a politicized militant unionism in the NRP's, at least prior to the advent of labor shortage in the 1970s.

In the NRRs, on the other hand, union activism is usually an endemic component of the politicized development process I have been describing. As inflation affects certain groups at the expense of others, unions may gain strength by leading protests, and usually achieve a perpetuation of their bilateral bargains with capitalists at the expense of the majority of nonunion workers. Union power is really given by the government and can be taken away by the government. Two monopolistic powers, the money-printing state and the wage-gap-creating union, can thus combine to create a situation that is often detrimental to the well-being of the working people of a developing country, as well as to the growth of the system as a whole—certainly before all the labor surplus has been mopped up.

As already noted, given the scarcity of natural resources, the NRP's primary import-substitution subphase (S_1) is likely to be both short and, judging from the way the major policy instruments are exercised, not as severe as in the NRR case. The comparative severity of the government's interventionist impact in the two cases can be seen mainly via comparative rates of monetary expansion, the level of the real rate of interest, the exchange rate, the rate of protection, the rate of taxation and the organized sector's real unskilled wage rate. There is an inherent tendency for inflation to result if restraint is not exercised in deploying these tools of government intervention. When deployed over extended periods of time in the fashion typical of NRR import-substitution regimes, they are likely to undermine the ultimate success of the very growth-oriented strategy they are intended to serve.

What is basically at work here is the relatively greater ability of the East Asian NRP to renounce the exercise of political muscle to "manufacture" purchasing power, in sharp contrast to the more typical Latin American NRR. It is this renouncing of power, or better, the more restrained exercise of power via "on the table" rather than "under the table" actions that is part of the deliberate trend toward NRP liberalization. Such depoliticization of the system implies that the government gradually learns to be more responsible and open about what it is doing, moving away from implicit taxes and covert transfers and toward explicit and more equitable and efficient types of influences on the economy. The willingness to avoid monetary expansion and the rejection of the printing press as a dependable source of revenue represent an important part of this liberalization movement. In monetary policy it means permitting the interest rate as well as the exchange rate to assume levels that might be closer to equilibrium over time. With less financial repression it also means greater reliance on a competitive institutional credit structure and the commercial banking system. The importance of policies that induce human resources to take over from natural resources in the NRP setting is indicated by the fact that gradual liberalization permits the opening up of opportunities not only for cultivating peasant households, but also for medium and small-scale industrial entrepreneurs in the rural areas—in strong distinction to what goes on in the more typical large-scale urban-oriented NRR case.

The liberalization process described for Taiwan has, of course, both a domestic and an international dimension. Domestically, the movement implies a reduction of government controls in order to accelerate the growth of saving and investment and the broader participation of human resources. Internationally, liberalization means an opening up of the economy with respect to trade and finance, and therefore enhanced economic integration with the rest of the world. Such an enhanced external orientation, of course, carries dynamic efficiency advantages as well as static gains from trade. Once domestic entrepreneurs become subject to the rigors of international competition, as they are forced to compete in world markets, they come to recognize the merits of quality and price and cease being a captive audience, as domestic consumers are. Instead, they become increasingly competitive risktakers, innovators, and production managers in the context of a "learning by doing" process.

The enhanced international competitiveness of the NRP case warrants mention for a number of reasons. One is that while a producer may dominate a local market, in the international arena the situation is much more likely to be workably competitive. The more open an economy to imports and foreign competition, the more this helps to control domestic market power as well as to force domestic entrepreneurs to select more appropriate technologies and innovate in more appropriate directions—both in the process and in the product sense. As long as traditional import-substitution strategies are maintained and domestic manufacturers are sheltered by political means, an intense fear of foreign competition is gradually built up. This represents one of the more vicious of the various vicious circles of development: the fear generated under political protection in turn generates demand for more political patronage, and for continued import substitution even when the initial infant industry argument has long lost its validity. This is very much a feature of the natural-resource-rich Latin American scene. It is only experience in world markets during an external orientation phase that can dependably allay these fears.

I have already noted that, while Taiwan shifted from quantitative restrictions to tariffs during its primary import-substitution subphase, and thus provided greater access to competitive imports and a milder form of infant industry protection, its overall levels of tariff protection did not diminish sharply for some time. This is because the effective rate of protection is not as sensitive to external short-term fluctuations as the other instruments of policy previously referred to. It is therefore not as vital that it be reduced early on. Moreover, a too-early radical reduction of tariffs could embarrass a government by reducing revenues before alternatives are in place or before industrialists have gained some confidence that they can manage competitively, and thus force a general policy reversal.

What Taiwan did instead was adopt a customs rebate system in the late 1950s and a policy of export-processing zones in the 1960s, amounting to a partial liberalization of trade as a first step. While the full meaning of liberalization is not to bias a system in favor of exports but to provide a more equitable game, this may have to be done in stages. Tariffs were further reduced in 1971, with the executive branch given the authority, without additional legislative approval, to adjust tariffs downward by up to 50 percent. Further across-the-board tariff reductions have taken place in the 1980s but, as is well known, Taiwan today is still far from a paragon of free trade. Its efforts at partial trade liberalization by first eliminating quantitative controls, subsequently introducing tariff rebates and export-processing zones, and only then reducing tariffs permitted some industries to continue to be protected and remain isolated from international competition as long as they sold only in the domestic market. This policy made it possible to continue to coerce the consuming public by political force in these areas not only to pay import duties but also to pay for the inefficiency of those protected industries. On the other hand, export-oriented sectors gradually and selectively increased their efficiency through the rebate system and the export-processing zones in areas in which the government gave up its political power. Since the government is clearly unable to coerce foreign consumers to pay for the inefficiency of domestic producers, these are also the industries that were the first to reduce their costs under the newly competitive pressures.

I hope it is by now clear that the gradual trend toward liberalization during the transitional growth process described here does not imply anything like a shift toward laissez-faire and an abandonment by the government of its major economic role.[9] What it does imply is that the NRP government gradually abandons its "under the table" efforts at shifting resources from some groups to others, including itself, via the exercise of its monopoly power in the fiscal and monetary arenas. For domestic monetary policy this means that, since the government cannot control both price and quantity, it must focus increasingly on quantity and let price (the interest rate) be market-determined. In the case of foreign-exchange management the same principle implies an increasing focus on the quantity of reserves and a more clearly (and cleanly) floating exchange rate. This means viewing money increasingly as a medium of exchange required for the internal division of labor, and viewing foreign-exchange reserves increasingly as a medium of exchange required to take advantage of the international division of labor. In this sense gradual liberalization is consonant with the notion that money is not simply purchasing power that can be artificially created to achieve socially desirable purposes, such as transferring profits among interest groups.

9. This point is also forcefully and effectively made in Wade 1985.

Increasingly, the view of a more independent central bank also means that the government must replace covert income transfers by explicit taxation, with consent. Basically what is involved here is avoiding the misapplication of the short-run Keynesian message (that large government deficits do not matter, that inflation is always cost-pushed, that an increase in the supply of money always lowers the rate of interest, that commercial bank lending does not represent the creation of purchasing power for investment finance, and that governments can and should manage economic affairs in general) to the development problem. The more or less linear trend toward liberalization in East Asia has depended to a large extent on a change in monetary thinking in regard to the role of money as a medium of exchange rather than as a means of providing purchasing power to the government, as well as on a different attitude toward the accumulation of foreign-exchange reserves.

As we have seen, such policy parameters as the interest rate, the exchange rate, and the growth rate of the money supply are the instruments that constitute the core of the politicization mechanism during import substitution and of possible depoliticization thereafter. In the NRP case they are used less and less over time as policy instruments to promote growth, with the government more and more assuming the role of a direct actor, as "on the table" taxes and expenditure patterns emerge, including a continued important role for public enterprise. In the East Asian countries, in fact, public enterprise continues to extend substantially into directly productive activities, well beyond traditional areas of public goods or external economies.[10] Domestic financial markets remain protected and underdeveloped to this day, rendering it difficult to collect a sufficient volume of savings to permit some relatively large-scale activities to take place. This bottleneck has become more important of late as Taiwan's comparative advantage has continued to evolve in favor of capital- and technology-intensive output mixes. Consequently, we may note that, while the relative role of public enterprise in directly productive activities declined during the 1960s, it is currently again on the upswing. Liberalization in this area, which may entail some privatization, has clearly been given a lower priority and must await improvements in the capital market.

Currently, as the NRPs enter the era of science- and technology-based production and exports, they have also turned to changes in the patent and trademark laws as an indication of the perceived need for more

10. Amsden (1985) points out that Taiwan's recent "ten major development projects" included public-sector involvement in integrated steel, shipbuilding and petrochemicals.

indigenous innovations in the context of the international technology-transfer environment, which has itself undergone marked changes. The Taiwan government, for example, has played an increasingly active role in providing for an improvement in the science and technology environment, including support for R&D, especially where there are external economies of sufficient magnitude that individual private enterprises cannot be expected to meet the costs. Its current reexamination of the required level of taxes, including the possibility of a value-added tax, relates to the need for additional resources to provide for the explicit expenditures of the mainline ministries where overhead creation is required, as well as to meet the costs of a second land reform (land consolidation in agriculture and the creation of new large-scale public enterprises in the nonagricultural sector).

When the natural-resource base is substantial and increasing in importance (the NRR case) both foreign-exchange accumulation and agriculture-based taxes are likely to be substantial, especially when the terms of trade are favorable. This often leads to the temptation to increase government expenditures out of line with long-run realities, especially once the terms of trade turn down. In the NRP case much more caution is likely to be exercised, given the need to shift taxes rather quickly from the natural-resource to the human-resource basis of production, and likewise with respect to foreign-exchange reserves.

Finally, an interesting and more complicated question is sometimes raised concerning the type of government required to carry out liberalization in a systematic, or more or less linear, fashion. It is argued that the problem with the East Asian case is that it seems to require a more or less hard, or authoritarian, type of government not acceptable to many of the contemporary LDCs. One could, of course, point out that there are many authoritarian governments (including some in Latin America) that have, in fact, been signally unsuccessful in effecting a successful transition. We also do not know what the proverbial man on the street would choose if confronted with the stark inevitability of a trade-off. What does seem to hold is that successful liberalization, once under way, is likely to mean moving in a direction in which organizational choices, like the structure of the system itself, ultimately approach those of a developed country—including an increasing role for markets and an increasing pluralism within the society in general. This certainly seems to be happening now, if not very rapidly, in contemporary South Korea and Taiwan. But at what stage in the transition process economic pluralism must be supported by political pluralism is less clear. The covert forms of income transfers typically seem to linger longer when a system is not yet politically a pluralistic society in which each of the multiplicity of interest groups can exercise only relatively small influence on the political stage and countervailing power exists. Yet we also know that the costs and benefits of overt government policy cannot be calculated, debated, or compromised as readily ex ante when political parties vie with each other in promising visible actions to various vocal, if often elite, minority interest groups.

It is difficult indeed to render a comparative judgment on Latin American versus East Asian authoritarianism, either in terms of its parliamentary or its human rights dimension. It is much easier to compare performance in terms of the speed of transition, growth, equity improvement, or poverty alleviation. Yet I am prepared to argue that parliamentary trappings may, in fact, constitute an aspect of the synthetic nationalism I see as an obstacle to early economic liberalization. If we assume, for example, that the quality of the policymakers in the East Asian and Latin American contexts is equivalent, it may well be true that acting sensibly in response to that vision may be easier for policymakers in more authoritarian NRP governments, which can take a longer view and need worry less about placating public opinion or their early reelection. In such a situation "accommodating" sequential policy reforms might be more readily carried out with less likelihood of protests by special interest groups, public demonstrations, or, worse, military coups.

But we also know that economic liberalization via enhanced mobility and participation is something which can be achieved in one or two decades. The emergence of an authentic differentiated political pluralism, on the other hand, is just as clearly a longer-run organizational accomplishment, different from the trappings of a multiparty system, and has to be dealt with differently. We must indeed try to distinguish between political pluralism as a plaything of the urban elite and mass participation plus the protection of habeas corpus for the many—just as we endeavor to assess the extent of participation and mobility in economic affairs by means of equity and poverty-alleviation indices.

In sum, an ample natural-resource endowment, like an ample supply of foreign capital available for the asking, can be a mixed blessing for a developing society attempting transition to modern growth. Such an abundance of resources contains the seeds of a generalized "Dutch disease" phenomenon extending well beyond the narrow impact on the exchange rate. On the one hand, it provides rents for both private parties and public decision makers that will likely induce second-best critical choices in the economic policy arena. On the other hand, it increases the society's exposure to terms-of-trade fluctuations and enhances the tendency over time to oscillate between liberalization and retreats to import-substitution policies. The problem is not that more natural resources (like more foreign capital) *cannot* be good for you—but that instead of being used to ease the pain of change, they are likely to be used to postpone change. Like individuals, societies that are not "up against it" prefer to avoid sustained changes in the policy mix that are perceived as potentially painful by powerful vested interest groups.[11] The natural-resource-poor society, on the other hand, is forced to "bite the bullet," so to speak; not being able to put off the day of reckoning, it is much more likely to begin relying in a sustained fashion on its human resources. This, in turn, implies a more competitive system over time and greater flexibility in adjusting to the inevitable changes in the international environment. And finally—though here we are admittedly on more speculative grounds—the productive participation of the majority resulting from the sequential liberalization in various markets is likely to generate its own pressure for a gradual liberalization in the political sphere as well.

REFERENCES

Amsden, Alice. 1985. "The State and Taiwan's Economic Development." In Theda Skocpol, Peter B. Evans, and Dietrich Rueschemeyer, eds., *Bringing the State Back In*. New York: Cambridge University Press.

Chenery, Hollis B. 1979. *Structural Change and Development Policy*. New York: Oxford University Press for the World Bank.

Fei, John C. H., Gustav Ranis, and Shirley W. Y. Kuo. 1979. *Growth with Equity: The Taiwan Case*. New York: Oxford University Press for the World Bank.

Fei, John C. H., Kazushi Ohkawa, and Gustav Ranis. 1985. "Economic Development in Historical Perspective: Japan, Korea, and Taiwan." In Kazushi Ohkawa and Gustav Ranis, eds., *Japan and the Developing Countries: A Comparative Analysis*. Oxford: Basil Blackwell.

Galenson Walter, ed. 1979. *Economic Growth and Structural Change in Taiwan: The Postwar Experience of the Republic of China*. Ithaca, N.Y.: Cornell University Press.

International Monetary Fund. Various years. *International Financial Statistics*. Washington, D.C.: IMF.

———— . Various years. *Yearbook*. Washington, D.C.: IMF.

11. Riedel, in a good survey of East Asian development, misspecifies the nature of the opposition. It does not come from agricultural interests resisting industrialization but from industrial interests, plus civil servants and organized labor, resisting the loss of rents that come from agriculture.

Krueger, Anne O. 1974. "The Political Economy of a Rent-Seeking Society." *American Economic Review* 64 (June): 291–303.

Kuznets, Simon. 1955. "Economic Growth and Income Inequality." *American Economic Review* 45 (March): 1–28.

————. 1966. *Modern Economic Growth*. New Haven: Yale University Press.

Mason, Edward S., Kim Mahn Je, Dwight H. Perkins, Kim Kwang Suk, and David C. Cole. 1980. *The Economic and Social Modernization of the Republic of Korea*. Cambridge, Mass.: Council on East Asian Studies, Harvard University.

Ranis, Gustav. 1955. "The Community-Centered Entrepreneur in Japanese Development." *Explorations in Entrepreneurial History* 8 (December): 80–98.

Ranis, Gustav, and John C. H. Fei. 1975. "A Model of Growth and Employment in the Open Dualistic Economy: The Cases of Korea and Taiwan." *Journal of Development Studies* 11 (January): 32–74.

Ranis, Gustav, and Chi Schive. 1985. "Direct Foreign Investment in Taiwan's Development." In Walter Galenson, ed., *Foreign Trade and Investment*. Madison: University of Wisconsin Press.

Riedel, James. 1985. "Economic Development in East Asia: Doing What Comes Naturally?" Paper presented to the National Centre for Development Studies, Australian National University, Canberra.

Scitovsky, Tibor. 1985. "Economic Development in Taiwan and South Korea, 1965–81" *Food Research Institute Studies* 19, no. 3: 214–64.

Scott, Maurice, 1979. "Foreign Trade." In Walter Galenson, ed., *Economic Growth and Structural Change in Taiwan: The Postwar Experience of the Republic of China*. Ithaca, N.Y.: Cornell University Press.

Shail, Jain. 1975. *Size Distribution of Income*. Washington, D.C.: World Bank.

Summers, Robert, and Alan Heston. 1984. "Improved International Comparison of Real Product and Its Composition." *Review of Income and Wealth* 30 (June): 207–62.

Taiwan. 1982. *The Trade of China*. Taipei: Inspectorate General of Customs.

————. Various years. *National Income of the Republic of China*. Taipei: Directorate General of Budget, Accounting and Statistics.

————. Various years. *Statistical Data Book*. Taipei: Council for Economic Planning and Development.

————. Various years. *Statistical Yearbook of the Republic of China*. Taipei: Directorate General of Budget, Accounting and Statistics.

United Nations. Various years. *Statistical Yearbook*. New York: UN.

————. Various years. *National Account Statistics*. New York: UN.

————. Conference on Trade and Development. Various years. *Yearbook of Trade and Development Statistics*. New York: UNCTAD.

————. Educational, Scientific and Cultural Organization. Various years. *Statistical Yearbook*. New York: UNESCO.

Wade, Robert. 1985. "State Intervention and 'Outward Looking' Development: Theory and Taiwanese Practice." In G. White and Robert Wade, eds., *Development States in East Asia*. Sussex, England: Institute of Development Studies.

World Bank. 1981. *World Tables, 1980*. Washington, D.C.: World Bank.

THREE

Public Finance for Developing Countries

Assar Lindbeck

FROM PLANNING PARADIGM TO MARKET PARADIGM

Opinions on the appropriate role of government policy, including budget policy, in developing countries have to be based on some *vision* of what the basic mechanisms of the development process are. The specification of such a vision is crucial also for the choice of analytical techniques when studying developing countries. This is why this chapter puts budget policy, or public finance, into the broad perspective of the development process. This also makes it natural to see budget policy as a complement and/or substitute for other types of policy.

The dominant vision of the development process during the 1940s, 1950s, and early 1960s was that the market failures in less developed countries were so huge that the market mechanism could not be much relied on in such countries. This view was certainly characteristic of economists such as Gunnar Myrdal, Ragnar Nurkse, Raul Prebisch, Paul Rosenstein-Rodan, and Hans Singer, even though their emphases on specific aspects of asserted market failures differed strongly.

Various forms of "structuralism" were also popular. Developing countries were asserted to be characterized by pronounced "structural inflexibility" in the allocation of resources; in other words, low (or even zero) elasticities and long time-lags with respect to the economic incentives of the supply and demand for goods, services, and factors of production,

I am grateful for useful comments on an earlier draft from Jorgen Appel gren, Jagdish Bhagwati, Arne Bigsten, Lawrence Krause, Anne O. Krueger, Deepak Lal, Sven-Olof Lodin, Mats Lundahl, and Amartya Sen. Karl Gustav Hansson and Reza Firuzabadi have assisted with statistical computation.

and, indeed, of productive effort and entrepreneurship in general, were thought to exist.[1] Also based on such structuralist views of the economies of developing countries was the idea of binding saving or balance-of-payments constraints on economic growth owing to asserted weaknesses in the response of saving and investment to changes in income and interest rates, as well as of exports, imports, and long-term capital movements to changes in exchange rates, the terms of trade, and the rates of return on assets. A special variant was the "two gap" theory of savings and balance-of-payments constraints, asserting strict limits on the raising of taxes by the national government and difficulties in turning domestic saving into capital formation via the exchange of traditional export products for capital goods on international markets owing to inelastic world demand for the former (Chenery 1965, 1979).

From views like these—which were far from uniform—followed both a strong distrust of the price mechanism and, as a mirror image, considerable enthusiasm for government regulation (such as licensing systems), as well as economywide central planning of inputs, outputs, exports, imports, and investment activity. Moreover, as the manufacturing sector, in contrast to agriculture, was often asserted to be characterized by constant or even increasing returns to scale, a high propensity to save, and rapid technological progress, government-enforced industrialization at the expense of agriculture and handicraft production was usually strongly advocated. Without drastic government actions in these fields, developing countries were asserted to be doomed to "underdevelopment equilibrium traps" or "vicious circles of poverty." Also popular was the notion that the entire manufacturing sector could be treated as an "infant industry," though this notion is difficult to distinguish from general political and ideological *preferences* for industrialization as the essence of economic and social "modernization."

The recommended, and indeed often also the actual, role of *public finance* during the first decades after World War II should be seen in this perspective: (1) as helping provide an industrial base by way of heavy public investment in both physical infrastructure and manufacturing, often in the form of large-scale government projects; (2) as squeezing private consumption by increasing the aggregate saving ratio by way of

---

1. *Structuralism*, as the term is used here, is thus something quite different from the idea that the initial structures of these countries, such as the proportions between various sectors and the existence of various disequilibria among factor rewards in different sectors, are important features to recognize in a realistic analysis of both the existing state and the development prospects of such countries.

taxes, in particular on traditional exports and on the large agricultural population (though in reality agriculture was perhaps squeezed more by overvalued exchange rates and regulated output prices than by explicit land or agricultural taxes); and (3) as directing the allocation of economic resources in general by means of government enterprises, subsidies, government credits, taxes, and tariffs (import-substitution policy)—as a complement to "command," which was to be implemented by physical regulations of various types.

These ambitions made the government budget a main tool of aggregate and disaggregate "national economic planning" for the mobilization and allocation of resources—a point emphasized, for instance, by A. Waterston (1965). While attempts to direct the economy by way of taxes, tariffs, and subsidies must have been based on the idea that private agents *do* react to economic incentives—though unguided markets were asserted to give the "wrong" incentives—the recommendations for reliance on public enterprises and on command of private firms by way of physical regulations were more consistent with a structuralist view of the world (in other words, weak responses of private agents to economic incentives).

It may be argued that the policy recommendation to raise the aggregate saving and investment ratio was the most valuable feature of the predominant development paradigm during the first few decades after World War II, and that the drastic increase in saving and investment ratios to some 20–25 percent of GNP in most developing countries was the most important achievement of actual development policies. Developing countries have usually been much less successful in increasing economic efficiency, and hence in speeding up the rate of productivity growth. For instance, while output in manufacturing in developing market economies increased by 5.1 percent per year during 1960–83, the accompanying increase in labor input was as high as 3.5 percent, which implies that the increase in labor productivity was only about 1.6 percent (calculations of time trends based on data in United Nations 1983).

By itself, a strong increase in labor input is, of course, favorable from the point of view of mitigating unemployment, or "underemployment," but output growth, and hence labor-productivity growth, has certainly been much weaker than would have been possible in reasonably efficiently functioning economic systems. Indeed, even if very labor-intensive methods of production are used, labor productivity should be able to grow by several percentage points per year "simply" by the introduction of better technologies and organization, as illustrated by the experience of developed countries, and indeed also of some developing countries. Many developing countries have simply been getting too small an increase in labor productivity from their investment. We also notice extremely high marginal capital/output ratios in many developing countries, such as in Africa and Latin America.[2]

It has in fact become obvious that vastly different rates of growth of GNP, and perhaps in particular of consumption, can be achieved with about the same rates of capital accumulation depending inter alia on the allocative efficiency of investment and production. For instance, reference is often made to the success of a number of countries in Pacific Asia (Taiwan, South Korea, Singapore, Hong Kong) that have relied to a considerable extent on economic incentives and an outward-looking development strategy—though active and competent governments in these countries have certainly also stimulated growth and economic efficiency by way of institutional reforms, redistributions of assets and infrastructural investment. To some extent, these countries have been engaged in growth forecasting ("indicative planning"), and, in varying degrees, operate state-owned firms, but it is difficult to have a definite opinion about the role of these features, which they share with many other, less successful nations. What has clearly differentiated these countries from many others is that governments have tried to *support* rather than restrict the activities and initiatives of the private sector.

It is for these various reasons natural that the emphasis in analytical discussions of economic policy in developing countries has gradually shifted to issues relating to the allocation, and not just the total volume, of investment, and indeed to *the allocative efficiency in general of production activities.* This is probably an important explanation for the increased respect for decentralized decision making by way of markets, price signals, and economic incentives, and, as a mirror image, an increased skepticism about the usefulness of direct government regulation and central planning.

2. These observations do not, of course, mean that when countries strive for better allocation of investment this will have to occur at the expense of the aggregate volume of saving and investment. There is not necessarily a conflict between high and efficiently allocated saving, as witnessed by, for instance, Japan. Indeed, several countries that have experienced particularly poor economic performance have been unsuccessful with both the volume and the allocative efficiency of saving—obvious examples being countries like Bangladesh, Chad, Ghana, Mali, Sudan, and Upper Volta, with gross saving rates in the neighborhood of zero or even with negative rates; see World Bank, 1985.

More generally, it has become increasingly understood during the past few decades that, contrary to previous assertions, both the aggregate and the "fine" (disaggregate) micro structure of the economies of developing countries respond quite strongly to economic reward, including profitability prospects and relative prices and wages—if governments allow such a response.[3] This is perhaps what we should expect, as poor people have no less reason to respond to the opportunities for improving their economic situation than do more affluent people, perhaps rather the reverse.

Moreover, after having brought about large infrastructural investments, and in some cases a considerable mobilization of resources, it is natural that problems of economic efficiency, and hence resource allocation, become more interesting. It has also become clearer over time that the potentialities of import substitution in manufacturing are rapidly exhausted in most countries owing to the smallness of domestic markets. It would also seem that the attractiveness of the Soviet planning model subsided when it became more widely understood that this was more of a "mobilization model" than a prescription for economic efficiency—indeed, that the model stimulated inefficiency.

When relying on markets, governments must, of course, help ensure that the market signals are "right," in the sense that prices reflect opportunity costs and preferences. However, it is also crucial that the price signals "work," in the sense that various institutional "filters" in society do not distort, or even "abort," the information and incentive content of market signals. Thus there is a potentially important role for the government both as regards improvement of the information and incentive structure and helping strengthen (and perhaps, at an early stage of economic development, even helping create) market-oriented institutions.

In broad terms, the main contribution of *public finance* to the economic development of market-oriented developing countries would then probably be (1) to provide infrastructure and public goods; (2) to help relative prices reflect opportunity costs and preferences, which is

3. Jacob Viner (1952), Gottfrid Haberler (1959), Theodore Schultz (1964), and Peter Bauer (1971) were pioneers in making these points, and early support for outward-looking strategies was provided by Hla Myint (1967). J. N. Bhagwati (1966) was also early in noting the potential importance for economic development of a relative price structure that is conducive to allocative efficiency. Similar views have more recently been reflected in, for instance, Little 1982 and Lal 1983, where liberal references are provided to research into the role of relative prices and economic incentives. However, the "watershed" book, symbolizing a shift among economists in general away from a regulation-and-planning paradigm to a market paradigm emphasizing outward-looking strategies, is probably Little, Scitovsky, and Scott 1970.

often more a question of avoiding and removing distortions previously introduced by the government itself than of fighting "spontaneous" market distortions; (3) to contribute to the redistribution of income and wealth (according to certain values concerning equity) by methods that are as market-conforming as possible; and (4) to contribute to the development of market-oriented institutions that respond satisfactorily to market signals, for instance, in the fields of finance, trade, labor markets, consulting, and the transfer of technology. However, it is also important to emphasize the crucial role of (5) macroeconomic stabilization policy, as failures in that field have often been extremely damaging to attempts to liberalize the economies of developing countries.

If governments start to rely more on markets for the supply of ordinary goods, the public sector can increasingly concentrate on those activities, mentioned above, that only the government can pursue, or where government at least has a comparative advantage relative to private agents. The administrative resources that are then released in the public sector can instead be used to improve the quality of the public sector's remaining functions, to the extent that such resources are not simply transferred to the private sector. This is an important consequence of the shift of a developing country to a more market-oriented system, as the majority of these countries are characterized by a shortage of competent civil servants. Administrative "overload," which has recently been much discussed in developed countries, is an even more characteristic feature of most developing countries—a problem that could be mitigated by a shift to a more market-oriented system. Indeed, managers of firms would then also be able to devote more time to "ordinary" business, rather than bargaining with government officials, or "rent seeking" (Krueger 1974), whereas today the latter often yields higher returns than do attempts to improve efficiency within firms. A removal of regulations could change that.

More generally, in market-oriented economies, the role of government planning and public finance is largely to "plan" the physical and psychological *environment* of private agents rather than to plan what those agents are supposed to do.

METHOD OF ANALYSIS

On the basis of the dominating view in the early post–World War II period that private agents in developing countries react (if at all!) completely differently to economic incentives than do agents in developed countries, and that markets in developing countries will not be able to function properly in the foreseeable future, there followed a profound skepticism about traditional methods of economic analysis. Developing countries were often asserted to be "different kinds" of economies, requiring both new tools of analysis and different behavior assumptions; indeed "development economics" was often asserted to represent a *new and separate branch of economic analysis.* By contrast, this chapter is based on the assumption that there are great enough similarities between behavior patterns and economic mechanisms in general in developed and developing countries to make standard economic analysis relevant for the latter type of country as well.

It is indeed quite easy to illustrate the relevance of standard economic analysis for developing countries. For instance, in a similar way as in developed countries, "overvalued" currencies, by keeping down profitability, tend to reduce output and employment growth in the tradable sectors, which often also results in (increased) budget deficits owing to the negative consequences for the tax base.[4] Moreover, it is well established by now, not only for developed but also for developing countries, that high real wage rates, in particular when combined with low real interest rates, tend to favor capital-intensive methods of production. Regulated wage rates tend to accentuate unemployment for certain types of labor (for instance where minimum wage rates are binding), while for other types of labor more or less permanent vacancies tend to prevail. Pegged interest rates create credit shortages, with "arbitrary" credit rationing and an inefficient allocation of credit and capital as a result. High tariffs and large subsidies to specific sectors tend to expand these sectors at the expense of others, in particular sectors for which government regulations have kept down prices, such as agriculture. Rent control hits house building, creates housing shortages, and results in a deterioration of the housing stock as well as a reduction in labor mobility.

We also note that, as in developed countries, regulations breed new regulations, as politicians and public administrators try to fight the unintended, and, for them, often unexpected, side effects of previous regulations. And, probably even more than in developed countries, regulation is "the mother of corruption," as corruption presupposes that politicians and administrators have "something to sell"—such as licenses, tax concessions, tariffs, or subsidies. Indeed, there is most likely

---

4. There may, of course, also be causation in the other direction—from budget deficits to cost increases that result in overvalued currencies (in fixed-exchange-rate regimes).

also a "reverse causation": corrupt politicians and public administrators have a strong self-interest in promoting regulations.

Moreover, the possibilities of substitution between labor and capital, and indeed between inputs in general, have come to be regarded as much more promising than they were earlier thought to be—a development that in economic theory is symbolized by the replacement of the rigid Harrod-Domar growth equation with more flexible aggregate growth models à la Solow and (in more detailed and quantified form) Denison. Such possibilities of substituting labor for capital in developing countries have proved to be particularly promising in multiple-shift operations and in ancillary services, such as maintenance, and handling of material and other transport services, such as packing (Morawetz 1976; White 1978).

My conclusion is that it is quite appropriate to regard "development economics" as an application of the standard tools of economic analysis (whether at micro- or macroeconomic levels) to long-term growth and development issues for *all* types of countries, in the same way as trade theory is the application of micro- and general equilibrium theories to issues of international trade regardless of what types of countries are studied. In particular, the traditional microeconomic theories regarding prices, markets, and incentives are probably no less useful for the analysis of developing countries than for that of developed countries. This also means that the entire arsenal of tools and insights from applied fields of economic analysis such as industrial organization, money and banking, labor economics, and, as illustrated by this chapter, public finance, can be put into operation in analyses of developing countries and not just of developed ones.

Of course, it is important to take into account various institutional peculiarities in the analyses, though by treating institutions not as insurmountable obstacles to development, which was typical for early postwar development theories, but rather as the "filters" through which incentives, as well as commands, necessarily have to pass. However, that cannot be done by assuming some kind of "standard" developing country institutional setup. Owing to the wide variations in institutional conditions among developing countries—heuristically speaking, with stronger variations than among developed countries—the institutional conditions have to be specified separately for each country.

The main contribution of the earlier evolution of economic analysis for less developed countries as a specific field of economics is then mainly that it has increased awareness of the importance in economic analysis (of both developed and developing countries) of watching out for various institutional peculiarities and the changes in these over time.

However, when discovering "institutional peculiarities," which sometimes makes markets look unfamiliar, it is important to realize that what in the light of traditional models may (superficially) appear as a "market distortion" may in fact be a simple reflection of costs that are not apparent when examining only conventionally defined production costs. It is, for instance, well known that price differences between apparently similar goods, services, or factors may reflect differences in risk, information costs, or "interlocking" markets (Stiglitz 1985).

Concern for the interaction between incentives and institutional conditions is important also in the field of politics and public administration, and not just in markets. Indeed, if it is agreed that differences in government policies are responsible for much of the variation in economic performance among nations, it must be a research topic of the uppermost priority to try to establish which institutional circumstances are conducive to various types of policies. More specifically, policy recommendations that do not rely on a realistic assessment of the functioning of the political systems and of the administrative capabilities of the countries concerned often do more harm than good. In particular, policy advice that is based on the assumption that governments and public administrators behave like well-informed, competent, and highly "benevolent guardians of the public good," maximizing some asserted social welfare function, are bound to lead to disappointing results. Indeed, it may be argued that a policy advisor should base his advice on a hypothesis about the *effects* of his advice on the actual policies (Lindbeck 1973).

Against this background it is important to include in the analysis not only traditional concepts of static efficiency and Pareto optimality, but also broader ideas about the functioning of the economic and political system, such as J. M. Clark's vision of competition as a dynamic process ("workable competition"); Joseph Schumpeter's idea of competition as "creative destruction" (when new kinds of competition, technologies, and products threaten existing ones); Friedrich von Hayek's view of competition as a decentralized search for ways of using existing knowledge more efficiently; Harvey Leibenstein's vision of X-efficiency, reflecting other types of economic efficiency than traditional allocative efficiency; and Herbert Simon's theory of "satisfying behavior," "bounded rationality," and endogenous changes in the aspiration levels of agents.

For instance, rather than taking the production function as given, it is important to analyze the process by which the production function is chosen or developed, not only via research and investment in physical and human capital, but also through organizational modification, innovation, and entrepreneurship. And when analyzing economic policy it is necessary to regard political and administrative decision making as an endogenous process with its own patterns of behavior, as suggested by the Public Choice School (Buchanan and Tullock 1962) and others. The latter point also emphasizes the importance of studying constitutional rules and political culture, including not only the distinction between democracies and authoritarian regimes, but also the rules of election, the degree of political centralization, the character of party competition, and the use of referenda (Lindbeck 1985). Moreover, Amartya Sen (1981) has argued that the existence of a free press and an active political opposition has helped prevent crop failures from resulting in starvation for various population groups.

In other words, analyses of the development process and appropriate government policies, including budget policies, have to include much broader, though often less rigorous, aspects than those on which formalized general equilibrium theory and optimization analysis are built. Institutional conditions and institutional change, the political and administrative processes, and the environment for human creativity and entrepreneurship are factors that seem to have played too small a role in economic analysis of both developed and developing countries.

This methodological point also implies that it is important that the genuine complexity and diversity of the development process are taken into consideration, and that evaluations of the performance of both markets and governments are made against much less ambitious benchmarks than perfect competition, perfect information, Pareto efficiency, and the maximization of social welfare functions. That we shall do below.

GOVERNMENT EXPENDITURES

If a country starts to rely more heavily on markets, economic incentives, and decentralized private initiatives, the "classical" roles of government spending for the allocation of resources come to the forefront: (1) *infrastructural investment* in physical and human capital, including the supply of goods that are produced with particularly high fixed costs relative to the variable costs, such as harbors, bridges, and some other transportation systems; and (2) the supply of *public (collective) goods*—including the legal system, education, basic research, and environmental protection. Moreover, as poor people in developing countries cannot be much helped by tax reductions, government expenditure policies become crucial also in (3) *redistributional policies.*

Infrastructural expenditures hardly need advertisement today. However, as the low productivity level in developing countries derives to a considerable extent from the lack of human capital, it may nevertheless be worth advertising infrastructural investment in the form of the accumulation of *human resources in a wide sense of the term*—including not only education, but also health, sanitation, and, in many countries, food supply to particularly poor sections of the population.

As it has been increasingly recognized that the social rates of return in most developing countries are higher for primary education and vocational training than for most forms of higher theoretical education (Psachropoulous 1981), a change in the composition of public spending on education in favor of the former seems to make sense for many developing countries. It is also important that public policies in the field of education and training recognize the need to build up competence that is relevant at the *microeconomic* level in society (for example, and in particular, within individual firms). This would probably be greatly facilitated if firms, rather than government institutions, were largely in charge of vocational training programs, so as to make them practically applicable and strongly market-oriented—the latter being particularly important in economies that follow a market-oriented strategy of economic development. However, as firms have suboptimal incentives to provide general training, owing to the mobility of labor between firms, it is natural to recommend combinations of general schooling provided by public institutions and specific training within firms, though the latter, too, could be at least partly tax-financed. Modified to fit the specific conditions in the countries concerned, the apprenticeship system in West Germany may be a model worth following.

It is also conceivable that the import and domestic dispersion of technology could be stimulated by government initiatives, even if the actual import is certainly best done by individual firms. For instance, government initiatives to help establish private import and service firms in the field of technology may be worth pursuing for a while in the least developed countries.

In many fields of technology it would certainly be useful if research could take place in the countries of the Third World themselves—though in many cases in cooperation with institutions and individuals in developed countries. The rationale is to increase the probability that the research will be relevant for the developing countries. Such activities could also perhaps, at least for a while, be stimulated by government initiatives. Obvious examples of such fields are aspects of agriculture and health care, such as tropical agriculture, soil analysis, integrated development in arid areas, aquaculture, and tropical medicine. As the results of research and development in these fields are characteristically public goods owing to the smallness of the firms and the externalities in the ecological systems, government spending programs have a particularly important role to play here. For instance, the experiences of agricultural extension services, financed by the government, often seem to have been rather good. Indeed, the atomistic structure of the agricultural sector makes it important that governments take initiatives to help establish such services in precisely this sector.

Beside basic general skills and technological competence, one of the most important bottlenecks in the area of human resources in developing countries is *managerial skills*—in the private as well as in the public sector. The role of managerial skill is not only an issue of the competence of managers at the top of organizations. Particular attention must probably be focused on middle-level management, supervisory staff, and people providing specialist services at the middle level—for example, procurement and inventory management; production management; control research; marketing; advertising; tool room service; raw material and product testing; machine assembly; equipment maintenance; staff recruitment; and project development. Government initiatives to stimulate training in such fields are clearly a promising type of government investment in developing countries.

Whereas the various types of training mentioned above are relevant for all types of developing countries, the buildup of *entrepreneurial capabilities* is particularly important in liberalizing developing countries. Experience from many countries over long historical periods illustrates the enormous role of entrepreneurship in the development process, not least in small and medium-sized firms and newly started firms. Because of the difficulties involved in formalizing and quantifying the role and importance of entrepreneurship, it easily "disappears," not only in economic theory, but also in domestic development plans and political and administrative discussion, which has often concentrated on existing firms and large firms. However, all developing countries that opt for industrialization and modernization along market-oriented lines are strongly urged to facilitate the emergence of vital entrepreneurship not only by way of formal education in business, but also, and in particular, *by allowing and stimulating entrepreneurial initiative.* Indeed, in addition to land, capital, and labor, it is reasonable to regard entrepreneurship as a fourth factor of production of crucial importance for economic development—a factor the government may promote by stimulating the buildup of facilities for the training of entrepreneurs and by deregulation, which tends to release entrepreneurial skills.

So much for the "creation" part of Schumpeter's vision of "creative destruction." It is, of course, also important that politicians allow the "destructive" part of the process to operate by avoiding subsidizing contracting or even "dying" sectors, firms, and production processes, even though the "demand" for such protection is certainly one of the most powerful forces in the political process in most countries. An important "constitutional" issue is then what types of political decision-making rules are conducive to preventing more subsidization than the electorate, and a majority of politicians, *on reflection* would like.

The stimulation of entrepreneurship is also an issue of the political and social attitudes in society toward entrepreneurial activities. Indeed, the attitudes in society toward entrepreneurship may be regarded as an important collective good in a private enterprise economy.

In the context of government expenditure policies, it is often also important to look over the rules, incentives, and practices of the management of publicly owned firms and agencies, which play an important role in many developing countries. Indeed, if governments of developing countries are serious about the shift to a more market-oriented system, it is important that this shift incorporate state-owned enterprises too, in the sense that these are either handed over to the private sector or given the same incentives and freedom of action as private business—and that they also feel the same need as private firms, by way of competitive pressure, to react to market signals. The withdrawal of "automatic" government financing of losses of government-owned firms is crucial from that point of view.

This chapter is not designed to deal with issues related to specific production sectors. However, it is nowadays well understood that the modernization and industrialization process is easily damaged, or may even fail completely, if *agriculture* is neglected, which may also have serious consequences for the distribution of income. "Negative" illustrations of this thesis are provided by several South American and especially African countries, while positive examples are found in several countries in Pacific Asia—countries that have also been strikingly successful in manufacturing.

Widespread experiences suggest, for instance, that government marketing boards in agriculture tend to destroy incentives. Such boards usually do not have either the competence or the incentives to create a level and structure of producers' prices that is even remotely rational for economic efficiency. Moreover, they tend to direct the rents from agriculture to inefficient and highly protected manufacturing firms by way of import-substitution policies. Thus, as a way of improving the production incentives for farmers, it is, as a rule, useful to abolish government marketing boards in agriculture. This would also contribute to the allocation of the rents and profits of agricultural production via market mechanisms rather than by bureaucratic fiat and government subsidies.

Favorable production opportunities in agriculture are important also for achieving a geographically dispersed income growth in society—among both regions and population groups. Obvious policies to promote this, besides a reasonably conducive price policy toward agriculture, are a decentralized public infrastructure and regionally dispersed public services in rural areas in general. Of course, this is something that is important regardless of whether the economy is liberalized or not. However, as decentralization of decision making may in some cases accentuate regional income differences, at least for a while, there is a case for conscious government attempts to speed up the process by which higher income in the national economy as a whole raises incomes in regions that lag behind.

This raises the general problem of poverty and income distribution. Considering the enormous misery among a minority at the bottom of the income distribution, humanitarian values should certainly make us emphasize redistributive actions in favor of the very poorest members of society, in the same way as redistribution policy in the presently developed countries started with "poor laws" even before the Industrial Revolution. On the expenditure side of the budget, such programs could very well to a considerable extent consist of what has been called a "basic needs strategy" for the purpose of providing basic food, shelter, water, sanitation, health, and education to the very poor, which is perhaps to some extent most effectively done by way of transfers in kind. Indeed, experience suggests that it is possible for a country to achieve substantial improvements in a number of "social indicators" at relatively low levels of per capita income (Balassa 1983), examples being life expectancy, infant mortality, and child death rates.

Thus there is evidence of the usefulness of "direct" attempts to satisfy some "basic needs" in nutrition and health, even at low levels of per capita income. A "basic needs approach" is therefore quite compatible with a growth-oriented approach based on economic incentives, provided that neither is pushed to the extreme. Indeed, a great number of studies indicate that increased spending on health, nutrition, and education—up to certain levels—may give considerable boosts to productivity growth (Balassa 1983).

So far, it has been typical for developing countries to provide income support via indirect subsidies of commodities rather than via direct transfers. One reason has certainly been administrative feasibility. However, another reason has simply been that strong pressure groups in the urban centers have "demanded" low food and housing prices, which has not only reduced production incentives in agriculture and housing but has often also assisted people with income levels considerably above those of the rural poor.

Sooner or later, when the "modern sector" starts to dominate the national economy, we would expect the same types of demands for social security systems for a broad section of the population as in developed countries. This is, again, not something which is confined to market-oriented systems. But market-oriented systems are certainly often blamed for creating inequalities and insecurities. Thus, in order to maintain their legitimacy among broad sections of the population, such systems need not only to pursue redistributions to the very poor, but also to provide social security systems for the population as a whole, though powerful urban pressure groups may benefit the most from such systems.

Indeed, while social security spending is only about 1.2 percent of GNP in low-income developing countries (with per capita income below $400 in 1983 prices), the figure is as high as 6.6 percent in upper-middle income countries (per capita incomes above $1,600); see figure 3.1. (Other categories of public spending do not differ much between developing countries with different per capita incomes.[5])

Eventually, of course, public spending programs may raise the same type of welfare state incentive problems that are intensively discussed today in most developed countries. Indeed, there may be a risk of the creation of "premature welfare states," in the sense that the economic

5. These statistics, covering "central government," are compiled from World Bank 1986, table 22, and International Monetary Fund 1985. A study by Tanzi (1986) indicates that total tax revenues of all levels of government, i.e., "general government," in developing countries are only slightly (one or two percentage points) higher than the figures for tax revenues of central government that are reported in fig. 3.2. (The countries are not exactly the same in the two samples, however.) Perhaps we could assume that the difference between general and central government is also on the expenditures side.

foundation for an elaborate system of social security, transfer payments, and redistributions of income among large population groups does not yet exist (Uruguay is often mentioned as an example). "Early" attempts to create elaborate social security systems may not only create severe incentive problems in the private sector; they may also strain the taxation system so much that governments will not be able to provide what they have a comparative advantage in supplying: collective goods and infrastructure facilities. These points lead directly to the problem of taxation.

TAXATION

The level and structure of taxes, subsidies, and tariffs differ so much between various developing countries that generalizations about their taxation problems are difficult. However, the general level of taxation in this group of countries is still usually much lower than that in developed countries—typically 10–25 percent of GDP, as compared to about 30–55 percent in Western Europe, 33 percent in the United States, and 25 percent in Japan. Among eighty-two developing countries for which information is available, the average tax share of GNP seems to have been about 18 percent in the early 1980s (Tanzi 1986), with taxes on goods and services and foreign trade playing a much more important part than in developed countries. (Figure 3.2 provides statistics for "central government" revenues; figures for "general government" are probably, on average, one or two percentage points higher.) Thus disincentive problems for private agents, owing to a *generally* high level of tax rates, cannot possibly be a serious problem in most developing countries. However, these figures underestimate the "tax bite" for those sectors that actually pay the bulk of the taxes. (For instance, if we assume, as an extreme case, that agriculture pays no taxes at all, the average tax rate for the rest of the economy would be about 24 percent as compared to 18 percent for the entire economy.)

One dilemma, though, is that a given level of taxes (as a percentage of GDP) may "hurt" people more in a poor than in a rich country by depressing an already very low level of private consumption. However, this is not really a problem of economic disincentives for private agents, but rather an issue concerning the ability, or disability, of the political process to generate a reasonable allocation and distribution of resources between private consumption, public consumption, and investment. However, it is also an issue of the efficiency of the allocation of investment.

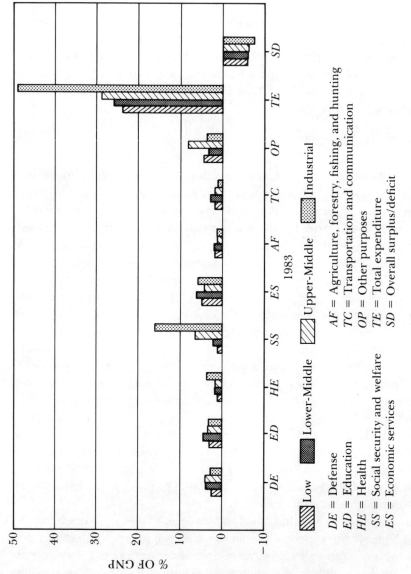

Fig. 3.1 Central Government Expenditure for Low, Lower-Middle, Upper-Middle, and Industrial Economies

Legend (within figure):

Low
Lower-Middle
Upper-Middle
Industrial

1983

% OF GNP

DE = Defense
ED = Education
HE = Health
SS = Social security and welfare
ES = Economic services

AF = Agriculture, forestry, fishing, and hunting
TC = Transportation and communication
OP = Other purposes
TE = Total expenditure
SD = Overall surplus/deficit

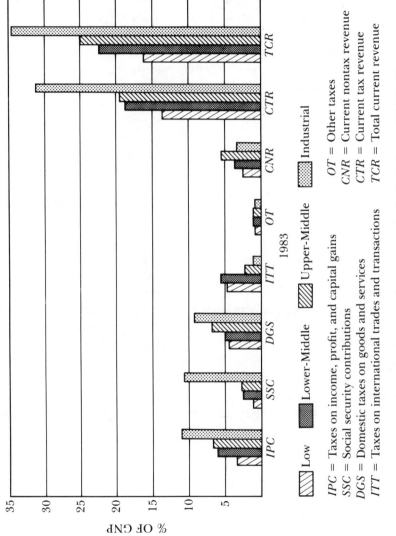

Fig. 3.2. Central Government Current Revenue for Low, Lower-Middle, Upper-Middle, and Industrial Economies

IPC = Taxes on income, profit, and capital gains
SSC = Social security contributions
DGS = Domestic taxes on goods and services
ITT = Taxes on international trades and transactions

OT = Other taxes
CNR = Current nontax revenue
CTR = Current tax revenue
TCR = Total current revenue

In a country where this allocation is more efficient than in other countries, it is not necessary to squeeze private consumption so much by way of taxes.

It is not clear whether liberalization of the economic system requires, or can be expected to result in, a higher or lower total level of taxation. Reductions in the level of tariffs no doubt raise the need for new tax sources. Moreover, if increased reliance on markets results in a more uneven distribution of income, and indeed if it is already *believed* that this is the case, the political process may generate strong pressure for more redistributions via public budgets, and hence a need for tax increases.

However, there are also factors that *reduce* the need for taxes in connection with economic liberalization, since some expenditure items would tend to disappear, or at least fall. In particular, a reduction in the need for subsidies to enterprises—private as well as government— would be an important part of a shift to a more market-oriented economic system, provided profitability is kept up sufficiently, which requires that the real exchange rate is not overvalued. The need for taxes would also recede to some extent if public authorities shifted to a greater reliance on users' fees for various types of public services, a reform for which there are well-known allocative and efficiency arguments. A reduction of the public bureaucracy and increased competition for public service agencies from private agents would further reduce the need for taxes—partly because competition would most likely increase efficiency in the public sector, and partly because the size of the public service sector would be smaller owing to private alternatives.

Another feature of economic liberalization is that increased incentives for private saving would reduce the need for public saving, though the recent fall in public saving in some developing countries is a reason for not advising the authorities to make substantial tax reductions on this ground.

However, even though the level of taxes in most developing countries cannot be regarded as excessive, or "harmful," the *structure* of taxes, subsidies, and tariffs is certainly already a serious problem. It is hardly necessary to say that high and strongly selective tariffs and taxes on foreign trade—*export discrimination policies*—often result in suboptimal foreign trade, and hence in an underutilization of the gains from the international division of labor. Indeed, it is today quite well established that such policies, often designed to promote "import substitution," when pursued for long periods (such as several decades), have been highly detrimental to most developing countries that have pursued them.

It is also quite clear that highly selective commodity taxes, as in fact implemented, have often created inefficiencies in the allocation of resources in the private sector, on both the consumption and production side, without always providing advantages in terms of the distribution of income. And in cases where selective taxes and subsidies have actually improved the distribution of income (on the basis of certain values), the same improvements could perhaps in many cases have been achieved by a structure of taxes and subsidies with smaller efficiency costs.

Severe distortions may also come out of some other taxes. The provision of accelerated depreciation for investment and subsidies to some investment, in combination with payroll taxes on labor, may contribute to raising the wage/rental ratio—though recent increases in interest rates may have reversed this feature in several countries. Moreover, some developing countries do have quite high statutory *marginal* income tax rates for high-income groups, and sometimes also for middle-high income earners—such as households with two or three times the national average. For instance, according to a study by Sicat and Virmani (1986) referring to the situation in the early eighties of married couples with one earner and a "standard" number of children (three), about half out of fifty developing countries studied had marginal income tax rates above 30 percent for incomes three times the average, and about a third of the countries had marginal income tax rates of at least 40 percent for that (relative) income bracket. (The mean marginal rate was 34 percent for that income bracket, as compared to 19 percent for the middle-income bracket.) If separate statistics had been available for the formal sector in urban areas, we would certainly have found much higher figures. Of course, legal avoidance and illegal evasion mean that many taxpayers do not in fact pay those rates, even remotely. However, the statutory marginal rates are an indicator of the incentives to avoid and evade, which is part of the process by which marginal tax rates distort the allocation of resources and human effort.

Of course, an overhaul of the tax system makes perfectly good sense even without a shift to a more market-oriented system. However, a reform of the price and incentive system is clearly more significant for a pronounced market-oriented system than for a highly regulated and centrally planned system, as the gains of shifting to a more market-oriented system cannot be fully achieved without reforming the price and incentive system in conformity with efficiency criteria. Indeed, this truth has been well illustrated in recent decades by the attempts of socialist countries in Eastern Europe to rely more heavily on markets and economic incentives. Moreover, if capital movements too are liberalized, it is important to adjust capital taxation to levels that make domestic and foreign wealth owners and firms willing to invest enough in the country in question, rather than abroad—and to allow remittances of earnings, as well as providing guarantees of property rights in general. Stability of the domestic currency is, of course, also crucial in this context. Indeed, the problem of "capital flight" in developing countries is to a large extent a "confidence problem" concerning property rights and the value of the domestic money.

What, then, are the most important specific changes to be considered in the tax system when an economy shifts from regulations and central command to increased reliance on markets? Some economists may want to base their policy advice on sophisticated calculations of *optimal* tariffs, taxes, and subsidies. There is no doubt that the literature on optimum taxation has helped us understand the general problems of taxes and subsidies in cases where compromises have to be made between the requirements of tax revenues, on one hand, and the losses of economic efficiency owing to the "excess burden" of positive marginal tax rates on the other. The literature on optimum income taxation has, for example, given precision to the old idea that marginal tax rates should be higher, the smaller the elasticity of effort with respect to rewards is, *ceteris paribus*. And the literature on optimum commodity taxation has formalized old views among economists about how to make a compromise between the allocative efficiency of consumption and concern for the distribution of income. While in the interest of economic efficiency tax rates should be relatively high on goods and services for which the demand and supply elasticities are small, the rates should, for distributional reasons, be high also on goods and services that play a relatively important part in the consumption pattern of groups of households that are supposed to be discriminated against in redistribution policy; these groups are often, of course, high income earners. Taxes should, *ceteris paribus*, also be high on goods and services that for the consumers closely complement untaxed, or indeed untaxable, goods and services, such as leisure. Quite complex formulas have in fact been derived to strike a balance between these different, often conflicting, aspects, using a Social Welfare Function as the criterion for the trade-off (Atkinson and Stiglitz 1980; Stern 1984).

However, there are strong objections to the strategy of using such calculations *as a basis for actual policy advice* in developing as well as in developed countries:

(1) First, formulas of optimum taxation catch only one, or possibly a few, types of mechanisms for adjustment by the individual agents, such as a shift between leisure and work, and/or between the consumption of different commodities. In reality there are, of course, myriads of other adjustment mechanisms for taxes, such as variations in the amount of do-it-yourself work and the intensity of work; adjustment of the level of saving and the composition of portfolios; changes in the level and type of investment in physical and human capital; changes of profession, workplace, or location of residence; emigration across national borders; the use of more time to search for tax loopholes, or even for cheating with taxes. Formulas that would simultaneously reflect all such major adjustment mechanisms, or most of them, are quite simply beyond the range of useful analysis.

(2) Second, even to derive an optimum tax formula that takes into account just *one single* type of adjustment mechanism, such as the choice between leisure and income, or between different consumer goods on the demand side, it is in fact necessary to rely on extremely special assumptions, such as identical preferences of all individuals, and special forms of the production function, such as Cobb-Douglas functions.

(3) Third, all optimum tax formulas, even rather modest ones, require statistical information that is not very reliable. Not only do we need an "arbitrarily" chosen Social Welfare Function, but also information about individual capabilities and preferences specific enough to quantify the sensitivity of the response to contemplated tax rate changes of the various types of adjustments that are supposed to be covered in the study. On most of this we shall never get sufficiently reliable information. This is serious, as the tax rates that are derived from optimum tax formulas are very sensitive to alternative specifications of the various functions and the statistical parameterization.

Indeed, if all the necessary information on individual capabilities and preferences that is required for empirical application of the theory of optimum taxation were available, we would not be too far from the type of knowledge that is necessary to design lump-sum taxes and transfers, and hence avoid the economic distortions that are the reason for choosing an optimum tax approach in the first place! More specifically, in order to design optimum tax systems, we would need information about both individual abilities and preferences, whereas it is simultaneously the difficulty in obtaining information about matters like these that is the basic reason why we are not able to use lump-sum taxes, and hence why there is a case for a second-best solution by way of "optimum taxation."

(4) Applications of the theory of optimum taxation are also confronted with a severe aggregation problem. More specifically, the tax rate that is assigned to a specific product in the context of an optimum tax formula depends crucially on the degree and type of aggregation of commodities. For instance, if furniture is put into the group of durable consumer goods, it gets one tax rate, but if it is put into some other group of goods, it would get a different rate—or even a zero rate or a subsidy. In other words, the tax rate of an individual good will be highly arbitrary depending on which other goods and services it is lumped together with. This means that optimum taxation will to a large extent be "arbitrary taxation." It is in reality also difficult to group the goods in such a way that only consumers' goods are included in the tax base. Many inputs in the production process will in fact also be taxed, which means that distortions of the allocation of resources will arise from the production side as well, without these distortions being considered in the calculation of the optimum tax structure. Attempts to differentiate the tax rates of one and the same type of good when used for direct consumption and when used as an input in the production process are bound to raise severe problems of administration and evasion.

Several of these difficulties with optimum taxation are, of course, well known by the adherents of optimum taxation. But it seems to me that they have not taken these problems seriously enough when ruling out "traditional" principles of uniformity of commodity taxes and tariffs, as well as "comprehensive" income taxation with similar tax rates for all sources of income (for instance, the so-called Haig-Simons principle).

(5) However, there is an even more fundamental objection to using optimum taxation as a basis for policy advice. There is no reason to assume that politicians and public administrators would follow advice that is based on calculations of optimum taxation by the help of some (assumed) Social Welfare Function. Politicians have their own targets and ambitions, which may not bear much relation to the ideas that lie behind calculations by economists of opti-

mum tax or tariff structures. Indeed, this is exactly the background for various attempts in recent years to endogenize the behavior of politicians and public administrators, as well as for suggestions tying the behavior of politicians to various types of "rules." More generally, there is no reason to assume that tax rates that are the outcome of political processes—with conflicts and compromises between various political parties and interest group organizations—would be much correlated to the tax structure that some economists may derive from optimization calculations.

This point about political behavior is important regardless of whether the main ambition of politicians is to satisfy some strong interest group, to increase the probability of being elected, or to adhere to some personal or ideological idiosyncrasy. Politicians and public administrators, with the help of their economic advisors, can always present some reasonable-sounding argument for their particular choice of a differentiated structure of taxes and subsidies—for instance, by referring to aspects that have not been considered in the calculations of the optimum tax specialist, or by exploiting the wide choice of "reasonable" elasticities of the demand and supply responses to taxes. The fact that calculated "optimum rates" for individual goods depend crucially on how goods are aggregated also opens the possibility of various interest groups arguing about the "proper" way of aggregating goods in official statistics.

If optimum tax theory then is not the most appropriate basis for tax policy advice in developing countries (or in developed countries for that matter), what types of considerations should be used instead? The general answer, in my judgment, is that it is better to rely on approaches that are less ambitious and less demanding concerning knowledge about private behavior patterns, statistical information, and administrative competence, but instead more ambitious with respect to basic insights about the functioning of the political process. In other words, it is important to focus on more "pedestrian," practical, and "commonsense" aspects than those emphasized in the optimum tax literature. For instance, the following types of tax reforms are worth considering in a great number of developing countries:

(1) As several developing countries, in particular those in Latin America, often have high and highly variable rates of inflation, an

adjustment of tax assessment and tax collection to inflation is often crucial. Though inflation functions as an implicit "inflation-tax" on the stock of money and government bonds (with less than fully adjusted interest to inflation), inflation often also implies that the government loses "explicit" tax revenues in real terms owing to the timelags in tax collection (the so-called Oliveira-Tanzi effect). Inflation often also erodes the tax base because of the deductibility of *nominal* interest rates, which in an inflationary situation means that part of the amortization of the debt, in real terms, can be deducted from the tax base. If the latter two effects dominate the former, inflation will generate (or accentuate) higher budget deficits (in real terms), which then often feed back into even higher inflation rates. Obvious reforms to solve these problems are to shorten the time lags in tax collection; make inflation adjustments to the tax rates (or tax brackets); and redefine the tax base in order to make a distinction in real terms between (deductible) interest payments and (nondeductible) amortization.

(2) As the tax base is often very narrow in developing countries, the tax rates are often relatively high for certain sectors and groups of taxpayers. For instance, in many developing countries today income taxation is, in fact, mainly a tax on public servants and the employees of large corporations rather than on capital owners or on employers and employees in agriculture or in the "informal" urban sectors. The tax system is also plagued with other types of "asymmetries" with respect to the effective tax rates for different agents and sources of income, and these asymmetries are often accentuated by inflation. These asymmetries could, of course, be mitigated by moving in the direction of a Haig-Simons type "comprehensive" income tax, with uniformity between different sources of incomes, different assets, and different types of income earners. Basically that would mean a broadening of the base and a lowering of the rates—as has recently been tried in some developed countries. The tax system would then most likely be improved in terms both of efficiency and equity (and perhaps even equality), whereas attempts to differentiate based on optimum tax formulas are likely to be exploited by various interest groups. In other words, uniformity, as the basic rule of taxation, is probably less vulnerable to manipulation by powerful interest groups than is the principle of "differentiation" according to optimum tax principles.

(3) As the small degree of household saving that exists in most developing countries largely takes place among the very top income earners, attempts to redistribute income from these groups *on a large scale* are likely to conflict with ambitions to stimulate private saving and to increase the supply of risk capital. This is a reason for being careful about heavy increases in income and wealth taxes for upper-middle and high income groups. Moreover, as corporate saving plays an important part in aggregate saving in some developing countries, and could play an even more important part in the future, there is a strong case also against raising taxes drastically on corporations.

Superficially, it may be argued that tax increases that reduce private saving are not really a problem, as it does not matter if saving is done by private agents or public authorities. However, this argument is seriously flawed for two reasons. First, it neglects imperfections in the political process in the sense that tax increases originally designed to increase public saving often, in fact, release increased public consumption or subsidies of private consumption. Second, public saving is *not* a perfect substitute for private saving in market-oriented economies, as private saving contributes to a decentralization of decisions regarding investment, the entry of new firms, and innovation. To keep down private consumption is not the only purpose of saving; another important role, which it plays in market-oriented economies, is to allow and stimulate the emergence of a system of *decentralized decision making,* and hence to help channel resources to alternative types of assets in an efficient way.

Indeed, it may be argued that one of the most important prerequisites for a successful shift to a more market-oriented economic system is just this, namely the stimulation of private saving—a conclusion that follows from *informal* commonsense views on the functioning of markets (such as those of Hayek and Schumpeter), rather than from formalized general equilibrium theories.

In fact, the history of economic development in the West during the past few hundred years illustrates vividly the importance of private saving and private supply of capital for the entry and growth of new firms, for "entrepreneurship," and hence also for innovation. In other words, it is difficult to preserve an important role for the entrepreneur if the private capitalist is "destroyed"—partly because these are often the same persons. Thus, while both centrally regulated economies and market-oriented economies have to be careful not to destroy incentives to work, it is also important in market-oriented economies to watch out for disincentive effects on private saving and entrepreneurship. This means, of course, that certain "sacrifices" have to be made in the ambition to redistribute incomes from high- to low-income groups—though less so in the case of redistributions from economically "passive" groups, such as "traditional" wealth holders who keep their assets in idle land and various types of collectors' items.

What, then, are the conclusions for indirect (commodity) taxation? My basic assertion is that if we opt for a reasonably nondistorting structure of taxes, tariffs, and subsidies, it is advisable to choose, at least as a starting point, a uniform structure (same tax rate on every commodity and the same tariff rate on every importable), rather than attempting to find some optimum tax structure. The rationale is simply to avoid a situation where something even further away from an optimum structure will in fact be implemented by way of party competition and the influence of strong interest groups. It is difficult for voters to judge if a highly differentiated tax structure reflects an attempt to implement "optimum tax rates" or if it is simply designed to assist politically powerful pressure groups. It is probably easier for voters to judge on this matter if the norm is a proportional structure of indirect taxes rather than some *asserted* optimum structure.

Moreover, it is likely that highly selective taxes and subsidies, like direct regulations, breed both corruption and "rent seeking" via political lobbying (Myrdal 1968). This means that while a liberalization of the economic system in developing countries is most likely a *necessary* requirement for a drastic removal of rent seeking and corruption, this outcome could partly be jeopardized if highly selective taxes and subsidies are introduced as suggested by proponents of optimum tax theory.

An obvious objection to this reasoning is that it may, in fact, be difficult to induce politicians to follow a norm about uniform indirect taxes and tariffs. However, it is well known that politicians sometimes may find it in their own interest to "straightjacket" themselves by accepting various types of norms—obvious examples being international GATT rules on tariffs. Indeed, commitment by way of binding rules has been discussed frequently in game theory in recent years, emphasizing that this may be a method of preventing various groups in society from exploiting the difficulties experienced by government, without such rules, in committing itself in advance to a policy it would like to pursue.

A braver strategy would be to use a uniform tax structure as the basis for the tax system, but to allow some additional selective taxes on goods for which there are really strong and uncontroversial reasons to believe

(1) that the supply and demand elasticities are very low, and (2) that the goods are consumed proportionally much less among citizens with low incomes than among high-income groups (assuming that an improvement in incomes of low-income groups relative to high-income groups is desired). Of course, there is then an equivalent case for deviating from the basically proportional tax structure by low tax rates (or even selective indirect subsidies) on goods and services that there is overwhelming reason to assume have the opposite characteristics.

Such a modification of a strategy of uniform indirect taxes would be a modest attempt to accomodate some of the basic ideas of the optimum tax theory without using that theory as the basic foundation for tax policy recommendations. It differs from the idea of optimum taxation in the sense that (1) attempts to adjust tax rates to differences in demand and supply elasticities would be the exception rather than the rule, and (2) considerations of the functioning of the political process would be paramount.

However, in a short- and medium-term perspective, the most important aspect of tax reform in developing countries is probably *to improve tax collection and tax compliance.* Not only is the administrative capacity of the tax authorities often weak, but in addition, firms are often small and difficult to control, and loyalty to the national state is often rather limited in some developing countries owing to historical experience. Greater uniformity and less differentiation in the treatment of different taxpayers, products, and sources of incomes may often facilitate both tax administration and tax compliance. Moreover, it may be advisable to use a sales tax on wholesale trade rather than a comprehensive value-added tax or a sales tax in retailing. Reductions in the element of "arbitrary discretion" by local tax collectors may also help to increase voluntary tax compliance, as would implementation of the earlier suggestion about a broader base and lower rates.

To summarize my general points on tax policies: policy that relies on (1) sophisticated analytical techniques, combined with (2) extreme oversimplifications of the functioning of the economic system, (3) enormous requirements of sophisticated statistical information, and (4) total neglect of the functioning of the political and administrative system is likely to create more distortions than simple rules of thumb using uniform and broadly based taxes and tariffs—possibly modified by selective taxes or subsidies where the case for such a modification is particularly strong. Thus, there is a strong case for the "traditional" recommendation in public finance of a "comprehensive" income tax with uniform rates between different sources of income assets and types of income earners, and a similar case for uniformity of the tax rates for commodity taxation as the basic starting point, though exceptions may be made where strong cases can be put forward.

GROWTH, DISTRIBUTION, AND POVERTY

Allocative efficiency and economic growth should not, of course, be regarded as "ends in themselves," but rather as means of raising the material well-being of "the ordinary man," and in particular of the poorest fraction of the population. This observation raises the classical question of the relation between the distribution of income, on the one hand, and allocative efficiency and economic growth on the other, hence highlighting the celebrated conflict between equity and efficiency—"the Big Trade-off" in Arthur Okun's terminology (Okun 1974). However, it is also obvious that equity and efficiency considerations are in many cases complementary rather than conflicting objectives. Indeed, it is important to try to find strategies and instruments of growth and redistribution policy for which such complementarities exist.

The most solid empirical observation on the relation between growth and distribution is perhaps that the fruits of economic growth, at least after a while, tend to become dispersed enough to result in an increase in the standard of living of both the great majority of the population and of the bulk of low-income groups (Kuznets 1955, 1963). Thus "immiserizing growth" (Bhagwati 1985) seems to be quite unlikely in a long-term perspective.

However, there is also rather strong evidence from time-series analysis that the *relative* overall distribution of income (as measured by, for instance, the Gini coefficient) often becomes more uneven during the very first decades of economic growth, with a reversal of this tendency later on. This is, of course, the empirical background to the celebrated "Kuznets' Law" about the inverted U shape of the relation between per capita income and the inequality of the overall distribution of income. Indeed, for a given point of time, cross-country studies, too, support the hypothesis of such an inverted U relation (Ahluwalia 1976 and references in Bigsten 1986).

The usual theoretical explanation for this asserted empirical regularity is that economic growth to begin with tends to be concentrated in the initially very small "modern" sector of the economy where per capita income is higher and more uneven, and often also tends to rise more rapidly than in the traditional (usually rural) sectors. When, later on during the growth process, the modern sector becomes a larger share of the total, and the intrasector distribution of skills tends to become more even, the overall distribution of national income, too, tends to become more even—possibly also more even than in the "initial" situation before the "take-off" of modern economic growth (Bigsten 1986).

A similar pattern seems to hold if we look at the relative position of low-income groups (such as the very lowest income deciles) rather than at measures of the overall distribution of income: though low-income groups often seem to gain absolutely also during the very first few decades of economic growth, they usually seem to lose ground relative to other groups during that phase of economic development.[6]

Thus, though there is hardly any reason to be pessimistic about the possibilities of raising the standard of living of low-income groups by way of economic growth, both concern for the relative positions of people during early phases of economic growth and an eagerness to help the very poorest certainly make a case for deliberate policy actions to help the fruits of economic growth spread to the poorest fraction of the population. Thus Kuznets' Law should be regarded as a "tendency" of given economic and social policies, rather than some "iron law of distribution" that cannot be repealed by appropriate economic and social reforms.

When discussing such reforms, it may be useful to distinguish between four (closely related) aspects: (1) attempts to redistribute the ownership of human, financial, and physical assets in favor of low- and low-middle-income groups; (2) removals of institutional obstacles keeping these groups from participating in the process of income growth; (3) redistributional considerations when designing general economic policies; and (4) fiscal policy actions specifically designed to improve the living standards of people in the above mentioned groups.

(1) It is true (and practically tautological) that a relatively even *initial* distribution of human and physical capital, in particular of land, helps to spread the fruits of growth widely. However, it would seem that successful land reforms have to fulfill two requirements: they should opt for private ownership, largely in the form of family farms, and they have to be once-and-for-all actions, so

6. It would seem that only a very modest part of the variations of the distribution of income among developed countries can be statistically "explained" by the level of per capita income. According to Bigsten (1986), about 80 percent of the inequalities remain to be explained by other factors.

that the owners of land can be sure about their property rights. Otherwise a serious conflict between equity and efficiency considerations easily arises in agriculture. We would also expect educational reforms during a process of growth to even out the overall distribution of income, in particular if there is a strong emphasis on literacy and vocational training for broad population groups.

(2) Obvious examples of methods to remove *institutional* obstacles to a dispersed distribution of the fruits of economic growth is the stimulation of the buildup of credit market institutions that reach low- and low-middle-income groups, in particular in rural areas. In the case of farm families characterized by ample availability of labor and scarcity of land, it is also important to remove legal and institutional obstacles for additional land tenure (such as the leasing of land). It is also obvious that the possibilities of poor farmers participating in the process of income growth may be drastically improved by government infrastructural investment, both to increase the productivity on the farms (for example, by irrigation systems) and by creating a favorable infrastructure for nonfarm activities in the countryside, where family labor may get additional earnings.

(3) The distributional consequences of alternative general policy strategies is a more difficult and controversial matter. However, both casual observations and systematic research indicate that a shift to an outward-oriented growth strategy tends to favor not only overall economic efficiency, but also employment and redistribution of income to unskilled labor (Krueger 1978; Bhagwati 1978). One of the explanations is that import protection in manufacturing turns the terms of trade against agriculture, where the majority of poor people are to be found in most developing countries. Another explanation is that such policies tend to increase competition and hence reduce monopoly profits. However, even more fundamentally, an outward-looking growth strategy in labor-abundant countries favors labor-intensive sectors and labor-intensive production techniques simply because free trade tends to allocate factors of production in conformity with comparative advantages, which tends to turn the composition of national income in favor of labor income, in particular for low-skilled workers. Poverty will then tend to be reduced, as there is overwhelming evidence that increased employment is of utmost importance of the removal of poverty (Fields 1984). Indeed, as

pointed out by Ranis (1978, 407), "The only sure method of achieving a sustained improvement in equity lies in hastening the advance of commercialization, i.e. the end of the labor surplus conditions."

The importance of high demand for labor for an even distribution of income, and for the mitigation of poverty, also creates a strong case for fighting various regulations in the labor market that keep low-skilled labor unemployed. Obvious examples are minimum-wage legislation and wage policies by unions with similar characteristics, though such legislation and policies do help some low- and middle-income employees—if they do not lose their jobs by way of such actions. Here then is another illustration that efficiency and equality do not always conflict.

However, when stimulating employment, it is, from the point of view of distributional considerations, important to avoid using methods, such as aggressive demand expansion, that generate high and fluctuating inflation, which easily hurts low-income groups. This is particularly important as inequalities generated by inflation are usually "nonfunctional," in the sense that they do not contribute to efficient economic incentives (probably the reverse), in contrast to inequalities that are caused by differences in productive effort. As high-inflation economies tend to get large distortions of relative prices, including the real exchange rate, here is another example where allocative and distributional aspects are complementary.

The upshot of all this is that those who, for efficiency reasons, are in favor of outward-oriented development strategies have certainly no reason to be shy about their position from the point of view of the distribution of income—rather the opposite. Recent experiences in countries like South Korea and Taiwan illustrate this point. There countries have demonstrated the possibility of reconciling efficiency and distributional considerations *both* by choosing an outward-looking development strategy *and* by making early redistributions of the ownership of land and human capital. Thus, even if examples are easy to find where specific tools of egalitarian policies, such as high marginal tax rates, do harm economic growth, there is no presumption of an unavoidable negative reverse causation, according to which increased economic growth would necessarily be unfavorable for income equality even in a short- and medium-term perspective.

The situation is more complex for countries with abundant natural resources rather than labor, as a growth process based on comparative advantage in this case tends to result in high rents. It is then often important to achieve institutional conditions, including a well-functioning capital market, dynamic entrepreneurship, and tax and expenditure policies that help these rents to flow to other sectors where the country has a comparative advantage, rather than using these rents for subsidies to import-substitution production.

(4) Of course, various arguments for institutional reforms in favor of low-income groups, redistribution of assets, and an outward-looking development strategy do not rule out the possibility of more direct policy actions specifically designed to improve the consumption of poor people. As pointed out in the section on expenditure policies, one obvious example is the provision of water, sanitation, health care, and food. It is, however, important to warn countries against choosing methods of redistribution that harm growth, as after a while economic growth usually tends to be accompanied by an equalization of the overall distribution of income.

PROBLEMS OF TRANSITION
AND MACROECONOMIC INSTABILITY

So far our discussion has been confined to various aspects of the allocation of resources and the distribution of income. However, when analyzing public finance, or economic policy in general for liberalizing developing countries, there is a strong case for emphasizing *stabilization policy* aspects as well. For instance, greater reliance on foreign trade, which is an expected consequence of more market-oriented economic policies, would be expected to accentuate the size of "imported" disturbances from world markets, though at the same time domestically generated disturbances will have smaller effects on the domestic economy, as part of the effects "leaks out" through the balance of payments.

However, it is conceivable that a market-oriented and outward-looking country will be so much more flexible than a highly regulated one (with the emphasis on import substitution) that the *effects* on the domestic economy of foreign shocks will not be greater in the former than in the latter type of country. Indeed, Bela Balassa (1984) asserts that a number of highly "outward-oriented" economies, in particular in Pacific

Asia, though being exposed to greater international shocks than most other developing countries, have recently been able to "absorb" the shocks better than more regulated, "inward-looking" developing countries. However, it is equally striking that attempts to liberalize the economies of some developing countries, in particular in South America, have backfired because of their inability to deal with problems of macroeconomic instability during the period of transition to a more market-oriented economic system. These important issues will be dealt with below.

One obvious problem during a period of transition to a more market-oriented economic system is that the redistribution of income and wealth, which is induced by the accompanying shifts in relative prices, profitabilities, and the composition of demand, will be resisted by various interest groups in society. New market uncertainties will often also be created during the transition period. One reason is that when an economy is originally in a situation characterized by pronounced disequilibria, which is a characteristic feature of a regulated economy, it becomes difficult to predict what will happen to various relative prices, demands, and supplies when the economy is liberalized. It is therefore important that there be confidence among private agents that the shift of system is *permanent,* as otherwise economic agents may not be willing to fully adjust their activities, in particular their investment, to the new information and the new incentives that are transmitted via the market system. An important explanation as to why the economic liberalization in West Germany in 1947–50 and in Pacific Asia in the 1960s and 1970s was so successful is probably just that there was considerable confidence that the shift to new rules of the game was permanent. More efficient market-oriented institutions in product and factor markets would also help smooth the transition, obvious examples being highly flexible credit institutes and labor exchange agents. It would also be useful if the government could adjust the public infrastructure rapidly, if possible even in advance of the liberalization of product and factor markets.

Another obvious transitional problem is the emergence of severe risks of large increases in frictional and structural unemployment, as the requirements of reallocations of labor may outstrip the ability of the labor market to achieve this smoothly. Thus, it may be hazardous to liberalize product markets without at the same time removing important obstacles to the flexibility of the factor markets. From that point of view it would be wise if, for instance, minimum-wage regulations and interest-rate ceilings were removed before, or simultaneously with, a liberalization of the product market. Recent studies indicate, however, that severe unemployment problems have not been caused by the liberalization attempts during the seventies—except in a few countries that pursued stabilization policies that severely damaged the employment situation (Michaeli 1986).

Indeed, experience suggests that the most important transition problem concerns macroeconomic instabilty—the difficulties of avoiding fluctuations in capacity utilization, inflation, and the balance of payments. For instance, inflation and balance of payments problems will most likely be accentuated when price controls and other types of regulations are removed. Indeed, this is exactly what has happened when socialist countries have experimented with a freer system of price and wage formation. The obvious, and generally accepted, conclusion is that a liberalization of the economic system has to be combined with increased concern for the management of stabilization policy—with fiscal, monetary, and exchange-rate policies as the main tools.

However, many years of experience in developed countries certainly show that even rather well designed macropolicies may not be enough to prevent high, and perhaps even rising, inflation. A main reason for this is that the mechanisms of wage formation are characterized by a pronounced inflationary bias in most, perhaps all, of the world's market economies. Some adjustment of these mechanisms is therefore worth considering when developing countries plan to liberalize their economic systems (in the same way as such modifications are today discussed in various developed countries). This argument may carry particular weight in countries with fairly strong labor unions, as in some Latin American countries.

Obvious candidates for such reforms are: removals of price index clauses in wage contracts, and the introduction of new contract forms with bonus systems that tie wage increases to productivity increases or profits. When developing countries introduce unemployment insurance systems, a strong case can also be made for letting unions and firms in each separate sector bear the bulk of the insurance costs, rather than shifting these costs onto the taxpayers. The idea is, of course, to internalize the negative consequences on the employment level of aggressive wage increases. Clearly, government budget policy has a direct responsibility for the rate of wage increases in the public sector, which in some developing countries has an important bearing on wages in the entire labor market. However, in some developing countries, where labor unions are weak, general macroeconomic policy—with a concentration on getting the budget surplus, the monetary aggregates, and the exchange rate right—may be not only a necessary but also a sufficient condition for reasonable macroeconomic stability if international disturbances are not too large.

In countries with large fluctuations in the terms of trade (owing, for instance, to heavy exports of raw materials), there is also a strong case for pursuing monetary and fiscal policies that avoid large swings in the real exchange rate for nontraditional exports to prevent a "Dutch disease" in that sector in connection to export booms. The "sterilization" of extreme export earnings (for example, by taxation) or of their consequences for domestic financial markets (by monetary policy actions) to reduce instability in the real exchange rate is a crucial aspect of a successful stabilization policy for such countries.

There are also a number of specific transition problems connected to the liberalization of foreign transactions—trade as well as capital movements. For instance, as a tariff reduction initially reduces the prices of import goods ("importables") relative to both export goods ("exportables") and nontraded goods ("nontradables"), both domestic absorption of importables and the production of nontradables are stimulated. In other words, there is an appreciation in the "real exchange rate." In combination with the reduced competitiveness of domestic production of importables, we would, in short-term perspective, expect temporary unemployment problems in that sector, and most likely also an increased current account deficit. This is, of course, the rationale for the traditional policy advice to devalue the currency in connection with a general tariff reduction—implying a slowing down (or reversal) of the appreciation of the real exchange rate. An additional complication is that the inflationary effects of the devaluation may dominate the deflationary effects of the tariff reduction, which is, of course, a reason to suggest that the devaluation be combined with restrictive demand management policies.

As direct regulations regarding imports are often more disruptive to the efficiency of the economy than tariffs, it is worthwhile starting a process of import liberalization not only with an "evening out" of the structure of tariffs between different groups of commodities but also with liberalizations of direct import controls. Attempts to reduce the *average* level of tariffs could then be delayed somewhat if rapid devaluations prove to be difficult.

With sufficiently restrictive management of domestic aggregate demand, the combination of tariff reduction and devaluation could then, in principle, bring about the desired shift of resources not only from less to more efficient parts within the tradable sector, but also from the nontradable to the tradable sector, with an expansion of foreign trade without a deterioration of the current account and without increased inflation.

However, if nominal wage increases (owing, for instance, to explicit or implicit indexation of wage rates) follow price increases closely, the result may be both stagflation and (with fixed exchange rates) a gradual disappearance of the gains in competitiveness that the devaluation was designed to provide. What would then remain of the entire operation would be a more efficient level and structure of tariffs, and hence a more efficient allocation of resources, though at the cost of more inflation and possibly also a deterioration in the current account of the balance of payments. Both the higher rate of inflation and the increase in the current account deficit then easily release political forces that result either in the reintroduction of a protectionist stance or in strongly restrictive unemployment-creating policy actions. *All this highlights the importance of an appropriate combination of trade liberalization and macroeconomic policy during a transition period.*

Of course, an increased current account deficit could, in principle, be financed by capital inflows, which are facilitated by the liberalization of capital movements, in particular if domestic interest rates are initially higher than the rates on world markets. However, such a development requires both high confidence in the permanence of the liberalization of capital movements and a sufficiently high real rate of return on domestically held assets, implying an appropriate and stable real exchange rate. As such conditions cannot always be taken for granted, a country that is about to liberalize foreign exchange should build up its reserve and/or lines of credit in advance, for instance by way of foreign borrowing by the government.

It would seem that the unsuccessful liberalization attempts in some countries in South America—in particular, in the so-called Southern Cone countries, Chile, Argentina, and Uruguay—in the late seventies and early eighties were closely connected with serious deficiencies just in short- and medium-term macropolicies. These policies were simply not "consistent" enough with the liberalization attempts (Khan and Zahler 1984). An overexpansion of domestic aggregate demand, often via a large budget deficit and a rapid increase of the money stock (partly to finance the budget deficit, partly owing to large capital inflows), during the process of liberalization contributed both to inflation and to rising current account deficits, which then resulted in severe liquidity and confidence problems for the national economy.

In these countries expansion of domestic aggregate demand pulled up prices in the nontradable sectors and wages in the entire economy, which with fixed exchange rates severely harmed production and employment in the tradable sectors. This also illustrates the dangers of trying to fight inflation with a fixed exchange rate if domestic aggregate demand policies are not kept under control—in particular, if wages are indexed to the domestic price level for consumer goods (with a strong component of nontradables). The experiences of Argentina and Chile during the late seventies illustrate this point.

Thus, the most important aspect of the transition problem is probably to avoid combining a liberalization of trade and capital movements with (1) an expansion of domestic aggregate demand by way of big budget deficits and a large expansion of the monetary aggregates, and (2) unstable real exchange rates, in particular heavy appreciations, for instance, owing to rapid wage increases with fixed (or lagging) exchange rates. Such policies have, of course, particularly serious consequences in an international environment characterized by drastically increased interest rates, a deterioration of the terms of trade, and a cyclical weakening of foreign markets, as in the early eighties.

However, it is also difficult to introduce trade liberalization in a situation in which the government tries to bring down inflation by restrictive demand policies, which will accentuate the unavoidable disturbances in the labor market resulting from the trade liberalization programs. This dilemma has induced some observers to suggest that a trade liberalization program has to be postponed until inflation has been brought down substantially (Bruno and Sachs 1985). It is also obvious that the order of trade liberalization is important. For instance, the experience of Argentina illustrates the danger of liberalizing imports before exports, and the experience of Chile illustrates the risk of liberalizing capital movements at an early stage of the liberalization process if effective action is not undertaken to prevent inflationary effects from capital inflows.

Finally, it is also important to avoid destabilizing macropolicies after a period of transition to a more market-oriented economic system, as both allocation and growth policies are likely to fail if the macroeconomic policy is not pursued with reasonable skill. An open economy, in particular a small one with large foreign trade, will be disrupted if aggregate demand is much too high, or much too low for that matter, and if the most important relative price of all—the real exchange rate— is excessive. Experience shows that this simple point cannot be stressed too much.

REFERENCES

Ahluwalia, Montek T. 1976. "Income Distributions and Development: Some Stylized Facts." *American Economic Review* 66 (May): 128–35.

Atkinson, Anthony B., and Joseph E. Stiglitz. 1980. *Lectures on Public Economics,* chaps. 12–14. New York: McGraw-Hill.

Balassa, Bela. 1983. "Public Finance and Social Policy—Explanations of Trends and Development: The Case of Developing Countries." In *Public Finance and Social Policy,* 41–58. Proceedings of the 39th Congress of the International Institute of Public Finance, Budapest.

———. 1984. "Adjustment Policies in Developing Countries: A Reassessment." *World Development* 12 (September): 955–72.

Bauer, P. T. 1971. *Dissent on Development.* London: Weidenfeld & Nicholson.

Bhagwati, J. N. 1966. *The Economics of Underdeveloped Countries.* New York: McGraw-Hill.

———. 1968. *The Theory and Practice of Commercial Policy: Departure from Unified Exchange Rates.* Essays in International Finance no. 8. International Finance Section, Department of Economics, Princeton University.

———. 1978. *Foreign Trade Regimes and Economic Development: Anatomy and Consequences of Exchange Control Regimes.* Cambridge, Mass.: Ballinger.

———. 1985. "Growth and Poverty." Lecture delivered at Michigan State University, East Lansing, April 4.

Bigsten, A. 1986. "Poverty, Inequality and Development." University of Gothenburg. Mimeographed.

Bruno, Michael, and Jeffrey D. Sachs. 1985. *Economics of Worldwide Stagflation.* Cambridge, Mass.: Harvard University Press.

Buchanan, James M., and Gordon Tullock. 1962. *The Calculus of Consent: Logical Foundations of Constitutional Democracy.* Ann Arbor: University of Michigan Press.

Chenery, Hollis B. 1975. "The Structuralist Approach to Economic Development." *American Economic Review* 65 (May): 310–16.

———. 1979. *Structural Change and Development Policy.* London: Oxford University Press.

Fields, G. S. 1979. "Decomposing LDC Inequality." *Oxford Economic Papers* 31 (November): 437–59.

———. 1984. "Employment, Income Distribution and Economic Growth in Seven Small Economies." *Economic Journal* 94 (March): 74–83.

Haberler, G. 1959. *International Trade and Economic Development* Cairo: National Bank of Egypt.

International Labor Organization. 1976. *Employment, Growth and Basic Needs.* Geneva: ILO.

International Monetary Fund. 1985. *Government Finance Statistics Yearbook.* Washington, D.C.: International Monetary Fund.

Khan, M. S., and R. Zahler. 1984. *Trade and Financial Liberalization in the Context of External Shocks and Inconsistent Domestic Policies.* IMF Document DM 84/44. Washington, D.C.: International Monetary Fund.

Krueger, Anne O. 1974. "The Political Economy of the Rent-Seeking Society." *American Economic Review* 64 (June): 291–303.

———, ed. 1983. *Trade and Employment in Developing Countries.* Vol. 3, *Synthesis and Conclusions.* Chicago: University of Chicago Press.

Kuznets, S. 1955. "Economic Growth and Income Inequality." *American Economic Review* 45 (March): 1–28.

———. 1963. "Quantitative Aspects of the Economic Growth of Nations: III: Distribution of Income by Size." *Economic Development and Cultural Change* 11 (January): 1–80.

Lal, Deepak. 1983. *The Poverty of Development Economics.* Hobart Paperback no. 16. Washington, D.C.: Institute of Economic Affairs.

Lindbeck, Assar. 1973. "Endogenous Politicians and the Theory of Economic Policy." Seminar Paper no. 35. Stockholm: Institute for International Economic Studies.

———. 1985. "What Is Wrong with the West European Economies?" *World Economy* (June): 153–70.

Little, I. 1982. *Economic Development: Theory, Policy and International Relations.* New York: Basic Books.

Little, I., T. Scitovsky and M. Scott. 1970. *Industry and Trade in Some Developing Countries: A Comparative Study.* London: Oxford University Press.

Michaeli, M. 1986. "The Timing and Sequencing of a Trade Liberalization Policy." World Bank papers prepared for conference in Lisbon, June 15–22. Mimeographed.

Morawetz, D. 1976. "Elasticities of Substitution in Industry: What Do We Learn from Econometric Estimates?" *World Development* 4 (January): 11–15.

Myint, H. 1967. "Economic Theory and Development Policy." *Economica* 34 (May): 117–30.

Myrdal, Gunnar. 1968. *Asian Drama: An Inquiry into the Poverty of Nations.* New York: Twentieth Century Fund. Reprint, Penguin Books.

Okun, A. M. 1974. *Equality and Efficiency: The Big Trade-Off.* Washington, D.C.: Brookings Institution.

Psacharopoulos, G. 1981. "Returns to Education: An Updated International Expansion." *Comparative Education* 17:321–41.

Ranis, Gustav. 1978. "Equity with Growth in Taiwan: How 'Special' Is the Special Case?" *World Development* 6 (March): 397–409.

Schultz, Theodore W. 1964. *Transforming Traditional Agriculture.* New Haven: Yale University Press.

Sen, Amartya. 1981. *Poverty and Famines: An Essay on Entitlement and Deprivation.* New York: Oxford University Press.

Sicat, G. P., and A. Virmani. 1986. "Personal Income Taxes in Developing Countries." World Bank. Mimeographed.

Stern, N. H. 1984. "Optimum Taxation and Tax Policy." *IMF Staff Papers* 31 (June): 339–78.

Stiglitz, Joseph E. 1985. *Economics of Information and the Theory of Economic Development.* NBER Working Paper no. 1. Cambridge, Mass.: National Bureau of Economic Research.

Tanzi, V. 1986. "Quantitative Characteristics of the Tax System in Developing Countries." In D. Newberg and N. Stern, eds., *Modern Tax Theory for Developing Countries.* Washington, D.C.: World Bank.

United Nations. 1983. *Industrial Yearbook.* New York: UN.

Viner, J. 1952. *International Trade and Economic Development.* Lectures delivered at National University of Brazil. Glencoe, Ill.: Free Press.

Waterston, A. 1965. *Development Planning: Lessons of Experience.* Baltimore: Johns Hopkins University Press for the World Bank.

White, L. J. 1978. "The Evidence on Appropriate Factor Proportions for Manufacturing in Less Developed Countries: A Survey." *Economic Development and Cultural Change* 27 (October): 27–59.

World Bank. 1985. *World Development Report, 1985.* Washington, D.C.: World Bank.

———. 1986. *World Development Report, 1986.* Washington, D.C.: World Bank.

FOUR

The Role of Medium-Term Plans in Development

Chen Sun

1. INTRODUCTION

The use of development planning to foster economic growth has been a general practice in almost all developing countries since World War II. It is perhaps pertinent, therefore, to enumerate at the beginning of this essay the major factors that are considered responsible for long-run economic growth. Economic growth means sustained increase in per capita output, which in the final analysis reflects continuing improvement in labor productivity.

Economists sometimes differentiate economic growth from economic development in that growth refers only to quantitative changes, while development involves not only quantitative but also qualitative changes, such as changes in industrial structure, economic institutions, and even the sociocultural environment. However, anything that grows changes. Without socioeconomic changes, economic growth could not be sustained for very long. This may be why certain economists, notably the late Simon Kuznets, use the term *growth* rather than *development* in dealing with the process of economic development (Kuznets 1966; see also Rostow 1960).

Economic growth can be attributed to the following factors:

(1) A growing stock of knowledge from which continuous technical progress, in the form of more efficient methods of production, new products, or the ability to take advantage of other countries' advanced science and technology, can be made. Without technical progress, existing sources of growth would gradually be

exhausted, and the growth rate would decline and eventually approach zero. The economy would become stagnant.

(2) A group of people who have the spirit of entrepreneurship to take the initiatives and risks necessary to apply new technology to production. Without entrepreneurs, there would be no innovation, and the increasing stock of knowledge would not be relevant to economic development.

(3) A healthy, disciplined, and well-educated labor force willing to work and responsive to the incentive systems of the economy.

(4) A well-organized social, cultural, and institutional framework within which economic activities take place. In a centrally planned economy government authorities make major decisions on resource allocation. In a mixed-market economy it is the private sector that functions as the major engine of the economy in cooperation with the public sector. As Barend A. de Vries has correctly noted:

> Without a viable private sector, government cannot (in most circumstances) stimulate or sustain economic growth. Conversely, without a reasonably efficient public sector capable of providing—at a manageable economic cost—the necessary infrastructure and an overall environment conducive to sound investment, the private sector is unlikely to make its full contribution to development. If government is inefficient and ineffective, or if it pursues policies that significantly distort private sector decision making, both the private sector and the overall prospects for economic development suffer. (de Vries 1981, 11–12)

(5) A constant flow of savings put aside from current production, and large enough in percentage of GNP to finance investment. A country cannot, however, save what it does not produce. A certain portion of what has been saved has to be exchanged, through international trade, for products consistent with domestic investment. Part of domestic investment could also be financed by foreign savings through trade deficits. A low saving ratio, underdevelopment of international trade, and lack of sufficient foreign capital inflow can all cause bottlenecks limiting the economic growth of a country.

Each of these factors can be interfered with by government action, and could therefore be included in development planning. Important though all of these factors are to economic development, none has been a major subject of economic analysis, with the exception of savings and investment. Modern articulated comprehensive development planning for mixed-market economies owes its origin to Keynesian economics, in which savings and investment play a key role.

This chapter consists of seven sections. Section 2 will trace the beginning of postwar comprehensive national economic plans and their later development. Types of plans, in terms of length, will also be discussed in this section. Section 3 deals with the objectives of planning in general and the relationship between growth and planning in particular. Section 4 is on resource mobilization and the allocation of resources between the public sector and the private sector and on determination of investment within the private sector. In section 5 education and research and development are discussed in connection with investment in human capital and technical progress. Section 6 is on price stability and income distribution. And the last section, section 7, contains concluding remarks.

2. DEVELOPMENT OF ECONOMIC PLANNING

Economic plans may mean many different things. Broadly defined, an economic plan is a systematic arrangement of policy measures designed to achieve certain objectives or goals in connection with the economy as a whole or with a particular aspect of the economy. In this sense, one can hardly think of any economy that has not adopted economic plans of one kind or another as a device for improving economic situations. But the use of comprehensive national development plans to promote nationwide economic development came into existence and emerged in developing countries only after World War II. Development planning improved only gradually and has reached its present level of sophistication as a result of both accumulated experience and advances in economics and econometrics.

During the early postwar years economic plans in many developing countries were often just wish lists and collections of proposed investment projects. W. Arthur Lewis included in a development plan any or all of the following parts:

(1) a survey of current economic conditions;
(2) a list of proposed public expenditures;
(3) a discussion of likely developments in the private sector;
(4) a macroeconomic projection of the economy;
(5) a review of government policies. (Lewis 1966, 13)

They were gradually developed into a body of consistent goals to be obtained and policy measures to be adopted. Modern articulated comprehensive national development planning would not have been possible without the existence of macroeconomics and national income statistics.

In the 1950s and the early 1960s, when post-Keynesian growth theory was prevailing, the Harrod-Domar model was widely used in development planning to calculate the capital requirement necessary to achieve a certain rate of growth or to determine a growth target given the financial resources available for domestic investment. Following the development of neoclassical growth theory, the Harrod-Domar fixed coefficient production function was replaced by more general forms of production functions. Manpower planning was brought into the picture at least partly as a result of the emergence of the investment-in-human-capital thesis. Of course, there were other factors that also had something to do with the inclusion of manpower and education in development planning, for example: (1) in order to raise production as the unlimited-supply-of-labor stage ended, improvement in the quality of labor by way of education was required; and (2) as capital accumulated and became abundant, availability of skilled workers gradually became a limiting factor to further growth.

In 1961 the General Assembly of the United Nations designated the 1960s as the Development Decade and called upon member countries to accelerate programs not only in economic growth but also in social development. In response to this idea of socioeconomic development, UN experts promoted the inclusion of social considerations such as employment, education, health care, housing, social welfare, income distribution, and regional development into overall development planning; they emphasized the need for intersectional coordination and integration (United Nations 1963).

However, the integration of economic and social development planning has never been successful. This is because we know very little about the interrelationships between economic and social variables. Although certain social aspects have been included in development plans, they are in most cases formal and superficial, and only passively involve the redistribution aspect of development—at most, in the sense that the benefits of economic growth should be widespread through social programs. After all, economic development is, in the final analysis, a sociocultural process, and sociocultural behavior is difficult to plan. Thus the basic nature of economic development largely limits the effect that can be expected from development planning.

Development plans can be put into three categories in terms of length: long-term plans, medium-term plans, and short-term plans. A long-term plan is a perspective plan that covers a period of fifteen, twenty, or even twenty-five years—strictly speaking, more a projection into the future than a plan for the future. It predicts certain major variables, such as population, labor force, and productivity in the distant future to serve as a background for the formulation of medium-term plans. Examples of long-term plans are the Soviet Union's 1960–80 twenty-year plan, and the French 1969–85 projection. Recently, the Republic of China on Taiwan completed a long-term projection into the year 2000, against which its 1986–1990 four-year medium-term plan was drafted.

The long-term plan is basically a supply-side plan. This is because, in the long run, economic growth is a result of increases in production capacity rather than in demand. And increases in production capacity involve improvement of the quantity and quality of the labor force, capital accumulation, and most important, technical progress, which reflects applications of advancing knowledge to actual production. Technical progress not only raises the productivity of labor and capital but also creates new products, offsetting the effect of the law of diminishing utility and opening up new dimensions for demand. Since knowledge concerning technical progress is limited, and is even more so as the period of observation extends, a long-term plan cannot be expected to be as comprehensive as a medium-term plan.

The duration of medium-term plans varies from three to seven years. Most countries adopt five-year plans, as have the Republic of Korea, India, and the Soviet Union. However, it is by no means necessary that a country always stick to the same duration in its medium-term planning. In the case of France, the first plan was for seven years (1947–53), but the following plans were for four years. Taiwan's medium-term plans have been four-year ones, except for a six-year plan in 1976–81. Medium-term plans are in operation in most developing countries. A complete medium-term plan consists of three basic components: objectives, projections, and policy measures. Objectives are the points we intend to reach with the help of certain policy measures; projections are the places we would arrive at without adopting any government policy. A medium-term plan consists of variables on both the supply side and the demand side. A key factor that connects supply and demand is investment, which is by definition an addition to the capital stock. Whenever net investment is not zero, the capital stock changes, and so does production capacity, or potential GNP.

The short-term plan is an annual plan, used for adjustment in order to keep development planning close to reality. It is also used to link economic plans to government budgets. A short-term plan is a plan on the demand side simply because potential supply is fixed in the short run. However, investment and certain elements of government budget expenditure, such as those on social infrastructure, education, and research and development, do add to supply capacity. This change in production capacity will not, however, be shown in the current plan period.

The characteristics of development plans, and the ways in which government actions affect economies through planning, vary with different economic systems. Plans in centrally planned communist countries are basically controlling plans, whereas those in mixed-market economies are mostly indicative plans. A controlling plan gives orders to the various units of the different sectors of the economy. Its effect on the economy is direct and by command. An indicative plan only indicates intentions and recommends policies to fulfill them. Its effect on the economy, apart from the public sector, is indirect and through the influence of public policies on the private sector. In a mixed-market economy, some sectors—such as the government and public enterprises—can be controlled by plans and others can only be influenced by policy actions. The control over the public sector may be tight or loose, and the influence on the private sector may be heavy or light in different countries and in the same country at different stages of development. This is what makes development plans different from one another.

The four-year and six-year economic plans of Taiwan may be taken as examples of indicative plans. Taiwan started its first four-year medium-term plans in 1953. During the first two four-year plan periods, 1953–60, the fundamental development strategy was the so-called inward-looking, import-substituting policy. Certain consumer goods industries, notably textiles, were selected for development under the protection of foreign-exchange controls and high tariff duties to supply the domestic market. Government intentions for private industrial development were carried out mainly through selective allocation of financial resources at differential rates of interest. And, until 1965, when it was terminated, U.S. aid was one major source of financing.

Toward the end of the 1950s, when the domestic market was becoming saturated with primary import-substituting products, the government undertook a series of foreign trade and exchange reforms. In so doing, it changed the development strategy to an outward-looking, export-promoting policy. The New Taiwan dollar was devalued. Import controls were relaxed. Throughout the 1960s, industrial development very much followed market forces rather than government decisions, with the importing sector still considerably protected by high tariffs and some import controls, and financial allocation in favor of exporting industries. In the mid 1960s export-processing zones were established to encourage development of the industries in which the economy possessed a comparative advantage.

The 1970s showed a reverting tendency toward more government intervention in private investment. The petrochemical intermediate products industry was established under government planning to supply the "downstream" industries. This is an example of so-called second-phase import substitution. Electronics and machinery were selected as "strategic" industries and enjoyed credit from banks with matching government funds to lower the interest rate. But the intervention was gradually reduced, and in the early 1980s the government eventually decided to liberalize the whole economy and go international.

3. OBJECTIVES OF PLANNING

The objectives that are commonly mentioned in medium-term development plans are:

    (1) high growth rate in terms of GNP and per capita GNP;
    (2) high level of employment or low rate of unemployment;
    (3) a stable general price level;
    (4) improvement in income distribution; and
    (5) improvement in the balance of international payments.

The last is not on the same level as the first four objectives, which may be considered the ultimate ends, in the sense that they are not used as means to achieve other ends. They are ends in themselves so far as development planning is concerned. The reason that balance-of-payments improvement is included as one of the objectives is that developing countries are often troubled by balance-of-payments deficit problems in the course of development. Additional objectives, such as improvement in industrial structure, diversification of production or exports, and more balanced development among regions, are also often found in development plans.

These objectives are not necessarily consistent, and may, in fact, conflict with one another in many cases. For example, rapid growth in production and full employment may be contradictory; rapid growth and a stable price level are difficult to attain at the same time; and many economists believe that high rates of growth and equitable income distribution conflict with each other. This, of course, may be oversimplified. Some of the conflicts could be resolved, or at least reduced to a certain extent, by incorporating appropriate policies into the plan. In the case of Taiwan, a high rate of growth, a low rate of unemployment, and improvement in the size distribution of income have all been achieved at the same time. The achievement may be at least partly attributable to two particular policies among its development plans:

(1) Method of production, in terms of labor/capital ratio, varies as relative prices (the wage rate and the interest rate) change over the course of development. To be specific, labor-intensive methods of production were encouraged when labor was an abundant factor in the economy, and only as labor gradually became scarce were more capital-intensive and technology-intensive production methods recommended in the 1970s and 1980s.

(2) Industries have been dispersed, helping factories to have easy access to labor (Ranis 1979, 222–24). This has not only raised the level of employment, and therefore reduced the rate of unemployment, but has also improved income distribution by way of raising labor's share of income in relation to capital's. This may also to some extent have been responsible for the price stability Taiwan was able to maintain prior to the early 1970s, since easy access to labor helped avoid an early labor shortage, which in turn prevented the wage rate from increasing excessively. But not every country has this kind of advantage. A prerequisite of the dispersion of industries is a well-developed system of transportation and communication.

If the objectives of planning are inconsistent in that the achievement of one may retard another, decisions must be made concerning the priorities of the objectives. Take the Republic of Korea and the Republic of China on Taiwan for example. In their respective development plans, Korea has assigned higher priority to growth, relative to price stability and equitable distribution, than has Taiwan.

Planning and Growth

While the priority system may differ in different countries and even at different times for the same country, economic growth is always the most important objective to be pursued in all development plans. At this point the following questions naturally arise: Does development planning really foster economic growth? If it does, then why, how, and to what extent does it do so? What are the factors that influence the effectiveness of a development plan?

Despite the prevalence of planning in almost all developing countries, economists have become skeptical about the effectiveness of economic planning on growth. After quoting Albert Waterston as saying that there have been many more failures than successes in the implementation of development plans in postwar planning history, and that the great majority of countries have failed to realize even modest output targets in their plans except for short periods, Michael Todaro concludes: "After more than two decades of experience with development planning in Third World countries, the results have been generally disappointing" (Todaro 1981, 459).

Another textbook writer, Clarence Zuvekas, even goes so far as to say:

> The macroeconomic plans adopted by developing countries vary in complexity and technical soundness, but with few exceptions they have one common characteristic: their ineffectiveness. The acceleration of economic growth rates since 1960 has had little to do with the preparation of planning documents which prescribe the speed and direction of growth and identify the policy instruments that are to be used to achieve national economic objectives and growth. Indeed, economic growth has often proceeded in directions not foreseen by the plan, or if in accordance with the plan, would have occurred even without the plan. (Zuvekas 1979, 191)

However, neither the poor record of growth rates nor the wide divergence of growth performances from planned targets is by any means clear proof of the dysfunction of development planning in promoting economic growth. There are areas that have to do with economic growth, but in which very little can be done in medium-term planning, such as entrepreneurship and cultural variables. And there are other areas where planning does carry a certain influence, such as the mobilization of physical and human resources. Ineffectiveness may result either from a deficiency of the plan or from its poor implementation. The often-mentioned shortcomings of development planning include inappropriate theory and techniques, inadequate and inaccurate data, and lack of willingness or administrative capability for implementation.

Economic growth in terms of per capita output (as it was defined in the introductory section of this chapter) results from increases in employment as a percentage of population, and in labor productivity.

The increase in the employment ratio is limited first by the size of the labor force and then by the age structure of the population. The difference between employment and the labor force is unemployment. And the size of the labor force is determined by the participation ratio, given the number of the population beyond a certain age, say fifteen years of age. Generally speaking, in a rapidly growing economy, the rate of increase in population first rises to a high level and then gradually declines. As a result, the proportion of the population that is of working age first declines and then increases. Usually, the labor-participation ratio also increases as the economy grows. Therefore, in the course of development, there is a period of time when the potential supply of labor increases as a percentage of the total population. However, this tendency does not last very long before the structure of the population ages.

The increase in labor productivity is a combined result of a number of factors, such as improvement of the quality of the labor force, increase in the amount of capital per worker (in other words, the capital/labor ratio, or the capital intensity), and, most important, technical progress. The contribution of the increase in capital intensity to productivity improvement would decline gradually to zero at a given level of technology because of the law of diminishing returns. There would be no incentives for investment, and the net saving ratio would fall to zero. In the long run, then, technical progress is the only source of economic growth in terms of both per capita output and labor productivity.

Technical progress is a simplified concept involving a multiplicity of factors. First, there has to be a constant flow of new technology that can be applied to production—in the form of either new products or new methods of production. Then a group of innovative entrepreneurs must exist who will take risks to apply new technology to actual production, otherwise advancement in technology would not be relevant to economic growth. Quality of the labor force has to be continuously improved, as do the sociocultural conditions under which investment and production are taking place.

The role of development planning in promotion of economic growth is (1) to mobilize idle labor for production, (2) to promote domestic savings and to attract foreign capital for investment, (3) to provide education and training or otherwise invest in human capital in order to upgrade the quality of the labor force, (4) to encourage or undertake research and development in science and technology, and (5) to improve sociocultural conditions in order to facilitate investment and production, among other things.

4. RESOURCE MOBILIZATION AND ALLOCATION

The mobilization of idle labor as a source of economic growth works only in the early stage of development, when there is large open and disguised unemployment. Furthermore, additional savings will be required to finance the mobilized workers. The mobilization-of-idle-labor thesis has never played a major role in development planning. However, the mobilization of savings has always been central to development planning.

In most developing countries, savings generated from the private sector are rarely adequate to sustain even a moderate growth rate. Therefore, public-sector savings and savings by state-owned enterprises have been heavily relied upon to finance investment in social infrastructure, such as transportation, communications, irrigation systems, and electric power. But the record is not impressive in most cases. According to an early study by the secretariat of the Economic Commission for Asia and the Far East of the United Nations, while net domestic saving as a percentage of national income was less than 10 percent for selected ECAFE countries (with the exception of Japan [27.7 percent] and Burma [15.6 percent]) during the 1950s, public saving was less than half of private saving in Burma, Taiwan, and Japan, less than one-fifth in India, and negative in South Korea. Public saving was equal to private saving in Ceylon and exceeded private saving in the Philippines, where net domestic saving was only 2.5 percent of national income. The same study reveals that the public sector was not able to generate enough saving to finance public investment in the period of 1950–60, with the exceptions of Ceylon and the Philippines. For four out of the eight selected countries, more than 60 percent was financed by external sources (United Nations 1962).

In a recent study Lin Wu-Lang reports that in most developing countries, net government saving (as a percentage of total current general government revenues) is generally less than 25 percent; that government net savings generally form not more than 3 or 4 percent of gross domestic product; and that within the public sector, public enterprises, instead of contributing to it, make large and growing claims on the government budget (Lin 1985).

In the early postwar years, when the saving ratios in most then underdeveloped countries were low and the public sector was sought as a major source of saving to finance investment, few came away with any significant results. In order to have a higher public-saving ratio, government revenues have to be increased relative to government expenditures. This, in turn, depends upon efficient administration and a sound and flexible system of taxation, both of which were lacking in underdeveloped countries. As development economists used to argue in the late 1950s and early 1960s, an underdeveloped country was under-developed because the administration was underdeveloped, and so was the tax system.

Even if public-sector saving could be increased by an increase in government revenues, whether it would be a net increase to the economy as a whole or merely an increase at the expense of saving in the private sector, so that total saving of the economy would not increase, is still difficult to say. The effect of an increase in public saving by way of an increase in tax revenues and the profits of state-owned enterprises is two-fold. On the positive side, through increasing public investment in social infrastructure, which would reduce costs of production and improve efficiency in the private sector, private investment would be encouraged. On the negative side, the increase in taxes might reduce private saving and weaken incentives to invest, therefore retarding economic growth. As a result, in the long run, increases in tax revenues might even decline rather than increase.

Alan Reynolds (1985) has demonstrated that in countries where average tax rates as a percentage of GDP were high, increases in real tax revenues over the seven-year period 1975–82 were generally low, and in many cases negative, while those countries where average tax rates were low nevertheless enjoyed rapid increases in real tax revenues. In promoting national saving to finance domestic investment in a developing market economy, behavior in the private sector is always of first importance.

In the early postwar years when development economics first emerged, many economists argued that an underdeveloped economy was underdeveloped because its saving ratio was inadequate to finance the high rate of investment required to sustain even a modest economic growth rate. The low saving ratio was a result of low per capita income, which in turn was owing to the low rate of economic growth. This process formed the so-called vicious circle of poverty that was so difficult for poor countries to break through.

Low saving ratios were a major characteristic of underdeveloped economies. Some people even went so far as to argue that there was a lack of thrift in underdeveloped countries—they simply would not save enough to get ahead. However, as T. W. Schultz has correctly pointed out, a stagnant poor economy fails to save enough to start growing not because of lack of thrift but because of lack of incentive (Schultz 1967, 28). At any given level of technology, capital will accumulate through investment until the marginal productivity of capital, and therefore its rate of return, approaches zero, at which point there will be no incentive for investment. Net investment will fall to zero, and so follows net saving if there is no opportunity to invest abroad. (Investing abroad prevents saving from declining to zero even though there is no return on investment at home.) Technical progress raises the marginal productivity of capital and incentives to invest on the one hand and improves profits and ability to save on the other. A country is never too poor to save a small portion of its production, but lack of technical progress makes saving and investment economically unjustifiable.

So a low rate of saving may be a limiting factor to growth in the early stage of economic development, as in the 1950s and early 1960s in many developing countries. But once they have started growing as a result of technical progress, developing countries will generate their own savings to finance at least part of the investment required for sustaining growth. And in many developing countries saving has considerably increased as a percentage of GNP since the late 1960s. This may be a major reason why saving has gradually become a less favored subject in development economics. Generally speaking, the saving ratio increases as the economic growth rate increases, which provides incentives and improves the ability to save. But there are other factors that also affect saving and help explain individual differences in the saving ratio among countries.

Among all developing countries, Taiwan has generated the highest saving ratio in the past decade or so. Its gross national saving as a percentage of GNP has exceeded 30 percent annually since 1972, the only exception being 1975, when it dropped to 26.19 percent as a result of the first oil crisis. In comparing economic development in Taiwan and South Korea, Tibor Scitovsky summarizes the factors responsible for Taiwan's high household saving as follows:

> The slightly faster growth of Taiwan's GNP; the slightly faster increase in the proportion of its labor force receiving part of its income in the form of bonuses; people's lesser spending and need to spend on education; the greater proportion of people saving up to establish independent businesses; the greater number of businessmen saving up to enlarge their already established independent businesses; and people's greater willingness to save especially for their old age, due partly to their greater affluence, and partly to the more secure and higher returns on their accumulated savings. (Scitovsky 1985, 249)

Savings can be encouraged by tax incentives, high interest rates, and price stability. Price stability provides certainty and security in saving. Governments that adopted expansionary monetary and fiscal policies to

provide forced financing for investment often found only worsening inflation and a declining saving ratio in the long run. S. C. Tsiang (1984)
criticizes the "misguided monetary policy," under the influence of
Keynesian economics, of keeping interest rates low in order to stimulate
investment and prevent cost-push inflation in the 1950s and 1960s for
discouraging, rather than promoting, saving by the public. He argues
that Taiwan was probably the first among the developing countries to
abandon a low-interest rate policy to combat inflation and encourage
saving, and was proven successful in the early 1950s and again in 1974.

In the past twenty years or so, Korea and Taiwan have achieved approximately the same average annual growth rate. However, since the
early 1970s, Taiwan has been able to generate more than enough savings to finance its domestic investment, while Korea (though also high
in saving ratio compared to many other developing countries) has had
to depend heavily on capital inflow in order to maintain its rapid growth.
The domestic saving–investment relationship has far-reaching effects
on the foreign sector, and the difference between saving and investment
at home always equals that between exports and imports. In recent years
Taiwan has suffered from an increasing trade surplus, and Korea from
trade deficits; both have their roots in saving-investment positions.

Determination of Investment

With regard to the allocation of resources available for investment, two
questions are essential in development planning: one is how much of the
resources should be allocated to investment in social infrastructure and
how much to productive investment; and the other is to what extent
should the productive investment be guided or intervened in by government policies. Whether investment in infrastructure should lead or follow productive investment has been an issue in development economics.
The advantage of low infrastructure investment is that more resources
can be available for productive investment, but the disadvantage is that
inadequate infrastructure investment may become a bottleneck and
therefore retard growth. The advantage of overinvestment in infrastructure is that it facilitates productive investment, but again, the disadvantage is that, in the face of limited resources, it may crowd out productive
investment. Intelligent planning serves the purpose of maintaining balance between the two categories of investment, and makes sure that the
growth rate is maximized. However, owing to both the large scale and
the indivisibility of social infrastructure, exact balance is neither possible
nor necessary. In this respect, the concept of balance applies only in the
long run.

As for government guidance or intervention in productive investment, it can vary from complete control (in the form of state-owned enterprises) at one extreme to total determination by market forces at the other. Even in the private sector there are various degrees of government intervention. The choices made will depend upon the ideology of the economic system, the theories believed by the decision makers and planners, and the stage of development of the economy, among other things. In order to influence private investment, the government may use protective tariffs, import controls, foreign-exchange policies, credit allocations, differential interest rates, direct assistance, and privileges and persuasion of influential government officials. In Taiwan in the 1950s, private investments were directed to the area of import substitution in order to save foreign exchange and to meet domestic demand. In the 1960s investments in exporting industries were encouraged in order to take advantage of the world market. As can be imagined, relatively more government measures (compared to market forces) were adopted to serve the purposes of the 1950s than the 1960s. In recent years the government has decided to go international and to further liberalize the economy in order to enjoy the benefits of comparative advantage, and thus to improve the economic efficiency of resource allocation.

The rationale behind government intervention in private investment is that while the market or the price system could achieve static efficiency by maximizing current output with given production factors under ideal conditions, it would not automatically lead to technological advancement and structural improvement. In this respect, government must play a role. As Oskar Lange once remarked: "Consequently, the problem of development planning is one of assuring that there be sufficient productive investment, and then of directing that productive investment into such channels as will provide for the most rapid growth of the productive power of national economy" (Lange 1964, 804).

Investment resources have been directed to import-substituting industries or to exporting industries in different countries and at different time periods in the same country. In recent years emphasis has been given to high-technology industries in many middle-income developing countries. Judged by past performance, there have been successes as well as failures. Generally speaking, those countries that pursued export-promoting development strategies have proven more successful than others. And of all the successes, four resource-poor export-oriented developing economies with small domestic markets (Korea, Taiwan, Hong Kong, and Singapore) have emerged as outstanding. The development of high-technology industries in developing countries has yet to be seen.

After reviewing more than three hundred plans, a World Bank report emphasizes the importance of consistency of development planning with the market and the price system, saying: "There is strong evidence to suggest that policies leading to high distortion in prices and incentives also lead to significant losses in growth and do not necessarily produce benefits in terms of equity" (Agarwala 1983, 13).

This report lists the following as policies that countries with relatively high growth rates have pursued:

- Avoiding appreciation of the real effective exchange rate
- Keeping the effective protection rate of manufacturing both low and even among products
- Avoiding the high taxation of agriculture by holding down producer prices
- Keeping interest rates positive and avoiding real wage increases not justified by rising productivity
- Applying cost-recovery principles in the pricing of infrastructure services
- Avoiding high and accelerating inflation

One common characteristic of these policies is that development incentives operate within the framework of the price system, not against it. Arnold Harberger advises:

- Make the tax system simple, easy to administer, and neutral and non-distorting with respect to resource allocation
- Avoid excessive income tax rates; high rates distort behavior and create disincentives to economic activity, while yielding little revenue
- Avoid excessive use of tax incentives to achieve particular objectives; excessive tax incentives too often direct scarce resources to less efficient investment
- Take advantage of international trade and modify tariff schedules in the direction of greater equality
- Let public enterprises operate like private interprises; when public enterprises and private enterprises compete, let their competition be governed by the same rules (Harberger 1984, 427–66)

Here again, the underlying principle is to be consistent with, and make use of, the market, not to distort it.

Government policy has universally been taken to provide the necessary incentives to channel investment resources to areas thought to be the most favorable to long-run growth. However, it should be kept in mind that economic growth is a sociocultural process that proceeds only gradually in terms of technological progress and improvements in industrial structure. The more ambitious the goal is, the larger the incentives offered will have to be. Too often in the history of the development of the Third World, government incentives have turned out to be so great that investments were induced in areas far from the reach of technology, and where little comparative advantage existed. And yet the burden had to be shared, in one way or another, by the economy as a whole. Whether a developing country chooses to be more or less ambitious in its industrial policy to push its economy to the developed state is a matter not only of economic calculation, but also of political philosophy.

Both South Korea and Taiwan have adopted export-led, outward-looking development strategies in their development plans to take advantage of international trade and their comparative advantages in labor-intensive industries. Both have pursued industrial policies to guide and influence private investments in order to speed up improvement in industrial structure and technological progress. And in recent years, both have moved to more technology-intensive industries and have emphasized the development of high-tech industries. The government of the Republic of Korea seems to have been playing a more energetic and aggressive role than has the government of Taiwan in promoting industrial development. In Taiwan, business leaders, and many government officials as well, have always admired the strong leadership of the Korean government and the prompt, extensive, and often efficient policy measures that it has taken to promote development. However, despite the aggressiveness of the Korean government and all the efforts it has made to accelerate economic development, the performance of the Korean economy in terms of growth has been no better, if not worse, than that of Taiwan over the past years. And Taiwan has achieved a more stable price level, greater equality in income distribution, and stronger balance-of-payments positions than has Korea, and indeed, perhaps any other developing country. The difference lies in the fact that development planning and government policies have been less forceful in Taiwan than in Korea, and more room has been left for market forces to operate. Whether Korea has built up greater potential capability for future development is yet to be seen.

5. PLANNING EDUCATION AND R&D

Economists have long realized the importance of education to economic development. "The progress and diffusion of knowledge are constantly leading to the adoption of new processes and new machinery which economize human effort," Alfred Marshall pointed out in his *Principles of Economics* (1920, 222). In fact, a major theme of Marshall's book at the macro-level was, in modern language, the promotion of economic growth by way of the progress and diffusion of knowledge. Thanks to T. W. Schultz, "human capital" has been a useful concept for analyzing economic development since the early 1960s.

The stock of human capital accumulates through investment in education. In the simplest form of the production function, total production is a function of technical progress, the amount of (physical) capital stock, and the labor force. Education has to do not only with the labor force, but also with technical progress. The level of economic development that a country has attained very much reflects the general level of the education of its people. Education is a means to achieve economic development as well as development in other areas. It is also more than a means; it is an end in itself. As a means, education is an investment good, but as an end, it is a consumption good. The importance of education therefore goes beyond the scope of economic development.

But investment in education is limited by scarce resources, as is investment in social infrastructure. This is especially true in the early stages of development, when there is a serious capital shortage. Given the condition of capital shortage, education and productive investment compete for scarce resources. How to allocate limited resources between the two is a difficult decision to make.

Education planning may have three main objectives: (1) to provide the people with the general knowledge, the basic skills, and the discipline that are required for living in a modern society; (2) to supply the economy with an adequate labor force of the quality required for growth; and (3) to develop higher education and the pursuit of advanced studies in order to provide a growing number of highly qualified people and to build up an increasing stock of knowledge, both of which are necessary for a country's long-run development, economically and otherwise.

Whereas inadequate education retards economic growth, too much education draws resources from productive investment, which also reduces the growth rate. The structure of education in terms of levels of education and areas of discipline has a great deal to do with economic growth. Too much emphasis on higher education at the expense of secondary and primary education does little to benefit growth. One can easily think of many formerly colonial developing countries that have quite a number of very well educated top people, but poorly educated or even illiterate general publics. These countries are characterized by slow growth and inequitable income distributions. The expensive investment in higher education seems to have contributed little to their economic development. This is understandable, because the structure of education was not consistent with the demand for labor. It is advisable for a developing country, in which national savings are inadequate to finance domestic investment, to plan its education in accordance with projected growth targets.

In planning education, it is important to keep in mind that economic development is a gradual process, and that an economy does not jump, but grows. Any country that has invested aggressively in higher education in its early stages of development, when the average qualification required of its workers is primary or at most secondary education, will find itself involved in a heavy cost that it can only expect to recover, with uncertain possibilities, in the very distant future.

In this regard, planning investment in education and planning investment in infrastructure are very similar, in that maintaining some kind of balance between education or infrastructural investment and productive investment is of utmost importance. A roughly balanced allocation of resources between education or infrastructure on the one hand and productive investment on the other is consistent with the basic principle of growth maximization.

In the case of Taiwan, the government has taken a gradual approach in educational development to correspond to its economic development. In the beginning, six years of free compulsory education were required as a minimum for all boys and girls of school age. Later the minimum requirement was extended to nine years, with the additional three years free from entrance examination, but not compulsory. Now, the government is talking about another extension to twelve years, with vocational education being the main stream at the senior high level. This new system is currently in the experimental stage. During the 1952–53 school year, only 33.8 percent of primary school graduates enrolled in junior high schools, 62.9 percent of junior high graduates enrolled in senior high schools, and 46.2 percent of regular senior high graduates enrolled in institutions of higher education. In 1985–86 the percentages increased to 99.4, 73.3, and 80.3 respectively (Taiwan 1986, 284).

As for the structure of secondary education, Taiwan has so far followed a 70:30 ratio between vocational senior high and regular senior high in terms of enrollment, on the grounds that vocational school graduates will go to work and regular senior high graduates will pursue higher education. However, as the economy becomes more and more sophisticated as a result of sustained development, the question of whether the country should produce more graduates from vocational senior high schools to take advantage of their technical skills, at the cost of a lack of general knowledge, or more from regular senior high schools to take advantage of their better basic knowledge and flexibility in adapting to changing technology deserves careful study.

When a country is getting rich and has more resources available for investment after a certain number of years of rapid growth, the time has come to consider allocating a higher percentage of resources to higher education. Too many college graduates may cause difficulties in employment at the beginning, but in the long run some people will create their own jobs and others will adjust by lowering their expectations and content themselves with positions that in the past would have been considered low for them. The general level of the society in terms of education and culture is upgraded in the process. There will be an increasing number of people considering an increasing proportion of education as a consumption good rather than an investment good. In this way, a country spreads its performance from the economic sphere to the sociocultural sphere and becomes, then and only then, a developed country.

Technical Progress

Education is the basic source of technical progress. However, as the final source of economic growth, technical progress does not necessarily have to come from research and development. In a developing country, whose general level of technology is low, new methods of production and new products can be learned and adopted rather easily from developed countries. In this sense, developing countries have the "advantage" of less development. Developed countries cannot do this; since they are at the top level of technology, almost everything new has to be developed by itself. It is natural, therefore, that the cost of technical progress is higher in developed than in developing countries. This "advantage" of less development helps explain why certain developing countries have performed better than developed countries in terms of economic growth in recent years.

Of course, a country cannot pick up technical progress from easy sources forever. Domestic capability for research and development has to be built up as the economy progresses. Enterprises in developing countries are often criticized for not doing, or not knowing how to do, research and development. And governments are often tempted to require enterprises in both the public and the private sectors to undertake R&D, or to allocate a certain percentage of total sales (or some other reference figure) for the purpose of R&D. However, if there are easy and inexpensive ways to make money, why should firms adopt expensive, uncertain, and sometimes even unnecessary ways, with which they may not be familiar? Businesses differ widely from one another. It is difficult for one general rule to apply to all firms as far as R&D is concerned. In planning technical progress and R&D, it may be useful to recall the basic principle of economics that incentive systems are always preferable to forceful, quantitative measures.

6. STABILITY AND EQUITY

It is often argued that price stability and economic growth conflict with each other, and that growth and equitable income distribution are also conflicting. Both arguments require clarification. The trade-off between the rate of growth and the rate of inflation is essentially a short-run relationship. In the long run, sacrificing price stability does not benefit economic growth. On the contrary, countries that suffered from serious inflation have seldom achieved significant performance in terms of growth. This is because in the long run, economic growth is a supply-side phenomenon, but inflation is mainly a demand-side monetary problem. In the short run, excessive demand causes both the price level and the growth rate to increase. But in the long run, economic growth results from real technical, economic, and sociocultural factors. Inflation discourages saving and productive investment and consequently is harmful to long-term economic growth.

Theoretically, development planning works better in the area of maintaining price stability than in other areas of development. All the government has to do is to manage the aggregate demand by means of monetary and fiscal policies so that it does not exceed the aggregate supply. But in reality it has been difficult for many developing countries to avoid budget deficits and rapid increases in the money supply. Therefore, this is not a problem of development planning, but rather a problem of implementation of the plans.

Whether rapid growth and equitable distribution of income conflict with each other depends on the definition of equity and on the government policies adopted to improve income distribution. Imposing high marginal rates on personal income tax as well as on corporate income tax in order to improve uneven distribution weakens incentives to work and to invest, thus reducing growth rates. In recent years, ideas regarding equitable distribution have been changing toward emphasizing improvement in the living standard of the people at the bottom of the distribution rather than taking away incomes from those at the top.

Taiwan adopted one particular industrial policy that has had a significant side effect on income distribution. Manufacturers were induced to establish their factories on industrial estates throughout the island, near the sources of the supply of labor, rather than concentrating in cities. This has the following advantages:

(1) There is easy access to workers, resulting in rapid increases in employment and growth without causing rapid increases in the wage rate.
(2) More people remain living in rural areas while taking jobs in nearby cities and the urban problems that often occur in the process of rapid industrialization are therefore reduced.
(3) The chances of cost-push inflation caused by large increases in the wage rate owing to rapid expansion in employment are reduced.

Taiwan was able to adopt this industrial policy because of its very well developed transportation and communication systems. Few areas on the island cannot be reached with modern means of transportation and communication. This has enabled Taiwan to achieve relatively balanced development between different regions and between urban and rural areas compared to many other developing countries. Since the main source of income of the rich is capital and that of the poor is labor, rapid increases in employment and in the real wage rate (as a result of rapid increases in labor productivity) have been the major factors that helped improve Taiwan's size distribution of income.

Social welfare programs have long been relied upon as a means of improving the well-being of the economically weak. Although strengthening social welfare programs is an increasing demand in developing countries, and many development plans have included social welfare schemes as an integral part, it is important to keep in mind that every dollar that goes to welfare could be used for productive purposes, and that the collection of an additional dollar through progressive income tax, as is usually the case, reduces the incentives to work and to invest. So the key issue of planning in social welfare is how to allocate scarce resources between investment and welfare in order to balance growth and equity. For a rapidly growing economy, increases in the real wage rate and expansion of employment would help solve many of the poverty problems that would otherwise call for welfare programs.

Another thing about welfare that is important and worthy of note is the substitutability between government programs for social welfare and private responsibility. In a traditional society, the family is the basic unit of social security. The family serves the functions of health insurance, unemployment insurance, retirement, and old age care. The more a government does to provide social welfare, the less private responsibility will be. From the private point of view, it is nice to have a comprehensive social welfare system taking care of all anxieties. But the negative aspect is that incentives to save, invest, and work hard will be weakened.

So, while a social welfare system is important for helping to improve income distribution and provide social security, a critical consideration in the early stages of development is whether an additional dollar should go to productive investment or to equitable income distribution. When the economy becomes richer, a major consideration is the choice between incentives to saving, investment, and hard work on the one hand and social welfare and equity on the other. These, however, are questions more of value judgment than of economic calculation. As an economy progresses, welfare expenditures as a percentage of the GNP usually increase. Many developed countries have come to the point where the percentage is so high that people have begun to wonder whether it should be reduced in order to give more incentives to economic growth. This is not yet a relevant question for most developing countries.

7. CONCLUDING REMARKS

Modern articulated comprehensive development planning for mixed-market economies owes its origin to Keynesian economics, which is fundamentally a theory of demand management. Although development of econometrics and growth modeling has helped make medium-term development plans more and more sophisticated, the basic framework of the plans is still demand-sided. But economic growth is in the long run a supply-side phenomenon. Planning affects long-run growth only when factors on the supply side are affected. Although medium-term planning has been extended to cover manpower, education, and sociocultural, institutional, and even environmental aspects of development, the core of almost all medium-term plans remains an aggregate demand management model formulated with simultaneous equations consisting of only economic variables. An economically sound development plan may not help long-run growth very much if the factors responsible for growth are left unaffected. There are three major functions that an economically sound medium-term plan may have:

(1) Prediction of aggregate growth targets such as the GNP growth rate, the rate of saving and of investment, the government budget, and the balance of trade and balance of payments. However, econometric models constructed mainly from the demand side work better in the medium term than in the long run. In the very long run, investment and the stock of capital are insufficient to predict growth potential. In predicting growth potential in the very long run, economists are no better, though no worse either, than experts in science and technology.

(2) Evaluation of major investment projects. Projects that are technically feasible may not necessarily be economically justifiable. Developing countries that are too ambitious and apply advanced technology to production, ignoring comparative advantages and market conditions, often retard, rather than foster, economic growth.

(3) Coordination of macroeconomic policies to avoid inflation and conflicts of objectives.

Realizing that economic growth involves more factors than just economic variables such as saving, investment, and employment, development planning should also take into consideration education, science and technology, research and development, manpower, and social and cultural factors. Market forces should be respected. Flexibility in implementation of development plans should be provided in order to allow for changes in external conditions and inadequate knowledge on the part of the planners.

At its present level of sophistication, good (from a purely economic point of view) development planning still does not assure rapid economic growth. Even growth models of the highest standard, neatly designed at the forefront of the science of economics, may not help growth in the real world very much, since the final sources of growth are not areas with which modern economics is accustomed to dealing. But without adequate planning, the growth rates realized will certainly be short of their potential.

REFERENCES

Agarwala, Ramgopal. 1983. *Planning in Developing Countries: Lessons of Experience.* World Bank Staff Working Paper no. 576, Management and Development Series no. 3. Washington, D.C.: World Bank.

Birmingham, W., and A. G. Ford, eds. 1966. *Planning and Growth in Rich and Poor Countries.* 1966. New York: Praeger.

Balassa, Bela. 1966. *Planning in an Open Economy.* Yale University Economic Growth Center Paper no. 90.

De Vries, Barend A. 1981. "Public Policy and the Private Sector." *Finance and Development* 18 (September): 11–15.

Donaldson, Loraine. 1984. *Economic Development, Analysis and Policy.* St. Paul: West Publishing Co.

Dubois, Paul. 1972. *The Use of Projections for Indicative Planning in Developed Countries: The French Experience.* Paris: UN Department of Economic and Social Affairs.

Dunlop, John T., and Nikolay P. Fedorenko. 1969. *Planning and Markets: Modern Trends in Various Economic Systems.* New York: McGraw-Hill.

Galenson, Walter, ed. 1979. *Economic Growth and Structural Change in Taiwan.* Ithaca, N.Y.: Cornell University Press.

Hagen, Everett E., ed. 1963. *Planning Economic Development.* Homewood, Ill.: Richard D. Irwin.

Harberger, Arnold C., ed. 1984. *World Economic Growth: Case Studies of Developed and Developing Nations.* San Francisco: Institute for Contemporary Studies.

Harris, Seymour E. 1949. *Economic Planning: The Plans for Fourteen Countries with Analyses of the Plans.* New York: Knopf.

Hasan, Parvez. 1984. "Adjustment to External Shocks: East Asia's Success Examined." *Finance and Development* 21 (December): 14–17.

Hope, Kempe Ronald. 1984. *The Dynamics of Development and Development Administration.* London: Greenwood Press.

Krueger, Anne O. 1985. "Import Substitution versus Export Promotion." *Finance and Development* 22 (June): 20–23.

Kuznets, Simon. 1966. *Modern Economic Growth.* New Haven: Yale University Press.

———. 1973. "Modern Economic Growth: Findings and Reflections." *American Economic Review* 63 (June): 247–58.

Lange, Oskar. 1964. "Economic Development, Planning and International Cooperation." In Gerald M. Meier, ed., *Leading Issues in Development Economics,* 487–91. Reprinted in Meier 1976.

Lewis, W. Arthur. 1966. *Development Planning: The Essentials of Economic Policy.* New York: Harper & Row.

———. 1980. "The Slowing Down of the Engine of Growth." *American Economic Review* 70 (September): 555–64.

Li, K. T. 1964. "Economic Development Planning." *Industry of Free China* 22 (September): 2–15.

Lin Wu-Lang. 1985. "The Role of the Public Sector in the Mobilization of Domestic Financial Resources for Promoting Social and Economic Development in Developing Countries: An Overview." Paper prepared for the International Seminar on the Role of the Public Sector in the Mobilization of Domestic Financial Resources for Social and Economic Development in Developing Countries, Bangkok, December 3–7.

Marshall, Alfred. 1920. *Principles of Economics.* 8th ed. London: Macmillan & Co.

Mason, Edward S. 1958. *Economic Planning in Underdeveloped Areas: Government and Business.* New York: Fordham University Press.

Meier, Gerald M., ed. 1976. *Leading Issues in Economic Development.* 3d ed. New York: Oxford University Press.

Onslow, Cranley, ed. 1965. *Asian Economic Development.* New York: Praeger.

Ranis, Gustav. 1979. "Industrial Development." In Walter Galenson, ed., *Economic Growth and Structural Change in Taiwan.* Ithaca, N.Y.: Cornell University Press.

———, ed. 1971. *Government and Economic Development.* New Haven: Yale University Press.

Reynolds, Alan. 1985. "Less Will Get You More." *Wall Street Journal*, January 23, 1985.

Reynolds, Lolyd G. 1980. "Long-term Growth in Third World Economies: Economic Development in Historical Perspective." *American Economic Review* 70 (May): 91–95.

———. 1982. "Inter-Country Diffusion of Economic Growth, 1870–1914." In Mark Gersivitz, C. F. Diaz-Alejendro, Gustav Ranis et al., eds., *The Theory and Experience of Economic Development*, 313–33. London: Allen & Unwin.

Rostow, W. W. 1960. *The Stages of Economic Growth.* Cambridge: Cambridge University Press.

Schultz, Theodore W. 1964. *Transforming Traditional Agriculture.* New Haven: Yale University Press.

Scitovsky, Tibor. 1985. "Economic Development in Taiwan and South Korea, 1965–81." *Food Research Institute Studies* 19, no. 3:214–64.

Taiwan. 1986. *Taiwan Statistical Data Book.* Taipei: Council for Economic Planning and Development.

Tinbergen, Jan. 1967. *Development Planning.* Trans. N. D. Smith. New York: McGraw-Hill.

Todaro, Michael P. 1981. *Economic Development in the Third World.* 2d ed. New York: Longman.

Tsiang, S. C. 1984. "Taiwan's Economic Miracle: Lessons in Economic Development." In Arnold C. Harberger, ed., *World Economic Growth.* San Francisco: Institute for Contemporary Studies.

United Nations. 1960. *Programming Techniques for Economic Development.* Bangkok: UN Economic Commission for Asia and the Far East.

———. 1961. *Formulating Industrial Development Programmes.* Bangkok: UN Economic Commission for Asia and the Far East.

————. 1962. "Design of Fiscal Policy for Increasing Government Savings." *Economic Bulletin for Asia and the Far East* 13 (December): 27–49.

————. 1963. "Social Development Planning." *Economic Bulletin for Asia and the Far East.* 14 (September): 1–60.

————. 1975. *Summaries of Industrial Development Plans.* Vol. 4. Vienna: UN Industrial Development Organization.

Zuvekas, Clarence. 1979. *Economic Development: An Introduction.* New York: Macmillan Co.

FIVE

Adjustment to External Shocks

Parvez Hasan

1. RECENT SHIFTS IN GLOBAL ECONOMIC ENVIRONMENT

The international economic conditions in the 1950s and 1960s were characterized by both unusually high growth and relative stability. In sharp contrast, during the past fifteen years, the international economy has been jolted by a series of unexpected and sudden changes, or economic shocks. The end of dollar convertibility in mid 1971 effectively ended the international gold exchange standard and ushered in the era of floating exchange rates. Under the new regime the key dollar exchange rates have shown quite wide fluctuations. The quadrupling of petroleum prices in 1973 ended the era of cheap oil and ushered in a period of rather large fluctuations in oil prices. After moderate real reduction in 1976–78, oil prices rose again sharply both in nominal and real terms in 1979–80, to touch a peak in 1981. In the following four years the real oil price dropped by 20 percent and then collapsed in early 1986.[1] World trade prices in U.S. dollars also showed wide swings, reflecting both the change in inflation rates in industrial countries and the sharp change in the value of U.S. dollars vis-à-vis other key currencies. During 1973–80 U.S. dollar prices of internationally traded manufactured goods increased by 12 percent per annum as accommodative monetary policy was followed in the United States. During 1980–85 they dropped by 6 percent, or over 1 percent per annum. The corresponding

This chapter expresses the author's personal views, which are not necessarily those of the World Bank.

1. In early 1986 the price of oil declined by more than 50 percent in less than two months to $13 per barrel.

changes in nonoil primary product prices were an increase of 14.5 percent per annum during 1972–80, and a drop of over 60 percent in 1980–85. The recent international price developments were essentially related to the disinflation in the United States, which, engineered through a sharp shift in U.S. monetary policy, has meant dramatic change in the real (ex post) interest rates on international lending. They went from highly negative in most of the 1970s to very strongly positive in the first half of the 1980s.

The highly volatile economic conditions after the early 1970s posed a major challenge to economic management in developing and developed countries regardless of whether the particular economic shock was initially favorable or not. Country responses to challenges varied widely. The purpose of this chapter is to discuss the comparative experience of developing countries in adjusting to external economic shocks during 1973–84, the period in which changes in oil prices and real interest rates were especially large. The focus is on major oil-importing developing countries, which witnessed a large loss in GDP owing to energy price increases, but the experience of a few oil-exporting countries, which gained large additional resources owing to rising oil prices and exports, is also analyzed.

Part 2 outlines the nature of external economic shocks and suggests that major initial economic shocks are more often than not accompanied by either reinforcing or compensating shocks. The impact of net economic shocks during 1973–85 on major oil-importing developing countries[2] is then discussed in some detail. Part 3 discusses the meaning of economic adjustment and discusses conditions under which increased foreign borrowing can be an appropriate response to negative economic shocks. Part 4 focuses on the country responses to significantly changed economic situations. Part 5 attempts to draw lessons from the country experiences and highlights the factors that are often crucial in successful adjustment to either positive or negative shocks.

2. THE NATURE OF EXTERNAL ECONOMIC SHOCKS

Coming in the wake of a period of extended economic stability, the recent economic shocks have indeed seemed exceptional. But external economic shocks, defined as major unexpected changes in external economic parameters affecting a country, are the rule rather than the ex-

2. Brazil, India, Korea, Morocco, Pakistan, the Philippines, Portugal, Thailand, Turkey, and Yugoslavia.

ception in the process of economic growth. As the following discussion suggests, these changes in external economic parameters can take various forms.

Terms of Trade Changes

The changes in the international terms of trade are perhaps the best known and most widely discussed of economic shocks. Quite clearly short-term year-to-year fluctuations in the terms of trade (a change reversed in a year or so) do not constitute an economic shock. In order to qualify as a major change in economic circumstances, the terms-of-trade loss or gain should be either sudden, significant, and lasting, or slow but secular.

Oil price increases in 1973 and 1979–80 have been estimated to have constituted a loss of about 2 percent of GNP for industrial countries on each occasion. The GNP loss for major oil-importing developing countries from this source was, however, relatively greater. Korea and Portugal suffered losses of national income over 1973–82 of 7–8 percent. For Turkey, Morocco, the Philippines, Thailand, and Pakistan, higher oil prices meant losses in GNP of 4–5 percent (see table 5.1). For India and Brazil, large continental economies with relatively small dependence on foreign trade, the corresponding loss of welfare was around 3 percent. In terms of relative impact on imports, the effect was especially large in Brazil, Turkey, India, and Pakistan precisely because trade is a small proportion of GNP in these countries. In terms of the impact of oil price increases on the import bill, Brazil, India, and Turkey were hit as hard as Korea. The relative impact of the oil price increase on oil-exporting countries was much bigger. Even leaving aside higher-income oil exporters (notably Saudi Arabia, Kuwait, and the United Arab Emirates) the impact of higher oil revenues on GNP and foreign-exchange earnings was dramatic in the case of Indonesia, Nigeria, Mexico, and Egypt. In the early 1970s oil income as percentage of GDP was either negligible or small in these countries, but by 1982 net oil exports were providing 9–12 percent of their GDPs.

Three examples of slow and secular decline in commodity terms of trade are declines in rubber export prices in Malaysia,[3] tea prices in Sri Lanka, and jute prices in Bangladesh.

3. With a ratio of merchandise exports to GNP of over 50 percent, Malaysia is heavily dependent on its export sector. In turn, in the early 1960s rubber and tin accounted for nearly two-thirds of merchandise exports. The real price of rubber declined 60 percent over the 1961–76 period and fell further by 30 percent during 1976–84. The real tin price

Loss of Markets

Major economic disturbances can also arise from the loss of established markets. This loss of markets should be distinguished from a long-term reduction in the demand for exports (inward shift of the demand curve) facing a country, which often translates itself into a secular decline in terms of trade. The loss of markets may be linked with noneconomic factors such as political shifts resulting in redrawing of national boundaries. Japan after World War II faced a major reduction in established markets in Korea, Manchuria, and Taiwan. The partition of the subcontinent in 1947 led to a major change in trade flows between India and Pakistan as trade ground to a virtual halt. The breaking away of Bangladesh from Pakistan in 1971 similarly affected trade flows, with Pakistan facing loss of outlets for manufactured goods exports to protected markets in former East Pakistan.[4]

New Market Opportunities

In contrast to the negative shock arising from loss of markets, opening of new markets provides positive opportunities. A striking example of

---

has also shown a large decline over the past twenty-five years. Malaysia was able to maintain a high rate of real growth of export earnings during the past two decades notwithstanding such a steep fall in the unit value of its principal exports. Indeed, overall purchasing power of exports expanded well over threefold between 1960 and 1980. This was made possible by (a) a strong diversification of exports to palm oil and manufactured goods and timber, (b) discovery of petroleum, and (c) improved productivity gains in rubber through massive replacement of old rubber trees by new technologically improved varieties, which made possible the expansion of rubber production and exports in the face of falling prices. Export experience in Bangladesh and Sri Lanka has been less fortunate, partly because these countries do not have the natural resources Malaysia enjoys. But lack of adequate policy response to the deterioration in external environment must also be considered a principal factor in the failure to compensate for loss in earnings from principal primary exports both in Bangledesh and Sri Lanka. In both countries export volume growth was negative over 1965–83, and resource transfers from abroad were 15 percent of GNP in 1983, providing for the very large bulk of investment in Bangladesh and more than 50 percent of gross investment in Sri Lanka.

4. A major devaluation was the policy instrument Pakistan used to redirect exports away from the former East Pakistan, and the opening up of large markets in the Middle East after the 1973 oil price increase further facilitated the shift. Nevertheless, it is difficult to avoid the impression that the setback to Pakistan's industry resulting from shrinking markets and the failure to set aggressive export goals in light of transformed conditions have been responsible for the relative decline of Pakistan as a manufactured goods exporter. In 1965 the manufactured exports of Pakistan (including East Pakistan, now Bangladesh) were valued at U.S. $190 million and were in fact larger than those of Korea ($104 million) and growing rapidly, helped perhaps by the sizeable domestic market. By 1982 late starters such as Turkey, Malaysia, the Philippines, Thailand, and Brazil, not to speak of Korea, had far outstripped Pakistan in the level of total manufactured exports.

TABLE 5.1 Impact of Oil Price Increase on Major Oil-Importing Countries

	GDP[a]	Total Imports[a]	Net Oil Import Bill[a]	Net Oil Import Bill as % of GDP	Net Import Bill as % of Imports	Net Oil Import Bill as % of GDP[b]	Net Oil Imports as % of Imports[b]
Brazil	248.5	23.3	7.9	3.2	33.9	0.6	5.6
India	150.8	16.0	5.6	3.7	35.0	0.6	5.8
South Korea	68.4	27.2	6.0	8.8	22.1	1.4	3.7
Morocco	14.7	5.2	0.9	6.1	17.3	1.0	3.0
Pakistan	24.7	6.7	1.5	6.1	22.4	1.0	4.0
Philippines	39.8	9.3	1.9	4.8	20.4	0.8	3.4
Portugal	21.3	10.6	2.1	9.9	19.8	1.6	3.3
Thailand	36.8	9.2	2.2	6.0	23.9	1.0	4.0
Turkey	50.0	8.9	2.6	5.2	29.2	0.9	5.6
Yugoslavia	68.0	14.6	1.8	2.6	12.3	0.5	2.0

SOURCE: World Bank 1985–86.

[a] In billions of 1982 U.S. $.
[b] Assuming 1973 constant oil prices. Real oil price in 1982 was six times the level in 1973. For simplifying purposes all direct and indirect effects of oil price increase on quantities demanded and/or growth rate of the economy are ignored here.

this is the remarkable expansion in incomes and wealth in the oil-exporting countries of the Middle East during the past decade. Imports into Saudi Arabia rose, in real terms, more than elevenfold over 1973–83. What is more, overseas construction contracts grew phenomenally in Saudi Arabia and other high-income oil-exporting countries as these countries undertook massive programs of infrastructure development and relied on foreign construction companies to supply both know-how and labor. These economic opportunities were to some extent an offset to the global oil shock. As it is, only a few countries, notably Korea, were able to organize themselves to fully exploit the opportunities that presented themselves.

Migration Flows

Another development related to the sharp rise in oil revenues was the tremendous growth in the demand for labor in oil-surplus countries. Saudi Arabia, Libya, Kuwait, and the United Arab Emirates (U.A.E.) are basically labor-scarce economies. They have thus had to encourage immigration flows to cope with the sudden growth in the volume of economic activity. Several million expatriate workers were present in the Middle East in the mid 1980s; the number of Egyptian and Pakistani workers was particularly large, and worker remittances became a very important part of foreign exchange earning in both Egypt and Pakistan. Worker remittances were, of course, not related exclusively to recent developments in the Middle East. Turkey and Portugal, and to a smaller extent Morocco and Tunisia, enjoyed large transfers from working populations in Europe. The opportunities provided by greater labor mobility and migration flows have historically been positive factors in international development. But the development of large pools of temporary, or guest, workers in Europe and Middle East had downside risks as well. OPEC (Organization of Petroleum Exporting Countries) oil revenues dropped very sharply after 1982 and were further drastically cut in early 1986, and oil-surplus exporters were thus running large current account balance-of-payments deficits. The completion of investment projects and retrenchment of economic activity in these countries was also likely to release labor. The pressures for reverse migration will grow, and what has been a positive impulse for countries like Egypt and Pakistan may therefore become a negative disturbance.

The broader point is that labor and population movements can be a positive or a negative shock, depending on the circumstances. In recent years Pakistan has had to cope with a large number of Afghan refugees,

176 PARVEZ HASAN

estimated at three million; the absorption of these unexpected and unlikely permanent migrants has imposed a heavy adjustment burden on
the economy, notwithstanding some additional foreign assistance.

Financial Shocks

Financial shocks can originate either domestically or abroad. The
changes in the availability and cost of external capital are generally exogenous to a country; on the other hand, capital flight is mainly rooted
in domestic developments. There were sharp changes during the past
decade in the cost of borrowed external capital, in other words, real interest rates. The real interest rate borne by market-borrowing developing countries averaged around 14 percent per annum during 1981–85
(see table 5.2), reflecting the combined effect of very high nominal interest rates, slowing down of inflation in OECD countries, and the sharp
rise in the value of the U.S. dollar. This was in sharp contrast to 1978–
79, just before the second oil shock, when average real interest rates
were negative to the tune of 7 percent per annum. In middle-income
oil-importing developing countries, the ratio of external debt to GDP
in 1984 was around 45 percent compared to 25 percent in 1980. The
swing in real interest rates thus meant, on average, a loss of foreign exchange of 6–7 percent of GDP during 1981–85 as compared to 1978–79
for this large group of countries. The highly negative interest rates in
1978–79 were, of course, exceptional, and could not be expected to continue. Still, even by using a "normal" real interest rate of 3 percent, the
excessive burden of high real interest rates on middle-income oil-
importing countries during the first half of the 1980s appears to have
been on the order of 3–4 percent of GDP per annum.

The changes in the cost have been accompanied by major shifts in the
availability of capital since 1973. During the 1970s there was a rapid
growth in net official capital flows—from $11 billion in 1972 to over $42
billion in 1980.[5] Even in constant 1982 prices and exchange rates, the increase was substantial, from $24 to $40 billion. There was a spectacular
growth of OPEC aid, OPEC bilateral official development assistance
jumping from only $450 million in 1972 to $4.2 billion in 1974, and to
a peak of over $8.7 billion in 1980. The early 1980s have seen an essen-
tial stagnation in net official flows, as growth in multilateral aid slowed
down and OPEC concessionary aid flows dropped by more than 40 percent between 1980 and 1985.

5. On official development flows, see World Bank, *World Development Report, 1985*, 95.

The changes in commercial bank lending to developing countries have been even more dramatic. The new international bank lending to developing countries rose from $10 billion in 1973 to $53 billion in 1981.[6] Much of this lending ($45 billion in 1981) was syndicated Eurocurrency loans carrying five- to ten-year maturities and floating interest rates. As debt difficulties in borrowing countries developed, the flows of new funds from international banks dropped sharply. The net new bank lending was estimated at less than $15 billion annually in 1984 and 1985, and a substantial part of this was in fact "involuntary" lending linked to rescheduling arrangements. In the 1970s the ample availability of capital from commercial banks provided an important, albeit easy, source of adjustment to external shocks. In the early 1980s the drying up of new flows from commercial banks in itself became an external shock.

Large-scale capital flight was another important source of balance-of-payments pressures on several countries in the early 1980s. Indeed, a good deal of the current debt problems in Venezuela, Argentina, and Mexico was attributed to domestic capital flight. According to World Bank estimates, annual capital flight averaged $22, 19.2, and 26.5 billion respectively in the above three countries during 1979–82.[7] In Argentina and Mexico nearly two-thirds and one-half of gross capital inflows respectively went to finance capital flight during this period. Strictly speaking, however, capital flight is not an external economic shock. As the following quotations suggest, capital flight is often related to a failure to adjust the domestic economy and the maintenance of overvalued exchange rates.

> In absolute terms, no country has suffered more from capital flight than Mexico. Mexico traditionally maintained a fixed exchange rate until a devaluation in 1976. In the late 1970s, the rapid growth in public spending and deficits fueled mounting inflation. Once it became clear the government would not reverse its expansionary policies quickly, the exchange rate came under strong pressure. The surge of official borrowing in 1980–81 helped to support the rate for a time, but it was running into waves of capital flight. In August 1982, Mexico was forced to suspend debt service payments, reschedule its debt, and devalue heavily. . . .
>
> Capital flight has not been confined to Latin America. In the Philippines, the government increased foreign borrowing sharply in 1981, anticipating that exports would soon recover and interest rates fall. The expected upturn in the world economy did not occur. Political uncertainty and lagging economic policy adjustment triggered capital flight. The government eventually had to devalue and reschedule. In Nigeria, official

6. Ibid., 110.
7. Ibid., 63–65.

TABLE 5.2 **Real Interest Rates**
(% per annum)

	1977	1978	1979	1980	1981	1982	1983	1984	1985
Actual Average Nominal Interest rate[a]	6.3	7.1	8.4	10.7	12.4	12.3	10.7	11.5	10.0
Change in World Trade Prices[b]	8.0	15.6	14.2	10.7	– 4.9	– 2.5	– 3.3	– 3.7	1.0
Real Interest Rate	– 1.7	– 8.5	– 5.8	—	17.3	14.8	14.0	15.2	9.0

SOURCE: International Monetary Fund 1986a, tables A20, A38, and A48.

[a] Actual interest payments in U.S. $ during the year as a percentage of total debt outstanding at the end of the year for market-borrowing developing countries. The average interest rate estimated here may be an underestimate because international reserves have not been netted out from external debt while interest payments are net of receipts. International reserves (including gold) were 30 percent of total debt of market-borrowing developing countries in 1977 but this percentage had dropped to 15 percent by 1984. So not only the actual interest rate but the increase in interest rate over 1977–84 may be understated. On the other hand, net interest payments include dividends and other investment income payments not related to foreign direct investment.

[b] The deflator used is the index of world trade prices for manufactured goods in U.S. $. Using an index that gives weight to prices of nonoil primary products would indicate an even higher real interest rate.

reluctance to devalue the exchange rate during 1981–83, when inflation was running at 20 percent a year, discouraged foreign direct investment, induced substantial capital flight, and encouraged firms to build up large inventories of imports.[8]

Compensating or Reinforcing Shocks

The above discussion suggests that it is not always easy to isolate the impact of a specific shock. More often than not major economic shocks are accompanied by either compensating or reinforcing shocks. The two periods 1974–78 and 1979–84 provide a sharp contrast in this regard.

In the period following the oil shock in 1973 there were many "compensating" external shocks for the oil-importing countries. The acceleration of international inflation while interest rates on international lending were fixed meant that real interest rates turned sharply negative. Not only were the interest rates negative, but there was also a very sharp increase in commercial bank lending to developing countries. The sharp rise in migration flows to oil-surplus Middle Eastern countries from neighboring countries like Egypt and Pakistan and, to an extent, India, the Philippines, and Thailand was another positive shock that helped offset the burden on the balance of payments. The availability of much larger concessionary assistance to certain countries, such as Jordan, Morocco, and Egypt, from oil-surplus countries was also a compensatory "shock." In the case of the Philippines, the terms of foreign assistance improved considerably after technocratic economic management introduced in the early 1970s led to the organization of an aid coordinating group under the chairmanship of the World Bank. The enlargement of markets in the Middle East, not only for foreign labor but also for imports and overseas construction services, was also an exogenous development that helped the adjustment process in oil-importing countries, depending on their ability to take advantage of the positive opportunities.

The developments following the 1979–80 oil price increase were strikingly different. The very large real interest rate shock greatly reinforced the terms-of-trade loss from the oil price increase, and generally more than offset the gain enjoyed by most borrowing countries during 1974–79 because of negative real interest rates. International economic activity slowed down even further, and opportunities for increasing worker remittances and overseas construction contracts were not available on the same scale. As the debt burdens grew, many countries found access to commercial banks drying up, and in many cases, there was virtual cessation of voluntary lending.

8.   Ibid.

TABLE 5.3   Balance-of-Payments
Impact of External Shocks in
Major Oil-Importing Countries
(average annual % of GNP)

	1974–76	1979–82
Brazil	− 3.9	− 5.7
India	− 2.1	− 3.0
South Korea	− 12.5	− 15.0
Morocco	− 2.8	− 6.9
Pakistan	—	− 2.8
Philippines	− 9.4	− 6.4
Portugal	− 13.0	− 1.4
Thailand	− 4.5	− 6.4
Turkey	− 7.5	− 5.4
Yugoslavia	− 10.2	− 6.1

SOURCES: Balassa 1984; Balassa and McCarthy 1984.

NOTE: External shocks during 1974–76 are defined as
the impact on the balance of payments of (a) changes
in the terms of trade, (b) a decline in the growth rate
of world demand for a country's exports. For 1979–82
the measurement includes increase in interest rates.
Data for 1974–76 show the change from 1971–73;
data for 1979–82 show the change from 1976–78.

Measurement of Shocks

Because of the multiplicity of external shocks and the difficulty of choosing appropriate base periods, precise quantification of external shocks
is not easy. Several attempts have been made, however, to measure the
impact of oil and related shocks in the period since 1973.[9] Studies by
Bela Balassa and Desmond McCarthy are among the most comprehensive. Their results for the major oil-importing countries are summarized
in table 5.3.

These figures show that external shocks were very large indeed for
most oil-importing countries. The shocks during 1974–76 and 1979–82
were largely, though not wholly, additive. During 1976–78 (which provides the base for the 1979–82 calculations), the real oil price was somewhat lower than in 1974–75, and the international economy had also re-
covered from the recession of 1974–75. Balassa's calculations tend to
overstate the net shocks during 1974–76, however, because they do not
take into account the effect of sharply lower real interest rates, which

9. See, e.g., Balassa 1984; Balassa and McCarthy 1984; Mitra 1984; Sachs 1985. Other
studies discussing adjustment experience include Jaspersen 1981 and Wallich 1981.

helped to soften the impact of higher oil prices. Inclusion of the other positive shocks, such as larger concessionary assistance and worker remittances, will further modify the calculations at least for some countries, specifically Morocco, Pakistan, and India. On the other hand, the estimates for 1979–82 underestimate the shocks because the focus is on measuring the changes in nominal interest rates rather than real interest rates, which have changed dramatically. For very heavily indebted countries, notably Brazil, Korea, Yugoslavia, Morocco, and the Philippines (which in 1984 had high ratios of total net external debt to GDP; see table 5.4), the large swing in interest rates after 1978–79 meant a massive loss of welfare, ranging perhaps from 8 percent to 12 percent of GDP compared with the base period of 1976–78. Even using the notion of normal real interest rate of, say, 3 percent, the interest-rate shock for Brazil and Yugoslavia during 1981–84 would appear to be over 4 percent of GDP. For Morocco and the Philippines the shock was much greater because of higher ratios of debt to GDP. The Balassa calculations of interest-rate shock equal to 1.9 percent of GDP for Brazil, 1.3 percent for Yugoslavia, 1.7 percent for the Philippines, 2.4 percent for Morocco, and 2.8 percent for Korea clearly understate the impact.

The central point is that the need for adjustment in the initial period (1974–78) was considered less pressing because the external borrowing option was available and sharply negative real interest rates (though relatively short-lived) lulled many countries into complacency. In the second round (1979–84) adjustment became inevitable. In many cases the net external shocks were larger in 1979–84. In any case the shocks were largely cumulative, and the borrowing option was increasingly less available.

Taking the past twelve years together, and accounting not only for oil and interest shocks but for other adverse terms of trade changes (notably in the Philippines) and positive shocks (worker remittances in India and Pakistan), the countries in our study affected most negatively (in terms of percent of GDP) were Korea, the Philippines, and Brazil, while India and Pakistan were probably the least adversely affected. Pakistan, on balance, probably benefited from the secondary effect of oil shocks because of a truly dramatic rise in worker remittances. Also, India and Pakistan suffered little from the rise in real interest rates owing to the highly concessional nature of their foreign capital inflows.

It should be stressed once again, however, that measurement of external economic shocks in terms of loss of GDP can be misleading. External economic shocks essentially impose a pressure on the balance of

TABLE 5.4 Major Oil-Importing Countries: Growth and External Debt

	Growth Performance (GDP growth per annum)			Net External Debt as % of Exports of Goods and Services				Total Debt Service Payments as % of Exports of Goods and Services			Net External Debt as % of GDP		
	1965–73	1973–83	1981–84	1973	1978	1980	1984	1975	1980	1984	1975	1980	1984
Brazil	9.8	4.8	0.2	88	313	271	306	43.2	63.0	41.2[d]	15.9	26.1	46.7
India	3.9	4.0	5.2	255	142	93	155	14.3	14.1	21.4	13.2	4.4	12.7
South Korea	10.0	7.3	7.4	70	84	116	119	12.4	19.1	20.0	26.8	42.8	49.5
Morocco	5.7	4.7	2.6	49	171	193	364	7.8	39.4	42.2[d]	15.3	42.2	102.1
Pakistan	5.4	5.6	6.1	285	N.A.	168	159	18.6	13.4	15.4	48.0	32.6	24.9
Philippines	5.4	5.4	0.8	31	177	166	293	12.7	24.8	29.5[d]	18.9	38.1	73.2
Portugal	7.0	2.9	0.5	20[a]	114[a]	95[a]	164[a]	4.0	14.5	33.9	8.1	37.4	77.8
Thailand	7.8	6.9	5.6	c	49	64	132	12.0	19.1	26.5	c	16.0	30.3
Turkey	6.5	4.1	4.7	21	319	249	171	8.4	23.6[d]	25.0	6.0	27.7	39.6
Yugoslavia	6.1	5.3	0.6	70[b]	137[b]	163[b]	185[b]	28.3	36.9	40.0[d]	16.1	24.4	41.4

SOURCES: Growth performance: World Bank, *World Development Report*, 1985 for 1965–73 and 1973–83; country sources for 1981–84. Other data: World Bank, 1985–86. Short-term debt figures for 1973 and 1975 are not readily available and have thus not been added to total external liabilities (including use of IMF credit) for those years. The short-term debt, however, was generally quite small in the early 1970s.

[a] Portugal has sizable gold reserves. Because of changes in valuations of gold over time, the figures given here are based on gross external liabilities. In 1984 the netting of reserves would reduce the net external debt ratio to 120 percent of exports of goods and services, and 40 percent of GDP.

[b] In the case of Yugoslavia the debt ratios relate convertible current debt to convertible currency exports.

[c] Negative figures as international reserves exceeded gross external liabilities.

[d] After rescheduling.

payments, so the ability of the economy to adjust depends critically on the size of the economic shock in relation to the foreign trade sector.

3. THE MEANING OF ECONOMIC ADJUSTMENT

What does adjustment mean? Negative shocks imply a loss of national income and/or import capacity. A rational response to these changes should involve both a reduction in national expenditure and a switching of expenditures to foreign-exchange saving or earning activities with a view to eliminating the deterioration in the current account balance of payments that invariably is the result of negative shocks. This adjustment need not be (indeed often cannot be) very quick, provided the foreign borrowing option is available. Increased net foreign borrowing must be an integral part of the adjustment process unless the country is already very heavily indebted or has been running an unsustainable current account balance-of-payments deficit in the period before the negative shock registers.[10] Increased foreign borrowing provides the opportunity to maintain imports and growth at a higher level than would otherwise be possible. But, more important, it provides time for orderly adjustment to the change in external economic parameters. If the increased borrowing is used merely to postpone adjustment, to sustain the past levels and pattern of growth, the external debt buildup will be rapid, borrowing capacity will increasingly become a constraint, and growth of the economy will ultimately be disrupted. In contrast, successful economic adjustment to negative shocks can be defined as maintenance (or resumption) of a satisfactory growth rate while keeping (or bringing down) the external debt burden within manageable limits over the medium term of, say, five to seven years. A country that borrows for adjustment must build up its capacity to service the additional debt, while at the same time reducing the initial disequilibrium caused in the balance of payments by negative external shocks.

This can be achieved only through export expansion and/or import substitution if maintenance of a reasonable rate of economic growth is also an important objective. Some reduction in growth rate, compared to historical levels, may be necessary if the negative external economic shocks are very large, but it is, of course, more desirable to bring about adjustment through a policy of switching national expenditures to

10. It is assumed that a typical developing country will have some net borrowing even in normal periods.

foreign-exchange saving or earning activities rather than a policy focused chiefly on reduction in national expenditures.

A policy of expenditure switching requires, above all, that the higher scarcity price of foreign exchange, which is inherent in a structural weakening of the balance-of-payments position through a lasting negative external shock, be reflected in domestic prices, if not immediately, at least over time. To the extent domestic prices correctly reflect international prices, higher scarcity prices of foreign exchange, energy, and capital (which have constituted the external shocks faced by oil-importing countries) will be passed on to the consumers and a good deal of the adjustment will be automatic. In a typical situation, however, the government response is critically important. For instance, very few developing countries have market-based exchange rates, and energy prices and interest rates are also often controlled by the government. In heavily energy-dependent oil-importing countries, the 1973 oil price increase fundamentally altered the balance-of-payments position. If the oil price increase was not seen as reversible, the response should have been a depreciation of the exchange rate and the *basing* of domestic energy prices on the new exchange rate and the new international oil price. Foreign borrowing decisions could be similarly based on the new exchange rate. This kind of market orientation was, however, rare, partly because political constraints clearly limit the reduction in consumption implied by a quick adjustment. The foreign borrowing option provides the possibility of adjustment to reduction in national income and import capacity without requiring a cut in absolute consumption. Instead, the adjustment in the balance of payments takes place in the context of overall growth, but with imports growing less fast than exports. Such an improvement in the balance of payments also implies a narrowing of the domestic savings and domestic investment gap. Indeed, domestic saving must improve relative to domestic investment not only to reduce the resource gap in the balance of payments, but also to accommodate the increase in interest payments abroad.[11] As the subsequent discussion shows, a persistent balance-of-payments deficit can easily be rooted in a domestic financial imbalance and may have little to do directly with the failure of policies to promote exports or saving foreign exchange.

11. Assume that as a result of negative shock, the resource gap in the balance of payments increases by 5 percent of GDP. In order to eliminate the gap over, say, five years, the domestic saving and investment deficit will have to decrease by 5 percent plus any *increase* in interest payments on external debt as a percentage of GDP.

Another dimension of the adjustment process is efficiency in the use of economic resources. The above discussion of growth implies that the relationship between economic growth and investment, and economic growth and import capacity, is more or less fixed. In actuality, substantial changes in incremental capital—output ratios (ICORs) and import elasticities—can and do take place over time.[12] If an improvement (reduction) in ICOR and/or import elasticity can be achieved, a given growth rate can be achieved with lower investment and/or lower imports. An important object of economic adjustment should be to improve efficiency in the use of scarce economic resources—especially foreign exchange, energy, and capital. The efficiency issue is linked with appropriate factor pricing but is broader. For instance, the effectiveness of the use of public investment resources and government efforts to encourage development of human resources and technological change can be important elements in improving the growth response of the economy somewhat, independent of whether severe price distortions exist.

4. A REVIEW OF COUNTRY RESPONSES, 1974–84

An Overview of Adjustment

Table 5.4 summarizes the growth performance of major oil-importing developing countries over the past two decades and highlights the changes in the burden of their external debt over the past decade.[13] By any reasonable measure, the burden of external debt has gone up sharply in all major oil-importing countries, with the possible exceptions of India and Pakistan, which have actually been able to contain the burden of debt while maintaining a reasonable growth rate. In all other countries there was heavy reliance on foreign borrowing in the wake of

12. A reduction in import elasticity would also show up as import substitution.

13. External debt burden can be measured in a number of ways. Until relatively recently, focus has been on medium- and long-term public and publicly guaranteed debt. It is now recognized that the inability to roll over short-term debt can be a source of serious balance-of-payments difficulties. Similarly, governments have found that they cannot allow a default on nonguaranteed private debt without creating a panic. Total external liabilities are thus increasingly being taken into account in judging the burden of debt. But if short-term debt is included, international reserves (i.e., short-term foreign assets) must be netted out from gross liabilities; otherwise countries that have large reserves would appear to be more vulnerable than they really are. It is this net external debt concept that is used in this chapter. The stock of net external debt can be measured either against GNP or against exports. Both measures are given in table 5.4. The ratio of net external debt to foreign-exchange earning, however, provides a better measure of debt burden than the ratio to GDP because ratios of foreign-exchange earnings to GDP vary widely among countries.

external shocks, and consequently the average growth rates remained relatively high during 1973–83. But by the early 1980s the heavy burden of debt was itself seriously inhibiting growth in a number of countries. Among countries heavily affected by both interest-rate and oil shocks, only Korea, and to an extent Thailand, can be deemed to have met our test of maintaining a high rate of growth while keeping the debt-service burden within reasonable limits over the past decade. In Thailand, the fact that net external debt was negative in the early 1970s provided substantial leeway for foreign borrowing. Turkey, neglecting adjustment until 1980, registered the sharpest relative increase in external debt between 1973 and 1980. But then, facing critical economic and political problems, Turkey embarked on a major economic adjustment program that has involved very significant shifts in economic policy and development strategy. By 1984–85 Turkey had succeeded in restoring a reasonable rate of growth of GDP while reducing the real burden of external debt and bringing the current account balance-of-payments deficit to manageable proportions (2 percent of GDP). A large number of major oil-importing countries, especially Brazil, Portugal, the Philippines, Morocco, and Yugoslavia, failed to adjust, or failed to adjust adequately, and are currently facing relative economic stagnation or major external debt problems or both.

Failure to Adjust

The seeds of the serious difficulties being faced in the mid 1980s by a number of oil-importing countries can be traced to an initial failure to take suitable action in 1974–79. Several policy weaknesses were common in their response to the 1973 oil price increase.

Excessive Domestic Expenditures. Even though oil-importing countries were faced with a decline in income and import capacity after 1973, a large number of them (notably Morocco, Brazil, the Philippines, and Turkey) maintained high rates of expansion of domestic expenditures (especially investment) relying on large foreign borrowing for financing growing current account balance-of-payments deficits (table 5.5). The inability to reduce domestic spending in line with the reduced availability of national resources was reflected in large fiscal deficits and high rates of monetary expansion, and ultimately in the large imbalance between domestic savings and investment.

In Morocco the effects of the oil price increase were initially offset by the ongoing boom in phosphate rock exports. The real price of phos-

TABLE 5.5   Major Oil-Importing Countries: Exports and
Balance of Payments

	Current Account Balance of Payments as % of GDP			Real Merchandise Export Growth % per annum		
	1973–80	1981–84	1984–85	1965–73	1973–80	1980–84
Brazil	− 4.4	− 3.3	0.3	10.1	7.8	12.5
India	+ 0.4	− 1.4	− 1.3	2.3	6.9	2.7
South Korea	− 5.1	− 3.6	− 1.3	31.7	16.8	16.0
Morocco	− 8.5	− 10.6	− 9.5	6.0	− 0.4	4.1
Pakistan	− 5.1	− 2.3	− 4.2	3.7	5.9	10.0
Philippines	− 4.1	− 6.3	− 2.6	4.2	12.3	− 3.3
Portugal	− 3.8	− 8.0	− 2.2	6.9	3.4	8.5
Thailand	− 4.8	− 5.5	− 4.7	6.9	9.0	9.0
Turkey	− 3.6	− 2.9	− 2.2	—	− 0.3	31.0
Yugoslavia	− 2.7	+ 1.2	+ 1.3	7.7	2.2	3.2

SOURCES: World Bank, *World Development Report*, 1981–85, and country sources.

phate in 1975 was 3.4 times the level in 1973. The government miscalcu-
lated the longer-term prospects of revenue from phosphate, did not
fully take into account the burden imposed by increased engagement in
the West Sahara war, and counted heavily on grant and loan assistance
from friendly Arab states, especially Saudi Arabia. Thus an extremely
expansional policy was followed at least until 1977. Gross investment expanded by 23 percent per annum during 1973–77, rising to 33 percent
of GNP. Turkey was another country that expanded gross fixed investment vigorously (nearly 14 percent per annum compared to 8.1 percent
per annum during 1972–77).

In Brazil domestic demand was maintained through public-sector
deficits and subsidies through the credit system. The interest rate
charged on credit programs administered through the Central Bank
and Bank of Brazil remained constant, while inflation accelerated from
13 percent in 1973 to 44 percent in 1977.

Brazil, Turkey, Portugal, Morocco, Pakistan, and Yugoslavia all
showed substantially worsened investment-saving balances in 1973–78
compared to 1965–72. The deterioration was the largest in Morocco (10
percentage points of GDP) as investment expanded vigorously while the
saving rate improved very little. Morocco was followed by Portugal (7
percentage points), Turkey and Pakistan (4 percentage points) and Yugoslavia and Brazil (3 percentage points each). Except for Yugoslavia
and Turkey, the situation worsened further during 1979–81.

TABLE 5.6   Changes in Domestic Savings/Investment Balance
(as % of GDP)

	1965–72/1973–78	1973–78/1979–81	1979–81/1981–83
Brazil	− 3 (3,0)	+ 1 (− 6,− 5)	—
India	+ 3 (3,6)	− 2 (3,1)	+ 2 (0,2)
South Korea	+ 6 (5,11)	− 2 (3,1)	+ 5 (− 5,0)
Morocco	− 10 (11,1)	− 2 (− 2,− 4)	—
Pakistan	− 2 (− 1,− 3)	− 3 (1,−2)	— (0,0)
Philippines	− 1 (7,6)	− 2 (3,1)	— (− 3,− 3)
Portugal	− 7 (2,− 5)	− 2 (5,3)	—
Thailand	+ 2 (1,3)	− 2 (2,0)	+ 2 (− 5,− 3)
Turkey	− 4 (4,0)	— (− 1,− 1)	—
Yugoslavia	− 3 (2,− 1)	+ 2 (4,6)	—

SOURCE: Adapted from World Bank, *World Development Report*, 1985, fig. 4.6.

NOTE: The first figure in parentheses is the change in the ratio of gross domestic investment to GDP. The second is the change in ratio of gross domestic savings to GDP. The
overall change is net of the two with the sign reversed.

Neglect of Exports.   High rates of growth of investment in Turkey, Yugoslavia, and Morocco during 1974–79 combined with the bias toward
capital-intensive investment and import substitution. In Turkey and Yugoslavia the authorities basically decided on an import-substitution
strategy of adjustment to external shocks, with emphasis on domestic
production of raw materials and basic industrial products. It was felt
that export possibilities were limited by high-technology competition
and protectionist barriers in the developed market economies and low-
wage competition in labor-intensive products from less-developed countries. Relatively little attention was paid to the creation of capacities for
exports. At the same time, the exchange rates, instead of being depreciated to reflect the greater scarcities of foreign exchange, were allowed to
become overvalued.[14] It is not surprising, therefore, that export performance during 1973–80 was poor in Yugoslavia and actually negative in
Morocco and Turkey (table 5.5), though in the case of Morocco the sluggish demand for phosphate exports was also a major factor. Because export volume growth was slow and external borrowing substantial, the
real burden of debt in relation to exports rose even though higher rates
of international inflation wiped out a portion of debt. In Turkey net external debt as a proportion of exports rose from a negligible level in

14. It is estimated that by 1979 the degree of overvaluation of the exchange rate was
about 100 percent in Turkey and over 40 percent in Yugoslavia. For a discussion of Yugo-
slavian and Turkish exchange rates, see World Bank, *World Development Report, 1984*, 45.

TABLE 5.7 Energy Consumption and Production
(growth rates per annum)

	Consumption		Production	
	1960–74	1974–79	1960–74	1974–79
Brazil	8.2	7.6	8.3	7.3
India	5.0	5.0	4.9	5.4
South Korea	13.9	12.0	6.3	4.6
Morocco	6.4	6.3	2.0	4.7
Pakistan	5.3	4.4	9.4	6.6
Philippines	8.4	5.6	3.0	24.4
Portugal	7.3	6.1	4.4	11.7
Thailand	16.2	7.4	28.3	− 0.2
Turkey	9.7	6.8	7.5	2.5
Yugoslavia	6.6	5.4	4.3	4.5

SOURCE: World Bank, *World Development Report,* 1981.

1973 to 250 percent in 1980. In Morocco the increase in debt was from less than 50 percent of exports to nearly 200 percent over 1973–80. If real interest rates had not been substantially negative, the debt problem in these countries would have emerged even earlier, though it can also be argued that persistence of high negative real interest rates provided a strong disincentive to adjust.

Energy Deficits. The failure to adjust was also related to less than satisfactory progress in the reduction of energy deficits after the first oil price increase. While the growth rate of energy consumption generally slowed down during 1974–79, the energy intensity of the economies increased in many oil-importing countries (notably Turkey, Portugal, and Morocco), and in a number of countries (notably Turkey and Yugoslavia) domestic energy production expanded at a slower pace than energy consumption (see table 5.7). Korea, India, the Philippines, and Brazil made relatively quick adjustments in domestic energy prices in contrast with Thailand, Pakistan, Turkey, Yugoslavia, Portugal, and Morocco.

Mixed Performance

While poor export performance was a key element in lack of adequate adjustment, good export performance did not guarantee a smooth adjustment. Brazil and the Philippines, for instance, achieved relatively satisfactory rates of growth of exports, but have ended up with very heavy debt burdens and very poor growth prospects. The Philippines was able to expand its manufactured exports by 30 percent per annum during the 1970s, and the share of manufactured exports had risen to 38 percent by 1980. The value added in manufactured exports was, however, limited, as the export sector's backward linkages with domestic industry did not develop. Unfortunately, the growth of consumption and investment remained high in the Philippines, and, what is more, a good deal of investment resources were not well directed, owing to heavy protection afforded to domestic industry. Thus pressures on the balance of payment remained high, and large recourse to external borrowing led to a growing burden of debt notwithstanding negative real interest rates and considerable improvement in the terms of foreign assistance.

In the case of Brazil also, export growth during 1973–80 was quite rapid (7.8 percent per annum), but the current balance of payments deficit remained large, as domestic outlays on consumption and investment were not restrained. It is also interesting to note that the rise in the burden of foreign debt in the case of Brazil was already very substantial by 1978 because, unlike the Philippines, all of Brazil's external financing needs were met from borrowing on commercial terms. Furthermore, the bulk of the growth in total external debt after the mid 1970s was on variable interest rates—thus greatly limiting the flexibility of debt management and increasing vulnerability to rises in interest rates. In 1984 the net external debt was over 300 percent of exports. This overhang of debt will clearly limit Brazil's room to maneuver in the remaining part of the 1980s. In retrospect, external borrowing was excessive in Brazil in the 1970s. Even though the current account balance-of-payments deficit during 1973–80 was as a percentage of GDP (4.4 percent) lower than in Korea (5.1 percent), the ability to service this debt was much more limited because of the limited size of the foreign-trade sector. Furthermore, Korea's export growth rate was double that of Brazil. Korea's external debt burden thus remained low, in sharp contrast to Brazil's.

The Case of Turkey

The only country that can be considered to have turned around an extremely poor record of economic adjustment during 1974–78 to a rather successful one in 1980–84 is Turkey. Turkey is almost unique among the oil-importing countries, reducing the relative burden of net external debt during 1980–84 from about 250 percent of exports at the end of 1980 to 170 percent at the end of 1984. At the same time its growth rate during 1981–84 (4.7 percent per annum) has been well above the average for other developing countries (2.4 percent per annum).

A fundamental shift from an inward-looking to an outward-oriented strategy has been the key element in the adjustment process in Turkey since 1980. The rise in Turkey's exports has been phenomenal. Helped by (a) exchange rate adjustments, (b) export incentives, and (c) liberalization of imports and sluggish domestic demand, merchandise exports rose from $2.9 billion in 1980, to $7.4 billion in 1984, an increase in volume terms of 200 percent in four years. The export growth was led by the manufacturing sector and involved a significant diversification of markets. Large exports to Middle Eastern markets have been an important factor in this expansion, but certainly do not tell the whole story. That Turkey, with a strong tradition of inward-looking policies, was able to stage such a major and quick turnaround in its exports— at a time when international economic conditions were sluggish—may be an important lesson for other developing countries. Indeed, outside East Asia, there are few cases of recent export performance matching Turkey's.

Other elements in Turkey's adjustment program include the following:

(1) A retrenchment of the public sector. Government consolidated budget expenditures, which stood at 24.2 percent of GNP in 1980, fell to 22.1 percent in 1983. The budget deficit to GNP ratio, which stood at 5.3 percent in 1980, decreased to 2.7 percent in 1981, to 2.1 percent in 1982, and was 3.3 percent in 1983. State Economic Enterprises (SEE) transfers as a percentage of GNP showed a decline from 4.8 percent in 1980 to 2.5 percent in 1983.

(2) Successful efforts to constrain the level of public investment in line with available resources, to limit the number of projects to a manageable level, and to ensure that priority projects received larger allocations in order to speed up their completion. Allocations for the energy, agriculture, and transport sectors were increased, and the share of manufacturing reduced.

(3) Substantial progress in import liberalization through the abolition of quotas, the freeing of a large number of items from licensing, rationalization of tariffs, and a simplification of administrative procedures.

(4) Adjustment of prices in the energy and agriculture sectors closer to economic levels, reduction of input subsidies in a phased manner, and introduction of measures to simplify the regulations surrounding banking operations and improve the performance of money and capital markets. As a result of action on energy prices, Turkish energy consumption expanded only at 3.4 percent per

annum during 1979–83, as compared to 8 percent per annum during 1974–78.

A high rate of inflation, running close to 40 percent annually, however, remained a major problem. A consequence of the persistence of the high rate of inflation was the sharp drop in real wage rates, which meant that the social cost of adjustment was spread unevenly. It can be argued, however, that costs of nonadjustment for the lower-income groups would have been even higher.

Successful Adjustment

Korea and India, and to an extent Thailand, are other good examples of not only successful, but also sustained adjustment. All three countries have been able to maintain relatively high growth rates during the past decade, have moderate burdens of debt, and have either kept or brought inflationary pressures under control. India's GDP growth rate during 1973–83 at 4 percent per annum was marginally higher than in 1965–73, and its net external debt burden, though it grew rapidly during 1980–84, was still relatively low (about 150 percent of export earnings).

India's case is interesting because, unlike Thailand and Korea, the export sector was much less dynamic. Though exports in India (at 4.9 percent per annum) expanded somewhat faster than did GDP (4 percent per annum) during 1973–83, and clearly faster than export growth in the previous period, 1965–73 (2.3 percent per annum), import substitution, especially in food, capital goods, and energy, has played a major role in reducing the rate of overall import growth (2.8 percent per annum) during 1973–83.

The common factor in adjustment in India and Korea, and to some extent in Thailand, was an exceptional savings performance (see table 5.6). The saving-investment balance improved in Korea (6 points), India (3 points), and Thailand (2 points) during the 1973–78 period compared to 1965–72, as saving expanded at a much faster rate than investment. In the following period (1979–83) there was further improvement in the saving-investment balance in Korea while the saving-investment balance did not deteriorate in Thailand and India. India's ability to restrain growth of investment and consumption following the oil price shock was undoubtedly a major factor in its successful adjustment. The first round of oil price increases in 1973–74 worsened India's already vulnerable external accounts and exacerbated inflation. Although the economy was already in recession, the government decided against borrowing abroad to absorb this new shock. Instead, domestic savings were boosted from 14 percent of GDP in 1965–72 to 19 percent in 1973–78 by raising taxes and interest rates, reducing public spending, and tightening monetary policy.[15]

In Thailand GDP growth during 1973–83 averaged 6.9 percent per annum, compared to 7.8 percent per annum during 1965–73. Though Thailand's external debt grew very rapidly during the past decade, the burden of total debt was still moderate in 1984 (130 percent of exports) because the initial level of debt was very low. Also, a large part of debt was owed to official creditors and was relatively long-term. The total debt-service ratio, including interest on short-term debt, was thus in 1984 not much above 25 percent. Adjustment was undoubtedly delayed in Thailand, as the government maintained a high level of aggregate demand and moved slowly on energy prices until 1979. However, the fact that export growth was strong and that there was not a major waste of investment resources suggests that the lag in adjustment was not too costly.

Adjustment in Korea

Korea is a very open and relatively energy-intensive economy, highly dependent on exports, borrowing, and oil imports, and thus felt the full impact of external shocks, sharply higher oil prices, rising international interest rates, and two international recessions during the past decade. Notwithstanding this, Korea was among the most successful oil-importing countries in terms of adjustment. Korea's case, therefore, deserves special attention.

The adjustment process in Korea falls into two clear phases: 1974–78 and 1980–83. During 1974–78 Korea was actually able to increase its growth rate to 12 percent per annum compared to 9.6 percent per annum during 1969–73, notwithstanding a sharp deterioration in terms of trade. Three factors contributed to these results. First and foremost, Korea maintained an aggressive export growth strategy and expanded exports in real terms by 150 percent between 1973 and 1978, increasing its share of world exports. The export drive was assisted by major efforts to diversify products and markets, a trade regime favorable to exports, and a major expansion of Korea's trading companies. Real wages, which had fallen by 6 percent during 1974, were held in check relative to foreign wages for two years after a 22 percent devaluation of the won in December 1974. This helped maintain the country's competitiveness though the real effective exchange rate actually appreciated after 1976.

15. World Bank, *World Development Report, 1985,* 52.

The fact that in the early 1970s the share of manufactured exports (out of the total) was already over 90 percent was a major structural strength of the Korean economy, because world trade in manufactured goods continued to grow rapidly until 1980. Second, the outstanding Korean success in obtaining construction contracts in the Middle East greatly strengthened the invisibles accounts in the balance of payments, and also provided support for export efforts; by 1978 the value of construction contracts stood at $15 billion and workers' remittances helped to swell foreign exchange receipts. Third, Korea borrowed heavily during the 1974–79 period, not to maintain consumption, which grew much less rapidly than GNP, but to sustain a higher level of investment directed at supporting diversification and deepening of industrial structure. Total Korean external debt (including short-term debt) expanded from less than $4 billion at the end of 1973 to $22 billion at the end of 1979. But because of the largely negative real interest rates and the very sharp expansion in exports, the burden of debt increased little.

However, strong economic expansion and the very success in adjusting the balance of payments during 1976–78 generated a number of structural problems. First, the Korean planners, assuming continuing buoyancy of the economy and of Korea's export potential, set out after 1976 to induce changes in the country's comparative advantage in order to accelerate its move into the next phase of industrial development.[16] For that purpose, large amounts of subsidized credits were made available to heavy industries (machinery, steel, shipbuilding, and petrochemicals) by the financial system under the government's direction. Since these industries are more capital-intensive than light industries, and since gestation periods tend to be long, the incremental capital/output ratio nearly doubled in comparison with the first half of the 1970s. Consequently, investment did not translate into rapid expansion in capacity and output, and domestic supply bottlenecks started to emerge— leading to increasing import requirements. Labor markets tightened, particularly for scarce skilled workers, and real wages increased at rates greatly exceeding productivity growth. The accelerating inflation, sharply rising unit labor costs, and a rigid exchange-rate policy resulted in progressively eroding export competitiveness. Real exports, which had grown rapidly for over a decade, fell in 1979. The current account

16. The original heavy industry plan was formulated in 1973 but was kept in check initially by the very large balance-of-payments disequilibria in 1974 and 1975. For discussion, see Hasan 1976.

balance deteriorated from a virtual equilibrium in 1978 to a deficit of almost 7 percent of GNP in 1979, even before the full impact of the second oil price increase was felt.

At the end of 1979, there was no doubt that Korea faced major adjustment problems. The domestic economy was severely overheated and faced major structural problems, with supply bottlenecks, excess capacities in heavy industries, and a relatively energy-intensive output mix. The difficult situation was greatly compounded by the simultaneous external shocks of doubling of petroleum prices, the shift from negative to highly positive interest rates in international financial markets, and the recession in OECD countries. The severe economic problems from external shocks were compounded by an equally difficult political and social crisis after the assassination of President Park in October 1979. At the outset of 1980, it was evident that in the absence of corrective policies the current account deficit would increase to critical levels during the year and beyond.

Early in 1980 the government started implementing a wide-ranging stabilization and adjustment program in response to the deterioration in economic conditions. The magnitude of the imbalances, which were partially rooted in the economic structure, left no doubt that the adjustment process would take concerted efforts over several years. The highest priorities were given to (a) wringing out structural inflation and (b) restoring a viable external position as the prerequisites for sustained growth. The government faced the challenges with a bold and resolute course of action. It involved the coordinated and flexible application of fiscal, monetary, credit, exchange-rate, and wage and price policies. Sharp depreciation of the real exchange rate in 1980, strict control of credit expansion, positive real interest rates, and wage restraint were important elements in the adjustment program.

The government used its considerable influence to moderate wage increases and to educate the public about Korea's economic problems. Real wages in manufacturing fell by 8 percent during 1980–81, though a part of this decline must be viewed as a correction to a very rapid growth in real wages during 1975–80.

Demand management policies were supplemented by measures designed to correct structural weaknesses in the economy. A major financial sector reform was initiated in 1980 to improve financial intermediation by relying more on market signals to alleviate financial resources. In 1982–83 the government denationalized all nationwide commercial banks, eliminated preferential interest rates, replaced direct credit controls through credit ceilings on individual banks by indirect controls through reserve money management, and authorized two near-commercial banks and numerous financial intermediaries.

A number of measures were also taken to rationalize the existing heavy machinery industry, including temporary protection and market-sharing agreements for some firms. The government committed itself to withholding special support for further investment in heavy industries, and to avoiding the excesses of the later 1970s. The extensive system of directed and subsidized credit was being phased out as part of the financial-sector liberalization, and the system of industry-specific fiscal incentives was abolished. Investment decisions were increasingly in the hands of private industry and autonomous banks.

The government also committed itself to a stepwise increase of the liberalization ratio to that of the industrialized countries (or about 90 percent) by the late 1980s. The liberalization ratio already had been increased from 54 percent in 1977 to 76 percent in 1982, and a further significant increase to 80.4 percent took effect July 1, 1983.

By 1983 Korea had once again succeeded in making a remarkable adjustment to the changed international economic environment. GNP growth averaged over 8 percent during 1983–84, inflation was negligible (3 percent compared to 18 percent in 1979) and the current account deficit was less than 2 percent of GNP. Declining oil and raw material prices helped the balance-of-payments position, but the burden of high real interest rates remained considerable. In quantitative terms, the expansion in merchandise exports from $14.7 billion in 1979 to $23.2 billion in 1983 was a major factor in overcoming the balance-of-payments disequilibrium. Korea was able to expand export volume by 12 percent per annum during 1980–84, notwithstanding the general sluggishness in world trade and the international economy at least until early 1983. In contrast, import growth in 1979–83 averaged only 3.5 percent per annum. This reflected slow growth of energy demand, only a modest growth in fixed capital formation, and considerable import substitution in industry. The ratio of net external debt to export (120 percent in 1983) was only moderately higher than in the early 1970s and compared favorably with other major oil-importing countries.

Positive Shocks

Oil exporters enjoyed large windfall gains during the decade following the oil price increase in 1973. Oil income became very sizable not only for capital-surplus oil-exporting countries (Saudi Arabia, Kuwait, U.A.E.) but also for a number of middle-income developing countries. In 1982 Mexico, Egypt, Indonesia, and Nigeria had net exports of oil ranging from 9 percent to over 12 percent of GDP and from 36 percent to 66 percent of total exports. In the early 1970s the volumes of oil exports were relatively small in the above countries, so much of the growth in oil revenues, representing both price and quantity factors, has come since 1973. The primary effect of the increase in oil income has been reinforced by increased ability to borrow abroad. This large increment of resources has, however, been a mixed blessing. Higher oil revenues have generally led to higher levels of public and private consumption. But it is not clear whether the positive shocks have helped to further the objectives of increasing the long-term growth rate of the nonoil economy or have increased the general viability of the development process, except perhaps in Indonesia. There is much to be said for the argument that sharp growth in petroleum revenues led to waste, corruption, consumption, and excessive debt. Indeed, of the four countries mentioned above, only Indonesia was able to avoid a serious debt problem. What is more, the growth in these countries had slowed down very considerably even before the dramatic fall in oil prices in early 1986. The factors that appear to have helped or hindered the effective use of windfall resources can best be illustrated by a comparative look at the experiences of Egypt and Indonesia since 1973.

Egypt gained large revenues not only from oil but also from very large worker remittances and concessionary aid flows. Total foreign exchange earnings in Egypt increased over fivefold between 1974 and 1983, implying an increase in real import capacity threefold higher than the relative increase in the case of Indonesia. Indonesia and Egypt, countries with roughly similar levels of per capita income, have responded very differently to the shifting economic circumstances. Egypt has been less successful than Indonesia in using its windfall gains to promote the nonoil sector and in avoiding heavy debt burden, even though its access to additional resources was somewhat greater than Indonesia's.

Both Egypt and Indonesia have enjoyed very high growth rates of GDP, consumption, and investment during the past decade (see table 5.8). Both face prospects of much slower growth in the second half of the 1980s owing to reduction in oil revenues and (in the case of Egypt) uncertain prospects about workers' remittances. But while by 1985 Indonesia had already achieved a degree of success in adjusting to the reduction in oil revenues after 1982, the adjustment process in Egypt had

TABLE 5.8   Egypt versus Indonesia: Comparative Economic Indicators
(1984 unless otherwise stated)

	Indonesia	Egypt
GDP in U.S. $ billions	75.9	31.9
GDP per capita in U.S. $	540	720
GDP per capita growth % per annum (1965–84)	4.9	4.3
Per capita private consumption growth % per annum (1973–83)	6.8	5.5
Investment growth % per annum (1973–83)	12.3	12.0
Total external debt (including short-term) in U.S. $ billions	32.5	23.2
International reserves in U.S. $ billions	5.7	1.5
Total debt service, including interest on short-term debt in U.S. $ billions	4.7	3.0
Total exports of goods and services in U.S. $ billions	22.2	12.9[a]
Current account balance of payments deficit in U.S. $ billions	2.1	2.1[b]
as % of GDP	2.8	6.6
Net external debt as % of		
(1) GDP	35	68
(2) Exports of goods and services	121	168

SOURCES: World Bank, World Development Report and World Debt Tables; International Monetary Fund, International Financial Statistics; and country sources (all 1986).

[a] Includes remittances.
[b] Net of official grants.

barely begun. Egypt's current account balance-of-payments deficit averaged about 7 percent of GDP in 1984–85, while Indonesia was able to limit the deficit to around 3 percent of GDP. Partly as a consequence of only moderate balance-of-payments deficits in 1973–84, Indonesia's external debt burden in relation to foreign-exchange earnings was not, in fact, excessive in 1984. In Egypt the debt burden has grown much faster than in Indonesia, notwithstanding a more rapid growth in foreign-exchange earnings, because current account balance-of-payments deficits have been large. With the reduction in oil prices in early 1986, Egypt's ability to borrow abroad is likely to be even more constrained than Indonesia's, in part because Egypt's initial debt burden is higher and in part because Indonesia has had at least modest success in expanding nonoil exports. Nonoil exports from Indonesia have nearly doubled in volume over the past decade, while in Egypt they have essentially stagnated.

Several factors can be singled out for the relatively greater success Indonesia has had in coping with both the positive external shocks and with the subsequent deterioration of the external exogenous economic situation.

Management of Investment Resources. In both Indonesia and Egypt gross domestic investment expanded rapidly over 1973–83. In both countries a substantial part of the expansion was concentrated in the public sector. The overall capital/output ratios, the relative growth rates in the agricultural sector, and the performance of nonoil exports suggest that Indonesia has, on the whole, been able to make more effective use of investment resources. Indonesia achieved an agricultural growth rate of 3.7 percent per annum during 1973–83, compared to less than 2.5 percent in Egypt; the rate of growth of domestic demand for agricultural products and rate of agricultural investments in relation to agriculture was actually higher in Egypt. Irrigation investments in Indonesia were a key factor in its ability to rapidly expand rice output and attain self-sufficiency in rice. Egypt's investments in land reclamation, in contrast, yielded low economic returns.

Price Distortions. The performance of the nonoil economy has also been related to the effectiveness of price signals. In both Indonesia and Egypt a large influx of foreign-exchange resources after 1973 enabled the real effective exchange rate to appreciate. Indonesia, however, followed an active exchange rate policy after 1977. The weakening of the underlying balance-of-payments situation triggered large devaluations in November 1978 and March 1983. The real effective exchange rate (which had appreciated by 14 percent between 1980 and 1982) declined by over 20 percent between 1982 and 1984. In Egypt, on the other hand, the real effective exchange rate appreciated by 40 percent between 1980 and 1984. The exchange-rate movement, in turn, had major disincentive effects on agricultural and industrial production.

Energy price policy provides another source of contrast between Egypt and Indonesia. In oil-exporting countries with ample government revenues, the pressures for keeping domestic energy prices low are strong. In Indonesia petroleum product (except gasoline) prices were kept low in the 1970s; consequently, the economic subsidy on energy sales was growing, and volume of domestic consumption doubled over 1973–78. Since 1982, however, Indonesia has raised energy prices sharply. Between the end of 1981 and 1984, domestic fuel oil prices increased more than fourfold, while the general price level increased less than 50 percent. This has had the effect of cutting the economic subsidy on oil products sharply (to less than 1 percent of GNP) and has also slowed down the growth of domestic petroleum consumption. Since 1981 domestic oil consumption in Indonesia has risen little, even though GDP has grown by over 12 percent. In Egypt real energy prices have actually declined by at least 40 percent over the past decade; in 1985 they were on average less than 20 percent of international prices. Consequently the economic subsidy on domestic sales of oil has grown enormously; it probably amounted, at prevailing world oil prices, to about 10 percent of GDP in 1985. This has had a very unfavorable impact on both the fiscal position and the balance of payments. The direct effects of cheap energy prices were compounded by the increased domestic and foreign-exchange costs of the large power investment program required to meet rapidly growing power demand.

Public-Sector Savings. Because economic subsidies on energy and other goods and services supplied by the public sector were very much smaller in Indonesia than in Egypt, government savings remained large (6–7 percent of GDP) in Indonesia. In Egypt government savings were actually substantially negative in the early 1980s. The fact that a large part of the oil revenue accruing to the government was saved was a major reason why the domestic saving-investment gap remained relatively small in Indonesia and external borrowing was kept within reasonable limits. On the other hand, in Egypt not only were government savings negative, but public investment was very high, so that public-sector deficits became very large indeed. It is these large public-sector deficits that were at the root of excessive external borrowing.

Quick Policy Response. Not only were Indonesian policies more prudent, but the government was also generally quick to act. In 1981–82 Indonesia's commitment to economic energy prices was relatively weak, the exchange rate was appreciating, and a very ambitious program of capital-intensive and foreign-exchange-intensive investment projects, based on large external borrowing, was planned. By early 1983 a weaker demand for oil, a reduction in oil prices, and a sharp decline in nonoil exports as a result of the deep international recession produced a fundamentally changed resource outlook. Within months the government allowed sharp increases in the prices of domestic oil and fertilizer, devalued the currency, and undertook a comprehensive reassessment of the public investment program. The major rephasing of large projects was aimed at an expected foreign-exchange saving of $10 billion. In addition to devaluation, longer-term structural improvements were initiated through a drastic overhaul of the tax system and a major reform of the financial sector that freed up deposit and lending rates of the state banks and removed credit ceilings. As a result of these concerted actions and the stimulus provided by international recovery, the current account balance-of-payments deficit, which had reached a peak of $7.1 billion in 1982–83, had dropped to $2.1 billion by 1984. The recent remarkable success of Indonesian decision makers in tackling adjustment issues might be related to unhappy experience immediately after the first oil price increase, when the Pertamina (state oil company) crisis erupted. In 1973–74 Pertamina, in the wake of an enormously expanded oil income base and growth in borrowing capacity, committed itself to a large number of uneconomic or marginal investments without proper government authority or approval. In the wake of the scandal, restructuring of a majority of Pertamina projects was undertaken, and the powers and influence of technocrats and economic coordination ministries were considerably strengthened.

5. THE LESSONS OF EXPERIENCE

Several major themes emerge from the foregoing discussion of external shocks. First and foremost, the ability to adjust successfully to external economic shocks depends on the quality of macroeconomic management. It is not very surprising that countries in East Asia (which had developed a tradition of good economic management in the 1960s) have by and large been able to survive the turbulent period of 1973 better than many other developing countries.[17] Second, the magnitude of external shocks generally has had only a limited relationship with the ability to adjust. Among oil-importing countries, Korea and Brazil have been amongst the most seriously affected by oil and interest-rate shocks— with Korea suffering larger GDP loss than Brazil over the past twelve years, though in relation to the foreign-trade sector the impact of shocks has been about the same in Brazil. Korea, however, has been able to adjust much more successfully to terms of trade deterioration and higher real interest rates. Korea's recent growth rate has been much higher than Brazil's, its current account balance-of-payments deficit has been

17. See Hasan 1984 and Sachs 1985.

brought down to modest levels, and its external debt burden is much more manageable than Brazil's. Third, the extreme swings in real interest rates of 20 percent between 1978–79 and 1981–84 have made adjustment difficult not only for a number of heavily indebted oil-importing countries (notably the Philippines, Yugoslavia, and Morocco) but also for a number of oil-exporting countries (notably Mexico and Nigeria). To the extent ex post real interest rates on private borrowings were, at nearly 10–11 percent, still very high in 1985, a part of the adjustment in heavily indebted countries must come through relief in the form of a decline in real interest rates to more normal levels. The expected further reduction in the value of U.S. dollar, some recovery in commodity prices, and further decline in U.S. nominal interest rates will, it may be hoped, bring about a much needed reduction ex post in real interest rates. But because, among other things, oil prices and interest rates may remain quite volatile during the next decade, reduction in real interest rates and the recent decline in oil prices must not be used by oil-importing countries to delay domestic economic policy adjustments and/ or to substitute for improvements in macroeconomic management.

Another theme of this chapter is that economic shocks and crises can prove a blessing. Turkey's case after 1980 suggests the value of alarming deterioration in the economic situation for forcing a fundamental change in economic strategy. It is an interesting question whether Turkey would have taken its economic problems so seriously and made such a major shift toward an outward-oriented growth strategy if adjustment had not been so greatly neglected during 1974–79 and if the external shocks after 1979 had not been so great. On the other hand, there is clearly a downside to positive economic shocks. Large unexpected gains in GDP or foreign exchange earnings often create a lax attitude toward economic management and resource use, or at the very least lead to a postponement of effort to deal with underlying structural and developmental issues. Indonesia's experience with Pertamina in 1974 and the external debt difficulties now being experienced by Egypt, Mexico, and Nigeria illustrate this point.

A real problem in dealing with external shocks is the inability to predict further shocks. Both at national and international levels, it was very difficult during the past decade to correctly forecast developments such as growth in international trade and interest-rate and oil price changes. Failure of reasonable assumptions about the international economy to materialize was a significant source of economic difficulty in a number of countries. But the ability to handle economic uncertainty, short of a major breakdown of the international economic system, must be considered an integral part of broad macroeconomic management at the national level. It is the quality of this management that is fundamental to successful adjustment.

Quality of Economic Management

But what is good economic management? Some of the key elements of economic policy that have enabled countries to adjust successfully to major and unforeseen changes in external economic circumstances are (a) outward orientation of development strategies, (b) a liberal economic framework, with reliance on market signals, including international economic parameters, (c) selectivity and effectiveness in the quality of public-sector interventions, (d) encouragement of high domestic savings in both public and private sectors, and (e) a high degree of flexibility and quick policy responses within the framework of stability and predictability of basic policy objectives. A high degree of political commitment to economic development, continuity of political and economic leadership, and societal consensus are, however, the essential prerequisites for sound economic policies.

Foreign-Trade Orientation. The past three decades constituted a period of unprecedented growth in world trade, and world trade grew substantially faster than world output. The growth of world trade was particularly rapid in manufactured goods. Even with the slowing down of OECD growth, world trade in manufactured goods doubled in volume during 1970–80 and manufactured exports of developing countries expanded by 12 percent per annum. World trade growth slowed down in 1980–84, but manufactured exports from developing countries held up reasonably well, growing at 9.7 percent per annum.[18] In this setting, countries that emphasized exports of manufactured goods, like Korea, Thailand, the Philippines, and Brazil, were able to expand their foreign-exchange earnings sharply. Others, notably Morocco and Yugoslavia, and, until 1980, Portugal and Turkey, neglected export development and thus faced an increasing scarcity of foreign exchange.

The economic rationale for the emphasis on manufactured goods exports lies in their potential for providing employment opportunities and foreign-exchange earnings at low capital cost. Import substitution, except in energy, foodgrains, and other natural-resource-based sectors, can conversely be quite capital-intensive. Notwithstanding growth in

18. World Bank, *World Development Report, 1985*, table 10.4, p. 140.

protectionist pressures in developed countries, low real wages in a large
number of developing countries (compared to OECD countries) will
continue to provide an important economic lever for increased international trade. Although the developing countries have increased their
share of industrial countries' markets in manufactured goods, it still remains small; in 1980 the share of developing countries' exports in consumption of manufactured goods was only 3.4 percent—up from 1.7
percent in 1970—but the import penetration by developing countries
was, at 7.6 percent in 1977–80, actually lower than it was in 1970–77.[19]
Finally, the potential for increased trade among developing countries is
growing.

The maintenance of realistic exchange rates, avoidance of discrimination against exports, and relatively low levels of effective protection are
central for a policy of effective export promotion. While it is not easy to
establish a direct and close relationship between export performance
and the real effective exchange rate in the short run except in a few circumstances, realistic exchange rates are perhaps the most important
instrument of export promotion.[20] There is no doubt that a realistic
exchange rate was a fundamental factor in the success of export-
promotion policies in East Asian countries, especially Korea. In Yugoslavia, Turkey, and Pakistan, appreciation of the exchange rate was a negative factor in export performance during 1973–79. In contrast, the
export performance of Thailand, India, and the Philippines during this
period was helped by depreciation of the real exchange rate. Over
1980–84 Turkey depreciated the real exchange rate substantially, and
this was a powerful factor in export expansion. Though Brazil's real exchange rate has shown wide variation, the net depreciation after 1980
was significant. This perhaps accounted for Brazil's impressive, though
erratic, export performance.

Liberal Economic Framework.   Outward orientation of the economy itself forces the need for market orientation. The effect of international
price signals is transmitted quickly, particularly if exchange-rate flexibility is maintained. There is a growing belief, not only in market economies but also in socialist countries such as China, Hungary, and Yugoslavia, that price distortions are inimical to growth. The issue of price
distortions has been widely researched and was a special focus of the
World Bank's 1983 *World Development Report.* In the context of dealing

19. World Bank, *World Development Report, 1983,* table 2.7, p. 14.
20. See Khan 1986, 84–87.

with external shocks, it is important to stress that oil and interest-rate shocks changed the scarcity value of energy, foreign exchange, and capital for oil-importing countries. The countries that maintained realistic exchange rates and were largely successful in reflecting these increased costs in their domestic price structures were able to adjust relatively quickly. On the other extreme, countries that enjoyed windfall gains from oil but were slow in adjusting domestic energy prices to international levels dissipated a part of the increased income subsidies to consumption.

Effectiveness of Investment.   Price signals also have great relevance for both the making and the effectiveness of investment decisions. In a number of countries that did not adjust, misdirection of investment resources and overinvestment were at the root of excessive domestic expansion. Overprotected industry and overvalued exchange rates encouraged allocation of resources to uses with low or marginal economic returns. Wasteful investment in the public sector was not, however, merely a question of price signals. In the 1960s and 1970s growth became synonymous with investment, and governments rushed to expand public-sector commitment to industry. The public-sector capacity to do economic analysis of large capital- and foreign-exchange-intensive projects was weak even in countries like Korea. Thus public-sector support for these projects often did not take into account the opportunity cost of these investments. Admittedly, many large industrial projects (fertilizer, cement, and steel plants; copper and aluminum smelters; heavy machinery complexes) have a role to play in the evolving pattern of industrial development. But economic justification, priority, and timing of major industrial investments require careful consideration, even in normal circumstances. In the sharply changed circumstances after 1973, many governments were not quick enough to adjust investment programs. The pressures for deepening industrial structure were strong and led to excesses even in Korea, where the broad shift toward the heavy industry and machinery sectors was generally well conceived. But in Korea and elsewhere sharp cutbacks in investment became inevitable after 1980. The ratio of gross investment to GDP in the middle-income countries dropped from 27 percent in 1980 to 22 percent in 1983 and probably fell further over the next two years. The cut involved an absolute decline in public investment and a sharp reappraisal of the public-sector role in industry and other productive sectors in countries such as Turkey, Morocco, and Portugal.

The share of public-sector investment to total investment cannot, however, in itself be considered an indicator of efficiency. It is the quality of public-sector investments that is relevant. In the Philippines in the early 1970s, public investment was at a very low level (2–3 percent) of GDP, and much of the increase during the decade was well directed. Important investments in rural infrastructure were responsible for the achievement of a high growth rate of 5 percent per annum in agriculture during the 1980s. Public-sector investment outlays in agriculture in India, Pakistan, Thailand, and Indonesia also had a high payoff. The very remarkable progress made in these countries toward attaining food self-sufficiency would not have been possible without these major investments.[21] The record of the large public-enterprise sectors was, however, less convincing. If price distortions are limited, and if there is no privileged access to credit, the reliance on a large state-enterprise sector need not be harmful. But in a typical situation where price adjustments are difficult and painful and access to public funds is relatively easy, the existence of a large public-enterprise sector becomes a drag on adjustment.

Fiscal Deficits and Savings Effort.   This is, in fact, what happened in the 1970s. The largely uncontrolled growth of public-sector spending led to large fiscal deficits in a number of countries (Mexico, Morocco, Turkey, and the Philippines). In Mexico, public spending grew from 17.6 percent of GDP in 1968–70 to nearly 26 percent in 1974–76. After oil revenues became available and foreign borrowing possibilities expanded, public spending in Mexico exploded from 30 percent of GDP in 1978 to 35 percent in 1980 and to 48 percent in 1982.[22] Consequently, the budget deficit rose steadily from 3 percent of GDP in the early 1970s to 18 percent in 1982. The large accumulation of external debt in Mexico, Morocco, and Egypt was closely linked to fiscal imbalances. In contrast, large public savings in India, Korea, Indonesia, and Thailand (until the late 1970s) helped to moderate the balance-of-payments deficits and the growth of debt.

An overall increase in the domestic saving rate is an essential element of economic adjustment. Initially the loss of income from, say, a terms-of-trade loss can be met at least in part from foreign borrowing, but this external borrowing must be serviced at least by making interest pay-

21. See World Bank, *World Development Report, 1982*, chap. 6, "Sources of Agricultural Growth."
22. World Bank, *World Development Report, 1985*, 64.

ments. This involves an improving trade balance (excess of exports over imports) on the one hand and an increasing domestic saving-investment balance (excess of domestic output over domestic expenditures) on the other. Merely increasing exports is not enough, as the experiences of Brazil and the Philippines have shown. If domestic savings are not increasing, the trade balance will not improve, notwithstanding the increase in exports. An important goal of the adjustment process should be for the public sector to contribute to the goal of improving domestic savings.

Handling Uncertainty: A Suggested Rule. By their very definition, external shocks cannot be predicted. But once a shock materializes, the judgment of governments as to its durability becomes critically important. Is the shock seen as lasting or temporary? Unfortunately, one observes an asymmetry in reaction to external shocks. Positive external shocks are often seen as permanent, whereas it is generally expected, or hoped, that negative shocks will be transient. Actually, countries that handled positive shocks well were those that treated them as essentially windfall gains and not as permanent changes in economic circumstances. For those countries that have suffered negative shocks, the opposite has been true. The very few oil-importing countries (notably Korea and India) that dealt decisively with the first oil shock were in much better positions to deal with a second round of shocks after 1979. A large number of countries basically neglected adjustment because they did not face up to the logical consequences of a fundamental change in the real price of oil. In designing a policy response to external shock, it is necessary first and foremost that change should be taken seriously and at least conceptually dealt with in the context of a medium- and long-term framework. But even in countries where the planning process is well established and macroeconomic management is stressed, this cannot be expected to take place automatically—especially as political constraints often tend to limit the ability to adjust consumption and investment and change relative prices. But if short-term adjustment is approached in a medium-term context, some of the short-term conflicts can be minimized, especially if foreign borrowing is available.

Flexibility and Speed of Response. The essential meaning of flexibility is that countries should be willing to review the assumptions of their development strategies and planning frameworks. In the case of Korea, a considered response to the first oil price increase was both an acceptance

of the need for domestic energy price adjustments, and a further step-
ping up of export efforts and a drive to make full use of construction
contract opportunities that opened up in the Middle East. In India the
emphasis was placed on energy price adjustments, domestic savings, and
import substitution. In both cases adjustment was given a high priority.
In many other countries emphasis was placed on sustaining aggregate
demand or stimulating investment, without a clear view of the long-
term consequences of the high borrowing strategy for the balance of
payments. For instance, in Turkey the risks inherent in continuation of
the import-substitution strategy were apparently never seriously ques-
tioned, though the country launched a massive expansion of external
debt in 1973. In Thailand also the external debt was allowed to expand
from a very low level without articulation of a medium-term debt-
management framework, and domestic adjustments were consequently
delayed.

Flexibility also involves relatively quick policy response to changing
economic circumstances. Korea, facing the crises of 1973 and 1979,
acted not only decisively, but also quickly. Again in 1982 when stabilization was in danger of overcorrecting the balance of payments and the
sharp drop in inflation threatened a very steep rise in real interest rates,
monetary and fiscal policies were adjusted to allow for reasonable economic expansion. Indonesian policies in the early 1980s provide another
good example of quick policy response. It is often the case that as sensible economic policies work, the confidence of the policymakers in their
own effectiveness increases and they are more willing to take risks atten-
dant on policy changes and are less and less wedded to the status quo.
In economic reform, as in other things, the first steps are often the most
difficult.

CONCLUSIONS

Large oil and interest-rate shocks after 1979 found most oil-importing
countries ill prepared to deal with adjustment issues. The shocks were
very great, and adjustment had generally been neglected after the first
oil price increase in 1973. Many compensating shocks, like negative real
interest rates, worker remittances, and aid flows from OPEC countries,
had helped to mitigate the impact of higher oil prices in the first round.
Even so, most countries, with the exception of Korea and India, borrowed to postpone adjustment. India borrowed very little and relied
mainly on restraints on consumption and investment, and Korea bor-

rowed to reinforce and strengthen adjustment policies. In all other countries borrowing, in retrospect, was excessive. This delay in adjustment proved costly. Either exports were neglected, and a base for additional debt service was not created, or domestic savings were inadequate and balance-of-payments deficits continued to be fed by large domestic imbalances, especially public-sector deficits. Adjustment was forced on a number of countries in the period after 1980. But the turnaround in international economic circumstances was too sudden and too drastic for many countries to cope with in an orderly fashion. Nonetheless, three major corrections to the course charted by developing countries in the 1970s appear to be under way. First, there is much less preoccupation with the level of investment and much more attention to quality of investment, its composition and effectiveness. By the same token, as factors in economic growth, policy framework and institutional capabilities are being stressed much more than the size of investment programs. Second, there is a general shift from inward-oriented strategies to outward-looking growth.[23] Third, a much needed reappraisal is going on in a large number of countries of the role of the public sector, and especially public-sector industry, in economic growth. As a result of these "corrections," economic policy in developing countries is likely to emerge stronger, and long-term growth will become more viable, provided growth in industrial countries recovers from the sluggish level of the first half of the 1980s, access of developing countries to markets in developed countries is not further restricted, and the international monetary system is able to deal satisfactorily with the problem of the debt-overhang.

REFERENCES

Balassa, Bela. 1984. "Adjustment Policies in Developing Countries: A Reassessment." *World Development* 12 (September): 955–72.

Balassa, Bela, and F. Desmond McCarthy. 1984. *Adjustment Policies in Developing Countries, 1979–85.* World Bank Staff Working Paper no. 675. Washington, D.C.: World Bank.

Hasan, Parvez. 1976. *Korea: Problems and Issues in a Rapidly Growing Economy.* Baltimore: Johns Hopkins University Press for the World Bank.

———. 1984. "Adjustment to External Shocks: East Asia's Success Examined." *Finance and Development* 21 (December): 14–17.

International Monetary Fund. 1986a. *IMF World Economic Outlook.* Washington, D.C.: International Monetary Fund.

23. This shift is not without some risks, as international trade trends look less robust than at any time during the past twenty-five years and the danger of growing protectionism is very real.

————. 1986b. *International Financial Statistics.* Washington, D.C.: International Monetary Fund.

Jaspersen, Frederick. 1981. *Adjustment Experience and Growth Prospects of the Semi-Industrial Countries.* World Bank Staff Working Paper no. 487. Washington, D.C.: World Bank.

Khan, Mohsin M. 1986. "Developing Country Exchange Rate Policy Responses to Exogenous Shocks." *American Economic Review* 76 (May): 84–87.

Mitra, Pradeep K. 1984. "Adjustment to External Shocks in Selected Semi-Industrial Countries, 1971–81." Discussion Paper, World Bank Development Research Department.

Sachs, Jeffrey K. 1985. "External Debt and Macroeconomic Performance in Latin America and East Asia." *Brookings Papers on Economic Activity,* no. 2: 523–74.

Wallich, Christine. 1981. *An Analysis of Developing Countries Adjustment Experiences in the 1970s: Low Income Asia.* World Bank Staff Working Paper no. 487. Washington, D.C.: World Bank.

World Bank. 1981–86. *World Development Report.* Washington, D.C.: World Bank.

————. 1985–86. *World Debt Tables, 1985–86.* Washington, D.C.: World Bank.

SIX

Export Liberalization

Juergen B. Donges and Ulrich Hiemenz

1. INTRODUCTION

There is a voluminous theoretical and empirical literature about the implications of alternative trade regimes for economic development. On balance it points out that export-oriented strategies, along with an efficient use of available resources, including indigenous labor, provide the most appropriate framework of economic incentives conducive to sustained and rapid growth (see, for instance, the surveys by Balassa 1980a; Donges 1983; and Krueger 1984a). Accordingly, an increasing number of developing countries have, in varying degrees, linked their economies to world production on the basis of comparative advantage and by doing so have been transformed into the now "newly industrializing countries" (NICs). South Korea is one of the outstanding cases in point. It committed itself to the notion of international specialization, adhering to it even when the world economic environment sharply deteriorated during the 1970s.

Yet, many governments of developing countries (and some influential academic economists as well) have remained skeptical about the implementation of outward-oriented trade regimes. The standard argument is that, after a long-lasting period of economic development based on policies of import substitution for industrialization, trade liberalization would cause excessively high adjustment costs, while the potential benefits from such a liberalization would only be small (if not negligible) in an unfavorable international economic environment such as the

The authors would like to thank Heinz W. Arndt, Lawrence B. Krause, and Rolf J. Langhammer for critical comments and suggestions on a previous draft of this chapter.

present one. The fact that some South American countries that embarked upon liberalization experiments during the 1970s fell into deep economic recessions, often accompanied by social and political upheavals, provides convenient support to such anxieties, despite pervasive evidence to the contrary in Asian countries. There are also instances, again mainly in Latin America, in which governments, faced with pressing foreign-exchange needs to service foreign debt, undid prior shifts to relatively outward-oriented trade regimes and readopted import-substitution strategies.

The purpose of this chapter is to reassess the case for outward-oriented trade regimes in the process of economic development. The nature of outward-orientation is briefly explained in the next section. As developing countries usually start their industrialization through import-substitution strategies, the shift from an inward- to an outward-oriented trade regime raises questions concerning the set of economic policies to be reshaped, the timing of the policy reform, and the feasibility of such changes, all of which are discussed in the third section. The fourth section provides evidence on both successful and unsuccessful liberalization attempts in the seventies and inquires into the causes for success or failure by relating the countries' experiences to the policy framework for export liberalization outlined in the previous section. In the fifth section, the revival of export pessimism is evaluated.

2. ESSENCE OF AN OUTWARD-LOOKING STRATEGY

Discussions of appropriate development strategies should start by recognizing that there are two dimensions of government policy that are analytically distinct, though sometimes mixed together. One is whether the government is intrusive in the process of economic development or is more "laissez-faire," and the other is whether government policies distort relative prices and markets or not. A government can be relatively "laissez-faire" and rely on market signals for the allocation of resources and economic growth (as in Hong Kong) or it can take a strong hand in steering the process of development without distorting markets (as in Singapore, South Korea, and Taiwan). It can distort prices but not try to plan the economy very much (as in Israel) or it can be both intrusive and distorting (as was the case in India and Mexico). Governments that do not want to rely heavily on market forces for development may resort to import substitution, but they could also apply an outward-looking strategy; in either case, the outcome of the chosen strategy will crucially depend on whether or not relative prices are in line with relative scarcities (of goods, services, and production factors). Though it is conceivable that an inward-looking government would pursue market-oriented economic policies, in reality such policies are more "normal" in countries integrated into the system of international division of labor, as shown below.

Export promotion and outward-oriented trade regimes have frequently been misinterpreted as policies that deliberately promote exports over other economic activities and beyond the level attainable under free-trade conditions (see, for instance, Streeten 1982). The crucial point to remember, however, is that government incentives for industrialization should be compatible with an optimal allocation of resources, to the largest extent possible (as elaborated in the rejoinders to Streeten by Henderson [1982] and Balassa [1983]). Disregarding externalities, an optimal allocation of resources requires that the domestic rate of transformation equal the international rate of transformation. Taking international prices as given (small country assumption), the ratio of relative domestic prices of importables and exportables over the respective world market prices must be unity (Krueger 1978). Then the system of incentives is neutral with respect to sales in domestic or in world markets. It is in this sense, and only this, that the export-promotion strategy is differentiated from the import-substitution strategy. Export-promotion strategies provide incentives to exports sufficient to compensate for the discrimination against export production inherent in import protection; they provide a uniform incentive to both import substitution and exports, and thus to saving and earning foreign exchange per unit of domestic resources used—they do not aim at boosting exports beyond free-trade levels. The emphasis is on specialization based on comparative advantage, not on export expansion, per se.

An outward-oriented trade regime does not provide sectoral preferences either; agriculture, industry, and services can expand in accordance to the natural-resource endowments of the countries concerned. Hence the pattern of production and the composition of exports will vary substantially among developing countries. Small resource-poor countries with an abundant supply of semiskilled labor are likely to specialize in the production and export of labor-intensive manufactures, while resource-rich countries by definition have a comparative advantage as producers and exporters of primary commodities. Even in the case of the latter group of countries, it is important, for at least two reasons, that industrialization not be impeded by policy-induced obstacles.

First, nonrenewable resources, by definition, are bound to run into depletion, and economic development sooner or later will have to be based on other activities; industrial production that promises high productivity gains and the creation of remunerative new jobs should be the prime candidate. Second, the sooner resource-rich countries diversify their export structures by including manufactures, the better the chances are that export earnings will be stabilized and the vulnerability to international commodity price fluctuations be reduced. A stable foreseeable framework is important if investors are to allocate their funds efficiently.

Judged in terms of the ideal of completely neutral policies, development strategies as actually applied can obviously err on both sides: too restrictive of imports or too promotive of exports. Both would probably raise marginal capital-output ratios and hinder economic growth. When the trade regime is biased toward import substitution based on a variety of trade barriers, ranging from high tariffs and restrictive quotas to outright import bans, too many resources are attracted by the protected industries. Moreover, as the process of import substitution goes on, encompassing the production of intermediate and investment goods, the incremental capital-output ratio will rise. This is likely to adversely affect the rate of economic growth, thereby leading to a vicious circle of generally lower saving and investment paths and weakening productivity and development trends. In the absence of corrective measures, exports will be discriminated against. On the one hand, exporters will have to pay higher prices than they otherwise would for protected locally produced or imported inputs (which they cannot pass on to potential customers on the world market unless they have a monopoly power, which is unlikely for most developing countries). On the other, the exchange rate tends to be overvalued owing to protection, a self-inflicted export obstacle par excellence.

It has been argued that in cases in which the private costs of export production are higher than the social costs, and this positive externality is higher than the corresponding externalities associated with import substitution, a bias of the incentive system in favor of exports could be justified on economic grounds (Mayer 1984). The general problem with this version of the "infant industry" argument is, however, that it may turn out to be very difficult in practice to accurately demonstrate the existence of significant externalities and, if this were possible, to discontinue the extra subsidies to exporting (or the protection of import substitutes) later on when the assisted activities have become mature. For these reasons, policy-induced export expansion runs the risk of favoring a composition of exports that is not in line with the comparative advantage of the exporting country and may ultimately slow down economic development in very much the same way an import-substitution strategy does.

However, economic reasoning suggests a greater danger of policymakers slipping into excessive import substitution than into excessive export promotion. A successful export-promotion strategy requires a framework of incentives to free producers of exportables from cost disadvantages vis-à-vis foreign producers. As long as import protection is granted on the grounds of nonpecuniary dynamic externalities, exporters have to be compensated by some form of subsidies and/or duty-free import allowances, as discussed below. Since subsidies constitute drains on government budgets, they provide a stimulus to policymakers to refrain from excessive export promotion, to maintain realistic exchange rates as an alternative to public subsidies, and to keep import protection at moderate levels.

By contrast, import-substitution strategies have revealed built-in tendencies toward reinforcing the inward bias of the incentive system (Bhagwati 1978; Donges 1983, 280–82; Krueger 1983, 32–33). Tariffs, if not prohibitive, create government revenues and thus lead to their implementation being abused, often for purposes totally unrelated to the chosen industrialization strategy. Furthermore, import-substituting industries replace fewer imports than are actually required as intermediate inputs or for investment purposes, thus aggravating existing, or giving rise to new, balance-of-payments problems. Growing current account deficits, as well as the exhaustion of narrow domestic markets by the newly established industries, put pressure on governments to implement additional trade restrictions and to intervene in foreign-exchange, capital, and labor markets—thereby further penalizing export activities.

3. THE FRAMEWORK OF EXPORT LIBERALIZATION

3.1. *Economic Objectives*

The outward-oriented trade regime aims at promoting sustained economic development and a rapid process of industrialization by exposing the domestic economy to international competition. The objectives are to improve the allocative efficiency of the economy as a whole by bringing the structure of production into line with the country's comparative advantage at each instant and to reap irreversible external benefits from the exploitation of economies of scale through exports, the stabilization of export earnings through export diversification into manufactured goods, the increase of savings for investment through raising real incomes, and the acceleration of technological innovation and human-capital formation through competition from, and contacts with, other countries. Such gains are forgone in an inward-oriented trade regime since import protection and the whole system of market regulations not only discriminate against exports and distort the structure of production and make it rigid, but also cause losses in efficiency through cartelization, rent-seeking behavior, the formation of a labor aristocracy, and the expansion of bureaucracy.

Export liberalization entails substituting price signals for administrative controls and adjusting domestic relative prices to international relative prices, either by gradual measures or shock treatment. Liberalization does not necessarily mean the implementation of free trade and nonintervention in all other markets; it rather means a reform of economic policies so that the price mechanism can work more effectively and competition is less distorted. Government measures to remove market failures are perfectly justified, provided that such market imperfections are real (nonpecuniary externalities, public interest in goods or services produced or consumed by the society, natural monopolies, and the like) and not the result of excessive encroachment of public authorities on the market process (as so often happens; see Krueger 1983; chap. 7).

A liberalization reform requires that ad hoc measures be replaced by a stable and foreseeable policy framework, uniform rather than selective interventions, and a return to price flexibility that allows for a proper response to market changes. What does this mean in detail? The answer will differ between countries, depending much on the nature of the inward-oriented trade regime previously in force. The common characteristics of an inward-oriented trade regime may therefore provide an appropriate starting point for a discussion of essential elements of a reform package.

3.2. The Inadequacies of Inward-oriented Policy Regimes

Once a country embarks on an import-substitution strategy, there seems to be a logic to the evolution of direct government controls on prices and quantities over time (Bhagwati 1978). Initial tariff protection for "infant industries" soon proves to be insufficient. Unprotected domestic sectors and discriminated-against export industries vehemently complain about unfair treatment, and protection creates an incentive to evade controls via smuggling, over- and underinvoicing, or black market transactions. The public authorities, yielding to political pressures of (often disparate) sectional interest groups, tend to react by moving from tariff protection to quantitative controls and import-licensing procedures, effected with ever-increasing product coverage and ever-finer selectivity. When easy import substitution possibilities have been exhausted, but the inward-looking policy approach is maintained, a complex control network is likely to evolve, encompassing direct import allocation by category of commodity, by type of domestic use, and by source of foreign exchange.

Despite proliferating import controls, import-substitution regimes will generally not come to grips with the balance-of-payments difficulties that typically afflict developing countries. As industrialization proceeds, the demand for imported intermediate and capital goods, which are complementary to domestic production, continues to grow at high rates, while the policy-induced overvaluation of the national currency retards or impedes export expansion. Rising trade deficits and subsequent shortages of foreign exchange make intervention in foreign-exchange markets inevitable and resort to external credits a pressing need. Hence, import controls are supplemented by a direct allocation of foreign exchange to domestic uses and also complemented by administrative credit rationing.

Capital-market interventions usually arise from two sources. First, unchecked import-substitution policies favor production of relatively capital-intensive products (as typically the industrial structure gets diversified in the vertical direction), the application of capital-intensive technologies (because of relatively low barriers to imports of capital goods), and an inefficient use of capital (owing to the lack of competition in domestic markets). High incremental capital-output ratios will soon slow down industrialization and economic growth unless access to financial capital at reasonable rates of interest can be maintained. To sustain the momentum of import substitution, intrusive governments will, therefore, impose interest-rate ceilings on both deposits and loans and/or provide preferential treatment for selected economic activities—as has actually occurred time and again. As these interventions usually are administered in a discretionary way, they create uncertainty among investors; as they tend to be guided by public preferences rather than by comparative advantages, investment patterns are likely to be distorted. In addition, interest rate and other subsidies to capital formation become an increasing burden to the public budget.

Second, interest-rate ceilings on bank deposits discourage domestic private savings and encourage capital flight, as well as an overvalued exchange rate—both of which augment demand for external funds. Reflecting donor rules or preferences for securing external financing by government guaranties, loans from abroad may largely be channeled through public institutions, reinforcing the heavy hand of the government in the allocation of credit. Foreign borrowing is not, however, an unlimited source for financing public budget deficits. Governments that are not able (or not willing) to reduce the deficits may be tempted to turn the screw of the inflation tax by accelerating the rate of growth of the money supply. To collect the inflation tax, the banking sector has to be exposed to tighter supervision of the central bank. High non-interest-bearing reserve requirements on bank deposits, forced lending to public-sector enterprises and, ultimately, nationalization of private banks, are tools to make sure that the inflation tax accrues to the government, but these tools further weaken the functioning of the capital market. The experience of Argentina until the implementation of the "Austral Plan" in mid 1985 is a case in point (Fischer, Hiemenz, and Trapp 1985, chap. 3).

Import protection and the availability of credit at subsidized interest rates promote expansion of capital-intensive lines of production and thereby boost labor productivity at the expense of creating sufficient employment opportunities to absorb a rapidly growing labor force. The distorted structure of production paves the way to nominal wage levels in excess of equilibrium wages in the formal sector of the economy, with the well-known consequences of labor migration and informal labor markets.

The situation worsens if governments pursuing inward-oriented development strategies do keep wages above their equilibrium levels by minimum-wage legislation and if they artificially increase labor costs to employers further by excessively rigid labor codes and generous social policies. Such interventions have, in fact, occurred in many developing countries (Squire 1981; Berry and Sabot 1984). They were meant to secure the political support of the (in most cases well-organized) urban labor force for the development strategy applied by the government. For this reason, governments also sought to shelter the urban labor force from the costs derived from high inflation through price controls for essential consumer goods, publicly decreed wage increases, and/or formal indexation of wages. Thus, labor markets become subject to a significant degree of government regulation and control as inward-oriented economic development proceeds over time, and the benefits of comparative advantage based on a relatively elastic supply of labor are not exploited.

It is against such a background (an economic environment character-ized by manifold interrelated and distorting government interventions in the economy) that export liberalization has to be contemplated. At-tempts to liberalize the economy have to take into account the nature of controls and regulations as well as the interactions between them. Wel-fare theory suggests that in a case of multiple distortions, removal of one distortion may make things even worse. Export liberalization will, there-fore, require a reform package that includes some degree of policy change vis-à-vis all major markets.

3.3. What Policy Reform Package?

From a theoretical point of view, export liberalization is best achieved by an instantaneous removal of all controls and regulations that distort the allocation of resources and contribute to an underutilization of available capacity. This best solution is, however, not likely to be feasible in the context of a highly regulated economy, since adjustment costs may become excessively high and even disrupt the political system as such. A more cautious approach to liberalization, which may therefore be chosen, raises a number of questions. Which are the key markets to be liberalized? What degree of deregulation is both necessary and feasible? What timing and sequencing of policy changes should be envisaged?

Under a fixed exchange-rate system, import liberalization can reduce the import-substitution bias of trade policies and may have a beneficial effect on inflation rates. It may, though, fail to achieve the desired ex-port expansion if capital and labor markets remain under tight control. Export prices do not change because of the fixed exchange rate. Al-though intermediate input costs decline as a result of import liberaliza-tion, labor costs remain high, and artificially low capital costs, owing to interest-rate ceilings, provide little incentive to redirect investment flows toward export activities—which usually yield a higher capital productiv-ity than does import substitution.

A devaluation of the currency might appear to be more promising than import liberalization with respect to export expansion, since, even with quantitative import controls persisting, the relative domestic price of exportables would increase. This result depends very much, however, on how the necessary exchange-rate adjustment is effected. In the pres-ence of high rates of inflation, the authorities may underestimate the difference between domestic and international inflation and thus cause a real appreciation of the exchange rate rather than a depreciation.

Even a freely floating exchange rate and a liberalization of the foreign-exchange market can have its drawbacks unless domestic financial markets are simultaneously liberalized. For, in the presence of controlled (and usually negative) interest rates, full liberalization of the exchange regime for both current and capital accounts, when coupled with a floating exchange rate, would surely result in capital outflows and rapid depreciation of the currency in excess of the rate of inflation. In countries with high and persistent inflation, a complete deregulation of financial markets will, however, hardly be feasible (at least not in the short run) since the tightly controlled banking sector will have lost the ability to collect and allocate financial resources efficiently.

Obviously, there are no recipes for initiating the transition from an inward- to an outward-oriented trade regime. Level of development, size of country, resource endowment, and relative importance of controls in individual markets will all have to be taken into account when designing an effective and feasible reform package. However, empirical evidence strongly suggests that trade interventions have been a major, if not the biggest, single source of distortion (Krueger 1984b, 417).

For this reason, it is a safe proposition that any policy reform will have to focus on the removal of obstacles to an expansion of exports in the first place. Depending on the nature and degree of protection, a combination of the following three elements of an import-liberalization strategy will have to be applied to accomplish this task: a transformation of quantitative trade interventions into tariffs, harmonization of tariff protection across sectors, and a reduction of the average level of protection.

As to the first aspect, tariffs are preferable to quantitative restrictions not only because the latter tend to veil the actual degree of protection, but also because the competition for import licenses diverts productive resources from more efficient uses elsewhere in the economy, apart from encouraging corruption in the bureaucracy.[1]

Second, reshaping the (new) tariff structure toward a uniform tariff system serves the purpose of eliminating, or at least reducing, the escalation and deescalation effects of selective nominal tariff protection on effective rates of protection. A more uniform effective rate of protection across sectors lowers artificial advantages for import-substituting activities through, for instance, duty-free imports of capital goods, and leaves

1. The beneficial effects of phasing out quantitative restrictions on imports have recently been shown in Turkey (Gönensay 1986).

the choice of efficient import-substitution possibilities to market forces rather than to bureaucrats. An intrusive government may be tempted to liberalize in a selective manner rather than across the board on the grounds that the benefits of comparative advantage will then be captured faster; this is dangerous, in that new sources of distortions emerge, to say nothing of the difficulty of accurately assessing comparative advantages in a dynamic setting.

Third, a more uniform tariff system in itself usually entails a lower overall degree of import protection for domestic industries, since sectors granted low protection in the past will now exert pressure on the government to treat other sectors equally. Obstacles to the expansion of exports are thus mitigated. However, additional efforts will be required if the general level of protection is to be lowered further.[2]

As long as some degree of import protection prevails, export activities remain discriminated against—both directly through higher prices for imported intermediate and capital goods, and indirectly through the effects of protection on the general level of product and factor prices. Direct cost disadvantages of export activities can be remedied by one or all of the following measures, which have been applied in a wide range of developing countries: duty-free importation of inputs for export production, drawback schemes for import tariffs, and the establishment of free export-processing zones. From the point of view of administrative ease, duty-free importation and export-processing zones are clearly superior to drawback schemes, and free zones, if appropriately established, may offer additional net benefits in terms of employment creation and strengthened linkages to the domestic economy.[3]

A closer vertical integration of the economy is also promoted by measures compensating export activities for indirect cost disadvantages. Such measures include income and sales tax rebates, special depreciation allowances, preferential credits, and straightforward subsidies (for details, see Wulf 1978). These various kinds of subsidies of either output

2. Chile, where the government removed quotas and reduced tariffs from an average level of 90 percent in 1974 to a uniform rate of 10 percent in 1979, following a pre-announced time schedule, is the most recent case in point—proving that a trade liberalization policy is feasible despite the opposition of vested interests (Sjaastad 1983).

3. The establishment of export-processing zones is sometimes criticized for the absence of linkages to the rest of the economy. Spinanger (1984) has shown, however, that such linkages have in fact emerged in, e.g., Malaysia (Penang) and Mexico (border trade areas) within a relatively short period of time. While more research is needed to fully explain the superior performance of some export-processing zones in comparison to others, one important condition for success is nondiscrimination of trade between domestic firms and firms in free zones.

or factor use can be compared to a partial, export-related devaluation of the currency, which may be necessary to balance the incentive system with respect to sales in domestic and foreign markets. However, this approach bears some risks. To begin with, it is almost impossible to determine the subsidy rate required to compensate for disadvantages accruing from import protection, which may lead to an undesirable overshooting. Moreover, the subsidies, typically related to the amount of investment, tend to encourage the use of capital over labor, and may thus be detrimental to a satisfactory rate of employment growth. And last, but not least, export subsidies can provoke retaliation from industrialized countries, which tend to ignore the compensatory nature of these subsidies, regarding them as price dumping. For these reasons, the emphasis of trade policy reform should be on import liberalization rather than on the implementation of export subsidies.

With import liberalization, the compensation of indirect cost disadvantages can be achieved by a more rational exchange-rate policy that increases the prices of exportables without inflating import prices. In the medium and long term, exchange-rate policy has to neutralize differences between domestic and foreign rates of inflation to shelter domestic suppliers from inflation-induced cost disadvantages vis-à-vis foreign competitors. This goal cannot be achieved if the exchange rate is used as a policy instrument to influence other macroeconomic variables as well, such as the rate of inflation itself. If the exchange rate is used to break the inflation mentality, as was done for instance in Chile in 1979–81, this is at best a short-term policy, the success of which depends on the credibility of the government's effort to contain inflation and the ability of the export sector to cope with the temporary discrimination implied by the real appreciation of the currency.

The choices for an appropriate medium-term exchange-rate policy are ad hoc devaluations in an otherwise fixed exchange-rate system; a sliding peg, or preannounced, devaluation schedule; or a freely floating exchange rate. The first can be dismissed as impracticable both on theoretical and empirical grounds. In a fixed exchange-rate system, the external value of the currency is adjusted retrospectively to inflation differences. This in itself contributes to permanently fluctuating real exchange rates, which discourage export orientation on the part of domestic firms, is detrimental to long-range investment planning, and induces destabilizing speculation. These negative effects are aggravated if necessary devaluations are delayed on account of national prestige considerations, as frequently occurs, so that further uncertainty is caused.

The choice between administered stepwise devaluations and freely floating exchange rates is a much more difficult one because the potential effect on resource allocation of either policy depends on monetary and credit policies pursued simultaneously. A controlled sliding peg has the advantage of leveling exchange-rate fluctuations and, hence, reducing exchange-rate risks for exporters and both local and foreign investors. Countries such as Brazil, Colombia, and South Korea successfully applied such a policy in the late 1960s and early 1970s (Donges and Müller-Ohlsen 1978, 112). Problems have been encountered with preannounced stepwise devaluations (*tablitas*) in some Latin American countries, such as Argentina and Uruguay, however, with high increasing rates of inflation (for details, see Barletta, Blejer and Landau, eds., 1984). In these countries, throughout the second half of the 1970s and early 1980s, the *tablita* has repeatedly failed to bring about the desired devaluation of the currency in real terms, since governments have usually underestimated future rates of inflation. The result was a real appreciation of the currency, since nominal devaluation rates fell short of international inflation differences. The lesson is that a *tablita* policy will only help to restore foreign-exchange equilibrium if governments simultaneously pursue a strict anti-inflationary monetary policy, which usually implies incisive cuts of public deficits (Sjaastad 1983; Fischer, Hiemenz and Trapp 1985). In order to alleviate short-term adjustment costs as much as possible, anti-inflationary policies will have to be accompanied by financial policies designed to enhance the restructuring of the economy according to comparative advantage, a topic to which we shall return shortly.

The other alternative, transition from a fixed, overvalued exchange rate to a freely floating one, usually implies a large initial devaluation, with an equivalent rise in the price level, which is difficult to cushion by import-liberalization measures—at least in the short run. Moreover, with low or negative real rates of interest in local capital markets, devaluation expectations are likely to give rise to an uncontrollable capital outflow, which will further reduce the ability of the economy to adjust to new relative prices. Yet a freely floating exchange rate may be the only feasible policy alternative as long as high inflation has not abated, since governments lack the foresight to predict future price increases correctly in an inflationary environment.

It thus seems clear that appropriate trade policies have to be combined with fiscal and monetary policies designed to curb inflation, and with a deregulation of capital markets as well, if the shift to an

outward-oriented trade regime is to succeed. The deregulation of capital markets gains particular significance once the adjustment process is
considered. With greater reliance on market forces and increased competition from abroad, parts of the installed capacity will be rendered ob-
solete, while expansion into new profitable activities creates demand for
credit to finance the necessary investment. The ease and the speed of
the adjustment process will depend heavily on whether this demand for
fresh funds can be met. Efforts have therefore to be made to mobilize
domestic savings and attract capital from abroad.

In both respects it is imperative that interest rates reflect the true
scarcity of financial capital so as to allow for a positive real rate of interest and to strengthen the ability of the banking sector to attract and allocate funds efficiently by removing excessive banking regulation.[4] In
some countries it may also be necessary to revamp investment legislation
so that existing "red tape" is reduced and foreign investors are guaranteed their property rights, which is much more important than the
provision of generous financial incentives by the host government,
as all available evidence indicates (see, for example, the overview in
OECD 1983).

Efficient capital-market policies are crucial, since the social acceptabil-
ity of liberalization hinges on swift achievements in terms of output
growth and employment creation. It need not be stressed that such
achievements depend not only on consistency between trade, monetary,
and credit policies, as pointed out earlier, but equally on the presumption that governments do not erode the potentially beneficial effects
of the new incentive system by some countervailing policy action,
such as controls on prices, profits, and dividends or interventions in
labor markets.

The positive welfare effects of liberalization arise from a reallocation
of resources following a shift in relative prices, including the wage rate.
Any attempt to maintain the privileged income position of workers in a
hitherto protected sector of the economy endangers the establishment
and growth of internationally competitive activities and prevents the
creation of additional productive jobs. Governments may find it difficult
to resist the claim of organized labor to secure, if not increase, real
wages, but this political pressure will relax only when the employment
and income effects of liberalization materialize. This will happen sooner

4. A relaxation of banking regulations, of course, requires adopting anti-inflationary
policies lowering the government's dependence on the inflation tax. This interrelationship
again, highlights the crucial interdependence of trade, monetary, and credit policies.

if real wages are allowed temporarily to decline until productivity gains accruing from better resource allocation again permit wage increases.

3.4 The Timing and Sequencing of Liberalization

Abrupt liberalization is the least painful way of proceeding provided (1) that with the new system of incentive firmly in place, adjustment proceeds rapidly without being hampered by resource misallocation during the transition; (2) that instantaneous adjustment prevents political opposition to the policy change from diluting it; and (3) that immediate transformation of the economic environment reduces uncertainty about the credibility of the policy initiative that could delay the response of economic agents to new incentives. If these considerations are overriding, the issues of timing and sequencing do not arise.

There is a widespread belief, however, that instantaneous liberalization of an economy hitherto subjected to exchange controls, import licensing, negative real interest rates, indexed real wages, and so on will completely disrupt economic activity and cause high adjustment costs in terms of declining output and increasing unemployment. Removing controls gradually so as to give economic agents time to prepare for adjustment (timing) and deregulating individual markets in a stepwise fashion, depending on the ease with which adjustment can be accomplished in these markets (sequencing), are therefore suggested.

Some of these problems have already been discussed above with respect to import liberalization and exchange-rate policy. Analytically, an optimal liberalization program depends on the degree of prevailing intervention, on the intensity of linkages between individual markets (the level of economic development), and on expectations that have been built up on the basis of past experience with economic policymaking (Lächler 1985). Although all of these factors do matter, very little is known about their precise relationships to the time schedule of a reform program. The basis for any proposal therefore remains largely judgmental. The advantages of graduation in import liberalization have been emphasized on the grounds that losses of capital and jobs, inevitable as they are in the process of moving toward a new production structure, will be minimized.[5] Whether this can be achieved depends on the

5. Similarly, gradualism has been advocated with respect to stabilization policy (Stein 1980). The main argument here is that unwinding inflation in smaller steps can avoid a head-on collision between monetary policy and price and wage determination that would result in a major economic recession. However, in a high inflation environment, any fine-tuning of monetary policies may be impossible and gradual stabilization may be

success of exchange-rate policy in shifting relative prices in favor of ex-portables without propelling domestic inflation.

Concerning the proper sequence of liberalization steps, Jakob Frenkel (1984) has argued that domestic distortions in the goods and asset markets should be removed before links with the rest of the world are liberalized. In addition, restrictions on capital flows should only be lifted after free trade has been introduced, because asset markets adjust more quickly to new policy regimes than do goods markets. The latter proposal also emerges from several studies of unsuccessful liberalization attempts in Chile, Uruguay, and Argentina (McKinnon 1982; Dornbusch 1984; Edwards 1984; Sjaastad 1984), which all conclude that liberalization of the capital account should be postponed because capital flows will either (under a freely floating exchange rate) push the value of the domestic currency to a level that impedes the structural transition of the real sector or (under a *tablita* or fixed exchange-rate regime) require extremely high real rates of interest in domestic capital markets to prevent large capital outflows and thus maintain the chosen parity.

Both effects are clearly undesirable, and there is little doubt that internal liberalization of capital markets alone could help improve the allocation of capital without risk of too much or too little (net) capital inflow or outflow. Yet, one could argue that the negative effects have actually resulted from an inconsistent mix of exchange rate and domestic economic policies rather than from the liberalization of the capital account as such. In particular, the attempt to use the exchange rate as an anti-inflationary device while distortions of domestic capital and goods markets remained in place has caused the severe economic recessions that each time marked the end of so-called economic liberalization in Latin America. Even if controls on capital flows had been maintained, the exchange-rate regime managed by the government would still have induced an appreciation of the real exchange rate. The resulting decline in the international competitiveness of the tradables sector, which was enforced by incompatible domestic policies such as wage indexation (Chile) or persistent monetary expansion (Argentina), would have been sufficient to prevent the necessary adjustment of the real sector of the economy and, thus, to provoke a new balance-of-payments crisis. Most

---

insufficient to break the inflation mentality. The experience of Germany in the early 1920s and that of Austria, Hungary, and Poland in the late 1940s show furthermore that shock treatment can achieve stabilization quickly and at low cost in terms of unemployment (Sargent 1982).

likely, the risks associated with the choice of a "wrong" exchange rate are by no means smaller than those stemming from destabilizing capital flows.

Furthermore, there is evidence (Corbo, de Melo, and Tybout 1985, 17–27) that policy inconsistency rather than liberalization of the capital account has caused the substantial capital movements into, and out of, the countries in the Southern Cone. The persistent policy-induced distortions of factor and goods markets undermined the credibility of the *tablita* policy. Expectations were that the government could not sustain this policy; hence the perception of the exchange-rate risks hardly changed. For this reason, interest rates remained high when inflation rates began to decelerate, and attracted much capital from abroad. The resulting real appreciation of the exchange rate then increased expectations of the collapse of the exchange-rate regime, and capital flows were reversed until a new balance-of-payments crisis made a maxi-devaluation inevitable.

This assessment suggests that appropriate liberalization policies for concrete cases can only be delineated after a careful economic analysis of the country concerned has been undertaken. With this qualification in mind, the history of successful liberalization in Asian countries and less successful liberalization attempts in Latin America's Southern Cone (to which we shall return in detail later) would at least suggest the following policy guidelines. Gradualism tends to be self-defeating with respect to stabilization and exchange-rate policies, while import and capital markets may be better candidates for a more cautious removal of controls. It has to be stressed, however, that at least a partial deregulation of the capital market is an urgent task, since capital markets have to play a key role in providing the funds needed for rapid and successful economic adjustment to a more outward-oriented trade regime. To facilitate financial flows, it may also be advisable in many countries not to postpone the liberalization of the capital account until the real sector of the economy has adjusted, even if there are some risks concerning an unwarranted appreciation of the currency. If the government abstains from interventions in the foreign-exchange market (and does not buy up the foreign-exchange inflow), a revaluation of the currency is unlikely. A steady course of the Central Bank with respect to monetary policy can prevent an inflationary increase of domestic money supply, while import liberalization will help to mitigate the revaluationary effect of capital inflows. The government should be prepared to accept a temporary deficit in the current account (J-curve effect) to accelerate productive investment based on imported capital goods and to limit the inflow of speculative capital. Once new investments go into operation and export growth is accelerating, the current account deficit will automatically be eliminated.

3.5 The Political Economy of Export Liberalization

Despite some open questions, the switch from an inward- to an outward-oriented trade regime has hardly been hampered by a lack of knowledge concerning the economic management of transition; it was rather impeded by a lack of political will to change the direction of economic development. The major problem with liberalization is that government officials, politicians, and the informed public can readily foresee those interests that are likely to be damaged in the short run by any liberalization effort. The damage accrues primarily to those benefiting most from controls and regulations, and it is in the logic of the system that the main beneficiaries of the regime, such as import-substituting industries, the labor aristocracy, and bureaucrats exerting power through controls, also tend to be well organized into political pressure groups. For them, it pays to invest in the continuity of an inward-oriented trade regime. Conversely, those who have to foot the bill for excessive regulations in terms of income and employment forgone, such as consumers, informal labor, export industries, and agriculture, often do not realize the price they are paying and, hence, have little incentive to organize themselves into special interest groups. They also usually find it difficult to perceive the medium- and long-term benefits that export liberalization holds out to them. For these reasons, there has always been a lot of opposition to, and little support for, a change of the trade regime.

Yet not just the so-called "Four Tigers" in Asia (Hong Kong, Singapore, South Korea, and Taiwan) but also quite a number of developing countries adopted export-promotion strategies in the 1960s and 1970s. This raises the question of which political conditions are conducive to liberalization. Bhagwati (1985, chap. 1) has hypothesized that authoritarian regimes can more easily choose appropriate policies than can democratic governments. His main argument is that the import-substitution strategy confers more political power than the export-promotion strategy, since it provides politicians with greater patronage. Hence, where politicians take power directly by authoritarian means, they have no need to use the economic system to generate and exercise power, freeing them to embrace economic liberalization. Though analytically appealing, Bhagwati's hypothesis does not carry very far in the light of empi.ical evidence. There are military dictatorships in some Latin American countries clinging to populist policies, while politicians in fairly democratic countries such as Malaysia and Thailand took the initiative to liberalize their economies in the 1970s.

So far we in fact know very little about the politicoeconomic background of economic decision making in developing countries and the constellation of power groups that provide governments with enough independence to implement appropriate policies for sustained economic development. Much more research is needed in this area. All that can be said at this stage is that the standard arguments against the political feasibility of export liberalization did not stand the test. The attempt to preserve national independence through a diversified domestic industrial sector, largely de-linked from the world economy, has increased dependence on imported intermediate and capital goods and has contributed to the currently intractable foreign indebtedness. Trade unions were not pacified by maintaining the course of import-substitution strategies—the political pressure exerted by organized labor against the government was as strong under inward-oriented trade regimes as when liberalization was attempted. And, finally, persistent reliance on import-substitution strategies for fear of political and social upheavals in case of a policy change has not protected many countries in Africa and Latin America from plunging into economic crises and civil disorder, with subsequent changes of government. The new governments, often military, then had little choice but to implement some liberalization measures to remedy the economic crisis.

4. EVALUATION OF THE EVIDENCE

4.1 Export Performance

The proposition that an open trading environment promotes an efficient use of available resources has received impressive support from the experiences of an increasing number of old and new NICs, which gradually opened their markets during the 1960s and 1970s. Export liberalization has caused manufactured exports from the Third World to expand spectacularly, outpacing both world trade expansion and domestic industrial output growth. As table 6.1 shows, manufactured exports of developing countries grew on average at an annual rate of roughly 14 percent in real terms in the period 1965–82—about twice as fast as world trade. Export expansion was predominantly achieved by the nineteen countries listed in table 6.1, which accounted for 79 percent of

TABLE 6.1 Manufactured Exports of Newly Industrializing Countries (NICs), 1965–82
(SITC 5 + 6 + 7 + 8 – 67 – 68)

	Value in millions of U.S. $			Share in total exports (%)		Annual real rates of growth (%)[a]	
	1965	1973	1982	1965	1982	1965–73	1973–82
First-Generation NICs	2,645.4	16,796.7	77,735.1	33.1	58.2	19.4	9.6
Predominantly inward-oriented (total)	1,062.6	3,426.0	8,859.3	24.6	23.5	9.7	2.7
Argentina	83.9	735.4	1,846.4	5.6	24.2	24.4	2.4
India	812.8	1,560.7	5,000.0[c]	48.3	55.5[c]	2.9	5.3[d]
Mexico	165.9	1,129.9	2,012.9	14.5	9.6	20.5	–1.4
Predominantly outward-oriented (total)	1,582.8	13,370.7	68,875.8	43.1	71.7	23.8	10.9
Brazil	124.3	1,216.9	7,720.9	7.8	38.3	26.1	13.5
Hong Kong[b]	819.7	3,649.5	13,161.0	93.2	96.3	14.3	6.6
Israel	276.3	1,108.8	4,243.2	64.3	80.4	12.8	7.3
Singapore[b]	72.1	1,004.0	5,034.3	52.1	37.0	31.8	10.6
South Korea	103.8	2,717.2	19,121.3[c]	59.3	90.0[c]	42.6	16.2[d]
Taiwan	186.6	3,674.3	19,595.3	41.5	88.8	37.6	11.3
Second-Generation predominantly outward-oriented NICs	230.1	1,500.6	10,326.2	0.7	20.5	20.6	14.6
Chile	15.0	44.5	780.0[c]	2.4	20.8[c]	8.6	30.2[d]
Colombia	33.8	307.3	745.5	6.3	24.3	24.9	2.0
Indonesia	—	60.6	808.1	—	3.6	—	23.3
Malaysia	64.3	346.5	2,734.9	6.4	22.7	17.0	16.3

Morocco	23.1	129.9	706.0	5.4	34.3	24.1	11.6
Peru	4.1	28.6	377.3	0.6	13.7	20.7	23.1
Philippines	65.8	219.6	1,145.7	8.3	22.9	10.2	11.1
Thailand	12.1	255.4	1,871.8	2.0	21.9	38.8	15.4
Tunisia	11.6	83.9	833.7[c]	9.9	33.3[c]	21.1	21.3[d]
Uruguay	—	24.4	323.2	—	31.6	—	23.2
Total (all NICs)	2,875.5	18,297.2	88,061.3	7.2	44.8	19.5	10.1
in % of developing countries' exports	68.3	79.0	79.0	—	—	—	—
in % of world exports	2.8	5.3	8.5	—	—	—	—
Manufactured exports of:							
Developing countries	4,212	23,148	111,519	—	—	17.3	10.1
World	102,137	346,851	1,042,052	—	—	10.5	4.5

SOURCES: United Nations, *Commodity Trade Statistics*, *Yearbook of International Trade Statistics*, and *Monthly Bulletin of Statistics*, various issues; UN Council on Trade and Development 1983 (with 1984 supplement); India 1984; Peru 1971; Singapore 1980 and 1984; Taiwan 1983; Uruguay 1973.

[a] Export values deflated by unit value indices for manufactured exports of industrialized countries.
[b] Excluding re-exports.
[c] 1981.
[d] 1973–81.

total Third World manufactured exports in 1982. With rapid domestic industrialization, the export portfolio of these countries significantly shifted toward manufactured goods, as shown by the shares of these goods in total exports, which increased from 7.2 percent in 1965 to 44.8 percent in 1982.

The nineteen countries in table 6.1 are quite diverse. Some (the first-generation NICs) had already established a substantial industrial base in 1965, whereas others (the second-generation NICs) were latecomers who began to promote industrialization and exports of manufactures only in the 1970s. Furthermore, a few first-generation NICs have pursued predominantly inward-oriented development policies, and for the reasons given in section 3 the consequences for their export performances were negative: either real growth of manufactured exports remained low throughout the whole period under observation (as in the case of India) or it slowed down considerably when the international economic environment deteriorated in the 1970s (as in the cases of Argentina and Mexico).

This is in clear contrast to the experience of the more outward-oriented first- as well as second-generation NICs. As to the latter, the interesting point to make is that they were able to launch export drives in spite of successive oil shocks, economic recession in industrialized countries, high interest rates, and new protectionism during the past decade. The unfavorable external environment did not prevent these countries from penetrating the markets of industrialized countries further and from intensifying trade within the Third World. The real rate of manufactured export growth of 10.1 percent for all countries taken together, which has to be compared to a rate of 4.5 percent for world trade in manufactures, indicates the continuity of export success in the period 1973–82. In this difficult period, the second-generation NICs were even more successful than their forerunners, as shown by rates of export expansion of 14.6 and 9.6 percent respectively.

Equally noteworthy is the fact that the early export drive of the old NICs has not clogged the markets of industrialized countries leaving no room for latecomers, as is often asserted. Most of the new NICs started industrialization based on relatively open trade regimes in the 1970s, and were able to compete successfully with old NICs and with suppliers from industrialized countries. All second-generation NICs except Colombia (which had abandoned outward orientation by then) have achieved rates of manufactured export expansion in excess of the group of old NICs (for further details, see Havrylyshyn and Alikhani 1982). An analysis of ASEAN countries (Indonesia, Malaysia, the Philippines, Thailand, and Singapore) (Hiemenz 1985) even suggest that the take-off to export-oriented industrialization may have been easier for the late-comers, since the experience of the old NICs served as an indication for choosing an appropriate product mix, tapping the right markets, and exploiting established trade links. Most important, however, the demon-strated superiority of choosing an outward-oriented development path in the old NICs created an expectation of success that all segments of society in the new NICs could focus on.

A great number of country studies show that exports, which ex-panded so rapidly under outward-oriented trade regimes, have been the major driving force of economic growth and employment creation, ex-ceeding any performance observed in countries pursuing import-substitution strategies (Donges 1983, and the references given there; Ram 1985). The domestic saving rate increased rapidly and so did the proportion of investment in GDP, both behind remarkable rises in the export-to-GDP ratios (table 6.2). Again, predominantly inward-oriented old NICs did not fare as well as the other NICs. Increments to savings and investment remained modest; hence real rates of GDP growth trailed far behind those achieved by most outward-oriented NICs.

What appears as an "export-led type" of economic development in most NICs in fact meant a continuous strengthening of the supply po-tential of the economy and a steady increase in productivity. Relatively low real wages provided the inducement to build up manufacturing-production capacities using labor-intensive technologies to a large ex-tent, which allowed the absorption of surplus labor. When later on labor became scarcer during the industrialization process, and consequently real wages increased more rapidly (particularly in the leading NICs), the economies had gained sufficient flexibility on the supply side to be able to shift the production structure toward more physical-capital and skill-intensive activities and to be internationally competitive in these new undertakings. Direct foreign investment has contributed to the success of export orientation and diversification, mainly by providing technical knowledge and marketing expertise and by upgrading skills of domestic workers. With the exception of Singapore, the significance of (totally or partly) foreign-owned firms, in terms of investment, production, ex-port, or employment shares, was much more modest than commonly believed.

The empirical evidence also confirms that these encouraging results have been brought about by improvements in trade and trade-related

TABLE 6.2 Indicators of Export-Oriented Development

| | Percentage Share in Gross Domestic Product of | | | | | | Annual Percentage Rates of | | | |
| | Exports | | Savings | | Investment | | Real Manufacturing Output | | Real GDP | |
	1965	1983	1965	1983	1965	1983	1965–73	1973–83	1965–73	1973–83
First-Generation NICs										
Predominantly inward-oriented										
Argentina	8	13	22	18	19	13	4.6	−1.8	4.3	0.4
India	4	6	16	22[a]	18	25[a]	4.0	4.2	3.9	4.0
Mexico	9	20	21	28	22	17	9.9	5.5	7.9	5.6
Predominantly outward-oriented										
Brazil	8	8[a]	27	21[a]	25	21[a]	11.2	4.2	9.8	4.8
Hong Kong	71	95	29	25	36	27	—	—	7.9	9.3
Israel	19	33	15	9	29	22	—	—	9.6	3.2
Singapore	123	176	10	42	22	45	19.5	7.9	13.0	8.2
South Korea	9	37	8	26	15	27	21.1	11.8	10.0	7.3
Taiwan	19	58	20	32	23	25	15.4	8.4	10.4	7.2
Second-Generation predominantly outward-oriented NICs										
Chile	14	24	16	11	15	8	4.1	0.5	3.4	2.9
Colombia	11	10	17	15	16	19	8.8	1.9	6.4	3.9

Indonesia	44	25	6	20	7	24	9.0	12.6	8.1	7.0
Malaysia	18	54	23	29	18	34	—	8.5	6.7	7.3
Morocco	16	23	12	11	10	21	6.1	4.0	5.7	4.7
Peru	17	21	19	14	21	13	4.4	0.4	3.5	1.8
Philippines	18	20	21	21	21	27	8.5	5.0	5.4	5.4
Thailand	18	22	19	20	20	25	11.4	8.9	7.8	6.9
Tunisia	19	35	14	20	28	29	10.3	11.1	7.3	6.0
Uruguay	19	24	18	14	11	10	—	—	1.3	2.5
For comparison:										
Middle-income countries	18	24	21	21	21	22	9.3	4.9	7.1	4.7
Upper-middle-income countries	19	25	24	23	23	22	—	—	7.4	4.9
Lower-middle-income countries	17	21	16	17	17	22	8.5	5.4	6.6	4.1
Industrialized countries	12	18	23	20	23	20	3.8	1.1	4.7	2.4

SOURCES: World Bank 1985; Asian Development Bank 1984.

[a] 1982.

policies along the lines discussed in section 3. A corrected and more sensible import-tariff and export-subsidy policy, combined with more realistically valued real exchange rates, more rational factor pricing, and less intervention in goods markets, have constituted the pillars of outward-oriented trade regimes. State intervention remained important in all NICs (with the exception of Hong Kong, which has always come very close to a laissez-faire economy), but the readiness of governments to consider comparative-cost criteria, to modify plans when circumstances changed, and to learn from past mistakes was much greater than elsewhere in the Third World. When export liberalization involved some kind of resource misallocation—for instance, because the government promoted exports bearing high marginal domestic resource costs per unit of foreign-exchange earnings—the country's industrialization process did not come up against a balance-of-payments constraint, as it almost inevitably would have under an inward-oriented regime; those exports at least provided foreign-exchange revenues.

It should also be noted that the transition from an inward-oriented to an outward-oriented trade regime nowhere caused traumatic dislocations in production and employment. On the contrary, the more or less gradual approach adopted by the governments in reforming policies greatly facilitated the needed adaptation. Even many of the inefficient producers, which lived so comfortably with the previous protectionist environment, demonstrated that they were actually quite able to reduce costs through process innovations and to develop new markets through product innovations—once the increased competitive pressures made such efforts imperative for survival.

4.2. *External Shocks and Foreign Indebtedness*

One frequently raised objection to export liberalization concerns the dependence of outward-oriented economies on conditions in world markets. It is argued that open economies are vulnerable to external shocks, while less trade orientation provides a protective shield against disruptive external demand or price changes. The experience of the 1970s and 1980s, when all developing countries were suddenly confronted with the need to overcome increasing balance-of-payments pressures in order to preserve the momentum of their development process, reveals the opposite. Outward-oriented economies commanded enough flexibility at both the macro- and micro-levels to meet the challenge of deteriorating world market conditions without falling into the debt trap, while inward-oriented economies suffered from severe economic depression and, in many cases, mounting foreign indebtedness. India is the major exception to this rule, perhaps because this country had previously not borrowed much abroad and has benefited from an improved performance of its agricultural sector more recently. Balassa (1984) has shown that outward-oriented economies relied largely on output-increasing policies of export promotion and import substitution to offset the balance-of-payments effects of external shocks in the 1974–76 and 1979–81 periods and accepted a temporary decline in the rate of economic growth in order to limit their external indebtedness. Inward-oriented economies, however, failed to apply output-increasing policies of adjustment; they financed the balance-of-payments effects of external shocks by foreign borrowing in 1974–76 and had to take deflationary measures in 1979–81 as their increased indebtedness limited the possibility of further borrowing. The policies applied led to economic growth rates substantially higher in outward-oriented than in inward-oriented economies, with the differences in growth rates offsetting the differences in the size of external shocks several times.[6]

4.3 Aborted Liberalization Attempts in Latin America

The liberalization attempts initiated in Uruguay, Chile, and Argentina in the mid 1970s (for details see the country papers in Barletta, Blejer, and Landau 1984) seem to run counter to the arguments presented in previous sections. True, all three economies experienced initial success in reducing inflation and accelerating the rate of economic growth, but the positive developments ended abruptly, as each country encountered a sudden economic downturn, large increases in external indebtedness, and internal financial crises.

Closer examination of the experiences of these countries underlines the extreme importance of internal consistency in the policy package implemented to liberalize an economy. In particular, a fixed exchange-rate system pegged against an appreciative currency (then the U.S. dollar) turned out to be incompatible with fiscal, monetary, and wage policies. In the Chilean economy, the momentum of economic development achieved by trade liberalization and anti-inflationary budget policies broke down when the exchange rate was fixed against the U.S. dollar in 1979. A sharply appreciating real exchange rate in 1980–81 combined with a considerable rise in real wages (owing to wage indexation to past,

6. A study undertaken at the Kiel Institute of World Economics with the focus on the effects of the oil price shocks has provided valuable confirmation of these conclusions. See Agarwal, Glismann, and Nunnenkamp 1983.

and higher, inflation rates) and persistently high interest rates (owing to bank regulations causing substantial arbitrage costs) could not but erode the international competitiveness of the tradables sector and provide strong incentives for speculative investment (mostly in construction activities).

A lack of consistency between exchange-rate policy and trade policies, as well as fiscal policies, also caused the failure of economic liberalization in Argentina, where a *tablita* was implemented, with a concomitant opening of the capital account, while protectionist trade interventions remained untouched and large fiscal deficits continued to fuel domestic inflation. This combination of contradictory policies put the trade sector under untenable pressure (as in the case of Chile) and gave rise to an unprecedented outflow of domestic capital. Both countries accumulated staggering levels of foreign debt within a relatively short period as a result of unresolved balance-of-payments problems.

These partial deregulation attempts can clearly not be used as examples against export liberalization based on a package of stabilization-cum-restructuring policies as suggested in section 2 and applied in most of the second-generation NICs. However, they do provide lessons with respect to the crucial link between exchange rate, interest rate, and wages, and with respect to the disastrous consequences of step-by-step approaches to liberalization. Sjaastad (1983, 19) makes the point unequivocally: "The fatal flaw is not to be found in the liberalisation programme per se, but rather in policy inconsistencies. Policy inconsistencies are of minor importance when markets are heavily regulated. Free markets, however, require a high degree of policy coherence."

5. WORLD MARKET CONDITIONS— OBSTACLE TO EXPORT LIBERALIZATION?

The above analysis has stressed that the main factors determining the success of outward-oriented economic development are to be found on the supply side of the economy. To be sure, world market conditions also matter, and when they are as favorable as they were in the 1950s and 1960s the chances for accomplishing a successful transition to an open trade regime are particularly good. But even a buoyant external demand can only be transformed into an impetus to economic development if there is adequate export potential. Nevertheless, persistent skepticism fuels new variants of export pessimism, resting on the assumption that the revival of protectionism will further restrict ac~ess to the markets of industrialized countries, that these markets cannot absorb expanding exports from a large number of developing countries, and that world demand will remain sluggish owing to the weak economic performance of the industrialized countries.

Though "new protectionism" in industrial countries has not completely eroded the gains from earlier rounds of trade liberalization (Hughes and Waelbroeck 1981, 131) and has not prevented export-oriented economies (in particular the East Asian NICs) from penetrating foreign markets, the danger is that it generates additional uncertainty among investors in developing countries concerning engagement in export-oriented activities. Investors may then turn to presumably "safe" investment opportunities geared toward production for local markets, and political forces favoring an import-substitution type of economic development may succeed in forestalling, or at least slowing down, any attempt to liberalize the system of economic incentives. In this sense, protectionists in the industrial countries play into the hands of protectionists in developing countries.

As to the proposition that it will be impossible for all developing countries to emulate success stories because the resulting surge of manufactured exports to Western markets would cause a glut on those markets and provoke further protectionist tendencies (Cline 1982; Spraos 1983, 140), it reflects a fallacy of composition. When moving in the direction of market liberalization, it takes a longer time for large, resource-rich countries, like those in Latin America, starting from a higher level of distortion, to arrive at the same manufactured export share in GDP than it does for small, labor-abundant countries like Korea, Taiwan, Singapore, and Hong Kong. In fact, it is likely that manufactured export shares in the former group will always fall behind those in the latter group, even at the same population and income levels. Nor, given differences in resource endowments and skills, will all developing countries export the same products. Even in the labor-intensive segment of the product range, there is a wide variety of manufactures that developing countries can specialize in, and market penetration is rather marginal in industrialized countries for most of these products.

Moreover, the implementation of an outward-oriented trade regime will provide for some degree of import liberalization. This offers the chance to expand South-South trade along with South-North trade, in particular with labor-intensive and standardized capital-intensive products. And, finally, should too many developing countries specialize in the same exports, their terms of trade will deteriorate (other things being equal), but this can be only a temporary effect, because it is unreasonable to assume that investors and exporters do not learn. Most likely, they will react to declining prices by changing the product mix.

As to export pessimism derived from slow economic growth in developed countries, it should be emphasized that for industrializing developing countries there is not a stringent and invariable link between the rate of expansion of world demand and that of exports (Riedel 1984). The composition of output changes and so does the structure of exports. In fact, the changing composition of exports has been the major reason behind rapid export expansion of developing countries over the past twenty-five years. Third World manufactured exports grew twice as fast as real GDP in industrialized countries in the 1960s, and more than four times faster after 1973, when industrialized countries experienced successive economic recessions.

6. CONCLUSIONS

This chapter has reviewed the arguments and the empirical evidence for the superiority of outward-oriented trade regimes in promoting industrialization and accelerating economic development. Trade policies that do not discriminate between local and foreign sales improve allocative efficiency and provide dynamic gains from economies of scale, enhanced transfers of technology, and better access to international financial markets. Beyond outward-oriented trade policies, internal liberalization of markets increases the flexibility of the economy, which is one necessary condition for successful economic development. These advantages accrue even in an international economic environment less buoyant than that of the 1960s and early 1970s. It is, however, of crucial importance that a high degree of coherence between trade liberalization and related economic policies be achieved, that the policies be credible, and that they be implemented rigorously.

REFERENCES

Agarwal, Jamuna P., Hans H. Glismann, and Peter Nunnenkamp. 1983. *Preisschocks und wirtschaftliche Entwicklung: Anpassungsprobleme in der Dritten Welt*. Tübingen: J. C. B. Mohr.

Asian Development Bank. 1984. *Key Indicators of Developing Member Countries of ADB*. Vol. 15. Manila: ADB.

Balassa, Bela. 1980a. "Prospects for Trade in Manufactured Goods between Industrial and Developing Countries, 1978–1990." *Journal of Policy Modeling* 3 (September): 437–55.

———. 1980b. *The Process of Industrial Development and Alternative Development Strategies.* Essays in International Finance no. 141. Princeton: International Finance Section, Department of Economics, Princeton University.

———. 1983. "Outward vs. Inward Orientation Once Again." *World Economy* 6 (June): 215–18.

———. 1984. "Adjustment Policies in Developing Countries: A Reassessment." *World Development* 12 (September): 955–72.

———. 1986. "Developing Country Debt: Policies and Prospects." In H. Giersch, ed., *The International Debt Problem: Lessons for the Future,* 103–22. Tübingen: J. C. B. Mohr.

Barletta, N. A., M. I. Blejer, and L. Landau, eds. 1984. *Economic Liberalization and Stabilization Policies in Argentina, Chile, and Uruguay: Applications of the Monetary Approach to the Balance of Payments.* A World Bank Symposium. Washington, D.C.: World Bank.

Berry, Albert, and Richard H. Sabot. 1984. "Unemployment and Economic Development." *Economic Development and Cultural Change* 33 (March): 99–116.

Bhagwati, J. N. 1978. *Foreign Trade Regimes and Economic Development: Anatomy and Consequences of Exchange Control Regimes.* Cambridge, Mass: Ballinger.

———. 1985. *Essays in Development Economics.* Vol. 1, *Wealth and Poverty.* Edited by G. Grossman. London: Basil Blackwell; Cambridge, Mass.: MIT Press.

Cline, William R. 1982. "Can the East Asian Model of Development Be Generalized?" *World Development* 10 (February): 81–90.

Corbo, Vittorio, Jaime de Melo, and James Tybout. 1985. *What Went Wrong with the Recent Reforms in the Southern Cone?* International Bank for Reconstruction and Development Report no. DRD 128. Washington, D.C.

Donges, Juergen B. 1983. "Re-Appraisal of Foreign Trade Strategies for Industrial Development." In F. Machlup, G. Fels, and H. Müller-Groeling, eds., *Reflections on a Troubled World Economy: Essays in Honor of Herbert Giersch,* 279–301. London: Macmillan & Co.

Donges, Juergen B. and Lotte Müller-Ohlsen. 1978. *Aussenwirtschaftsstrategien und Industrialisierung in Entwicklungsländern.* Tübingen: J. C. B. Mohr.

Dornbusch, Rüdiger. 1984. *External Debt, Budget Deficits, and Disequilibrium Exchange Rates.* NBER Working Paper no. 1336. Cambridge, Mass.: National Bureau of Economic Research.

Edwards, Sebastian. 1984. *The Order of Liberalization of the External Sector in Developing Countries.* Essays in International Finance no. 156. Princeton: International Finance Section, Department of Economics, Princeton University.

Fischer, Bernhard, Ulrich Hiemenz, and Peter Trapp. 1985. *Argentina: The Economic Crisis in the 1980s.* Tübingen: J. C. B. Mohr.

Frenkel, Jacob A. 1984. "Economic Liberalization and Stabilization Programs." In N. A. Barletta, M. I. Blejer, and L. Landau, eds., *Economic Liberalization and Stabilization Policies in Argentina, Chile, and Uruguay: Applications of the Monetary Approach to the Balance of Payments,* 12–27. A World Bank Symposium. Washington, D.C.: World Bank.

Gönensay, Emre. 1986 "From Bankruptcy to Revival: The Turkish Experience with Restructuring Economic Incentives, 1980–1984." In B. Balassa and H. Giersch, eds., *Economic Incentives: Proceedings of a Conference Held by the International Economic Association in Kiel*, 348–68. London: Macmillan & Co.

Havrylyshyn, Oli, and Iradk Alikhani. 1982. "Is There Cause for Export Optimism? An Inquiry into the Existence of a Second Generation of Successful Exporters." *Weltwirtschaftliches Archiv* 118 (December): 651–63.

Henderson, P. D. 1982. "Trade Policies and 'Strategies': Case for a Liberal Approach." *World Economy* 5 (September): 291–302.

Hiemenz, Ulrich. 1985. "Die Aussenhandelsverflechtung von Entwicklungsländern: Eine Analyse von Markterschliessungsstrategien." In H. Giersch, ed., *Probleme und Perspektiven der weltwirtschaftlichen Entwicklung*, 159–77. Berlin: Duncker & Humblot.

Hughes, Helen, and Jean Waelbroeck. 1981. "Can Developing-country Exports Keep Growing in the 1980s?" *World Economy* 4 (June): 127–47.

India. 1984. *Economic Survey, 1982–83*. New Delhi: Economic Division, Ministry of Finance.

Krueger, Anne O. 1978. *Foreign Trade Regimes and Economic Development: Liberalization Attempts and Consequences*. Cambridge, Mass.: Ballinger.

——— ed., 1983. *Trade and Employment in Developing Countries*. Vol. 3, *Synthesis and Conclusions*. Chicago: University of Chicago Press.

———. 1984a. "Comparative Advantage and Development Policy Twenty Years Later." In M. Syrquin, L. Taylor, and L. E. Westphal, eds., *Economic Structure and Performance*, 135–56. Orlando, Fla.: Academic Press.

———. 1984b. "Problems of Liberalization." In A. C. Harberger, ed., *World Economic Growth*, 403–26. San Francisco: ICS Press.

Lächler, Ulrich. 1985. "Credibility and the Dynamics of Disinflation in Open Economies: A Note on the Southern Cone Experiments." Kiel: Institute of World Economics. Mimeographed.

McKinnon, Ronald. 1982. "The Order of Economic Liberalization: Lessons from Chile and Argentina." In K. Brunner and A. Meltzer, eds., *Economic Policy in a World of Change*. Amsterdam: North Holland Publishing Co.

Mayer, Wolfgang. 1984. "The Infant-Export Industry Argument." *Canadian Journal of Economics* 17 (June): 249–69.

Organization for Economic Cooperation and Development. 1983. *International Investment and Multinational Enterprises: Investment Incentives and Disincentives and the International Investment Process*. Paris: OECD.

Peru. 1971. *Estadisticas de exportación hasta 1969*. Lima: Banco Industrial del Perú, División de Comercio Exterior.

Ram, Rati. 1985. "Exports and Economic Growth: Some Additional Evidence." *Economic Development and Cultural Change* 33 (June): 415–25.

Riedel, James. 1984. "Trade as the Engine of Growth in Developing Countries, Revisited." *Economic Journal* 94 (March): 56–73.

Sargent, Thomas J. 1982. "The Ends of Four Big Inflations." In R. E. Hall, ed., *Inflation: Causes and Effects*, 41–97. Chicago: University of Chicago Press.

Singapore. 1980. *Yearbook of Statistics, 1979/80*. Singapore: Department of Statistics.

————. 1984. *Economic Survey of Singapore, 1983*. Singapore: Ministry of Trade and Industry.

Sjaastad, Larry A. 1983. "Failure of Economic Liberalism in the Cone of Latin America." *World Economy* 6 (March): 5–26.

————. 1984. "Liberalization and Stabilization Experiences in the Southern Cone." In N. A. Barletta, M. I. Blejer, and L. Landau, eds., *Economic Liberalization and Stabilization Policies in Argentina, Chile, and Uruguay: Applications of the Monetary Approach to the Balance of Payments*, 83–103. A World Bank Symposium. Washington, D.C.: World Bank.

Spinanger, Dean. 1984. "Objectives and Impact of Economic Activity Zones: Some Evidence from Asia." *Weltwirtschaftliches Archiv* 120 (March): 64–89.

Spraos, John. 1983. *Inequalizing Trade? A Study of Traditional North/South Specialisation in the Context of Terms of Trade Concepts*. Oxford: Clarendon Press.

Squire, Lyn. 1981. *Employment Policy in Developing Countries: A Survey of Issues and Evidence*. New York: Oxford University Press.

Stein, Herbert. 1980. "Achieving Credibility." In W. Fellner, ed., *Contemporary Economic Problems. 1980*. 39–76. Washington, D.C.: American Enterprise Institute.

Streeten, Paul. 1982. "A Cool Look at Outward-Looking Strategies for Development." *World Economy* 5 (June): 159–69.

Taiwan. 1983. *The Trade of China, 1982*. Chinese Maritime Customs, Statistical Series no. 1. Taipei: *Inspectorate General of Customs*.

United Nations. Various years. *Commodity Trade Statistics*. New York: UN Department of International Economic and Social Affairs, Statistical Papers.

————. Various issues. *Monthly Bulletin of Statistics*. New York: UN Department of International Economic and Social Affairs, Statistical Office.

————. Various years. *Yearbook of International Trade Statistics*. New York: UN Department of International Economic and Social Affairs.

United Nations. Council on Trade and Development. 1983. *Handbook of International Trade and Development Statistics*. New York: UNCTAD. Supplement, 1984.

Uruguay. 1973. *Análisis estadístico, importación-exportación*. 17th ed. Montevideo: Centro de Estadísticas Nacionales y Comercio Internacional.

Wulf, Luc de. 1978. "Fiscal Incentives for Industrial Exports in Developing Countries." *National Tax Journal* 31 (March): 45–52.

SEVEN

Import Restriction and Liberalization

Wontack Hong

1. THE "PROTECTIONIST," EXPORT-ORIENTED ECONOMY

Unless exorbitant costs will result from their adoption, economic theory favors general taxes and subsidies over tariff protection. Whatever its objects, tariff protection is bound to generate by-product distortions in factor intensity, in consumption, and toward home-market bias (see Corden, 1971). Furthermore, quantitative restrictions on imports are considered even more distorting than tariff protection.[1] Despite this knowledge, however, many countries relying on export promotion, such as Korea, have maintained fairly severe import-restraining systems in the form of both tariff protection and quantitative restrictions, partly because of political considerations of vested interest groups (as in the case of agricultural protection) and partly because import restriction is believed by many policymakers—regardless of trade theorists' statements to the contrary—to be the best available policy measure at an early phase of economic development. Import restriction is thought to pro-

1. Tariff protection (TP) implies perfect competition at tariff-inclusive prices. Under a quantitative restriction (QR) system, however, firms' output levels are often determined by the imports of intermediate goods directly allocated to them. If licenses for imports of intermediate goods are allocated in proportion to each firm's capacity, the associated quota premium encourages the development of excess capacity in the economy. Furthermore, when firm-specific allocation of intermediate imports determines market shares, there is little competition among firms, ensuring the growth of inefficient firms. Under the QR system, government officials may also deny imports of certain products whose roles in production processes they do not understand, and thereby inflict unwarranted hardships on the related industrial activities. It is believed that private-sector response to unintended incentives created by QR systems has led to the frustration of many of the goals of import-substitution (IS) regimes. See Bhagwati and Krueger 1973 and Keesing 1967.

mote infant industries (and rapidly convert them into exporters) and also to maximize the foreign sales of currently exporting industries (at the expense of domestic consumers' surplus).[2]

Countries such as Hong Kong and Singapore have pursued export-oriented growth strategies while maintaining free-trading regimes almost from the beginning. Countries such as Korea, Taiwan, and Japan, on the other hand, maintained fairly protectionist import regimes for long periods of time. It was not until the 1960s that Japan eliminated the bulk of its formal quantitative restrictions: the nominal import liberalization ratio (by items) expanded from less than 70 percent in 1960 to about 93 percent in 1964, and to 97 percent by 1976. Similarly, Taiwan did not eliminate the bulk of its formal quantitative restrictions until the early 1970s: the nominal import-liberalization ratio increased from 61.5 percent in 1970 to 96.5 percent in 1973.[3] As a result, in both Japan and Taiwan, quantitative import restrictions are now essentially limited to special laws and other invisible unofficial means. Korea is scheduled to eliminate the bulk of its quantitative restrictions during the period of 1984–88.[4]

This chapter analyzes the efficiency and welfare implications of import restriction and import liberalization in an export-oriented developing economy. In light of the Korean experience, it addresses the

2. Export promotion (EP) and QR do not necessarily make an inconsistent policy set. For instance, an export industry can maintain a monopolistic domestic market structure because of QR. It is well known that an industry exports more with a domestic monopoly and price discrimination than with a perfectly free trade regime. See Davies and McGuinness 1982.

3. Data from Young et al. 1982, 78.

4. Economists seem to agree that a prudent policy should be based on liberalization of the current account first of all, and that whenever possible, the QR system should be removed before tackling the TP system. The capital account of the balance of payments should only be opened after the domestic capital market is freed, and this can happen only after the fiscal deficits, if any, have been substantially reduced. See Edwards 1984. This suggestion is consistent with the well-known immiserizing growth that can result from the free inflow of foreign capital in the presence of domestic distortions. See Brecher and Diaz-Alejandro 1977 and Brecher and Findlay 1983. Moreover, if one postulates that the supply price of foreign capital is an increasing function of the magnitude of its supply, then one can argue for restricting the inflow of foreign capital on the basis of monopsony power. First, there may be significantly diminishing returns on foreign capital owing to limited absorptive entrepreneurial capacities, and the international financial market not supplying larger amounts of capital without raising the risk premium. Second, if the government acts as a monopsonistic agent in importing foreign capital and allocating it competitively among domestic entrepreneurs, the difference between the average rate of return on investment and the average interest rate on foreign borrowing will accrue to the government as monopsonistic profits, which in turn may be used as subsidy funds.

question of whether extensive import liberalization is always a necessary condition for the successful growth performance of an export-oriented economy. If not, it asks, when does it become a necessary condition?[5]

In order to give the complete picture, section 2 discusses the unified analytical framework. Section 3 examines the experience of Korea in its early phase of export-oriented growth and analyzes the effect of its import policy on economic growth. Section 4 examines the Korean experience in the later stage of growth, when Korea's comparative advantage started to shift away from the simple labor-intensive consumption goods toward more capital-intensive intermediate and investment goods. The effect of sustained protectionist import policy and the need for more extensive import liberalization are analyzed. Section 5 delineates the liberalization effort of the Korean government during the period 1983–86. Emphasis is given to the politics of protection versus liberalization. The chapter concludes that in order to initiate export-oriented growth, a developing economy must undertake some minimum level of import liberalization, because an extremely protectionist regime would simply frustrate any kind of incentives given to the export sector. However, extensive import liberalization is not a necessary condition for initiating and sustaining successful export-oriented growth. Only at a later stage of development, when the economy starts shifting into the intermediate and investment-goods sectors, might extensive import liberalization become a necessary condition for maintaining production efficiency and maximizing consumer welfare.

2. ANALYTIC FRAMEWORK

2.1 Earning versus Saving Foreign Exchange:
Export Promotion versus Import Substitution

This section summarizes the analysis of Keesing (1967) and Bhagwati and Krueger (1973). They argue for the promotion of exports (earning foreign exchange) and against the substitution of imports (saving foreign exchange).

First of all, the argument is made that the most important source of economic growth is the upgrading of human resources and production technology rather than the simple accumulation of physical capital. It is

5. The TP and QR systems are often identified with IS regimes, but it is one of the main emphases of this chapter that an EP regime such as Korea's is never free from tariff or nontariff import restrictions and IS biases.

persuasively argued that under an export-promotion regime, entrepreneurs are mainly concerned with cutting costs, keeping production facilities and techniques up to date, and improving product quality and marketing to suit consumer taste (both at home and abroad), whereas workers are subject to great pressure to perform and train others. Under an import-substitution regime, on the other hand, entrepreneurs presumably spend most of their energy manipulating government officials (who have mastered the finer arts of lobbying, corruption, and graft), in order to improve their protection, while workers learn lackadaisical ways, as they are not pressed to raise their quality and productivity performances. A developing country should therefore gain higher-quality industrial experience and undergo greater pressure for quality and efficiency performance by selling the same value of output abroad under competitive conditions than at home with protection. In short, an export-promotion regime is believed to create human resources more suitable for sustained growth than is an import-substitution regime, which, by encouraging the wrong skills and habits, casts a long shadow over the future of the economy.

It follows, then, that one of the important gains to be made from trade is rapid technical progress arising from innovative imitation. Adam Smith long ago emphasized the "educative effect" of "mutual communication of knowledge of all sorts of improvements which an extensive commerce to all countries naturally, or rather necessarily, carries along with it" (Cannan ed., 1950, 125). Exporting firms must face both price and quality competition in international markets, and consequently the survival and success of each exporter depends on adaptive innovations and active absorption of available production techniques.[6] The export-promotion strategy also enables an economy to take full advantage of economies of scale. Even when the initial markets are found at home, the physical layout of manufactures permits a ready exploitation of scale economies and an easy transition into export markets.

Both export-promotion and import-substitution regimes may be characterized by a mistrust of laissez-faire and free trade. However,

6. International competition enhances communication, and entrepreneurs pay close attention to the possibilities of innovation and speeding up learning processes because survival, advancement, and success depend on these. On the other hand, in an IS regime, protection is accepted as a legitimate major instrument for promoting industrialization. Every industry is thus spurred to demonstrate its need for shelter from the cruelties of foreign competition, and eventually the country ends up allowing each industry protection according to its inefficiency.

foreign governments respond to the extreme abuse of export subsidies not tolerated by international trade conventions. Hence the potential for arbitrary government intervention is more restricted under an export-promotion regime than it is under an import-substitution one. Furthermore, it is believed that in an effort to make local prices and wages appear cheap, less inflationary policies are pursued under export-promotion regimes. This, in turn, restricts the size of subsidies and tax exemptions a country can afford, providing a built-in check on excessive intervention.[7]

For a developing economy, foreign products may mostly reflect locally unattainable natural resources, skills, and technology. Most likely there will be a lack of substitutability between local resources and foreign-supplied resources. The ability to pay for needed imports may, then, severely limit economic growth. An export-promotion regime is believed to relieve the foreign-exchange constraint on growth more readily than is an import-substitution regime.

Another advantage of export-promotion regimes is that they naturally tend to rapidly expand the volume of exports and consequently also the volume of imports, while import substitution regimes tend to reduce (or increase less rapidly) the volume of a country's trade. According to Corden (1971), the opening up of an economy to trade (which may be measured in terms of the export/GNP ratio) generates a "static" efficiency gain that is very similar to a "once-and-for-all" technical advance that raises the absorption-possibility frontier of a country at a given factor-supply level. Furthermore, with a given constant propensity to save, the static efficiency gain may itself induce the rate of capital accumulation to rise. Consequently, it will raise the growth rate of the economy. This can be described as the "induced-growth gain" from trade. If investment goods are mostly imported, then this induced-growth gain will also include the effect of reduced prices of investment goods. Moreover, it is possible that the opening up of trade (or the rising trade-volume/GNP ratio) will also raise the rate of growth of an economy by directly increasing the country's propensity to save.

7. Assuming realistic exchange rates, EP can be sustained mostly by subsidies. Since the costs of excess subsidies are quite visible, there are built-in forces against excessive EP. The equivalent costs of IS are borne by firms and consumers; hence opposing pressures do not emerge as rapidly. Under IS, government officials have the power to remove or enhance the domestic monopoly positions of firms, and consequently the firms can be subject to intolerable interventions into their decision-making processes. Under an EP regime, with firms engaged primarily in the export market, officials simply do not have the same degree of power.

2.2 Protection, Offsetting Policy Measures, and Growth

In a typical developing economy, with typical political power balances, import restrictions—in the form of both tariffs and quotas—have to be accepted as a fact of life. However, as shown by Johnson (1967) and Bhagwati (1968), when industrial promotion and growth are by and large biased in favor of the production of commodities in which the country has a comparative advantage, the adverse efficiency and welfare effects of the protection (which is attuned to the sectors with comparative disadvantage) are alleviated as the economy grows and as policy measures promoting industry are enforced.

Figure 7.1 illustrates such an economy. With free trade the country produces x and y at f. In order to highlight only the aspect of "protection-cum-second-best-policy," we now postulate a small open economy in which all kinds of external economies are completely taken care of by a set of ideal taxes and subsidies. Consequently, the production-possibility curves represent the "true" ones and, in the absence of tariff protection, production and consumption are determined at the welfare-maximizing optimal points.

With a tariff-distorted domestic price ratio p^*, however, the country finds itself producing outputs at q, adversely affecting the production of the exportable, y. Consumption is at c where an international price line, p, passing through q intersects the Engel line corresponding to the domestic price ratio p^*. Postulating a set of well-behaving homothetic social indifference curves, we have drawn a linear Engel line that represents the income-consumption path corresponding to the given commodity price ratio; bq of y is exported, and bc of x is imported, but an amount equivalent to tc of x is taken away as government tariff revenue. To avoid cluttering the geometry, the diagram omits the social indifference curves, one of which passes through C with a slope equal to that of p^*. It is assumed that tariff revenue is not redistributed to the private sector as an income subsidy, but instead is spent by the government.[8]

When import restrictions are a fact of life, there are always second-best policies to consider: in the presence of irremovable import-substitution-biased commodity-market distortions, a country can adopt certain offsetting policy measures to promote production and exports of the unprotected sector. At the given factor-supply level, and holding

---

8. Figure 7.2 elaborates this aspect: tariff revenue is equivalent to d^*d units of x which is spent on gc of x and gc^* of y by the government, resulting in exports of bq of y and imports of bc of x for the country as a whole.

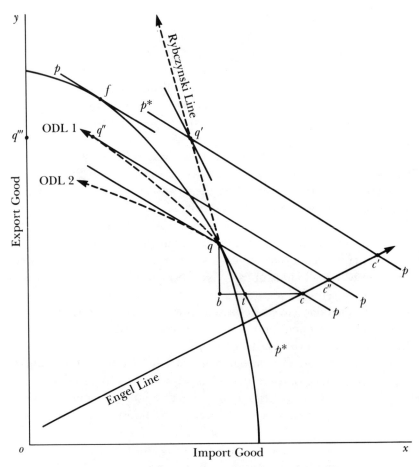

Fig. 7.1. Tarriff Protection and Second-Best Policies

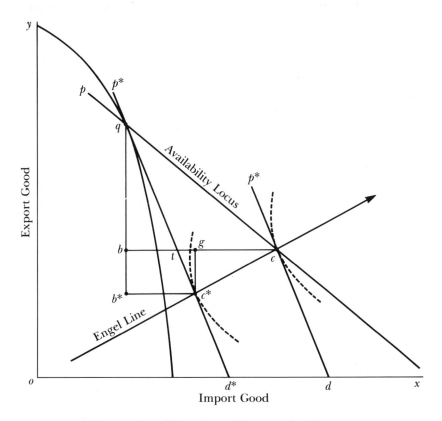

Fig. 7.2. Tariff Revenue and Aggregate Consumption Pattern
NOTE: *do* represents national product at domestic market prices, *d*o* national product at factor cost, and *dd** the total revenue from tariffs. This represents the case of balanced trade and no factor payments to other countries. National expenditure and product are equal in size.

the distorted domestic price ratio unaltered at p^*, the government can try to shift the output pattern in the direction of f by introducing a second-best policy measure such as subsidized credit rationing in favor of y. This will necessarily result in by-product efficiency losses in production, and place the economy inside the given production-possibility curve. In figure 7.1 such a policy leads the output pattern to move along a path like "Offsetting Distortion" (OD) line 1 (ODL 1).[9] This implies that the stronger the offsetting factor-market distortions, the larger the domestic production and exports of y at the expense of x will be.

In a two-factor (capital and labor) framework, we may let y represent the consumption good, which is capital-intensive, and x the agricultural product, which is labor-intensive, completely ignoring the existence of any other raw materials and intermediate and capital goods. In figure 7.1, a shift in output pattern to a point like q'' along the OD line is equivalent (in terms of the increase in output level of y) to the capital accumulation and growth along the familiar Rybczynski line up to the point q'. The Rybczynski line is the locus of tangencies of the fixed (tariff-distorted) domestic price ratio with the (undrawn) production-possibility curves resulting from successive accumulation of capital. Both movements will imply an increase in real income and a rise in export/GNP ratio.

As mentioned earlier, such second-best promotion policies will inevitably create efficiency losses. These losses, if large enough, could cause real national income to become smaller than it was in the absence of offsetting intervention—even though there may be substantial shifts in the output pattern and an increase in the export/GNP ratio. Offsetting Distortion line 2 (ODL 2) in figure 7.1 shows the immiserizing path of declining real national income.

In a dynamic context, there will be continual increases in factor supplies and technical progress that shift out the production-possibility curve. In figure 7.1 growth (or capital accumulation) is biased in favor of the unprotected export industry and hence is not immiserizing. So long as import-restriction-induced distortions in commodity markets are maintained, the need for continuous policy-induced structural adjustments through offsetting government policy measures,

9. When the policy measure takes the form of, say, factor-market distortions, the feasible production-possibility curve will shrink in, and there will be no tangency between the commodity price ratio and the feasible production-possibility curve. The Offsetting Distortion lines in figure 7.1 represent the locus of distorted domestic commodity price ratios (p^*) intersecting the various shrunk-in feasible production-possibility curves.

though perhaps reduced with growth, will never disappear—even in the absence of external economies. The trade triangle may, for instance, shift along the Rybczynski line from the one with the hypotenuse qc to the one with the hypotenuse $q'c'$, or shift along the ODL 1 from the triangle with the hypotenuse qc to the one with the hypotenuse $q''c''$. In a real economy, a combination of both movements will be present.

2.3 Protection, Reinforcing Distortion, and Growth

Just as policies favoring the comparatively advantaged (nonprotected) industries can offset some of the adverse effects of protection, this section illustrates how industrial promotion of the protected (comparatively disadvantaged) industries aggravates, or reinforces, these effects.

In figure 7.3 y represents the intermediate and capital goods sector, which is capital-intensive, and x represents the consumer goods sector, which is labor-intensive. Output and consumption are at q and c, respectively, with tariff protection of the now import-competing y sector. Tariff revenue is equivalent to ct of y. Since the international price line p has been drawn steeper than the Rybczynski line, capital accumulation results in immiserization. We further postulate that the government promotes the import-competing y sector by, say, maintaining a credit-rationing system. The capital-intensive sector is now not only protected by tariffs, but is also promoted by other policy measures. Hence figure 7.3 presents the case in which the government nontariff policy measure induces the immiserizing structural adjustments along RDL (the Reinforcing Distortion line). In the growth process, the nontariff policy measures will reinforce the decline in y imports and also the immiserization.

Evidence suggests that aspects of immiserizing growth did exist in Korea, especially in the late 1970s, that were serious enough to substantially reduce the allocative efficiency of the economy.

2.4 Protection of Monopolistic Export Industries

In figure 7.3 growth by capital accumulation will (with or without the reinforcing distortions) eventually lead the output point to reach the Engel line, beyond which y becomes exported. With a perfectly competitive market structure, protection of the y sector beyond the Engel line is meaningless. However, Robinson (1969) shows that when the export sector consists of a monopolistic producer, import restriction of export goods can have the effect of expanding the proportion of export sales to total sales (at the expense of consumers' surplus) without resulting in allocative inefficiency. Monopolistic profit maximization through

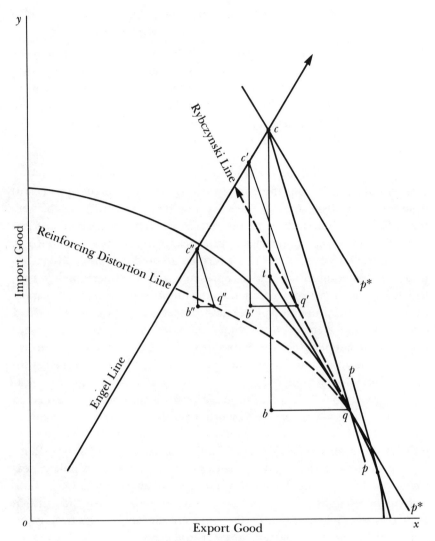

Fig. 7.3. Immiserizing Growth

price discrimination in the domestic market does not cause the total output of the good to differ from that of free trade; it only expands the proportion of the export sales out of a given quantity of total output. That is, protection of the monopolistic export sector raises the export/ GNP ratio, results in a redistribution of income in favor of the monopolist and against the domestic consumer, and may even cause a premature exportation of the import good, but it does not affect allocative efficiency.

3. PROTECTION AND LIBERALIZATION IN THE EARLY PHASE OF KOREA'S GROWTH

3.1 1961–67: Import Liberalization and an Export-Promotion Regime

As a result of the heavy bias toward import substitution in the 1950s, Korea's commodity markets were significantly distorted. As a result, the labor-abundant Korean economy had not actively taken advantage of the gains to be made from trade à la Hecksher-Ohlin, and maintained an only half-open economy. With the initiation of the export-promotion strategy in 1961, the Korean government replaced its multiple exchange-rate system with a unitary one, made a series of exchange-rate adjustments to rectify the extremely overvalued domestic currency, and above all tried to prevent the direct impact of its own extremely protectionist import-restriction regime from negating the newly created incentives for export activities.[10]

Four principal policy measures were adopted in Korea in order to pursue this new export-oriented growth strategy: vigorous administrative support for export promotion, a preferential tax system, a subsidy allocation for export activities, and, finally, a reduction of the import-substitution biases of the economy. This last was especially important, because extreme import restrictions may well more than offset any kind of incentives given to export activities. For example, both tariffs and quotas are equivalent to taxes on imports, which, in turn, can become taxes on exports. Also, when direct import restraints are used as the instrument for correcting balance-of-payments deficits, exports will suffer—the exchange rate will be overvalued, and hence the competitive power of the export industries will be reduced.

In other words, a country cannot launch an export-promotion strategy while maintaining extreme forms of import restriction. Thus,

10. For details of the shifts in trade policies during 1961–67, see Frank, Kim, and Westphal 1975, chap. 4 and Hong 1979, chap. 5.

when it was decided that this was the policy to be followed, the Korean government had to free export producers from the negative effects of tariff protection and quantitative restraints at the outset, by allowing tariff-exempt imports of the raw materials and investment goods that were directly used in the export-production process. Furthermore, the government tried to reduce the general level of quantitative import restrictions, culminating in the introduction of the negative list system in the second half of 1967.

In the period 1961–63, the number of items positively listed as importables (subject to government import licensing, quotas, foreign-exchange allocation ceilings, linkages to exports, and other regulations) fluctuated in the range of 1,000 to 1,600. Feeling the pressure of balance-of-payments deficits, the government reduced the number of importable items to fewer than 500 in late 1964, but then restored the 1961–63 level in 1965; the number of importable items was increased from 1,778 to 2,491 in 1966, and 3,852 by July 1967, when the switch to the negative list system occurred. Now just the "prohibited" or "restricted" import items were recorded.

Under the negative list system, only a handful of the manufactured goods belonging to SITC (Standard International Trade Classification) code numbers 6 and 8, as well as certain food products, got classified as "Automatic Approval" import items. Most finished consumption goods were either classified as "Restricted Import" items or as "Prohibited Import" items.[11] The government effectively controlled the import of these restricted items by imposing annual import ceilings. Furthermore, there were numerous special laws for selected industries that, purely incidentally or with expressly protectionist intentions, restricted the import of related "automatically approved" commodities. In principle, restricted imports that competed with domestic production were allowed only to fill the estimated gap between domestic supply and demand. Quantitative import controls of noncompetitive raw materials and intermediate and capital goods (which were classified as restricted items and were not directly related to export activities) seem to have been influenced entirely by the overall balance-of-payments situation.

11. From 1967 to 1981 the Ministry of Trade and Industry (MTI) announced the semi-annual or annual lists of "Prohibited Import" items separately from the list of restricted items. Since 1982, however, the prohibited items have been listed together with the restricted ones, noting that such items may be imported subject to procedures as may be separately announced by the MTI, but without actually making such separate announcements.

Imports of raw materials and intermediate inputs and investment goods for foreign exchange-earning activities, on the other hand, were approved automatically, irrespective of their classification.[12] Furthermore, imports financed by government-contracted foreign loans were permitted after consultation with the Trade Committee, irrespective of classification.[13] All in all, according to Frank, Kim, and Westphal (1975, 58), out of 30,000 SITC commodities, the number of "automatic approval" items expanded from 2,760 in the first half of 1967 to 17,128 in the second half, while the number of "prohibited import" items was reduced from 26,148 to 2,617.[14]

Since the old system of commodity classification (used prior to the second half of 1967) was significantly different from the more systematic classification (into 30,000 items based on the UN's SITC manual), these numbers can only serve as a crude first approximation of the degree of liberalization. Nonetheless, we still conclude that the minimum requirements of import liberalization were satisfied in Korea, and that the remaining import-substitution biases could have been more than offset in the 1960s and 1970s by various policy measures to promote exports of manufactures.

3.2 1967–78: Protectionist Regime

This section gives a rough description of Korea's protectionist regime during the period 1967–78, and shows that little progress in import liberalization was made after 1967.

Following the introduction of the negative list system, the average basic legal tariff rate (weighted by import value of each commodity) was raised from about 17 percent in 1963–67 to about 26 percent in 1968–72. From 1964 to 1972 there was also a special tariff law that empowered the Ministry of Finance to collect additional special tariffs (up to 90 percent of the differential between the estimated wholesale value and the import cost) on nonessential imports.[15]

12. Until 1977 imports of plant facilities for export production were permitted after consultation with the Trade Committee.

13. Since the second half of 1975 imports financed by foreign loan funds have been permitted according to special procedures set by the MTI. The clause on imports financed by government-contracted loans disappeared in the first half of 1977.

14. Even the negative list system in principle, allowed the import of restricted items when the prices of competing domestic products were extremely high or their quality extremely poor.

15. There was another important form of import restriction that had tariff equivalent effect: since 1961 importers have had to make advance deposits of varying amounts as specified for each category of commodities.

It was only after the 1973 tariff reform (which abolished the special tariff system) that the tariff rate was reduced to a 20 percent level (the average legal tariff rate for all commodities amounted to 20 percent in 1973–74 and 1976) and to 19 percent in 1978.[16] However, because of the tariff exemptions or reductions that were granted on the imports of raw materials directly used for export production and on the capital goods imported for foreign direct investment projects, export production, and other important industries, the actual tariff rate (the amount of tariff revenue collected divided by the total c.i.f. value of imports) amounted to only about 9 percent on average during 1962–71, and about 7 percent throughout the period 1972–83.[17] The average tariff rate actually collected, then, does not seem to have been extremely high in Korea— but since those tariffs collected were mostly from the commodities whose imports were "approved," they do not tell the magnitude of the import premium, or the effective rates of protection, generated by the quota system (see tables 7.1 and 7.2).

When the government changed from the positive list of quantitative restrictions to the negative list system in 1967, the nominal import liberalization ratio by item (on the basis of 1,312 SITC 5-digit classification) amounted to nearly 60 percent. However, as mentioned above, there was no further movement toward liberalization after 1967, and in fact the import-liberalization ratio rather steadily declined thereafter to become about 50 percent by the first half of 1978. According to table 7.3, the number of restricted import items, as well as their share in total value of imports, was substantially larger in 1978 than it had been in 1967. There were significant increases in import restrictions (both in terms of number of items and value of imports) of machinery, chemicals, and other manufactures (except textiles) during 1967–78. Even raw materials were subject to increased import restrictions. It was only after the

16. Data from Hong 1979, 322–49, and Republic of Korea 1983b, 8. According to Frank, Kim, and Westphal (1975, 61 and 63), the simple arithmetic average tariff rate amounted to about 42 percent in 1966–68, about 39 percent in 1972 (including the special tariffs), and about 31 percent after the 1973 tariff reform.

17. For instance, in 1982, 25 percent of commodity imports constituted materials for export production that were tariff exempt, another 25 percent was crude oil, which was subject to a zero tariff rate, 3.7 percent were minerals that paid no tariffs, and 5.3 percent of imports were exempt from tariffs by various provisions. As a result, about 59 percent of imports were duty-free. The average actual tariff rate for raw materials and intermediate inputs (which amounted to 14 percent of total imports) was 17.6 percent, the rate for capital goods (17 percent of total imports) was 13.1 percent, and that for grains (8 percent of total imports) was 2.3 percent. The actual tariff rate for consumption goods (3 percent of total imports) was 32.1 percent. See Republic of Korea 1983a, 10.

second half of 1978 that the import-liberalization ratio (both by items and by value) began to increase.

Between 1970 and 1975, out of Korea's total commodity imports the share of consumption goods amounted to only about 5 percent. The share of foodstuffs amounted to about 16.6 percent in 1970 and 14.3 percent in 1975. Consequently, about 80 percent of Korea's imports during this period consisted of raw materials, intermediate-input materials, and capital goods.[18] On the basis of this observed composition of trade, Korea's protectionist regime may be characterized as follows: imports of agricultural products were restrained to the minimum necessary levels, while preferential treatment was given to the import of capital goods (in order to accelerate investment activities) and to raw materials and intermediate goods (in order to raise the utilization rate of existing production capacity). As a result, at least until the mid 1970s, the quantitative import restrictions were essentially set against agricultural products and finished consumption goods. This is important; it means that the import restrictions did not directly affect the production of other (export) goods.

3.3 Growth Performance of the Korean Economy

In the 1950s Korea's imports were mostly financed by foreign grants-in-aid. The opening up of the Korean economy to trade (through the switch to an export-oriented growth strategy) occurred over an extended period of time, spanning the 1960s and 1970s. The efficiency gains from this action materialized in the form of both rapidly increasing real wage rates and rising rates of return on investment. The average gross rates of return on investment in the Korean manufacturing sector increased from about 12 percent in 1954–61 to about 23 percent in 1972–79 (see table 7.4). Over the period 1962–79, there were also rapid increases in domestic savings, which, together with the productivity gains from trade, allowed nearly 10 percent average annual growth rates of GNP. The average annual growth rate of GNP rose from about 4 percent in 1953–61 to about 8 percent in 1962–66 and to almost 10 percent in 1967–79 (see table 7.5).

18. Owing to the drastic jump in the price of crude oil, the share of raw materials in total commodity imports rose from about 18 percent in 1970 to about 27 percent in 1975, while the share of capital goods fell from 28 percent in 1970 to 22.5 percent in 1975. However, the share of intermediate-input materials did not change much, amounting to about 32 percent of Korea's total commodity imports through 1970–75. The import data were obtained from material provided by the Bank of Korea Input-Output Tables.

TABLE 7.1   Nominal and Effective Rates of Protection by Sector in South Korea
(in %)

	Agricultural Sector	Manufacturing				All Tradable Sectors			
		Total	Export Sector	Export-Import	Import-Competing	Total	Export Sector	Export-Import	Import Competing
Nominal Rates of Protection									
1963	27	39	47	55	33	33	29	49	29
1970	28	24	16	76	46	25	9	74	39
1978	83	25	28	38	39	36	34	38	53
Effective Rates of Protection for Domestic Sales (Corden Method)									
1963	31	26	50	78	15	30	7	77	30
1970	31	18	5	79	64	24	− 4	74	44
1978	92	13	18	22	29	38	29	22	57

SOURCE: Kim and Hong 1982.

NOTES: Sectors that exported more than 10 percent of total output as of 1970 are classified as Export Sectors, sectors in which imports took more than 10 percent of total domestic supply are classified as Import-Competing Sectors, and sectors that exported and imported more than 10 percent are classified as Export-Import Sectors. Others (not shown in the table) are regarded as Noncompeting Sectors and are taken into account in the estimation of the weighted average rate for total sectors.

Nominal rate of protection represents the percentage difference between domestic and c.i.f. price of an equivalent item. Effective rate of protection refers to the protection granted to domestic value-added activities in a particular production line, quantified by the percentage difference between the value-added in domestic prices and that in world prices.

TABLE 7.2 Import Liberalization Ratios and Rates of Protection in South Korea
(in %)

	Liberalization Ratio in 1982		Nominal Rate of Protection		Real Rate of Protection (Corden Method)	
	Proportion of Automatic Approval Items	Excluding Special Law Items	1978	1982	1978	1982
Agriculture and fisheries	75.8	36.8	43.4	66.3	54.5	70.6
Tobacco	100.0	25.0	19.3	16.3	73.7	50.0
Mining and energy	94.5	82.7	0.5	0.3	– 1.3	– 1.5
Beverages	10.9	6.5	11.3	8.8	– 0.1	– 8.6
Processed foods	50.1	29.1	16.8	19.8	– 30.0	– 33.8
Durable consumption goods	56.5	49.8	54.7	26.1	119.4	36.0
Nondurable consumption goods	73.1	53.9	28.7	21.3	42.2	28.1
(textiles)	(79.2)	(79.2)	(30.5)	(27.2)	(61.0)	(60.6)
Construction materials	99.2	96.2	7.0	26.3	8.5	33.5
Intermediate goods I	85.2	76.0	11.1	14.6	25.5	39.7
Intermediate goods II	91.9	57.9	13.8	19.2	13.3	24.3
(Chemical products)	(94.7)	(31.5)	(29.1)	(31.5)	(55.4)	(49.7)
(Nonferrous metal)	(82.9)	(80.1)	(8.0)	(23.9)	(9.3)	(28.1)
(Iron and steel)	(91.7)	(91.3)	(16.0)	(14.5)	(20.0)	(24.9)
Machinery	65.0	63.1	28.9	22.6	41.6	21.2
Electrical machinery	47.0	39.1	42.1	27.5	78.7	41.3
Transport equipment	48.2	48.2	46.6	31.1	97.5	52.1
All manufacturing	76.5	56.8	19.1	19.4	20.6	18.5
All industries	76.8	56.1	25.2	31.7	34.1	38.4

SOURCE: Young et al. 1982.

TABLE 7.3 Shifts in Proportion of Restricted Imports in South Korea by Sector
(value in millions of U.S. $)

	1967 Total Imports	1967 Restricted Imports	1978 Total Imports	1978 Restricted Imports	1981 Total Imports	1981 Restricted Imports
All commodities—by item	1,312	546 (41.7)	1,312	652 (49.7)	1,312	443 (33.8)
—by value	994	331 (33.3)	14,609	8,424 (57.7)	24,912	8,756 (35.2)
All manufactures—by item	976	456 (46.7)	976	491 (50.3)	976	313 (32.1)
—by value	624	284 (45.4)	8,717	6,607 (75.8)	10,783	7,124 (66.1)
0,1.[a] Foodstuffs, raw—by item	114	38 (33.3)	114	68 (58.8)	114	61 (53.5)
—by value	93	12 (12.8)	944	398 (42.2)	2,742	659 (25.1)
2,4. Raw materials—by item	198	48 (24.2)	198	92 (46.5)	198	69 (27.8)
—by value	215	32 (14.6)	2,495	1,414 (56.7)	3,645	943 (25.9)
3. Mineral fuels—by item	24	4 (16.7)	24	1 (4.2)	24	— (—)
—by value	62	4 (6.5)	2,453	6 (0.2)	7,742	— (—)
0,1. Food manufactures—by item	37	24 (62.2)	37	31 (83.8)	37	25 (67.6)
—by value	2	2 (83.3)	30	28 (93.6)	34	30 (88.5)
5. Chemicals—by item	195	43 (22.1)	195	52 (26.7)	195	28 (14.4)
—by value	113	26 (22.8)	1,312	789 (59.5)	1,995	1,164 (58.4)
65. Textiles—by item	97	75 (77.3)	97	55 (56.7)	97	27 (27.8)
—by value	71	62 (88.0)	322	214 (66.4)	399	182 (45.7)
67. Iron and steel—by item	60	17 (28.3)	60	45 (75.0)	60	32 (53.3)
—by value	56	20 (35.4)	965	880 (91.2)	1,000	469 (46.9)
6-. Other manufactures—by item	246	121 (49.2)	246	94 (38.2)	246	40 (16.3)
—by value	58	24 (41.4)	750	509 (67.9)	1,151	396 (34.4)
7. Machinery—by item	145	49 (33.8)	145	86 (61.4)	145	82 (56.6)
—by value	307	140 (45.6)	4,787	3,768 (78.7)	5,504	4,404 (80.0)
8,9. Misc. manufactures—by item	196	127 (65.0)	196	125 (63.8)	196	79 (40.3)
—by value	17	10 (56.4)	552	428 (77.6)	700	478 (68.3)

SOURCES: Korean Traders Association 1968; Republic of Korea, Ministry of Trade and Industry, *Semi-Annual Export-Import Notice* (first half of 1978 and of 1981), *Yearbook of Foreign Trade Statistics*, and *Standard Korean Trade Classification*; and United Nations 1963.

NOTE: Figures in parentheses are percentages.

During the 1953–61 period of import substitution, Korea was insignificant as an exporter of primary products, and the export/GNP ratio amounted to only about 0.01. By pursuing the export-promotion strategy, Korea became an exporter of manufactures, and the export/GNP ratio rose rapidly from about 0.04 in 1962–66 to about 0.26 in 1977–79. Commodity exports expanded from a mere $33 million in 1960 to about $15 billion in 1979, and the proportion of manufactures out of total commodity exports increased from about 15 percent in 1960 to more than 90 percent by 1979.

As the case of Korea proves, an export-oriented economy can achieve both high growth performance in output and export expansion with just a minimum (but necessary) degree of import liberalization. Obviously, the fairly extensive quota and tariff systems that Korea maintained throughout the period 1967–79 did not prevent it from achieving high rates of growth in either of these areas. Hence it is fair to say that the export-promotion policy measures more than offset any possible adverse effects from the tariffs and quotas. In fact, the system of tariff protection may even have contributed positively to Korea's growth. Real GNP grew about 9 percent per annum during 1962–84, and domestic savings expanded from about 4 percent of GNP in 1953–61 to about 25 percent in 1976–85. Government saving was negative prior to 1964, and negligible in 1964–66. However, it amounted to an average of about 5.5 percent of GNP during 1967–85, and about 40 percent of this was financed by tariff revenue—in spite of the fact that the actual rate of tariffs was reduced from about 9.1 percent in 1967–71 to about 6.2 percent in 1980–85. Because the Korean government has been directly involved in various productive investment activities, the static negative effects of the tariff system have to be weighed against its positive contributions of reducing consumption, enhancing domestic savings, and increasing productive investment. (This possibility has been indicated in figure 7.2.)

Owing to the fact that prior to the mid 1970s imports of intermediate and capital goods were subject to less severe quantitative controls than were consumption goods, import substitution of these products had not been as profitable as it had been for consumption goods, and hence was relatively slow. It might sound paradoxical, but Korea's early failure to extensively promote the intermediate and capital-goods industries seems to have contributed positively to rapid export expansion. That is, manufacturers of export goods were relatively free to use low-cost imported intermediate and capital goods rather than having to use high-cost domestic products—even when these products were classified as

TABLE 7.4 Gross Rates of Return on Investment in Manufacturing in South Korea

Annual Average	(a) Incremental Output-Capital Ratio	(b) Share of Capital in Value-Added (I-O data)	(c) Ratio of Net Working Capital to Fixed Assets	(d) Estimated Capital Gain (per annum)	Estimated Rates of Return		
					(e) $= (a \times b)$	(f) $= e/(1+c)$	(g) $= (f+d)$
1954–61	0.345	0.493	0.300	−0.01	0.17	0.13	0.12
1962–66	0.448	0.489	0.300	−0.03	0.22	0.17	0.14
1967–71	0.448	0.503	0.227	−0.01	0.23	0.18	0.17
1972–76	0.679	0.590	0.269	−0.09	0.40	0.32	0.23
1977–79	0.594	0.551	0.112	−0.06	0.33	0.29	0.23
1980–83	0.279	0.466	−0.043	−0.06	0.13	0.14	0.08
1981–83	0.382	0.468	−0.051	−0.02	0.18	0.19	0.17

SOURCES: Bank of Korea, *Price Statistics Summary, Financial Statement Analysis, National Income Accounts,* and *Input-Output Tables of Korea* (various issues).

[a] Gross incremental value-added/fixed capital ratios were computed allowing a one-year time lag between the increase in value-added (at 1980 constant factor cost, which does not include indirect taxes) and gross fixed-capital formation.

[b] Imputed wages for unpaid family workers were excluded from the share of capital in value-added.

[c] In order to take account of the fact that average firms also use (net) working capital in addition to fixed capital, the rates of return figures were deflated by the amount of net working capital.

[d] Capital loss was approximated by the differences between the rates of increase in average prices of capital goods and those of the wholesale price index for all commodities.

[e] These estimates differ from those of Hong (1979, 189): 12% in 1954–61, 17% in 1962–66, 26% in 1967–71, and 27% in 1972–75. Estimates in this table use income statistics of 1980 base year and incremental value-added/gross-investment ratios while Hong's estimates use income statistics of 1970 base year and the inverse of ICOR (incremental capital/output ratios) in computing output attributed to gross investment. Further, estimates of this table exclude indirect taxes (subsidies) from total value-added in computing the share of capital in value-added. For a more detailed discussion of the estimation of rate of return on investment, see Hong 1979, 176–96.

TABLE 7.5 Growth, Trade, Savings and Tariff in South Korea

Average Annual	Growth Rate (%)		Ratio to GNP (%)					Actual Tariff Rates[c]	Nominal Import-Liberalization Ratio[c]
	GNP	Manufacturing	Commodity Exports[a]	Commodity Imports[a]	Gross Investment	Foreign Saving	Government Saving[b]		
1953–61	4.0	10.5	1.1	10.6	12.4	8.0	−2.6	—	—
1962–66	7.9	15.1	4.4	15.3	16.3	8.6	0.6	9.5	—
1967–71	9.7	21.8	9.5	22.8	25.7	10.1	5.6 (35.4)	9.1	57
1972–76	9.7	19.2	23.7	31.0	27.0	6.7	3.9 (49.1)	6.2	51
1977–79	9.6	15.9	25.9	30.0	31.5	3.6	6.1 (38.3)	8.1	61
1980	−5.2	−1.1	29.8	36.9	32.2	11.5	5.4 (38.5)	5.4	69
1981	6.6	7.5	32.7	37.0	30.3	9.8	5.6 (35.2)	5.1	75
1982	5.4	4.1	31.5	33.9	28.6	7.0	6.1 (32.5)	5.7	77
1983	11.9	12.2	32.9	33.8	29.9	4.8	7.2 (34.3)	7.1	80
1984	8.4	14.8	34.4	34.4	31.9	4.0	7.1 (34.0)	6.8	85
1985	5.1	3.5	33.9	33.9	31.2	3.1	6.3 (37.1)	6.9	88

SOURCES: Bank of Korea, *National Income Accounts* and *Economic Statistics Yearbook*; Republic of Korea, National Tax Administration, *Statistical Yearbook of National Tax*; Republic of Korea, Ministry of Trade and Industry, *Semi-Annual Export-Import Notice*. Various years.

[a] c.i.f. values.
[b] Figures in parentheses represent the proportion of government savings financed by tariff revenue.
[c] Percentage.

restricted import items. This factor, combined with the low cost of labor, seems to have helped Korea achieve an extremely rapid export expansion.

4. PROTECTIONIST POLICIES IN THE LATER STAGES OF GROWTH

4.1 The Mid 1970s: Protection of Intermediate and Investment Goods Sectors
As noted, until the mid 1970s, both Korea's industrial production and its exports were dominated by final-consumption goods, whose production was labor intensive and depended heavily on imported intermediate and investment goods. Import restrictions were mostly on consumption goods, at the expense of Korean consumers. This apparently was not fatal to the growth performance of the economy. However, with the beginning of the third five-year economic development plan (1972–76), the Korean government began to promote "heavy and chemical" industries, and actually implemented various tax-cum-financial incentives for these industries[19] (see Hong 1979, chap. 4). As a result, there was extensive domestic production of hitherto imported intermediate and investment goods by the late 1970s. Unfortunately, many of the so-called heavy and chemical industries promoted by the government were excessively capital-intensive, and Korea did not have the comparative advantage necessary to successfully compete against foreign products. As a result, promotion came to imply somewhat extensive import restrictions on these capital-intensive intermediate and investment goods, and both the growth rate of exports and of GNP would be affected.

As early as 1972 when the first petrochemical factories began operation, MTI changed ten petrochemical products from "automatically approved" to "restricted import" items. Such practices intensified and became more frequent in the late 1970s. Since 1976 those wishing to import machinery worth more $1 million, and financed either by foreign loans or foreign-currency loans from domestic banks have had to report in advance to MTI (and after 1985 to the Korea Machine Industry Promotion Association). As a condition for approving the import of the domestically unproducible portion of the machinery, MTI specified

19. The Korean government had already established a legal foundation for promoting the so-called heavy and chemical industries. During the second five-year economic development plan period (1967–71), "promotion laws" were introduced for the machine industry and shipbuilding (1967), for electronics (1969), and for steel and petrochemicals (1970). Each of these laws specified various tax-cum-financial supports for the respective industry.

a certain portion that must be produced domestically. MTI also specified the required domestic-content ratios for selected plant facilities that cost more than $3 million and were financed by foreign loans or foreign-currency loans.[20]

According to table 7.3, the proportion of restricted import items in the machinery sector (in value terms) amounted to about 46 percent of total machinery imports in 1967, rising to about 79 percent in 1978, and to 80 percent in 1981. In the chemicals sector, the share of restricted items increased from about 23 percent in 1967 to about 60 percent in 1978, and was 58 percent in 1981. As shown in table 7.6 chemicals imports have been restricted mostly by special laws rather than by MTI classification notices.

4.2 Impact on Export Production and Trade Pattern

The Korean government's decision to change its emphasis and promote the "infant" intermediate and investment-goods industries was not simply for the sake of self-sufficiency in these sectors, but also so that they would eventually become the new generation of leading exports. The government believed that tariff protection and quantitative restraints were indispensable policy measures for initiating the domestic production of these products. Unfortunately, such policies could not help but generate the familiar efficiency-reducing effects associated with import substitution, and they immediately affected the production costs of related downstream domestic industries. Eventually, the adverse effects were passed on to export-production activities. Unlike in the earlier period, this time government promotion activities did not offset the efficiency losses of protection, but rather encouraged them.

Until early 1971 any intermediate input that was needed for export production could be freely imported, even if it were classified as a restricted import item. However, in October 1971 MTI made 41 intermediate input materials for export production (including even important textile fibers) subject to pre-import approval. In 1975, 12 more items were added to the list, and by 1982, 61 intermediate input items (based on the 4-digit CCCN classification) were subject to the prior-to-import approval system. Moreover, the import of selected plant facilities for eight industries was completely prohibited, even when they were to be

20. Selected plant facilities have included cement, fertilizer, ethanol, thermal and hydro power generation, oil refinery, formalin (since 1976); polyethylene, synthetic rubber, polyester, steel (since 1977); ethylene, PVC, polyprophylene, caustic soda (since 1978); caprolactam, paper, paperboard, atomic power generation (since 1979); radial tire, liquid gas, naphtha cracking (since 1980); VCM, EDC, soda ash (since 1981); and so on.

TABLE 7.6 Restricted Import Items and Their Import Values in South Korea by Sector, 1984

| | Number of Items Imported | | | Value of Imports (Million U.S. $) | | |
| | | Imports Restricted by | | | Imports Restricted by | |
	Total Items	MTI Notice	Special Law	Total Imports	MTI Notice	Special Law
All commodities	7,915	1,203 (15.2)	1,302 (16.5)	30,631	8,508 (27.8)	9,823 (32.1)
All manufactures	6,595	952 (14.4)	987 (15.0)	17,636	7,732 (43.8)	1,451 (8.2)
0,1.[a] Foodstuffs, raw	515	180 (35.0)	138 (27.2)	1,586	411 (25.9)	1,087 (68.5)
2,4. Raw materials	680	71 (10.4)	117 (17.2)	4,113	365 (8.9)	772 (18.8)
3. Mineral fuels	125	— (—)	60 (48.0)	7,296	— (—)	6,513 (89.3)
0,1. Food manufactures	172	118 (68.6)	6 (3.5)	101	79 (78.2)	1 (0.7)
51. Organic chemicals	557	31 (5.6)	348 (62.5)	1,247	624 (50.0)	483 (38.7)
58. Resins and plastic	138	21 (15.2)	22 (15.9)	469	160 (34.3)	101 (21.5)
5-. Other chemicals	944	14 (1.5)	397 (42.1)	995	176 (17.7)	383 (38.5)
65. Textiles	578	52 (9.0)	8 (1.4)	631	133 (21.0)	2 (0.3)
666. Pottery	25	18 (72.0)	— (—)	1	1 (80.6)	— (—)
667. Precious stones	23	18 (78.3)	— (—)	13	7 (53.8)	— (—)
67. Iron and steel	249	15 (6.0)	9 (3.6)	1,324	97 (7.4)	4 (0.3)
68. Nonferrous metal	149	28 (18.8)	2 (1.3)	531	348 (65.5)	— (—)
6-. Other manufactures	914	25 (2.7)	40 (4.4)	1,278	168 (12.9)	71 (5.6)
76,776. Electronics	122	69 (56.6)	12 (9.8)	2,068	1,306 (63.2)	9 (0.4)
78. Road vehicles	97	58 (60.0)	— (—)	239	215 (90.0)	— (—)
79. Other transport eq.	130	25 (19.2)	— (—)	3,401	2,441 (80.3)	— (—)
7-. Other machinery	1,188	290 (24.4)	92 (7.7)	4,470	1,520 (34.0)	203 (4.5)
895-7. Jewelry, art work	77	51 (66.2)	5 (6.5)	30	25 (83.8)	1 (3.3)
8,9. Other misc.	1,232	118 (9.6)	46 (3.7)	1,193	432 (36.2)	193 (16.2)

SOURCES: Republic of Korea, Ministry of Trade and Industry, *Yearbook of Foreign Trade Statistics* (1984); *Semi-Annual Export-Import Notice* (second half of 1984 and first half of 1985); *Standard Korean Trade Classification* (1984).

NOTE: Figures in parentheses are percentages.

[a] Standard International Trade Classification (SITC).

used for export production. In 1985, 54 intermediate input materials for export production were subject to the requirement of a prior recommendation. Among them, about 20 items (mostly petrochemical products) could obtain the recommendation when domestic supply prices exceeded c.i.f. import prices by more than 3 to 10 percent.

By 1974 the tariff exemption on capital equipment for export production had also been changed—to tariff "payments on an installment basis," and in 1975 the tariff exemption on raw material imports for export production was changed to a "tariff drawback" or refund, after making initial payments to the government. In late 1977 the Korean government introduced the "limited tariff drawback" system on materials imported for export production. Out of the 117 items subject to this system, 87 were given zero percent drawback (no tariff exemption at all) and the other 30 were allowed between 2 and 97 percent drawbacks of the tariffs that been paid at the time of customs clearance.[21]

The number of items subject to the limited tariff drawback system was reduced to 62 in early 1980, and then expanded to 128 by mid 1981, to 212 by early 1982, and to 266 by mid 1983.[22] By the end of 1984, 170 items were subject to zero percent drawback, and 84 items were subject to between 2 and 90 percent drawback. In principle, the tariff drawbacks on these items are allowed only on the portion that cannot be satisfied by domestic supply, regardless of domestic price. This has generated continuous conflicts between the users (export producers) and the suppliers (domestic import-competing producers) of the specific intermediate inputs.

According to Young et al. (1982, 49), in 1978 the average effective rate of protection for heavy and chemical industries amounted to 71.2 percent, while that for light industries amounted to − 2.3 percent. According to the input-output table data, the share of raw materials (excluding crude oil) in Korea's total commodity imports increased from 9.4 percent in 1975 to 11.3 percent in 1980, but the share of intermediate-input materials decreased from about 32 percent in 1975 to about 29 percent in 1980. Presumably, the protection and promotion of heavy and chemical industries was responsible for the declining share of intermediate-input materials in Korea's total commodity imports.

21. These items consisted mostly of (petro)chemical products such as naphtha, methanol, urea, polyester resin, PVC tube, film and resin, viscose rayon F yarn, PP filament yarn, polyprophylene staple fiber, polyester staple fiber, acrylic fiber, ammonium chloride, nitrobenzene, etc.

22. After 1981 many nonferrous metal products such as lead ingot, zinc ingot, aluminium ingot, brass bar, tin ingot, copper wire, etc., became subject to limited tariff drawbacks.

The labor-intensive consumption-goods sector had dominated Korea's commodity exports in the early phase of export-oriented growth. By the late 1970s, however, a new group of leading exports (including machinery, transport equipment, and iron and steel products) had emerged. These belonged to relatively capital-intensive sectors, making Korea's overall commodity composition of exports shift toward a more capital-intensive one. Hong (1987) shows that the value of capital per worker directly and indirectly employed in the Korean manufacturing sector for the production of commodity exports rose from $3,000 in 1966 to $8,900 in 1980 (in constant 1980 dollar prices). At the same time, owing to the promotion of capital-intensive import-substituting sectors (that included various petrochemical products), the value of capital per worker that was employed in replacing competitive imports rose from $4,800 in 1966 to $12,200 in 1980. The average capital intensity of Korea's manufacturing sector itself rose from $3,800 in 1966 to $10,400 in 1980.

With capital accumulation in a country, one naturally expects to observe a rising wage/rental ratio, and a rising capital/labor ratio in both production and exports. Unfortunately in Korea many of those intermediate and investment-goods sectors promoted by the government in the 1970s turned out to be excessively capital-intensive (for that particular stage of growth), and these sectors ended up having to be protected by tariff and quotas, which in turn raised the production costs of downstream industries.

During the period 1965–76, Korea had maintained an average annual growth rate of real exports as high as about 34 percent. However, the growth rate of real exports started to decline in 1977, making the average growth rate of real exports only 12 percent per annum for the period 1977–85.[23] Furthermore, Korea's performance in GNP growth began to look less impressive after 1980. The growth rate of GNP fell from nearly 10 percent per annum on average in 1967–79 to around 7.5 percent in 1981–85. The significantly reduced rates of export expansion and GNP growth may at least partly be related to tariff protection and quantitative restrictions. Consequently pressure arose for the government to search for more efficient policy measures with which to promote the intermediate and investment-goods sectors.

23. The growth rate of real exports represents the growth rate of the export quantum index (1980 = 100) estimated by the Bank of Korea.

4.3 The Late 1970s: Abortive Import-Liberalization Attempts

In an early stage of export-promotion-based development, complete import liberalization is obviously not a necessary condition for successful growth performance. In the later stages of export-oriented development, however, an extensive import liberalization may become a necessary condition, not only for maximization of hitherto much neglected consumer welfare,[24] but also for efficiency maximization. Efficient domestic production is clearly important if exports are to be internationally competitive. Indeed, in Korea, by the end of 1970s nationwide pressure to initiate further import liberalization seems to have appeared.

In 1977 Korea's current account of the balance of payments registered a small surplus for the first time since 1966. This was followed by an import-liberalization effort. In February 1978 the Korean government established the Committee for Import Liberalization to formulate the direction of liberalization and then to determine the items to be liberalized. The import-liberalization ratio by item jumped from about 54 percent in the first half of 1978 to about 65 percent in the second half.[25] However, MTI seems to have assumed the task of import liberalization in 1978 with reluctance and skepticism.

According to MTI, the items to be liberalized were those that did not compete with domestic production, those for which there were no plans for domestic production, and those that already enjoyed strong international competitive power. The items *not* to be liberalized were those produced by heavy and chemical industries and other strategically promoted industries, those produced by small- and medium-sized industries, those produced by infant industries that still had to expand further in order to enjoy scale economies, those produced by industries that had substantial forward and backward linkage effects, those produced by industries that supplied necessary intermediate inputs and basic materials to the heavy and chemical industries, agricultural products, and

24. The share of consumption goods in Korea's commodity imports had declined from 4.5 percent in 1970–75 to 3.8 percent by 1980. The share of foodstuffs declined from 16.6 percent in 1970 to 14.3 percent in 1975, and to 9.3 percent in 1980. According to Young et al. (1982, 92), the high prices that Korean consumers paid because of protection amounted to about 13 percent of the national income in 1978. This indicates that the dividends to consumers also became large enough to generate strong pressure for an extensive import liberalization.

25. Based on 1,097 4-digit CCCN classification. In order to maintain consistency with the 1967 import liberalization ratio, the number of RI items in table 7.3 was counted on the basis of 1,312 5-digit SITC classification.

luxury goods.[26] In other words, MTI wanted to liberalize the import of only those items that would have minimal impact on the domestic economy. The number of restricted import items did substantially decrease in the second half of 1978, but most of the newly import-liberalized items were either economically unimportant ones or were classified as "import surveillance" items that could be reclassified as "restricted" should a surge of imports follow.[27] When the balance on the current account deteriorated seriously in 1979, the halfhearted liberalization movement was brought to a halt in 1980.

5. IMPORT LIBERALIZATION IN THE 1980s

5.1 The Protectionist Regime as of the Early 1980s

During the second half of 1981 and the first half of 1982, the import-liberalization ratio by item (or the share of automatically approved items in the 7,915 8-digit level CCCN classification) amounted to about 75 percent. However, if those items whose imports were subject to special laws are excluded, then the import-liberalization ratio amounted to only about 55 percent (see table 7.2). In value terms, as estimated by Luedde-Neurath (1984, chap. 8), the import-liberalization ratio for the first half of 1982 amounted to 58.7 percent (not taking into account the special laws), and to only about 22.7 percent if imports subject to special laws are excluded. Since many of the special laws controlled imports of related commodities purely incidentally, and since many of the import items that were only partly controlled were counted as full "restricted import" items, these figures may represent a significant underestimation of the actual degree of import liberalization in Korea in the early 1980s.

A study by Kim and Hong (1982) shows that there were steady decreases in the effective rate of protection for the manufacturing sector as a whole throughout 1963–78. During the first half of the period (1963–70), the decreases in the effective rates of protection occurred most drastically in the export sectors, while the rates of protection for import-competing sectors rather significantly increased. During the period 1970–78, however, the drastic decreases in effective rates of protection occurred in import-competing sectors and in sectors that both ex-

26. Data from Republic of Korea 1978.
27. According to Young et al. (1982), the effective rates of protection for durable and nondurable consumption goods and machinery and transport equipment declined substantially during 1978–82. However, the effective rates of protection for construction materials and intermediate-input materials rather significantly increased during the same period (see table 7.2.)

ported and imported, while there was a significant increase in nominal, as well as effective, rates of protection for export (manufacturing) sectors (see table 7.1). The implications of this somewhat paradoxical phenomenon were examined in section 2. As of 1983 only 38.9 percent of Korea's major export commodities were classified as "automatic approval" items, but the average liberalization ratio by item reached 80.4 percent.[28]

5.2 Import Liberalization as a Long-Term Policy Goal

The liberalization movement that was halted in 1980 was resumed in 1981 despite the enormous current account deficit, but was again halted in 1982. The current account situation substantially improved in 1983, and a renewed movement toward import liberalization followed. This time, however, it was approached as a long-term policy goal with a definite annual liberalization timetable. According to the schedule, Korea will reach the OECD level of import liberalization by 1988.

The simple arithmetic average tariff rate was reduced from about 36 percent in 1977–78 to about 25 percent in 1979–81. The weighted average tariff rate also fell steadily from about 19 percent in 1978 to about 12 percent in 1981. In early 1983 the Ministry of Finance (MOF) took decisive initiative in the import-liberalization movement and presented a long-term (1983–88) tariff reduction scheme: the simple arithmetic average tariff rate was scheduled to fall from 23.7 percent in 1982 to 20.6 in 1984 and to 16.9 percent in 1988.

Following the MOF initiative, MTI presented its own schedule of import liberalization: the share of "automatic approval" items was to increase from 76.6 percent in 1982 to 80.4 percent in 1983, to 91.6 percent in 1986 and 95.2 percent in 1988. MTI also presented a list of the "restricted import" items that would be liberalized during 1984–86.

Theory suggests that it is desirable to eliminate quantitative restrictions first, even if this means raising the rate of tariff protection. Since MOF took the initiative, MTI had to follow, and faced the difficult task of selecting a large number of new automatically approved items all at once. Many of the items produced by politically influential monopolistic firms escaped the early round of liberalization, and most of the items scheduled to be liberalized first were produced by less influential small firms. The former included many heavy industrial and chemical products, and the latter included many finished consumption goods. Owing to the existing political power balances, the consumers' surplus problem

28. Republic of Korea 1983a, 2.

was, quite unintentionally, significantly taken care of in the early phase of import liberalization.[29] Furthermore, the government officials seem to have pursued import liberalization indiscriminately, with no clear idea of priority between consumers' surplus and efficiency enhancement at the beginning stage.

5.3 Progress in Import Liberalization

In accordance with MTI's long-term import liberalization schedule, out of the total importable items the proportion of restricted imports declined from about 25 percent to about 12 percent during 1981–85, and the proportion of "special law" items declined from about 19 percent to about 16.6 percent. According to the 1982 Luedde-Neurath data and the table 7.6 data of 1984, the import-liberalization ratio by value (the share of commodities imported as "automatic approval" items out of the total value of commodity imports) increased from about 59 percent to 78 percent during 1982–84 without taking into account special laws, and increased from about 23 percent to about 40 percent excluding the special law items.

Among primary products, imports of raw foodstuffs and mineral fuels were mostly subject to special laws. Among manufactures, the import of chemicals was largely subject to special laws. Not only did the absolute number of restricted items in the chemicals sector decrease in 1981–85, but the proportion of chemical imports subject to special laws also declined (from about 60 percent to 47 percent of total importable items). In the case of machinery and other manufactures (SITC 6, 7, and 8, excluding textiles and electronics products), the number of restricted import items has substantially decreased, but the proportion of imports subject to special laws has significantly increased.[30] Apparently, in cer-

29. In order to cope with the possibly severely damaging effects of import liberalization on the competing domestic industries, an adjustment tariff was introduced in early 1984 that enables the government to raise the tariff rate up to 100 percentage points on a commodity whose import has been liberalized within the past three-year period. The application of this adjustment tariff rate cannot exceed three years. There have also been antidumping tariffs, countervailing tariffs, and retaliatory tariff systems, but none of them has even been actually enforced.

30. During 1981–84 the proportion of RI items in the machinery sector (SITC 7) was reduced from about 45 percent of total importable items to about 28 percent, while in value terms the share was reduced from about 72 percent to 54 percent. In the chemicals sector the proportion of RI items was reduced from about 6 percent to about 4 percent during this period, while the share in value terms was reduced from about 58 percent to about 35 percent. In the meantime, the proportion of chemicals out of total imports increased from 8 percent to about 9 percent, and that of machinery from about 22 percent

tain sectors there has been a tendency to replace a "restricted" classification with special laws.[31] On the whole, however, not only did the number of restricted import items decline significantly during 1981–85, but the proportion of items subject to special laws did too (see table 7.7).

As of 1984, imports of electronics and telecommunication equipment, road vehicles, ships, and other machinery and equipment were heavily restricted. In value terms, nonferrous metal products were also significantly restricted (see table 7.6). However, if we examine table 7.3, we can see that imports of textiles have been steadily liberalized since 1967. Import restrictions on raw materials and iron and steel products very much expanded during 1967–78, but then were substantially liberalized after 1978. About 46.5 percent of raw materials were classified as restricted import items in 1978, but this has been reduced to about 10.4 percent by 1984. As of 1978, about 75 percent of iron and steel products were subject to import restriction in the form of a restricted-import classification, and more than 90 percent of total iron and steel imports were imported subject to some restriction. By 1984, however, less than 10 percent of iron and steel product imports (either by item or by value) were subject to restriction either in the form of restricted-import classification or special laws. Furthermore, as the growth rate of commodity exports slowed down in 1985, the government reduced the number of items subject to the limited tariff drawback system from 254 to 79.

In 1983 the simple arithmetic average tariff rates for raw materials, intermediate inputs, and finished goods were 11.9 percent, 21.5 percent, and 26.4 percent respectively.[32] By this time, increasingly fierce resistance to import liberalization by the big monopolistic business groups could be detected. The following guiding principles on import liberalization set out by MTI in 1984 reflect this reality:

> [Monopolistically produced] commodities will be subject to early liberalization in principle. Although import liberalization should lead to increased competition among firms, it should not be pursued to such an extent as to bankrupt firms. The import liberalization program should also allow for preservation of basic material industries even if they are not.

---

to about 25 percent. Ship repair, which amounted to $418 million in 1981 and $2,445 million in 1984, was excluded from the percentage estimations for the machinery sector. See Korean Traders Association, 1984.

31. In the cases of textiles and electronics, the number of restricted items decreased substantially, but there was no change in the number of special law items. In the case of mineral fuels, the proportion of special law items increased from about 37 percent to 50 percent.

32. Data from Republic of Korea 1983a, 2.

TABLE 7.7 Reductions in Number of Restricted Import (RI) and Special Law Items in South Korea, 1981–85

	Number of Items	RI Items (% Share)			Special Law Items (% Share)		
		1981	1985	Change	1982	1985	Change
All commodities	7,915	2,014 (25.5)	979 (12.4)	−1,035 (−13.2)	1,495 (18.9)	1,317 (16.6)	−178 (−2.3)
All manufactures	6,595	1,675 (25.4)	749 (11.4)	−926 (−14.0)	1,145 (16.4)	1,001 (15.2)	−144 (−2.2)
0,1.ª Foodstuffs, raw	515	231 (44.9)	166 (32.2)	−65 (−12.6)	151 (29.3)	133 (25.8)	−18 (−3.5)
2,4. Raw materials	680	108 (15.9)	64 (9.4)	−44 (−6.5)	153 (22.5)	120 (17.7)	−33 (−4.9)
3. Mineral fuels	125	0 (—)	0 (—)	— (—)	46 (36.8)	63 (50.4)	+17 (+13.6)
0,1. Food manufactures	172	141 (82.0)	102 (59.3)	−39 (−22.7)	9 (5.2)	6 (3.5)	−3 (−1.7)
51. Organic chemicals	557	44 (7.9)	31 (5.6)	−13 (−2.3)	424 (76.1)	351 (63.0)	−73 (−13.1)
58. Resins and plastics	138	32 (23.2)	13 (9.4)	−19 (−13.8)	39 (28.3)	22 (15.9)	−17 (−12.3)
5-. Other chemicals	944	21 (2.2)	11 (1.2)	−10 (−1.1)	524 (55.5)	394 (41.7)	−130 (−13.8)
65. Textiles	578	143 (24.7)	47 (8.1)	−96 (−16.6)	8 (1.4)	8 (1.4)	0 (0.0)
666. Ceramics	25	25 (100.0)	18 (72.0)	−7 (−28.0)	— (—)	— (—)	— (—)
667. Precious stones	23	21 (91.3)	18 (78.3)	−3 (−13.0)	— (—)	— (—)	— (—)
67. Iron and steel	249	29 (11.7)	14 (5.6)	−15 (−6.0)	1 (0.4)	1 (0.4)	0 (0.0)
68. Nonferrous metal	149	37 (24.8)	16 (10.7)	−21 (−14.1)	1 (0.7)	2 (1.3)	+1 (+0.7)
6-. Other manufactures	914	59 (6.5)	21 (2.3)	−38 (−4.2)	17 (1.9)	39 (4.3)	+22 (+2.4)
76,776. Electronics	122	111 (91.0)	52 (42.6)	−59 (−48.4)	12 (9.8)	12 (9.8)	0 (0.0)
78. Road vehicles	97	81 (83.5)	38 (39.2)	−43 (−44.3)	— (—)	— (—)	— (—)
79. Other transport eq.	130	38 (29.2)	25 (19.2)	−13 (−10.0)	— (—)	— (—)	— (—)
7-. Other machinery	1,188	466 (39.2)	215 (18.1)	−251 (−21.1)	61 (5.1)	90 (7.6)	+29 (+2.4)
895-7. Jewelry, art	77	58 (75.3)	46 (63.6)	−12 (−15.6)	4 (5.2)	5 (6.5)	+1 (+1.3)
8. Misc manufactures	1,186	367 (30.9)	77 (6.5)	−290 (−24.5)	18 (1.5)	42 (3.5)	+24 (+2.2)
9. Other	46	2 (4.4)	5 (10.9)	+3 (+6.5)	27 (58.7)	29 (63.0)	+2 (+4.4)

SOURCES: Republic of Korea, Ministry of Trade and Industry, *Semi-Annual Export-Import Notice* (second half of 1981 and first half of 1982, second half of 1985 and first half of 1986); Korean Traders Association, *Export-Import Procedures by Item* (second half of 1982 and first half of 1983, second half of 1985 and first half of 1986).

ª Standard International Trade Classification (SITC).

internationally competitive and also for the need to protect economies of scale industries and those industries in which we are still acquiring technology. Thus, while the petrochemical, steel and metal products, automobile, and electronic product industries are oligopolistic, they are also the basic materials and strategic industries. (translated from the Korean by Young [1984, 79])[33]

Nevertheless, import liberalization did progress more or less on schedule in 1983–85. The import liberalization ratio by item increased from 76.6 percent in 1982 to 87.7 percent in 1985, and is scheduled to reach 95.4 percent by 1988. The government also reduced the number of so-called "automatic approval" items whose imports were subject to special laws, and intends to keep reducing it in the future. Moreover, the simple arithmetic average of legal tariff rates for all commodities, which amounted to 22.6 percent in 1983, kept falling. It reached 16.9 percent by 1988. It is true that most of the important agricultural products were not included in the 1984–88 import-liberalization scheme, but as far as manufactures are concerned, if everything goes as presently scheduled, Korea will have the most liberal import regime of all the Third World countries in its income class.

5.4 The Political Economy of Import Liberalization

It is also important to consider the political economy of import liberalization in an export-oriented economy. It is well known that consumers are one of the least organized groups in any economy. Hence, they cannot exert concentrated pressure against the protection accorded to the domestic producers of final-consumption goods. Therefore, in the early phase of growth, when domestic outputs as well as exports are dominated by labor-intensive consumption goods, there is usually little pressure for the government to undertake extensive import liberalization. Only a certain minimum level of import liberalization, enough to facilitate industrial growth and export expansion, has to be enforced.

In a later phase of growth, however, a large number of intermediate and investment-goods producers emerge. They sell substantial portions of their products to domestic industries. These buyers, or so-called

---

33. The ministerial guidelines laid down for import liberalization for the one-year period starting in mid 1983 included statements to the effect that the manufactured commodities whose import was to be liberalized should be those for which there were no competing domestic substitutes and in whose case liberalization was unlikely to produce an import surge. Should there be an import surge, such commodities would be put on a surveillance list, and their imports could be restricted again. Furthermore, newly developed commodities may be entitled to temporary protection by being classified as new restricted import items. See Young et al. 1982, 22–23.

end-users, are better organized than consumers in general to mobilize a
concerted effort against the protection accorded to the producers of
intermediate and investment goods. Sellers' domination and uncontested
protection rents tend to disappear in these sectors since there finally exists an equally powerful group who stand to benefit by eliminating import restrictions. Often, end-users are themselves producers of other
intermediate and investment goods. When this happens, their stance on
import liberalization becomes very complicated.

Since it sounds more noble for end-users to insist on import liberalization in general, rather than for just those intermediate and investment
goods that are directly related to their production activities, it sometimes happens that imports of consumption goods also tend to be liberalized. This may, however, be regarded as rather unintended. The government is under pressure to liberalize imports, but it is also subject to
opposing pressure from the strong vested interest group of intermediate
and investment-goods producers. Consumption-goods producers are
comparatively weaker in political influence. What happens, then, is that
the preannounced target of import liberalization is partly met by liberalizing the import of some final-consumption goods. The purpose is not
to enhance consumers' surpluses per se, but simply to give the impression that the government is liberalizing imports on schedule.

The question faced by the protected industries in Korea, however, was
simply whether they were to be liberalized during 1984–86 or during
1987–88. Imports of almost all manufactured products, regardless of
whether they are consumption goods, intermediate goods, or investment goods, had been liberalized by the end of 1988.

Under the import-liberalization schedule for 1987–88 that was announced on October 30, 1985, a 100 percent import liberalization was
achieved for metals and iron and steel products by 1987, and for electronics goods and both electrical and nonelectrical machinery by 1988.
The imports of pulp and paper, ceramics, and chemicals were liberalized up to 99.6 percent, and textiles imports up to 97.8 percent, by
1988. Among textile products, only those related to sericulture (such as
raw silk, silk yarn, and silk fabrics) will continue to be subject to import
control. Among chemicals, only ethyl alcohol and some toxic insecticides
(8 items altogether) will continue to be subject to import controls.

As of 1986, 56 monopolistically produced manufactured commodities
(out of 254) were subject to import restrictions. However, by 1988, only
3 monopolistically produced commodities (milk powder, fruit juice, and
fermented lactic bacteria) continued to be subject to import controls.

Out of 7,915 importable items, 369 remained "restricted" in 1989, and of those, only 32 were manufactured products. The other 337 items consisted almost entirely of agricultural products and certain special items, such as precious stones.

6. SUMMARY AND CONCLUSIONS

When the "growth" or "promoted" industries are mostly in the export sector, the harmful effects of protecting other import-competing sectors are alleviated as time passes. However, if the growth or promoted industries are in the major import-substituting sectors, then the harmful effects of protecting these industries can be very much exaggerated as capital is accumulated and sector-specific industrial promotion policies are enforced.

In Korea the consumption-goods sector was promoted as the leading export sector in the 1960s and early 1970s, and it also constituted the major growth sector (as compared to agriculture or intermediate and investment goods). Until the mid 1970s, therefore, capital accumulation and export promotion in Korea did not seem to seriously aggravate the harmful effects of protecting the import-substituting sectors. Even the severe restriction of imports of consumption goods did not by itself seriously reduce allocative efficiency, though there apparently were substantial losses of consumers' surplus.

Since the mid 1970s, though, a host of highly capital-intensive heavy and chemical industries began, as a promising new generation of infant industries, to be protected by severe import restrictions and, at the same time, were promoted as export industries. These newly promoted industries began supplying increasing amounts of intermediate and investment goods to domestic producers, but in many cases at excessively high costs, because Korea still did not have comparative advantages in many of these products. The adverse efficiency effects of both tariff and quantitative protection of capital-intensive heavy and chemical industries were then inevitably amplified as capital was accumulated and sector-specific promotion policies were enforced. Since Korea was not expected to gain a comparative advantage in the production of many of these intermediate and investment goods for a long time, pressure arose for import liberalization—not so much to enhance consumer welfare as to enhance the production efficiency and the international competitive power of Korean industries in general. That is, by the beginning of the 1980s, pressure arose for the Korean government to search for better measures than tariff protection and quotas to promote infant (intermediate and investment-goods) industries. At this same time, by pure coincidence, the United States also dramatically increased pressure for import liberalization, which could by no means be ignored by the Korean government.

On the basis of the Korean experience, we can conclude that, in the initial phase of export-oriented growth, extensive import liberalization does not constitute a necessary condition for high growth performance. In a later phase, however, it is more likely to become a necessary condition for maintaining the competitive power of domestic industries in the international market and the high growth performance of the domestic economy. Infant intermediate and investment-goods industries with reasonable chances of becoming internationally competitive have to be promoted, but by more efficient means than tariff protection and quantitative restrictions.

The evolution of Korea's import-restriction policy suggests that an export-promotion regime is much more conducive to early import liberalization than is an import-substitution regime. Owing to enhanced ability to earn foreign exchange, once low domestic saving ceases to constrain growth, an export-promotion regime can afford to reduce or eliminate its import-restriction system much more rapidly than could an import-substitution one.

REFERENCES

Bank of Korea. Various years. *Economic Statistics Yearbook (Kyongje tonggye yonbo)*. Seoul: Bank of Korea.
———. Various years. *Financial Statement Analysis.* Seoul: Bank of Korea.
———. Various years. *Input-Output Tables of Korea (Sanop yon'gwan p'yo)*. Seoul: Bank of Korea.
———. Various years. *National Income Accounts.* Seoul: Bank of Korea.
———. Various years. *Price Statistics Summary (Mulka ch-ongnam)*. Seoul: Bank of Korea.
Bhagwati, J. N. 1968. "Distortions and Immiserizing Growth: A Generalization." *Review of Economic Studies* 35 (October): 481–85.
Bhagwati, J. N., and B. Hansen. 1973. "Should Growth Rates Be Evaluated at International Prices?" In J. Bhagwati and R. Eckaus, eds., *Development and Planning: Essays in Honour of Paul Rosenstein-Rodan.* Cambridge, Mass.: MIT Press.
Bhagwati, J. N., and Anne O. Krueger. 1973. "Exchange Control, Liberalization, and Economic Development." *American Economic Review* 63 (May): 419–27.
Brecher, Richard A., and Carlos F. Diaz-Alejandro. 1977. "Tariffs, Foreign Capital and Immiserizing Growth." *Journal of International Economics* 7 (November): 317–22.

Brecher, Richard A., and Ronald Findlay. 1983. "Tariffs, Foreign Capital and National Welfare with Sector-Specific Factors." *Journal of International Economics* 14 (May): 277–88.

Corden, W. Max. 1971. "The Effects of Trade on the Rate of Growth." In J. N. Bhagwati, ed., *Trade, Balance of Payments and Growth.* Amsterdam: North Holland Publishing Co.

Davies, Stephen W., and Anthony J. McGuinness. 1982. "Dumping at Less Than Marginal Cost." *Journal of International Economics* 12 (February) 169–82.

Edwards, Sebastian. 1984. *The Order of Liberalization of the Current and Capital Accounts of the Balance of Payments.* NBER Working Paper no. 1507. Cambridge, Mass.: National Bureau of Economic Research.

Frank, Charles R., Kim Kwang-Suk, and Larry E. Westphal. 1975. South Korea. Vol. 7 of *Foreign Trade Regimes and Economic Development.* New York: National Bureau of Economic Research.

Hong Wontack. 1979. *Trade, Distortions and Employment Growth in Korea.* Seoul: KDI Press.

———. 1987. "A Comparative Static Application of the Heckscher-Ohlin Model of Factor Proportions: Korean Experience." *Weltwirtschaftliches Archiv* 123: 309–24.

Johnson, H. G. 1967. "The Possibility of Income Losses from Increased Efficiency or Factor Accumulation in the Presence of Tariffs." *Economic Journal* 77 (March): 151–54.

Keesing, Donald B. 1967. "Outward-Looking Policies and Economic Development." *Economic Journal* 77 (June): 303–20.

Kim Kwang-Suk and Hong Sung Duck. 1982. *Long Term Changes in the Structure of Nominal and Effective Rates of Protection.* KDI Research Report no. 82-02. In Korean. Seoul: KDI Press.

Korea, Republic of. Ministry of Finance. 1983a. *Reform of Tariff System (Kwan-se ku-jo gae pyon).* In Korean. Seoul: Ministry of Finance.

———. 1983b. *Tariff Reform Data.* In Korean. Seoul: Ministry of Finance.

Korea, Republic of. Ministry of Trade and Industry. 1978. *Detailed Work Plan for Import Liberalization.* Seoul: Ministry of Trade and Industry.

———. Various years. *Yearbook of Foreign Trade Statistics.* Seoul: Ministry of Trade and Industry.

———. Various years. *Semi-Annual Export-Import Notice.* Seoul: Ministry of Trade and Industry.

———. 1984. *Standard Korean Trade Classification.* Seoul: Ministry of Trade and Industry.

Korea, Republic of. National Tax Administration. Various years. *Statistical Yearbook of National Tax.* Seoul: National Tax Administration.

Korean Traders Association. 1968. *Trade Yearbook (Moo-yuk yon-gam).* Seoul: Korean Traders Association.

———. Various years. *The Trend of Foreign Trade (Muyok tonghyang).* Seoul: Korean Traders Association.

———. Various years. *Export-Import Procedures by Item (Pum-mok byul soo-chul-ip yo-ryong).* Seoul: Korean Traders Association.

Luedde-Neurath, Richard. 1984. "Import Controls and Export-Oriented Development: A Reexamination of the South Korean Case, 1962–1982." Ph.D. diss., University of Sussex.

Nam Chong Hyun. 1981a. *Analysis of Korea's Industrial Incentive Policies and the Structure of Protection by Industry.* In Korean. Seoul: KDI Press.

————. 1981b. "Trade, Industrial Policies, and the Structure of Protection in Korea." In Wontack Hong and Lawrence B. Krause, eds., *Trade and Growth of the Advanced Developing Countries in the Pacific Basin.* Seoul: KDI Press.

Robinson, Joan. 1969. *The Economics of Imperfect Competition.* 2d ed. New York: St. Martin's Press.

Smith, Adam. 1950. *An Inquiry into the Nature and Causes of the Wealth of Nations.* 1776. Edited by Edwin Cannan. London: Methuen.

United Nations. 1963. *Commodity Indexes for the Standard International Trade Classification.* Revised. Vol. 1. New York: UN.

Westphal, Larry E., and Kim Kwang-Suk. 1982. "Korea." In Bela Balassa and Julio Berlinski, eds., *Development Strategies in Semi-Industrial Economies,* 212–79. Baltimore: Johns Hopkins University Press.

Young Soogil. 1984. "Problems of Trade Liberalization in Korea." Paper presented at a workshop meeting organized by the Trade Policy Research Center, London, October 22–25.

Young Soogil, Soo-Young Kim, Young-Son Lee, Jung-Ho Yoo, Sung-Duck Hong, Seung-Jin Kim, Bon-Young Koo, Joon-Kyung Park, Jin-Woo Kim, Kwang-Ha Kang, Koo-Hyun Chung, Jai-Won Kim, Kwang-Doo Kim, See-Chun Koh, and Seung-Hoon Lee. 1982. *The Basic Role of Industrial Policy and a Reform Proposal of Industrial Incentives.* In Korean. Seoul: KDI Press.

EIGHT

Agriculture in the Liberalization Process

D. Gale Johnson

Liberalization of trade in agricultural products has a number of implications not commonly associated with liberalization of trade in manufactured products. Without attempting to order them in terms of significance or difficulty of achieving liberalization, several differences between trade liberalization for agricultural and manufactured products may be noted.

One difference is that trade liberalization for agricultural products means moving toward more market-oriented policies not only in international markets but in domestic ones as well. Though it is not as common for the manufacturing sector, virtually all countries have domestic policies that directly intervene in farm product markets. In the vast majority of these cases, trade policy becomes an adjunct of domestic agricultural policies. Thus it is commonplace for countries to argue that it is inappropriate to require that they negotiate about trade interventions that are required as a part of their domestic price support and subsidy policies. To permit negotiations on such trade policies would mean that domestic policies were subject to negotiation.

Another difference is that in the agricultural sector governmental interventions appear to be as likely to reduce farm product prices below international market levels as to increase the prices above them. Many countries follow a policy of low prices for consumers for important food products, either through lowering farm prices or by subsidizing the difference between producer and consumer prices. Thus liberalization of the agricultural sector is about as likely to result in higher producer and/or consumer prices as in lower prices, and thus the interests affected by agricultural liberalization may take quite different positions than would be the case for liberalizing trade in most manufactured products, where the likely outcome is both lower producer and consumer prices.

Security of food supply is an argument often used as a rationalization for protecting domestic farm production. It is relatively easy to gain acquiescence, if not support, for maintaining a large domestic agriculture on the grounds that to do otherwise subjects the ordinary citizen to unacceptable and unnecessary risks of going hungry. Aside from the military sector, it is less easy to make similar arguments for nonfarm activities.

A final difference between agricultural and manufacturing policies is that in many countries, including all of the advanced industrial countries and the NICs (the newly industrializing countries such as South Korea and Taiwan), farm policies have significant income objectives for the farm population. The unavoidable fact is that as economic growth occurs, resources—especially labor—must be shifted out of agriculture into nonfarm sectors. This will generally result in somewhat lower income in farm areas than in urban areas. Most governments attempt to use price interventions to reduce such apparent income differentials, even though quite simple analysis indicates that such interventions have little or no long-run effect upon the returns to mobile factors of production, especially labor.

While this chapter concentrates on the issue of liberalization, it begins by providing an analytical framework for the overall role of agriculture in the development process. Though at unprecedented levels today, intervention in the agricultural sector is nothing new, and section 2 contains a historical summary of the worldwide pattern of agricultural protection. Looking at some of the studies that have been done, section 3 tries to explain why protection of the agricultural sector (both positively and negatively) is so prevalent, and why it varies so greatly from country to country. Section 4 then focuses on some of the institutional barriers to liberalization of this sector, and the chapter ends with a brief conclusion.

1. AGRICULTURE AND ECONOMIC DEVELOPMENT

At low levels of per capita income, most of a country's economically active population is engaged in agriculture. This is true in the low-income developing countries of the world today, just as it was true in the industrial countries in the not too distant past. In some industrial countries three-fourths of the economically active population were engaged in agriculture well into the present century. When such a large percentage of the population is required to produce a country's food and fiber, it is important that agricultural productivity increase. Increasing such productivity depends upon providing farm people with appropriate incentives to contribute the investments and effort needed to make both land and labor more productive.

A productive agricultural sector has three important contributions to make to economic growth and development. One is to provide an adequate supply of food and fiber at reasonable prices. The second is to provide an export surplus so that foreign exchange will be available to provide for the import of capital goods and technology to modernize and expand the nonfarm sectors of the economy. The third is to increase productivity so that resources can be transferred to the rest of the economy. These transfers involve both labor and capital. In a rapidly growing economy there will be large and continuous transfers of labor from agriculture to urban areas. Eventually (as evidenced by the industrial countries today), the labor force in agriculture declines to less than 5 percent of the total labor force. The rate of the decline in the percentage of the labor force in agriculture is related both to the rate of productivity improvement in agriculture and the rate of growth of the nonfarm part of the economy. Where both changes occur at significant rates, agriculture's share of national employment can decline by one or more percentage points per year. This is approximately what occurred in upper-middle-income developing countries between 1960 and 1980, when the percentage of the labor force in agriculture declined from 49 percent in 1960 to 30 percent in 1980 (World Bank 1982).

Capital transfers from agriculture to the rest of the economy are more difficult to document than is the labor transfer, yet it is generally agreed that such transfers do occur. How large the transfer will be depends upon institutional arrangements, such as the importance of landlords with large holdings who find greater expected profits from investments in industry than in agriculture, and the nature of the tax system. It is evident that over time agriculture's share of national investment declines.

The relative decline of agriculture as a source of national employment and output results from two important factors. One is that as real per capita incomes increase, the percentage of income spent upon farm products falls, declining from nearly 70 percent at income levels such as those prevailing in India to less than 20 percent in Western Europe and

North America. The other factor is the increased productivity of agriculture. Despite the long-standing view that the supply of agricultural land is fixed and diminishing returns prevail, the growth of resource productivity in agriculture has in fact been sufficient to more than offset both. Through research, the use of nonfarm inputs such as fertilizer and machinery, and increased human capital, the agricultural-production frontier has been continuously pushed outward, more than compensating for whatever negative effect diminishing returns may have when the supply of land is limited.

The relative, and eventually absolute, decline of the farm labor force causes serious adjustment problems for rural communities, but the transfer of labor to the nonfarm economy makes it possible for farm people to participate in economic growth. If the transfer of farm workers to nonfarm jobs is inhibited, economic growth is slowed, and the disparities between farm and nonfarm incomes grow. Because labor must transfer out of agriculture as economic growth occurs, the returns to farm labor must be less than urban earnings to induce farm people to migrate. The relative earnings of farm people depend upon how easy it is for them to find nonfarm job opportunities.

A World Economic System for Agriculture

If there were free trade in agricultural products or even liberal trade regimes based upon low ad valorem tariffs, the world would produce its food at or near minimum cost. The arguments for liberal trade in farm products are the same as those for liberal trade in general: consumers everywhere would have access to a wide variety of foods at low cost, and efficient producers would find ready outlets for their production.

If the world's agricultural resources, both natural and human, were efficiently used, most present market interventions would have no place. Freedom of trade—domestic and international—is required if food is to be both abundant and low in cost and if farm people are to participate fully in economic growth. The levels of income of farm people depend primarily upon two things: the per capita incomes of the country in which they live and the access they have to nonfarm earning opportunities. Economic growth requires that farm employment decline, first relatively and then absolutely. Thus interventions that interfere with the smooth transfer of labor out of agriculture have an adverse effect upon the welfare of farm people.

However, not all government interventions or activities are inconsistent with domestic and international liberal trade. Many interventions are economically and socially productive—the education of farm youth, support of agricultural research and extension, and the creation and maintenance of the rural infrastructure (markets, highways, roads, and communication facilities) that lowers the cost of marketing farm products and helps to integrate farm people into the economy. These activities do not create distortions; they are basically public goods that cannot or will not be provided through the market.

In fact, of course, trade in farm products is subject to wide-scale governmental intervention. Some interventions increase farm output prices; others depress them. In the latter case, the price system is used to transfer income from farm people to the urban economy. The interventions can be measured through estimates of nominal protection coefficients (that is, estimates of the ratio of domestic farm prices to adjusted border prices, which reflect adjustments for marketing and transportation costs, for quality differences, and for overvaluation of the exchange rate). If the nominal protection coefficient is 1, then domestic and international prices for farm products are the same. If the coefficient exceeds 1, agriculture is receiving positive protection. If the coefficient is less than 1, domestic prices are below international market prices and agriculture is being taxed, or there is negative protection.

Subject to a number of qualifications that will be noted later, it is possible to indicate in a simple way the relationships between per capita income and the protection of agriculture. At low levels of per capita income, say below $1,000 per capita (1982 U.S. $), the protection coefficient is generally below 1. As per capita incomes approach $1,500 to $2,000, the protection coefficient becomes positive, and it increases gradually as incomes rise. As will be noted later, the explanation of the size of the nominal protection coefficients is complex and requires a considerable number of variables. The level of per capita income, or a proxy for it (the percentage of gross national product produced in agriculture), has a major influence on the size of the coefficient.

What Differences Do the Distortions Make?

The market distortions in agriculture have many effects. Some are in terms of income transfers; others lower productivity by encouraging inefficient use of resources.

Since the protection coefficients vary from country to country, the effects of the interventions upon the incomes of farmers and the welfare of consumers differ, depending upon the particular setting. Where the protection coefficient is positive, and the higher returns are achieved through raising market prices, income is transferred from consumers to farmers. When the protection coefficient is less than 1, and the lower domestic prices are achieved through export taxes, consumers have access to food at prices below world levels at the expense of farmers.

After a period of time the magnitude of the protection coefficients in excess of unity have little positive effect upon the returns to farm labor. The primary income effect of positive protection coefficients is to increase the price of land; the return to farm labor is determined primarily by the level of nonfarm wages and the access that farm people have to these jobs (Johnson 1973). Negative protection, on the other hand, may have serious adverse effects upon farm people. Low output prices (below international levels) will result in lower land prices than would prevail under free trade. And since negative protection occurs primarily in low-income developing countries, where rural areas are still generally isolated from urban areas, nonfarm jobs are not readily accessible to farm people. Access to such employment is also reduced by both limited education and restraints upon job availability in the formal sectors of the urban economies.

Agricultural price stability is often considered a desirable policy goal, and domestic prices can be stabilized in one of two ways: by varying imports and/or exports so that domestic demand and supply are made equal at a predetermined price, or by variations in stocks of particular commodities that absorb significant variations in world demand and supply. The first approach utilizes quantitative import quotas, or variable levies and variable export subsidies that make international market prices irrelevant to domestic producers and consumers. (Examples are the import quotas on dairy products and sugar in the United States; quotas for beef and oranges in Japan and state trading in Japan; and the variable levies on imports and subsidies on exports of the European Community's Common Agricultural Policy.) This form of protection affects the variabilty of international prices. Governments that stabilize domestic prices for their producers and consumers by adjusting international trade do so at the cost of increased instability of world market prices (Johnson 1975). The reason for this effect is, first, that when domestic prices are stabilized, neither consumers nor producers are required to adjust to domestic variations in demand and production, and second, that the markets in such countries do not respond to changes in production and demand in the rest of the world, since imports and/or exports respond not to external prices but only to variations in local demand and supply.

The other method of domestic price stabilization need not lead to international price instability. By being willing to buy and sell grains, for example, at reasonably fixed and stable prices, and then storing any excess of purchases over sales, or selling from the large stocks that were accumulated, domestic support prices can still be established in excess of equilibrium prices—if this is the policy objective. (The United States and Canada have both used this technique.)

If the argument for high and stable prices of food is to provide for national food security (often defined in terms of self-sufficiency), then almost any level of prices and incentives can be justified.

Market interventions for agricultural products are also often used to provide high levels of protection for the processing of agricultural products. As will be discussed later, seemingly modest levels of tariffs on semi-processed products—say, 10 percent—may lead to effective protection rates of 100 percent or more if the raw farm product is imported free.

With the high rates of effective protection often provided for the processing of farm products, developing countries have placed export taxes on agricultural raw materials in order to encourage processing in the country where the raw product is produced. The high protection of processing in developed countries and the counterimposition of export taxes by the developing countries have two adverse effects. The first is that processing will not be done where it can be done at lowest cost; in fact, with the import duties and the export taxes, there is no way that the market can reveal where processing can be done at lowest cost. The second effect is that the farmers in the developing countries definitely lose through bearing the cost of the export tax, which often goes to support a relatively high-cost domestic processing industry. Once processing in the developing country is made possible by an export tax on the raw product, the finished products face import duties in the developed countries. Thus the farmers in the developing countries must pay for the processing wherever it is done.

2. PATTERNS OF AGRICULTURAL PROTECTION

Some Historical Background

It is important to note that significant protection of agriculture is nothing new. There has been but a brief interlude in modern history when there was something approximating free trade in agricultural products in Europe and North America. For Europe this period began with the abolition of the Corn Laws by the United Kingdom in 1846. Starting in

1860 there was free trade in agricultural products in Western Europe. However, free trade was maintained for less than two decades—Italy reintroduced protection in 1878, Germany in 1879, and France in 1881. Only Denmark and the Netherlands, in addition to the United Kingdom, resisted the move to protection until the Great Depression of the 1930s.

The British Corn Laws, as they evolved over at least four centuries, were a complex set of laws, regulations, and interventions in domestic and international markets. They included every protective device in use today, save one. Included were variable import levies, quantitative restrictions upon imports (including seasonal quotas), export subsidies, export taxes, and, of course, tariffs. There were also special preferences for the use of British ships, a precursor of the U.S. cargo preference rules for farm products. The only twentieth-century innovation I have discovered is the use of direct payments to producers to meet a price or income commitment. Even this device is but a slight modification of various bounty schemes that have existed, at least briefly, in a number of countries.

The abandonment of free trade in farm products in Western Europe has been attributed to the Franco-German war of 1870–71 and the Great Depression of the last quarter of the nineteenth century. However, protection of agricultural products in Western Europe prior to World War I was quite modest compared to recent levels.

In many countries, primarily low-income developing countries, governments intervene to reduce the prices of agricultural products. But even negative protection of agriculture is not new. The British Corn Laws included provisions for an export tax on grain when internal prices exceeded a certain level. However, there is no historical precedent for the wide prevalence of negative protection extending over long periods of time such as prevails in many developing countries today. The difference in degree is great indeed.

Agricultural Protection Rates before 1940.   Estimates of the levels of tariff protection in Europe exist for 1913, 1927, and 1931 for three broad groups of products: foodstuffs, semimanufactures, and manufactures.[1]

1. The estimated tariff rates were based on an analysis of 144 commodities. The tariff levels are the unweighted averages of the tariff levels divided by export prices. In this calculation a commodity is included even if the tariff rate is prohibitive—even if none of the commodity were imported. This method of estimation results in a somewhat higher estimate than would a comparison of internal prices and import prices of each commodity,

For the larger European countries, the tariff levels for agricultural products were generally in the range of 20 to 30 percent (see table 8.1).

The upper group of six countries in table 8.1 were industrial countries with significant imports of agricultural products. The bottom group consists of countries that as of 1913 were exporters of timber products (Sweden and Finland) and timber, agricultural, and other raw products, and were only modest importers of agricultural products. Countries in this second group had much higher rates of protection for agricultural products than did the countries in the upper group.

Protection of foodstuffs changed very little between 1913 and 1927 for the countries in table 8.1. Except for Belgium, there were sharp increases in protection between 1927 and 1931. Remember that three European countries—the United Kingdom, Denmark, and the Netherlands—had free trade in agricultural products in 1913 and until the early 1930s.

The United States did not protect its agriculture until 1890, and then protection remained at a relatively low level until the Smoot-Hawley tariff of 1929. Japan was nearly isolated from world trade prior to 1868 and did not move to a free-trade position for agriculture as it opened up to the rest of the world. South Korea was a part of the Japanese empire from 1910 to 1945, as was Taiwan for approximately the same period, and both were subject to about the same degree of protection from non-Japanese sources as was Japanese agriculture.

The earliest available Japanese rice price data are for mid 1880s. Comparisons of Thai export prices with Japanese producer prices indicate that in the 1880s there was a modest degree of protection for rice (table 8.2). For the five years centered on 1885, the producer price in Japan exceeded the Thai export price by 34 percent. Because of quality differences between Thai and Japanese rice, the 34 percent difference should not be taken too literally. However, comparisons of the same data series for the next half century indicate a sharp increase in the ratio of Japanese producer prices to the Thai export price, reaching a ratio of approximately 2.5 in 1920. The ratio declined to 1.8 in 1930 and then rose to 2.9 in the late 1930s.

The available price data indicate that the Korean export price was essentially the same as the Japanese producer price from 1915 to 1935.

but seems clearly preferable to an estimate of tariff levels based upon the ratio of tariff receipts to either total imports or to dutiable imports. Tariff rates weighted by consumption would be preferable, but are not available.

TABLE 8.1 Estimated Tariff Levels in Europe, 1913, 1927, and 1931 (in % of export prices, European products only)

	Foodstuffs			Semimanufactured Goods			Industrial Manufactured Goods		
	1913	1927	1931	1913	1927	1931	1913	1927	1931
Germany	21.8	27.4	82.5	15.3	14.5	23.4	10.0	19.0	18.3
France	29.2	19.1	53.0	25.3	24.3	31.8	16.3	25.8	29.0
Italy	22.0	24.5	66.0	25.0	28.6	49.5	14.6	28.3	41.8
Belgium	25.5	11.8	23.7	7.6	10.5	15.5	9.5	11.6	13.0
Switzerland	14.7	21.5	42.2	7.3	11.5	15.2	9.3	17.6	22.0
Austria[a]	29.1	16.5	59.5	20.0	15.2	20.7	19.3	21.0	27.7
Czechoslovakia[a]		36.3	84.0		21.7	29.5		35.8	36.5
Sweden	24.2	21.5	39.0	25.3	18.0	18.0	24.5	20.8	23.5
Finland	49.0	57.5	102.0	18.8	20.2	20.0	37.6	17.8	22.7
Poland[b]	69.4	72.0	110.0	63.5	33.2	40.0	85.0	55.6	52.0
Romania	34.7	45.6	87.5	30.0	32.6	46.3	25.5	48.5	55.0
Hungary[a]		31.5	60.0		26.5	32.5		31.8	42.6
Yugoslavia	31.6	43.7	75.0	17.2	24.7	30.5	18.0	28.0	32.8
Bulgaria	24.7	79.0	133.0	24.2	49.5	65.0	19.5	75.0	90.0
Spain	41.5	45.2	80.5	26.0	39.2	49.5	42.5	62.7	75.5

SOURCE: Liepmann 1938, 413.

[a] In 1913 Hungary and the lands that subsequently formed Czechoslovakia were components of the Austrian Empire. The figures for Czechoslovakia and Hungary in 1913 are thus included in those for Austria.

[b] In 1913 most of the subsequent (pre–World War II) Polish state was part of the Russian Empire. Figures for 1913 Poland are thus equivalent to the Russian figures.

TABLE 8.2   Estimated Protection of Rice in Japan,
1885 to 1938–39

Year[a]	Producer Price (yen/kg) (1)	Thai Export Price (yen/kg) (2)	Protection Coefficient (1) / (2)
1885	3.8	2.8	1.34
1890	4.5	2.9	1.54
1895	6.4	3.4	1.85
1900	8.6	4.9	1.77
1905	10.0	5.8	1.74
1910	11.5	7.3	1.57
1915	11.9	5.4	2.20
1920	26.7	10.7	2.49
1925	24.7	11.3	2.19
1930	15.8	8.9	1.78
1935	19.7	8.9	2.21
(1938–39)	27.5	9.5	2.89

SOURCE: Saxon and Anderson 1982, 5.

[a] Five-year averages centered on year shown except for 1938–39, which is a two-year average.

Since after 1920 rice from both Korea and Taiwan entered Japan without duty, the similarity in prices in the three areas is explained.

Agricultural Protection Levels since 1950.   Estimates of the degree of protection for agriculture at the end of the first decade after World War II and in the early 1960s for major Western European economies are given in table 8.3, along with similar estimates for the United States and Japan. The rates of protection for the 1950s and early 1960s now seem to be quite moderate, even in the case of Japan.

The estimates of the average protection rates for agriculture in tables 8.1 and 8.3 are not directly comparable, but the rates of protection in Western Europe in 1913 and the mid 1950s probably differed rather little. The Netherlands and Denmark remained virtual free traders, and Belgium had a very low level of protection. The United Kingdom, however, had adopted a protectionist stance with respect to producers, though not to consumers. The consumer had access to most foods at international market prices; farmers received protection through deficiency payments.

In the decade following 1956, the degree of protection of the Western European countries increased significantly, except for Ireland and Denmark. Prior to the formation of the European Community, the original

TABLE 8.3   Estimated Price Support Costs
as a Percentage of Gross Agricultural Output

	1956	1965–67
West Germany	22	54
France	18	47
Italy	16	64
Belgium	5	54
Netherlands	5	37
EEC (original six)	(16)	52
Ireland	4	3
United Kingdom	32	28
Denmark	3	5
Sweden	27	54
Japan	42[a]	76[b]
United States	2[c]	8[d]

SOURCES: McCrone 1962, 51; Howarth 1971, 29; and Saxon
and Anderson 1982, 29. The McCrone and Howarth estimates have been adjusted to measure protection in terms of
international prices instead of domestic prices. See Honma
and Hayami 1984, table 1 (no page number).

NOTE: Valuation is at international market prices.

[a] 1955–59.
[b] 1965–69.
[c] 1955.
[d] 1965 only.

members had an average rate of protection of 16 percent; a decade later
in the Community the average was 52 percent. The creation of the EC
clearly increased the average rate of protection.

A comparison of the rates of nominal protection for agricultural
products in the East Asian economies of Japan, South Korea, and Taiwan given in table 8.4 may be of interest. There are a number of paral-
lels in the protection coefficients. Each country had relatively low levels
of protection in the late 1950s, with South Korea and Taiwan having
negative rates of 15 and 21 percent respectively. The rates of protection
increased rapidly in Japan, reaching more than 100 percent by the early
1970s. In South Korea the level of protection remained modest until the
early 1970s and then rapidly moved to the high Japanese level before
the end of the decade. Taiwan followed a very different pattern during
the period. The level of protection in Taiwan was modest through the
early 1970s, gradually increasing until reaching the Japanese level of the
late 1950s and the South Korean level of the early 1970s, but remaining
much below the current protection levels of the other two.

In just two decades South Korea changed from a slightly negative rate of protection to one that is among the highest in the world. Later I shall indicate possible explanations for changing patterns of protection and why there has been an increase in protection everywhere.

Generally, the estimates of protection have included only the added costs to consumers—basically the difference between domestic and international prices multiplied by the amounts consumed domestically. Costs to taxpayers have not been included. Failure to include taxpayer or governmental costs may distort the comparisons somewhat.

Estimates of the total costs of agricultural protection for the United States and the European Community as of 1979–80 are presented in table 8.5 on as comparable a basis as seems possible. This table gives the value of domestic human and industrial use at world prices, and the excess costs imposed upon consumers by the difference between domestic and world prices. For the EC the excess consumer costs were 45 percent of what consumer costs would have been under free trade. For the United States the excess consumer costs were 12 percent. Taxpayer costs were 20 percent of the world value of domestic use of EC farm output and 7.2 percent in the United States. Thus the total costs—consumer plus taxpayer—implied a cost of protection of 65 percent for the EC and 19 percent for the United States in 1979–80.

Fluctuations in exchange rates such as have occurred over the past few decades can have major effects upon agriculture and on the effects of particular agricultural policies. If real exchange rates increase, agricultural exports are adversely affected—as occurred from 1981 to 1985 in the United States. The EC's Common Agricultural Policy was financially viable after 1980 owing to the declining value of the European Currency Unit (ECU) in terms of the dollar. In 1980 the exchange rate was $1.39 per ECU, but by 1982–83 the exchange rate was $0.89 per ECU. This change meant that world market prices denominated in ECUs rose and the cost of export subsidies declined. Consequently, the EC could maintain its price supports at high levels during these years; had the value of the ECU not declined by more than a third, the financial costs would have increased substantially, perhaps to an untenable level.

Declines in the real exchange rate can encourage a country's exports of farm products, as was the case in the late 1970s and early 1980s in the United States. Such a growth in exports can result in unrealistic expectations concerning the prospective demand for exports. In other words, fluctuations in real exchange rates result in added uncertainty and may

TABLE 8.4 Estimated Nominal Rates of Agricultural Protection in Japan, South Korea, and Taiwan (%)

	1955–59	1960–64	1965–69	1970–74	1975–79	1980–82
Japan						
Rice	50 (51)	72 (62)	99 (69)	160 (116)	263 (207)	249 (204)
Wheat	37 (36)	62 (33)	97 (28)	127 (21)	276 (31)	278 (26)
Barley	39 (37)	66 (35)	101 (26)	129 (15)	312 (32)	399 (31)
Soybeans	37	43	53	124	173	287
Beef[a]	113	142	165	146	284	181
Pork[a]	−11	27	23	26	16	3
Chicken[a]	−12	27	21	23	20	5
Weighted average[b]	44	68	87	110	147	151
South Korea						
Rice	−14 (−12)	−9 (−6)	6 (4)	55 (46)	138 (130)	154 (163)
Wheat	−22 (−5)	−8 (−20)	18 (19)	16 (−2)	47 (6)	128 (23)
Barley	−14 (−4)	7 (10)	−6 (−6)	35 (20)	77 (11)	107 (24)
Corn	—[c]	31	17	43	67	101
Soybeans	−23	5	51	63	109	226
Beef	3	5	55	88	281	326
Pork	−11	−5	82	111	113	208
Chicken	−27	7	132	103	153	140
Weighted average[b]	−15	−5	9	55	129	166
Taiwan						
Rice	−31 (−28)	−8 (−5)	−13 (−8)	4 (11)	58 (64)	144 (162)
Wheat	48 (50)	25 (16)	39 (30)	32 (15)	57 (−2)	92 (0)
Barley	15 (—)[c]	73 (—)[c]	67 (—)[c]	33 (—)[c]	49 (−18)	99 (−3)

Corn	2	21	37	29	41	91
Soybeans	69	47	37	13	16	56
Beef	−4	8	20	37	162	153
Pork	15	32	40	38	13	3
Chicken	−50	−2	21	27	29	36
Weighted average[b]	−21	2	2	18	36	55

SOURCE: Tyers and Anderson 1984, 8.

NOTE: Defined as the percentage by which the domestic price exceeds the border price. The producer price is used in the case of grains and soybeans and so underestimates the rate of protection by the producer-to-wholesale marketing margin. The numbers in parentheses show the extent to which wholesale prices for food grains exceed border prices. The wholesale price is used for meats, which again provides an underestimate of the rate of protection to the extent of any producer subsidies. Thus these estimates are slightly biased downwards. In cases where no import or export price data are available because of lack of trade, proxy border prices have been used (for example, Hong Kong unit import values for some livestock products in the absence of Korean import data).

[a] The rates of protection to Japanese meat production (particularly pork and chicken) may be seriously underestimated, since they are based on the assumption that the average quality of domestic meats is the same as the extremely high quality of meats that Japan imports. Producer prices for cattle, pigs, and chickens in Japan in 1977–79, for example, were 5.8, 2.3, and 1.6 times producer prices in Australia (cattle) and the United States (pigs and chickens) according to FAO sources.

[b] Averages are derived using weights based on domestic production of the commodities listed valued at border prices.

[c] Not available.

TABLE 8.5   U.S. and EC Taxpayer and Consumer Costs of Farm Price
Support and Income Stabilization Programs, 1979–80

	United States		European Community	
	Million U.S. $	%	Million U.S. $	%
Value of domestic human and industrial use at world prices	69,939		63,901	
Excess consumer costs as % of value at world prices	8,406	12	28,858	45
Taxpayer cost as % of value at world prices	3,833[a]	5	12,945[b]	20
Total costs as % of value at world prices	12,239	17	41,803	65

[a] Includes only direct expenditures on price support and supply management. Does not
   include expenditures for food and nutrition programs.
[b] Does not include expenditures by member states.

result in farmers and governmental officials permitting themselves to be
misled about future prospects.

Our discussion of agricultural protection has thus far emphasized the
established industrial countries and rapidly growing developing countries such as South Korea and Taiwan. The data on nominal protection
indicates that during the 1950s and into the 1960s the latter two countries had negative nominal protection coefficients—domestic prices
were lower than world market prices. On the assumption that they will
spur urban and industrial activity, negative rates of protection are in fact
common in low-income countries, one might say all too common. Data
on 120 commodity protection coefficients for both high- and low-income
countries show that there were 54 with positive coefficients, 59 with negative protection, and 7 with domestic prices equal to international prices
(Miller). All of the commodities with negative protection were found in
low-income countries.

Table 8.6 presents data on protection coefficients calculated by
Binswanger and Scandizzo (1983) for fourteen developing countries.
While I have biased the selection slightly by excluding two members of
OPEC, it is worth noting that out of 57 coefficients, only 5 indicate positive levels of nominal protection. There were 13 instances in which the
negative protection was 50 percent or greater—the price received by
farmers was less than half the international price.

This review of the historical development and the current status of
agriculture protection clearly shows that governmental intervention in
agricultural markets has been, and is, pervasive. In fact, it is now quite

TABLE 8.6 Protection Coefficients for Low-Income Countries

	Cocoa	Coffee	Cotton	Groundnuts	Maize	Rice	Wheat
Malawi	—	—	0.72	0.62	1.50	—	—
Mali	—	—	0.48	0.48	—	—	—
Senegal	—	—	0.65	0.57	—	0.70	—
Sudan	—	—	0.48	0.53	—	—	0.95
Zambia	—	—	—	0.58	0.62	—	—
Pakistan	—	—	0.61	—	0.90	0.68	0.76
Thailand	—	—	0.91	—	0.81	0.58	—
Togo	0.30	0.26	0.57	—	—	—	—
Ivory Coast	0.39	0.43	0.76	0.73	0.83	0.97	—
Egypt	—	—	0.44	—	0.67	0.34	0.76
India	—	—	—	—	0.80	0.65	0.80
Brazil	—	0.43	0.65	—	0.87	0.57	—
Kenya	—	0.74	0.85	—	0.91	1.30	1.13
Philippines	—	—	—	—	0.72	0.73	—
Cameroon	0.32	0.40	0.62	—	—	0.50	—
Ghana	0.05	—	—	—	—	0.06	—
Turkey	—	—	0.83	—	1.20	1.50	0.94

SOURCE: Binswanger and Scandizzo 1983, 20–23.

NOTE: The coefficient of less than unity means that protection is negative; farmers receive less than the international market price. A coefficient greater than 1 means protection is positive. A coefficient of 0.72 means that the farm price is 28 percent less than it would be if farmers were permitted to export their product without governmental intervention. A coefficient of 1.30 means that the domestic farm price exceeds the international market price by 30 percent. The international market prices are adjusted to reflect potential farm gate prices by reflecting marketing and transportation costs and, where possible, quality differentials.

clear that it is inappropriate to always describe the interventions as protection—at least as that term is normally used. In far too many cases, governments intervene to reduce prices received by farmers.

There is a way to reduce consumer prices without necessarily resulting in intervention adverse to farmers. This is the policy of reducing prices paid by consumers not only below international market prices, but also below the prices actually paid to farmers. Such policies are common in the Centrally Planned Economies (CPEs), with the USSR having the most expensive such effort. There, meat and milk prices have remained constant in nominal terms since 1963, and some other prices since the mid 1950s. As of 1989 all of the Eastern European CPEs and China had significant consumer subsidies on food products. Some low-income countries such as Egypt and Sri Lanka have subsidized consumer prices or have held food prices at low levels through periods of greatly overvalued currencies (World Bank 1982).

In light of the foregoing discussion, it is clear that liberalization of agricultural markets would have quite different effects from country to country, and within countries. Let us now turn to what we know about why there is such a wide array of interventions in agriculture.

3. WHY AGRICULTURAL PROTECTION VARIES

The information contained in tables 8.1 and 8.6 reveals enormous variation in the degree of protection. The rates of protection vary widely by country and by commodity within countries. In recent years there have been a number of studies that have attempted to explain the variations in protection rates. While much remains unexplained, some important results have been obtained.[2]

The studies of protection that I summarize can be said to assume that there is a market for protection. There is a demand for protection, which may be strongest when agriculture loses its comparative advantage. There is a supply of protection as the politicians respond to effective political power. As the studies indicate, effective political power is not measured by the number of farmers or their relative importance in the population, but rather by certain characteristics that permit them to press their demands upon politicians effectively and obtain a response. In these studies an implicit assumption is that the actors in the political process are rational in pursuit of their objectives and that they use the resources available to them in an effective manner. Thus politicians supply protection as one part of their effort to maintain their position of influence and authority or, to put it more crassly, to stay in office. The motivations influencing the supply of protection appear to be similar for various forms of political authority.

Binswanger and Scandizzo (1983) tested a model in which they included nominal protection coefficients for a cross section of 151 commodities in 33 countries. The protection coefficients ranged from the highly negative (0.44 for cotton in Egypt) to the highly positive (2.81 for wheat in Japan). Both low-income and high-income countries were included; however, four major exporters were not included—Australia, Canada, New Zealand, and the United States. In Binswanger and Scandizzo's analysis, country characteristics (per capita income, agriculture's share of GDP, farmland per capita) and dummy variables for tropical beverages, exportable commodities, and importable commodities were

2. This section draws heavily on Miller 1985.

included. Regressing the logarithms of the nominal protection co-efficients on the variables resulted in R-squares of 0.43 to 0.48, depending on the particular regression. Per capita income, agriculture's share of GDP, and farmland per capita, and the tropical beverage dummy were important in explaining the protection coefficients.[3]

Honma and Hayami (1984) undertook to explain differences in agricultural protection levels in industrial countries, utilizing data for ten countries and six periods between 1955 and 1980. Their analysis was intended to determine if they could explain both differences over time and between countries in the amount of protection afforded agriculture. They included the following variables: a measure of comparative advantage, the share of agriculture in the labor force, the international terms of trade between agricultural and industrial commodities, and two dummy variables—one for the formation of the European Economic Community and its Common Agricultural Policy (CAP) and the other for a country maintaining self-reliance (food self-sufficiency) to support a policy of neutrality. This dummy variable was positive for Sweden and Switzerland. Two measures of comparative advantage were used. One was the ratio of labor productivity in agriculture to labor productivity in the entire economy. The U.S. 1975 value of the ratio was set equal to 100 and the ratios for other countries in specific years were compared to that ratio; the U.S. ratio for other years was also indexed to 1975 as a base. The other measure of comparative advantage was the ratio of the average amount of farm land per farm worker to the average capital endowment per worker in the entire economy. Lacking a measure of the capital endowment per worker, the average per capita GDP in 1975 constant prices converted into U.S. dollars by purchasing power parities was used. Again the U.S. value in 1975 was set equal to 100.

The following hypotheses were supported by the empirical analysis:

(1) In the process of economic growth, the comparative advantage of agriculture declines or shifts from agriculture to industry. This shift increases the demand for protection of agriculture.

3. The tropical beverage dummy was negative, as was the coefficient for agriculture's share of GDP. First, because tropical beverages are tree crops, it is assumed that the elasticity of supply is low in the short and intermediate terms. Thus output is expected to be relatively irresponsive to the price received. Second, local consumption represents a small percentage of production and the price elasticity of demand is low so that even a sharp decline in consumer price will have little effect upon consumption. Finally, the only market is the export market, which is much easier to control than the domestic market.

(2) The relative contraction of the agricultural sector (as measured by agriculture's share of GDP) makes it easier for farmers to organize to press their interests (owing to greater ease of organizing smaller numbers of farmers) and the reduction in the burden upon the nonfarm population of a given degree of protection.

Tracy Miller, in his Ph.D. dissertation (1985), applied interest group theory to the analysis of differences in rates of protection. He undertook to explain two things. One was whether nominal protection coefficients were negative or positive. If domestic prices were below border prices, nominal protection coefficients were negative; if domestic prices were exactly equal to border prices, the coefficient was zero and if the domestic prices exceeded border prices, the coefficients were positive.

The other aim was to explain the size of the nominal protection coefficients. Miller's model was quite robust in explaining the magnitude of the nominal protection coefficients, since he applied it to all commodity-country combinations, including both negative and positive protection coefficients. In this summary, only the results based on nominal protection coefficients adjusted for overvaluations of currencies (the adjusted nominal protection coefficients) will be presented.[4]

In explaining the sign of the protection coefficient, the most important variable was national per capita gross domestic product. With the addition of one of two variables, the correct classification of the nominal protection coefficients occurred 82 percent of the time (there were more than 100 coefficients in the analysis). One additional variable was exports of agricultural products per capita; the other was the amount of agricultural land per capita. In the analysis, imports are counted as negative exports. Given the level of per capita GDP, "The smaller the imports or the greater the exports of a commodity, the more likely that it will be taxed and the less likely that it will be subsidized" (Miller 1985, 82). The amount of agricultural land per capita had a negative coefficient in the model; that is, the less land there is per capita, the more likely it is that the protection coefficient will be positive. With little land per capita, a country is likely to be a net importer of agricultural products.

4. There is no exact formula for determining the degree of overvaluation of currencies. The method used was to start from a period when it was assumed that the foreign-exchange value was in equilibrium and then determine the change in the nominal exchange rate relative to the weighted nominal exchange rates of major trading partners compared to the changes in domestic prices of tradable goods relative to prices of tradable goods in the major trading countries.

As these studies indicate, there seems to be little mystery as to why in some economies (generally the more developed ones) agriculture is taxed and in others (usually LDCs) it is subsidized. At least there seems to be considerable agreement concerning the country and commodity characteristics associated with the differences. Differences in either agriculture's share of GDP or per capita GDP, in net exports per capita, and in land per capita seem to explain most of the observed differences. The interest-group analysis as applied by Miller adds something to the explanation in terms of specifying what interests are affected by the degree of protection and what variables influence whether the various groups will find it worthwhile to organize and push their interests in the political process.

Robert H. Bates presents a picture of governmental policies toward agriculture that is generally consistent with the results just presented. Based on his studies of Africa, he argues that as the number of large farmers increases, "the farming community will tend to grow politically more assertive." Bates adds:

> Countries with greater numbers of larger farmers will tend to have agricultural policies that offer more favorable prices to farmers. The Ivory Coast and Kenya are cases in point. Planters, large farmers, and agribusiness in the two countries have secured public policies that are highly favorable by comparison with those in other nations. Elsewhere the agrarian sector is better blessed by the relative absence of inequality. But it is also deprived of the collective benefits which inequality, ironically, can bring. (Bates 1981, 95)

Bates summarizes his results by indicating that there were three factors that were important in determining the degree and nature of governmental intervention in the agricultural markets: the nature of the product (whether an export crop or a food crop), the structure of production (large versus small farms), and the degree of relative advantage that producers have in the production and marketing of the crop. The last point implies that the stronger the comparative advantage of a particular crop, the greater the potential for exploitation through low prices, since the high degree of relative advantage means farmers can continue to produce at very low prices for a considerable period of time.

The role of the structure of production is related to the political influence of large farmers relative to many small farmers. "Large farmers ... often possess close social and political ties with governing elites. ... One consequence is that crops whose production is dominated by large farmers tend to be less heavily taxed" (Bates 1981, 126). This result occurs because it is easier for a small number of large farmers to organize to protect their interests than it is for a large number of very small farmers. It is this phenomenon that explains the increased political influence of farmers in industrial countries as the number of farmers declines. Miller's analysis gives weak supports for this conclusion, but the reason for the weak support may be the large negative correlation between the number of farmers and the level of GDP per capita or agriculture's share of GDP.

Protection of Processing of Farm Products

Not only is agricultural protection divorced from general trade policies, but similar differentiation often applies to the processing of agricultural products. Countries that import raw agricultural products that they do not produce often have zero tariffs on such products but have positive tariffs on processed product. Similarly, in response to the importers' actions, exporters often impose an export tax upon the raw product but no tax upon the products derived from it. Soybeans can be used to illustrate both phenomena: Brazil has had an export tax on soybeans of approximately 10 percent, with nil or much lower export taxes on meal and oil derived from the soybeans. As an importer, the EC permits the free entry of soybeans, but imposes duties on the importation of oil and meal. In both instances, the rate of effective protection of the processing activity is very high—probably on the order of 100 percent. And it is the Brazilian soybean producer that pays for the protection of the processing sectors.

Both the EC and the United States have used subsidies to increase their exports of flour. Flour milling is not exactly a high-technology undertaking and is performed in many economies at much different levels of income and technology. Except to serve the interests of domestic flour millers, there is no reason industrial countries should subsidize the export of flour at a rate that differs from the subsidy, if any, on wheat.

Examples of the differences in LDC export taxes and developed country tariffs on agricultural products by the degree of processing are given in table 8.7. These data are for the early or mid 1970s, but the Tokyo Round did little to change the tariffs and obviously had no influence on the LDC export taxes.

To some degree the structure of LDC export taxes is a response to the structure of developed country import tariffs. If the industrial

TABLE 8.7   Average LDC Export Taxes and DC Tariffs
(in %)

	LDC Export Tax	DC Tariffs
Copra	6.0	0
Coconut oil	4.0	10.1
Natural rubber	6.3	0
Rubber articles	0	7.6
Cocoa beans	26.5	3.2
Cocoa butter and powder	5.6	10.2
Raw cotton	11.9	.7
Cotton yarn and fabric	0	9.9
Raw wool	11.8	1.3
Wool yarn and fabric	0	11.4
Hides and skins	23.4	0
Leather	13.3	6.9
Logs	11.3	0
Sawn logs	4.0	1.1
Coffee beans	30.0	3.3
Soluble coffee	6.0	8.9

SOURCES: The average tariffs were in all but one case (coffee) calculated from Yeats's 1976 tabulation. For coffee, the tariffs were obtained from tariff tables for the EEC, the United States, and Japan. The export-tax information was obtained from a U.S. government interagency report on export restrictions (United States 1976). Export taxes and tariffs were averaged across countries using weights based on 1973 trade flows.

NOTE: The above table and accompanying information originally appeared in Golub and Finger 1979, 560.

countries have no tariff on a raw product, such as copra, and 10 percent duty on coconut oil, the LDC that produces the copra is precluded from extracting the oil from the copra unless the LDC imposes a tax on the export of the raw product or controls the amount of the raw product exported.

Golub and Finger have presented estimates of the gain in LDC export revenue if the escalation of tariffs by the degree of processing were abolished in the industrial countries. For eight commodities as of the mid 1970s the elimination of developed country tariffs on processing would have resulted in an annual increase of LDC export revenue of $1.6 billion. If both the tariffs and export taxes were eliminated simultaneously, the gain in LDC export earnings was projected to be $1.2 billion. The authors compare this gain in annual revenue to projected increases from the Generalized System of Preferences of approximately $500 million (Golub and Finger 1979, 573).

The magnitude of the barrier confronting the LDC processor of raw farm products from what appear to be very low rates of tariff turns out to be surprisingly high. Assume that the industrial country permits the import of a raw product, such as soybeans, free of duty, but has a tariff on oilmeal and oil at the seemingly low rate of 10 percent. If the raw product accounts for 90 percent of the value of the two processed products, the effective protection of the processing turns out to be in excess of 100 percent. Assume that soybeans have a landed price of $250 per ton and that the value of the oilmeal and oil derived from a ton of soybeans is $275 per ton. This means that processing adds 10 percent or $25 per ton to the value of the soybeans. For the present example, it is assumed that the $25 per ton is the value added from processing; actually, the value added will be significantly less than this because of the costs of power and certain materials required for proper handling of the processed products. As noted, the tariff on the products processed from soybeans is just 10 percent. A developing country that attempted to export the oilmeal and oil from a ton of soybeans would have to pay a tariff of $27.50 per ton of the original raw materials. The tariff paid would be more than the value added in processing, and the effective protection of the processing would be a minimum of 110 percent. This is a remarkable effect from a seemingly modest tariff of 10 percent. It also explains why much of the processing of agricultural products occurs in industrial countries.

Alexander Yeats has compared the nominal and effective rates of protection for several processed farm products. A few examples will suffice. The EC had an 11 percent tariff on soybean oil; Yeats estimates that the rate of effective protection—the protection of the value added in processing—was 148 percent. For the same product, the Japanese had a tariff rate of 25.4 percent, which generated an effective protection rate of 268 percent. Somewhat less extreme, there was a Japanese tariff of 7.2 percent on palm kernel oil, which gave an effective rate of protection of 49 percent. The United States had a tariff rate of a mere 2.6 percent on cocoa powder and butter, but the effective protection turned out to be 22 percent (Yeats 1981, 6–7).

In the industrial countries farmers have an ally in the firms that process agricultural products, especially from raw farm products that are imported. It is unlikely, however, that most farmers realize that their allies are receiving a much higher degree of protection than they are.

An interesting case of mutuality of interest between producers of a farm crop and processors is to be found in U.S. sugar policy. During the period of time of the U.S. sugar acts—from 1934 to 1974, and since 1978—essentially only raw sugar could be imported into the United States for consumption. Thus producers agreed to support a monopoly for domestic processors of imported raw sugar. In recent years there has been a rather different confluence of mutual interests. This has arisen because of technological changes that reduced the cost of producing sugar from corn. It is in the interests of the producers of high-fructose sugar to have a very high price support for cane and beet sugar in the United States. The domestic raw sugar price since 1981 has been approximately 20 cents per pound. The production of high-fructose sugar is very profitable at a price significantly less than 20 cents per pound dry weight equivalent. As a result, the share of the U.S. sweetener market captured by high-fructose sugar increased rapidly and in 1985 accounted for 40 percent of all caloric sweeteners consumed in the United States. One consequence was that U.S. imports of raw sugar declined from approximately 5 million short tons in 1980 to approximately 2 million tons in 1985 to as low as 1 million tons in 1989. During 1985 the U.S. sugar price was at least four times the international market price and for some months as much as six times.

There are now fewer than 12,000 producers of sugar cane and beets in the United States. The domestic production of beet and cane sugar has remained approximately constant over the past several years. Since there are no controls over the production of these sources of sugar, this means that the current high price of sugar is not especially profitable to the producers. In other words, the farmers are receiving a net income from producing sugar that on the average is approximately what they could obtain from producing the next best alternative farm product. The primary beneficiaries of the existing policies are the processors of cane and beet sugar and the producers of products that substitute for sugar, such as high-fructose sugar and the noncaloric sweeteners such as aspartame. Even the refiners of cane sugar are beginning to feel the pinch of reduced imports of raw cane sugar.

Food Security

Except for Honma and Hayami 1984, none of the studies of protection reviewed have included food security as a persuasive argument for positive protection. Even the Honma-Hayami analysis is rather ad hoc, since it is achieved by introducing dummy variables for Sweden and

Switzerland and obtaining highly significant coefficients. But in the case
of Sweden, at least, it may be that other explanations for the high level
of protection are as relevant. The Swedish protection levels are not all
that high compared to either Italy or Germany and are significantly
lower than the Japanese ones.

The supporters of agricultural protection in Japan have made persuasive and effective use of the food security objective. The Ministry of
Agriculture, Forestry and Fisheries (MAFF), with the support of politicians from all of the major political parties, has been an active propa-
gandist for a high level of food security. The cynic might well argue that
the emphasis upon food security is designed primarily to support the
heavy taxpayer and consumer costs of Japan's agricultural policies. Public opinion polls indicate, however, that a large percentage of the Japanese people favor a high degree of food self-sufficiency.

The self-serving nature of MAFF's promotion of food security as an
important national objective has been its emphasis upon the results of
the "Projection for the World Food Supply and Demand Model" study.
In June 1982 MAFF summarized the findings of this study in *Farm Product Imports, Present State of Agriculture and Direction of Agricultural Policy.*
Included was the categorical statement that in the year 2000, if prices
were constant, "a shortage of 53 million tons [of grain] will occur in the
case of normal crop and a shortage of 198 million tons in case both the
United States and the Soviet Union are simultaneously hit by crop failures. There will also be considerable shortages of livestock products." In
terms of 1978 real prices, and assuming a normal crop and "a 2-to-3 percent increase in the prices of fertilizers, the prices will turn upward in
the latter half of the 1980s. And in the year 2000, the prices of grains
and soybeans will be about 1.7-fold to 1.8-fold and the prices of meat
will be about 1.3-fold." And in a scenario in which the United States and
the USSR were hit by simultaneous crop failures in 1985 and 1986, "the
peak prices of wheat and coarse grains will be about 4-fold and those of
rice and soybeans 2-fold to 3-fold (of the 1978 real prices)" (MAFF 1982,
24–26).

The first section of the report containing these statements is entitled
"Problems about Farm Product Import Liberalization." The quoted material is from a section entitled "The Necessity for Maintenance of Domestic Agricultural Production." I have seen nothing to indicate that
MAFF has repudiated the rather wild price projections or supplanted
the earlier study by one more consistent with other reputable projections of future world demand for and supply of food.

A speech given by an official of MAFF in 1980 painted a gloomy picture of world food demand and supply in an effort to justify the maintenance of the existing amount of land in rice paddy:

> If Japan's agricultural production falls sharply, necessitating increasing grain and soybean imports, problems may arise in connection with the world demand and supply of grains. The world population will continue to grow, especially in developing countries. It will take a long time for those countries to improve their domestic agricultural production to a point approaching self-sufficiency. In addition, demand for feed grains for livestock production will rise steadily in developed and semi-developed countries. In the meantime, while demand for grain will increase in centrally planned economies, production remains somewhat unstable. In view of these tendencies, it is expected that the world demand-supply situation of feed grains and soybeans will become very tight, and the fragility of the demand-supply balance with regard to good or poor harvests will appear more frequently, thus throwing prices into instability. (Matsuura 1980, 6–7)

Later in the same speech, Matsuura declared that as an Asian nation, Japan should follow an import policy that would not adversely affect "those countries, particularly those in Southeast Asia, where people are suffering from serious food shortages" (8).

The view that food prices in world markets will be unstable and display an upward trend persists in the face of overwhelming evidence to the contrary. In the summary of the 1983 agricultural white paper, released in April 1984, this position was taken by MAFF: "When we also consider the irregular weather conditions in recent years and the growth of the world population, it appears that the international supply-demand situation leaves little room for optimism in either mid- or long-term projections" (MAFF 1984, 24).

Essentially the same point was made in a handout at a small meeting with officials of MAFF in late 1984, with added comment about concerns of the population that have been reinforced, perhaps consciously, by ministry officials: "Under the probable unstability [sic] of world food supply and demand in the future, concerns over the low level of food self-sufficiency rate have been growing among people."

Among the benefits that MAFF claims for its agricultural and trade policies is that they contribute to stability of world markets. Again, in the handout referred to above: "We think our country has been contributing to the stability of world markts through the stable imports of agricultural commodities." This is an incorrect conclusion; Japan does not adjust its imports either when world prices decline or when they increase, thus leaving consumers and producers elsewhere in the world to cope with the variability of supply and demand.

Given the projections and speeches by important public officials that point to the possible disastrous consequences of further declines in the self-sufficiency ratio, it is not surprising that opinion polls indicate that the majority of the Japanese population support efforts to maintain or increase food production in Japan. Kenzo Hemmi reports the results of surveys made in 1975 and 1980 that asked whether domestic production of food should be increased whenever possible. In 1975 affirmative responses were given by 71 percent; in 1980 the affirmative responses increased to 75 percent. Hemmi also reports the results of a poll by a major newspaper (no date) in which 65 percent of the respondents agreed with the statement that "import liberalization of agricultural commodities must be promoted *if it is not harmful to domestic producers*" (emphasis added) (Hemmi 1983, 324).

For Japanese who have any memory of World War II and the years immediately thereafter, it is relatively easy to arouse fears related to food security. In those years many Japanese went hungry. But it is somewhat ironic that Japan was nearly self-sufficient in rice, and in food generally, before 1940—yet this did not provide food security. Before 1940 Japan itself produced approximately 85 percent of the rice it consumed (the rest came from Taiwan and Korea) and imported hardly any other food products.

The lesson that could be emphasized from the World War II experience is that a high level of domestic food supply is not enough to provide security. And what was true four decades ago is even truer today. Japan today is self-sufficient in the capacity to produce rice, but if Japan were blockaded or its trade with the rest of the world significantly reduced, its dependence upon fertilizer produced from imported materials would rapidly result in a sharp decline in rice production. This could readily occur in one year. There would be other negative output effects of a sharp reduction in energy imports.

I do not want to leave the impression that national food security is an inappropriate objective of national policy. But even rather casual analysis shows convincingly that most countries have made no effort to devise a food security policy that would, in fact, protect their citizens against the more likely adverse circumstances. Nor can it be said that the particular policies that are followed are carried out with minimum cost. For example, assuming that the objective of rice self-sufficiency were appropriate for the circumstances that Japan faces, its current rice policy is not an efficient means. The recent and current levels of rice

prices have resulted in more rice production than can be consumed domestically. The solution to that embarrassment has been an expensive
land diversion program. There is clearly a lower rice price that would
be consistent with rice self-sufficiency without the costly land diversion
effort. The current program obviously pursues objectives other than
food security, presumably increasing the incomes of farmers who produce rice. These, it may be noted, are primarily part-time and not full-
time farmers.

But there are other approaches to security of rice supplies. Domestic
use is about 10.5 million tons and declining. One approach would be to
set rice prices at a level required to produce about 5 million tons or
about half domestic use and to continuously hold a beginning-
of-the-year stock of 11 to 12 million tons. Against the types of interrup-
tion of supply that might adversely affect Japan, this policy could well
provide a greater degree of food security than the current policy and at
a significantly lower consumer and taxpayer cost. The cost of the storage
program would be no more than a fifth of the budgetary costs of the
present rice price policy.

This discussion of food security and the manner in which governmental and political groups have created and used the fears of the Japanese
population for the benefit of the majority party is not meant to imply
that what is done is in any way unique to Japan. Politicians everywhere
make those expenditures and commitments that they believe will maximize their own interests.

In the European Community, for example, the CAP has been supported on several grounds that are without substantial foundation. The
major appeal to consumers has been one related to security and stability.
The EC's *Guidelines for European Agriculture* justifies the high and stable
prices as follows:

> Comparisons with world market prices may easily lead to misleading con-
> clusions. It is highly unlikely that European consumers could be supplied
> for long at low and stable world prices if Community supply, because of
> reduction in production, would depend to a greater extent on imports.
> World market prices are notoriously volatile because the quantities in-
> volved in international trade are often marginal in relation to total pro-
> duction (e.g., sugar, cereals, dairy products) and may reflect short-term
> fluctuations in production. For several products (e.g., beef, wine, tobacco)
> there is no real world market and prices vary according to the destination
> of exports.
>
> Therefore the Commission is convinced that a generalized and system-
> atic alignment to world market prices would not be a practical policy
> guideline. (Commission of the European Communities 1981b, 8)

The fact that the CAP is a major source of price instability in world markets is entirely ignored by the Commission of the European Communities. Also ignored is the available empirical and analytical evidence that with liberal trade among OECD countries there would be adequate supplies at prices much more stable than now prevail in the world markets. The commission does not recognize that the internal price stability resulting from the CAP is bought at the expense of greater instability of prices for many developing countries and consumers and producers in countries that permit domestic prices to vary with international prices. But failure to recognize the effect upon others outside the borders of the European Community is not unexpected, since there is no direct loss to EC policymakers from the costs imposed upon those who have no voice in EC policy determination.

4. WHY THERE HAS BEEN MODEST SUCCESS IN LIBERALIZING AGRICULTURAL TRADE

By explaining why countries choose to intervene in agriculture (be it positively or negatively), the previous section has gone a considerable distance in suggesting why trade liberalization has made so little progress. The low-income countries could not carry out many of their urban-oriented or urban-biased policies if trade in agricultural products were liberalized. And in the high-income countries, the political influence of agricultural interests, including the processors and distributors of farm products, has become so great that the political process apparently does not have the capacity to deal with the issues involved.

But there are aspects of the General Agreement on Tariffs and Trade (GATT) rules and principles for agricultural products that also have responsibility for the lack of success. I have dealt with these issues in some detail elsewhere (Johnson 1950, 1984) and will only summarize the main main points here.

The general GATT principles for international trade were that both quantitative restrictions and subsidies, including but not restricted to export subsidies, were prohibited. However, exceptions to these principles were made for primary products at the insistence of the United States.

Article XI, paragraph 2, exempts certain quantitative restrictions from the general ban on all "restrictions other than duties, taxes or other charges:

(c) import restrictions on agricultural or fisheries products, imported in any form, necessary to the enforcement of governmental measures which operate:

(i) to restrict the quantities of the like domestic product permitted to be produced . . . ; or

(ii) to remove a temporary surplus of the like product . . . by making the surplus available to certain groups free of charge or at prices below the current market level; or

(iii) to restrict the quantities permitted to be produced of any animal product the production of which is directly dependent, wholly or mainly, on the imported commodity, if the domestic production of that commodity is relatively negligible."[5]

The following important guideline was indicated: "Moreover, any restrictions applied under (i) above shall not be such as will reduce the total of imports relative to the total of domestic production, as compared with the proportion which might reasonably be expected to rule between the two in the absence of restrictions. In determining this proportion, the contracting party shall pay due regard to the proportion prevailing during a previous representative period and to any special factors which may have affected or may be affecting the trade in the product concerned."

But these exceptions, inserted by the United States to placate Congress, were not enough to permit the United States to carry out some farm programs.[6] To a considerable degree the failure of GATT to be an appropriate instrument for dealing with agricultural protection stems

5. There are two other permitted exceptions related to agriculture: Temporary export prohibitions or limitations "to prevent or relieve critical shortages of foodstuffs or other products essential to the exporting contracting party"; and import or export prohibition or restrictions used to enforce standards or regulations "for the classification, grading or marketing of commodities in international trade." In addition, quantitative import restrictions were permitted for countries with balance of payment difficulties (article XII). This exception was used extensively during the 1950s and early 1960s to justify quantitative restrictions on agricultural products (Dam 1970, 261–62).

6. Section 22 of the Agricultural Adjustment Act of 1933, as amended, includes the following: "No trade agreement or other international agreement heretofore or hereafter entered into by the United States shall be applied in a manner inconsistent with the requirements of this section" (Hillman 1978, 211). It was this provision that required the United States to obtain the GATT waiver for quantitative restrictions on agricultural products that causes other nations to be somewhat skeptical of our interest in achieving a liberal trade regime and of our capacity to modify our domestic farm programs in ways that would be required by much freer trade. The Trade Expansion Act of 1962 reads: "The authorization for U.S. participation shall not be construed to affect in any way the provisions of Section 22 of the Agricultural Adjustment Act (of 1933), or to apply to any import restrictions heretofore or hereafter imposed under such section." In more than three decades we have done nothing to eliminate the arrogance implicit in section 22—namely, that the U.S. Government is bound neither to live by its international obligations with respect to agriculture nor to abide by even the rather loose GATT principles for the use of quantitative restrictions.

from the unwillingness of the United States to abide by the exceptions that it designed and insisted upon.[7]

In the late 1940s and early 1950s unwillingness by the United States to subject its farm programs to the discipline of international trade or serious international negotiations resulted in the insertion into the GATT of exceptions for agricultural subsidies, including export subsidies. Article XVI of GATT contains a general provision against subsidies of all kind, including price and income supports, that might result in increasing exports. After January 1, 1958, subsidies on all products other than primary products were prohibited.

An attempt was made to include a clause that might hold subsidies on agricultural products in check, but it was written in such ambiguous language that it is without any effect. The export subsidy provision for primary products was that for any subsidy "which operates to increase the export of any primary product from its territory, such subsidy shall not be applied in a manner which results in the contracting party having more than an equitable share of world export trade in that product, account being taken of the shares of the contracting parties in such trade in the product during a previous representative period, and any special factors which may have affected or may be affecting such trade in the product."

This exception, which was designed to permit the United States to hold some of its farm prices above world market prices, especially those of cotton and wheat during the 1950s, is now being used by others for the same objective. Had the United States agreed to the prohibition on all subsidies after 1957, the shape of the Common Agricultural Policy might now be quite different. This point was well put in a recent book on the CAP:

> Ironically the Community's creation of the CAP in its current form, with its use of variable import levies and export refunds as its principal agricultural trade measures, was only possible as a result of earlier actions by, principally, the USA. Thus, in 1955 the US achieved a formal waiver from GATT provisions so that it could continue to use import quotas and fees to the extent necessary to prevent material interference with its domestic agricultural support programmes, so legitimizing the primacy of such programmes over international trade obligations. Then, in 1958, the USA was foremost among those countries which refused to endorse an absolute prohibition on the use of export subsidies. As a result, GATT allowed export subsidies to continue to be used for primary products, sub-

7. See Johnson 1984 for further elaboration of the inconsistencies in the position of the United States with respect to application of GATT trade principles to agriculture.

ject to the condition that they did not allow a country "more than an equitable share of world trade" (Article XVI of the GATT). Hence the EC has been able to use export refunds as a principal CAP policy instrument. (Harris, Swinbank, and Wilkinson 1983, 275)

As long as the United States retains the 1955 GATT waiver that permits it to use import restrictions as it sees fit, there can be no significant progress toward liberalization of agricultural trade. Generally speaking, the United States makes no pretense of abiding by the GATT exceptions for quantitative import restrictions—exceptions the United States wrote. We have done nothing to bring our dairy price support program into conformity with the GATT exceptions. Our current sugar program is in clear violation of the GATT principles, as are our beef import restraints. The fact that we use "voluntary" export restraints by our suppliers rather than import quotas is beside the point. The voluntary restraint procedure is one designed to keep exporters from complaining, since we cooperate with them to exploit the American consumer. The same principle applies to our sugar quotas: for the diminishing amounts of the quotas, we permit the exporters to receive the U.S. domestic price, currently several times the world price.

The United States has never taken seriously the requirement that quotas are not to be used to reduce imports more than domestic production is limited. The GATT provisions were designed to assure importers that their share of a market would not be reduced by the use of quantitative restrictions. We have never seriously accepted this obligation. Thus it is not surprising that the EC has never accepted responsibility to administer the variable levies—which are comparable to quantitative import restrictions—in such a way as to assure exporters·a constant share of the EC market.

The United States, so far as I know, has never attempted to explain how the deficiency payments that result from our target prices are consistent with the mild GATT provisions on subsidies. The deficiency payments affect U.S. farm production and thus inevitably the volume of our exports. It is true that the deficiency payments are usually associated with acreage diversions, but this is not always the case. Nor has there been any public indication of whether the output-increasing effects of the deficiency payments outweigh the output-reducing effects of acreage diversions.

The United States and the EC continue to talk past each other, each accusing the other of various violations of appropriate behavior. Japan continues grudgingly to resist opening its markets to agricultural products. It makes minor adjustments, though it has so far completely resisted any significant modification of its expensive rice policy. Until these three entities decide to approach trade negotiations in a serious manner, with the positive objective of reducing barriers to trade in agricultural products, there is little chance that there will be significant trade liberalization during this century.

5. COSTS AND BENEFITS
OF AGRICULTURAL LIBERALIZATION

The unwillingness to embrace liberalization of agriculture is almost universally attributed to the effect that it would have upon the incomes of farm people. There is also the associated argument, frequently noted in Japan and the European Community, that liberalization would drastically reduce the number of persons engaged in agriculture and would greatly diminish the role of the rural community in the nation's political and social life.

Let us consider first the effect of trade liberalization upon the incomes of farm people. The fear that trade liberalization would adversely affect farm incomes is derived from the proposition that the level of farm prices has a significant long-run effect upon farm incomes. The argument for protection and prices above market equilibrium is that farm incomes are enhanced thereby. This conclusion rests upon the proposition that incomes are determined by demand. If you increase the price of a product by a government commitment to purchase at the higher price, you increase the demand for that product and, in turn, the demand for the labor, capital, and land used to produce the product.

What this line of argument ignores is that prices of resources are determined by the interaction of demand *and* supply of those resources. The position or shape of demand is not sufficient to determine the price of any resource. True, increasing the prices of farm products does shift the demand for farm resources and does increase the amount of such resources demanded at any given price. But how large the effect of the increase in demand for labor will be from any increase in the price of a product depends upon its supply response to a change in wage. In the extreme, if the elasticity of supply of the resource is very high, an increase in demand for it will have almost no effect upon its price; the primary effect will be upon the quantity employed.

Increasing the demand for farm inputs, such as labor and capital, has no measurable long-run effect upon the return to a farm input or resource unless the supply of the input can be limited. Since it is not possible to limit the amount of labor or capital engaged in farming, any increase in the return to labor through higher output prices will be quite temporary, because adjustment in supply of both labor and capital occurs quite promptly, especially in countries where agriculture is well integrated into the national economy. The lesson that the returns to labor and capital in agriculture are little affected by the level of farm prices is one that is very difficult for the layman, and I include politicians in this category, to learn and to accept. It seems self-evident that higher prices mean higher returns to labor and capital. But it just isn't so.

The supply of labor to agriculture in the industrial economies and in the newly industrializing economies (NICs) is very elastic. In other words, any increase in the returns to labor, other things being the same, results in an increase in amount of labor offered (Johnson 1973). This refers to both family and operator labor and to hired labor. As demand increases, whether owing to economic growth or to governmental intervention through higher output prices, the main consequence is to increase farm employment (compared to what it otherwise would have been) and not in any significant increase in the returns to farm families for their labor. There are a number of statistical studies that show that the supply of labor to agriculture is very responsive to differences in the returns to farm labor compared to nonfarm labor (Trychniewicz and Schuh 1969).

In the United States between 1960 and 1980, farm output prices declined by 15 percent relative to the prices of farm production inputs. Yet during the same period the incomes of farm people relative to nonfarm people increased from 50 to 80 percent. Dale Hathaway, a prominent agricultural economist who became under secretary of agriculture, strongly supported the view that adjustments in the labor market and not commodity programs were the source of the improvement in the relative income position of farm families that occurred after 1940.

> During the war, the differential began to narrow. In the last half of the 1940's, per capita income of farm people averaged 60 percent of the per capita income of nonfarm people from all sources.
> In the 1950's, however, farm income per person again fell behind—remaining mostly static while the per capita income of nonfarm people rose by more than a third. In the last half of the 1950's, the per capita income of farm people was only one-half the per capita income received by people living off the farm.
> In the early 1960's, we could see the beginning of adjustment. By the end of the decade, per capita income on farms averaged above $2,000

compared with around $3,000 for nonfarm people. For the 5 years 1965 through 1969 people living on farms averaged 71 percent of the per capita income of people living off the farm.

In more recent years, this percentage has risen to 85 or more—although this of course varies from year to year.

So—the labor market did adjust. But the adjustments were difficult for many. Despite government efforts to deal with these difficulties, it appears in retrospect that no government policy or program was significant in aiding the adjustment or softening the pain of adjustment for farm people. (Hathaway 1980)

What, then, does determine the incomes of farm people if it is not the level of output prices? The principal determinants of the return for the work of farm people are the amount of human capital (education) they possess, the level of wages in the rest of the economy, and the access that farm people have to available nonfarm employment. One need only look at the experience of the industrial economies, especially the European Community, the United States, Canada, and Japan, to verify this.

There are large differences in farm incomes within the EC—regional differences of 5 or 6 to 1. It is worth quoting the Commission of the European Communities on the wide regional differences in farm incomes and the reasons why they exist:

> During the period from 1964/65 to 1976/77, regional disparities in agricultural incomes (as measured by gross value-added per agricultural worker) increased in the Community. The ratio between the regions with the highest agricultural incomes and those with the lowest rose from 5:1 to 6:1.
>
> Generally speaking, the regions with an above-average-level of agricultural income are to be found in a favourable general economic context; the converse is true of regions with a low level of agricultural incomes. (Commission of the European Communities 1981a, 52)

What the commission is saying is that high farm output prices, even when maintained over a long period of time, have no significant effect upon the relative income positions of the low-income farm communities. Clearly the large differences in farm incomes cannot be explained by differences in output or input prices, since such prices are more or less the same in all countries. What does explain the differences are the opportunities for nonfarm work, as noted by the commission, and the amount of education farm people have acquired, something the commission tends to ignore.

If you find the previous line of reasoning unconvincing, compare data on the level of national income per capita with the percentage of the population engaged in agriculture. It is evident that the incomes of farm families are not going to exceed those of nonfarm families, except in a few high-income countries where farm people own much more wealth than nonfarm families. As of the early 1980s, countries with less than $400 per capita gross national product had about 70 percent of their labor force engaged in agriculture, those with incomes of about $1,000 per capita had about 50 percent; those with incomes of $2,000, about 30 percent; and those with per capita incomes of $11,000, about 6 percent (World Bank 1985). A similar relationship has prevailed for decades, either across countries or in the same countries over time.

It is easy to exaggerate the potential effects of the level of output prices upon farm employment. One effect of economic growth—increasing real per capita incomes—upon agriculture cannot be modified or offset. As economic growth occurs, agriculture's share of both national income produced and of national employment declines. There is no escape. As people's incomes increase, they spend a smaller and smaller fraction of that income upon food. And agriculture has shown the capacity to increase productivity, at least labor productivity, as rapidly as the nonfarm sectors of the economy have. In fact, in the industrial countries labor productivity in agriculture has outpaced labor productivity in manufacturing and in the remaining nonfarm sectors. Japan is the only important exception to this rule.

The only effect that higher output prices could have upon farm employment is to slow down the rate of decline. But a comparison of the relationships between the levels of farms prices for wheat and corn and the decline in farm employment since the mid 1950s shows that the level of farm prices seems not to have had a significant effect upon the rate of farm employment decline.

Tables 8.8 and 8.9 provide simple comparisons between the levels of grain prices and the decline in farm employment. Employment change is presented for three time periods from 1955 to 1979; the grain prices are for 1970 and 1979. However, the relative grain prices in 1960 were about the same as in 1970. As noted, there is no apparent effect of high output prices in slowing down the decline in farm employment.

International Price Effects of Agricultural Protectionism

Before there can be consideration of the welfare and income-distribution effects of trade liberalization, it is necessary to have estimates of the effects of existing forms of agricultural protectionism upon international market prices. There have been a number of studies made of such effects, and several more are now in process.

320   D. GALE JOHNSON

TABLE 8.8   Prices Received by Farmers in Major
Industrial Countries
(U.S. $ per metric ton)

	1970		1979	
	Wheat	Coarse Grain	Wheat	Coarse Grain
Belgium	100	86	212	214
Denmark	—	62	224	214
France	84	75	232	214
Germany	99	89	274	247
Italy	110	93	231	210
Netherlands	102	—	212[a]	202[a]
United Kingdom	74	68	160	—
Ireland	76	—	—	181
Canada	61	—	117	100
Japan	162	131	770	582
United States	48	52	118	95

SOURCE: Johnson 1982, 359.
[a] 1978.

TABLE 8.9   Annual Rates of Decline in Farm Employment
(% per year)

	1955–60	1960–70	1970–79
European Community	− 3.2	− 4.6	− 3.4
Belgium	− 3.7	− 4.9	− 4.6
Denmark	− 2.1	− 3.1	− 2.7
France	− 3.7	− 3.7	− 4.6
Germany	− 3.3	− 4.6	− 4.8
Ireland	− 2.5	− 3.0	− 3.1
Italy	− 3.2	− 5.8	− 2.2
Netherlands	− 2.7	− 3.4	− 1.8
United Kingdom	− 2.5	− 3.8	− 1.0
Canada	− 3.6	− ·2.7	− 0.7
Japan	− 2.6	− 4.0	− 4.1
United States	− 3.3	− 4.5	− 0.5

SOURCE: Johnson 1982, 359.

Protectionism has two effects upon international market prices: one
is upon the average level of prices, and the other is upon the variability
of prices. The studies that I now summarize generally include both.

It is important to note that the effects of the trade interventions in
agriculture upon international market prices depend upon the level of

protection that existed for the time period covered by the estimates. Some studies are based on the levels of protection that existed in 1975–77; others are based on 1978–80. Protection levels in the first period were significantly less than in the second one. As a result, the international price effects based on the 1975–77 period are the smaller of the two periods.

The studies undertaken by Tyers and Anderson (1984) and Chisholm and Tyers (1985) have been the most extensive. These studies included five commodities or groups of commodities: rice, wheat, coarse grain, ruminant meat, and nonruminant meat. In one exercise it was assumed that there was free trade in the six principal market economies, four NICs, and eight LDCs as of 1978–80. The results are presented in table 8.10 in terms of changes in projected prices. The 1990 estimates, which allow sufficient time for all production and consumption adjustments to occur, indicate that the expected level of wheat and coarse grain prices under liberalization would differ from the prices under continuation of present policies by an increase of 20 percent for wheat and 16 percent for coarse grains. The increase for nonruminant meat was projected at 2 percent. Liberalization was estimated to result in a 27 percent increase in the price of ruminant meat, but part of this difference may be owing to the difficulty of making appropriate adjustments for quality differences.

Valdes and Zietz have estimated the effects of the agricultural protection of the OECD countries upon the exports of farm products by the developing countries (mimeographed paper). These estimates, based upon 1975–77 levels of protection, involved projecting the price effects of the trade restrictions. Based on reducing protection levels by 50 percent, Valdes and Zietz obtained results comparable to those reported in table 8.10, though not as large, owing to the smaller degree of liberalization. Their study included 99 commodities, with the price increases resulting from reducing the barriers to trade reported for 47. There were only 4 commodities with price increases greater than 10 percent— and all of these were processed products: roast coffee, cocoa paste and powder, malt, and wine. Other price increases were 2 percent for maize, 4 percent for wheat, 8 percent for raw sugar, 7 percent for beef, and 9 percent for pork. (The degree of protection for sugar from 1975–77 was much lower than in subsequent years.)

Ulrich Koester, using the model and data bases developed by Valdes and Zietz, estimated the effect of removing the grain protection by the European Community upon the level of international market prices for

TABLE 8.10 Projected Outcomes of Hypothetical 1980 Agricultural Trade Liberalization

	Rice	Wheat	Coarse Grains	Ruminant Meat	Nonruminant Meat
World Price[a] *(% change)*					
LDCs, 1981	− 8 (− 71)	+ 10 (− 40)	+ 1 (− 7)	+ 1 (− 9)	+ 1 (− 8)
LDCs, 1990	− 10 (− 71)	− 5 (− 55)	+ 2 (− 12)	+ 2 (− 12)	− 0.1 (− 14)
OECD/NICs, 1981	+ 45 (− 10)	+ 36 (− 37)	+ 28 (− 27)	+ 38 (− 36)	+ 23 (− 18)
OECD/NICs, 1990	+ 17 (− 12)	+ 21 (− 46)	+ 16 (− 26)	+ 26 (− 22)	+ 3 (+ 3)
All eighteen countries,[c] 1981	+ 8 (− 71)	+ 32 (− 54)	+ 26 (− 30)	+ 37 (− 39)	+ 22 (− 23)
All eighteen countries,[c] 1990	+ 6 (− 70)	+ 20 (− 63)	+ 16 (− 32)	+ 27 (− 27)	+ 2 (− 11)
World Trade[b] *(difference and % change)*					
LDCs, 1990	+ 1.4 (+ 10)	+ 1.5 (+ 2)	+ 4.1 (+ 4)	0 (0)	0 (0)
OECD/NICs, 1990	+ 2.4 (+ 18)	− 4.7 (− 6)	+ 27.6 (+ 27)	+ 2.5 (+ 73)	+ 3.3 (+ 61)
All eighteen countries,[c] 1990	+ 3.3 (+ 25)	− 3.8 (− 5)	+ 28.3 (+ 27)	+ 2.4 (+ 72)	+ 3.2 (+ 60)

SOURCE: Chisholm and Tyers 1985.

[a] World prices are percentage changes in forecast means, with changes in standard deviations in parentheses (based on 100 simulations), for the first year (1981) and the tenth year (1990) after trade liberalization respectively.

[b] World trade volumes are quantity changes as of 1990, measured in million metric tons, with percentage changes in parentheses.

[c] I.e., the eight LDCs (Bangladesh, Burma, India, Indonesia, Pakistan, the Philippines, Sri Lanka, and Thailand), the four NICs (South Korea, Malaysia, Singapore, and Taiwan), and the six OECD members (Australia, Canada, EC, Japan, New Zealand, and the United States).

grain (mimeographed paper, 1982). The projected increases in world grain market prices ranged from less than 1 percent for millet and sorghum to almost 20 percent for oats. For wheat the projected increase was 9.6 percent and for maize, 2.2 percent. The price increase for barley was projected at 14.3 percent. If the grains are weighted by the value of world exports in 1975–77, the average increase in price would have been 6.7 percent.

Maurice Schiff (1983) has estimated a model of the world wheat market, based on econometric estimates of his own. Free trade is assumed for the European Community, the United States, Canada, Australia, Japan, and Argentina. The model includes estimates of the wheat trade functions of the USSR and the rest of the world for continuation of existing policies. Schiff estimates that if there had been free trade in wheat in the designated countries from 1964 to 1978, the average increase in world wheat price would have been 15 percent. He also estimates that if there had been free trade in the European Community only, with all other countries continuing their actual policies, the world market price of wheat for the same period would have been 17 percent higher. This result may seem somewhat surprising until it is remembered that during most of the years included in the analysis the major exporters, especially the United States and Canada, had limited the output of wheat by domestic supply-management programs. If there had been universal free trade, exports of wheat by the major exporters would have been somewhat higher than they actually were.

Stefan Tangerman and Wolfgang Krostitz (1982) have estimated the effects of trade liberalization on the beef sector and calculated the implicit tariff equivalent of the restraints on trade that existed during 1977–79. Elasticities of supply and demand were also estimated. With this information plus the actual levels of production and consumption of beef in each country or region, changes in production, consumption, and net trade were made for reductions in the implicit tariffs of 25, 50, and 100 percent. They estimate that with full trade liberalization, the international market price for beef would increase by 47 percent.

One very interesting result is that no one of the three degrees of reduction of the implicit tariffs would have any noticeable effect upon domestic prices of beef in the United States or Canada. The reason for this rather striking result is that the increases in world market prices would be approximately equal to the reduction in the implicit tariff for each of the three cases: 25, 50, or 100 percent. For example, if the United States reduced its implicit tariff by 50 percent, this would have amounted to a decrease in the tariff by $230 per ton (slaughter weight). However, if all countries reduced their implicit tariffs by 50 percent, the world price would increase by $220 per ton. For the European Community a reduction of its implicit tariff of 118 percent by 50 percent would have resulted in a decrease in the domestic price of 15 percent. The decline in the domestic price in Japan was projected to be 28 percent, or $163 per ton.

Roy Allen, Claudia Dodge, and Andrew Schmitz (1983) arrive at a much more modest estimate of the effect of the voluntary export constraints for beef on beef prices in the United States. For 1976–77, when there were voluntary restraints on beef exports to the United States, the U.S. price of frozen boneless beef was increased by about $85 per ton, or about 8 percent of the free-trade price. However, the price increase for all U.S. beef would be significantly smaller than the estimated 8 percent, since beef of the quality that is imported accounts for no more than a quarter of U.S. beef consumption. An interesting result of the study was that the average price received by the exporters was slightly higher than it would have been under free trade. Under the voluntary quotas the exporters realized the price gain from the reduced level of U.S. imports. It may be noted that there were no voluntary restraints in effect during 1980, 1981, and 1982, though such restraints were imposed for the second half of 1983.

The trade intervention policies not only affect the average level of international market prices but also influence the variability of prices. The figures in parentheses in table 8.10 are measures of the price variability under current policies and free trade. The measure is the coefficient of variation, which is in percentage terms and represents the relationship between the standard deviation of prices and the average prices. For wheat and rice the estimates indicate that current policies have substantially increased the variability of international market prices.

The much greater variability of international market prices under current policies than under free trade results from the nature of agricultural protection that prevails in many countries. Agricultural protection per se need not result in increasing price variability in international markets and in the countries where international prices are directly reflected in domestic prices. It is the form of protection that causes the increased variability. Protection of agriculture that functions by stabilizing domestic prices by varying imports and exports of commodities destabilizes international market prices. It does so by using import and export changes to meet any variations in domestic supply-and-demand variability and by preventing internal price changes that would absorb at least part of the variability.

Consider the following example. A country has a fixed price of $100 per ton for grain, average use is 55 million tons and average production is 50 million tons. The price of $100 is maintained by varying the amount imported, with average annual imports being 5 to 10 million tons. The internal price remains at $100. In the next year production is 55 million tons and there are no imports, since none are required to keep the price at $100 if demand has remained unchanged. As this example indicates, all of the variability in domestic production is imposed upon the international market. None of the variability is absorbed by changing domestic use; since the price remains at $100, the users have no incentive to change. Nor are producers encouraged to increase their production in the year following the short crop. In effect, the country achieves domestic price stability by exporting its instability through varying imports to exactly offset production departures from the average.

Welfare Gains and Losses from Agricultural Liberalization

Chisholm and Tyers (1985) have provided estimates of the worldwide welfare impacts of full agricultural trade liberalization by the eighteen countries included in table 8.10. Their results are presented in table 8.11. Despite the likely increases in international market prices of many commodities, the welfare gains from liberalization are very large for Japan and the EC, two entities with high rates of agricultural protection. The per capita gains are also large for New Zealand, owing to the impact of greater market access at improved prices for farm products, in which it has a great comparative advantage. Australia also gains, while the United States is estimated to have a very modest gain.

Among the NICs, South Korea has a large gain at $158 per capita, and Taiwan has a significant, though smaller, gain in welfare. Most of the other developing countries are little affected by free trade in agricultural products as measured by per capita welfare effects. Bangladesh is an important importer of cereals, for example, and would lose as a result of higher international market prices. Some of the modest effects for the developing countries may result from the limited range of commodities included in the exercise.

The welfare gains and losses are measured as the sum of the changes in consumer surplus and producer surplus minus the net change in government revenue. I have argued elsewhere (Johnson 1973) that the

TABLE 8.11 Projected Welfare Impacts in 1990 of Hypothesized Complete Agricultural Trade Liberalization in 1980

	Free Trade by LDCs		Free Trade by OECD–NICs		Free Trade by Eighteen countries	
	Total (mill. U.S. $)	Per Capita (U.S. $)	Total (mill. U.S. $)	Per Capita (U.S. $)	Total (mill. U.S. $)	Per Capita (U.S. $)
OECD						
Australia	− 27	− 2	1,098	67	1,126	69
Canada	− 87	− 3	650	25	697	27
EC	− 426	− 2	34,157	129	34,156	129
Japan	240	2	30,923	247	30,896	246
New Zealand	40	13	607	193	637	202
United States	356	1	3,805	16	4,158	17
Total	96		71,240		71,670	
NICs						
South Korea	− 11	0	6,959	156	7,036	158
Malaysia	− 46	− 3	− 269	− 16	− 289	− 17
Singapore	6	2	− 44	− 16	− 36	− 13
Taiwan	30	1	1,291	61	1,229	58
Total	− 21		7,937		7,940	
LDCs						
Bangladesh	− 33	0	− 106	− 1	− 150	− 1
Burma	− 19	0	5	0	3	0
India	− 346	0	− 1,647	− 2	− 1,830	− 2
Indonesia	374	2	− 337	− 2	− 66	0
Pakistan	− 77	− 1	41	0	− 54	0
Philippines	− 93	− 2	− 93	− 2	− 166	− 3

Sri Lanka	7	0	− 13	− 1	− 12	− 1
Thailand	72	1	28	0	234	4
Total	− 114		− 2,122		− 2,041	
Aggregates						
Africa	231	0	− 1,264	− 2	− 1,025	− 2
China	− 60	0	− 66	0	− 181	0
Central & South America	64	0	− 1,053	− 2	− 1,016	− 2
USSR	79	0	− 492	− 2	− 424	− 1
Middle East and other						
Asian countries	142	0	− 1,157	− 4	− 1,027	− 3
Other European countries	− 46	0	− 170	0	− 62	0
Total	410		− 4,202		− 3,735	

SOURCE: Chisholm and Tyers 1985.
NOTE: Figures represent changes in total and per capita mean annual welfare measured in 1980 U.S. dollars.

conventionally measured welfare costs of market intervention are only a part—perhaps a minor part—of the economic effects. These policies frequently involve very large income transfers from one group to another within each of the economies. In the industrial economies the income transfers are from consumers to producers, whereas in many, though not all, developing countries, the transfers are from producers to consumers. What social and economic benefits are realized by such transfers is almost never asked. In the industrial countries, the transfer from consumers to farmers results in net transfers from at least half of the consumers to at most a fifth of the farmers, who have significantly higher incomes than the median consumer. Even where governmental expenditures are involved, there is a significant transfer from low-income taxpayers to farmers with much higher incomes.

At the time when Great Britain was considering joining the European Community, estimates were made of the distribution of costs and benefits of the EC agricultural policy compared to free trade (Josling et al. 1972). This study indicated that consumers with incomes in the lowest six quintiles would pay £581 million more for their food with the EC prices than under free trade. Of this total £366 million went to farmers who had incomes higher than the designated group of consumers. Farmers in the same income group as the consumers would have received £77 million in extra income if the EC prices had prevailed. These results are comparable to what occurs in industrial countries today when most of the transfer to producers is through higher prices.

6. CONCLUDING COMMENTS

What does the future hold? There was agreement among the OECD countries to include agriculture in the Uruguay round of trade negotiations. True, agriculture was also included in past GATT negotiations, though in the prior negotiations none of the participants were willing to seriously discuss the changes in their domestic programs that would be required to achieve significant trade liberalization. Nor has it been possible to achieve a modification of GATT rules governing the use of quantitative restrictions on trade or reasonable restraints upon the use of subsidies, including, but not restricted to, export subsides.

The current round of GATT negotiations could show more positive results. The financial costs of the farm programs of the EC and the United States and other OECD countries are enormous, with a total annual cost to consumers and taxpayers of more than $200 billion.

The hope for positive results rests upon the combined effects of the large budgetary costs and the growing recognition that the needed changes in domestic farm policies can only be made if all the industrial countries act in unison. It is generally agreed that no country can unilaterally reduce its subsidies and trade restrictions and permit more liberal trade. To do so would result in the flooding of its market with large quantities of highly subsidized farm products. Politically none of the industrial countries can accept this outcome. But if in unison each gradually reduced the protective measures, including domestic subsidies as well as border measures, then the scope of the required adjustments would be reduced for all. This would be true because the gradual reduction in protection would result in increases in international market prices.

There may also be greater recognition among politicians that the current policy measures have not been effective in guarding farmers against the loss of income and financial difficulties. In neither the EC nor the United States have the high costs of the current programs been adequate to maintain the level of farm incomes, to say nothing about increasing such incomes. As of the mid 1980s in the United States, the total governmental expenditures upon farm income and price supports have, in some years, exceeded the net income of all farm operators from their farm operations. In the EC the sum of governmental expenditures plus consumer costs exceeds net farm income. One can have some hope that the combination of high costs and a recognition that these costs are not translating into increased farm incomes may lead the political process to try other means for improving the economic situation of farm families. Yet there is a significant probability that the Uruguay round will fail owing to the inability to devise an acceptable agreement for reducing agricultural subsidies.

REFERENCES

Allen, Roy, Claudia Dodge, and Andrew Schmitz. 1983. "Voluntary Export Restraints as Protection Policy: The U.S. Beef Case." *American Journal of Agricultural Economics* 65 (May): 291–95.

Bates, Robert H. 1981. *Markets and States in Tropical Africa: The Political Basis of Agricultural Policies.* Berkeley: University of California Press.

Binswanger, Hans P., and Pasquale L. Scandizzo. 1983. *Patterns of Agricultural Protection.* Washington, D.C.: World Bank.

Chisholm, Anthony H., and Rodney Tyers. 1985. "Agricultural Protection and Market Insulation Policies: Applications of a Dynamic Multisectoral Policy."

In J. Whalley and J. Piggott, eds., *New Developments in Applied General Equilibrium Analysis.* Cambridge: Cambridge University Press, 1985.

Commission of the European Communities. 1981a. *The Agricultural Situation in the Community: 1980 Report.* Luxembourg: Official Publications of the European Community.

———. 1981b. *Guidelines for European Agriculture.* COM(81) 608 final. Brussels.

Dam, Kenneth W. 1970. *The GATT: Law and International Economic Organization.* Chicago: University of Chicago Press, 1970.

Golub, Stephen S., and J. M. Finger. 1979. "The Processing of Primary Commodities: Effects of Developed-Country Tariff Escalation and Developing-Country Export Taxes." *Journal of Political Economy* 67 (June): 559–77.

Harris, Simon, Alan Swinbank, and Guy Wilkinson. 1983. *The Food and Farm Policies of the European Community.* New York: John Wiley & Sons.

Hathaway, Dale E. 1980. "Shifting Markets, Government Policies, and the Implications for Agricultural Financing." Speech at Farm Credit/Universities Conference, Louisville, Kentucky, April 26, 1980. U.S. Department of Agriculture Press Release.

Hemmi, Kenzo. 1983. "A Japanese Perspective." In John W. Rosenblum, ed., *Agriculture in the Twenty-First Century.* New York: John Wiley & Sons.

Hillman, Jimmye S. 1978. *Nontariff Agricultural Trade Barriers.* Lincoln: University of Nebraska Press.

Honma Masayoshi and Hayami Yūjirō. 1984. "Structure of Agricultural Protection in Industrial Countries." Unpubished paper. Tokyo Metropolitan University.

Howarth, Richard W. 1971. *Agricultural Support in Western Europe.* London: Institute of Economic Affairs.

Japan. Ministry of Agriculture, Forestry, and Fisheries. 1982. *Farm Product Imports, Present State of Agriculture, and Direction of Agricultural Policy.* Tokyo: MAFF.

———. 1984. *The State of Japan's Agriculture, 1983: A Summary Report.* Tokyo: MAFF.

Johnson, D. Gale. 1950. *Trade and Agriculture: A Study of Inconsistent Policies.* New York: John Wiley & Sons.

———. 1973. *World Agriculture in Disarray.* London: Macmillan & Co.

———. 1975. "World Agriculture, Commodity Policy, and Price Variability." *American Journal of Agricultural Economics* 57 (December): 823–28.

———. 1982. "International Trade and Agricultural Labor Markets: Farm Policy as Quasi-Adjustment Policy." *American Journal of Agricultural Economics* 64 (Mar): 355–61.

———. 1984. "Domestic Agricultural Policy in an International Environment: Effects of Other Countries' Policies on the United States." *American Journal of Agricultural Economics* 66 (December): 735–44.

Josling, T. E., Brian Davey, Alister McFarquhar, A. C. Honnale, and Donna Hamway. 1972. *Borders and Benefits of Farm-Support Policies.* Agricultural Trade Research Paper no. 1. London: Trade Policy Research Centre.

Liepmann, H. 1938. *Tariff Levels and Economic Unity of Europe.* London: Allen & Unwin.

McCrone, Gavin. 1962. *The Economics of Subsidizing Agriculture.* London: Allen & Unwin.

Matsuura Akira. 1980. "Japan's Agricultural Policy." *Japan's Agricultural Review* 80 (February): 1–11.

Miller, Tracy C. 1985. "Explaining Agricultural Price Policy across Countries and across Commodities Using Political Interest Group Theory." Ph.D. diss., University of Chicago.

Ogura Takekazu. 1980. *Can Japanese Agriculture Survive?* 2d ed. Tokyo: Agriculture Policy Research Center.

Saxon, Eric, and Kym Anderson. 1982. *Japanese Agricultural Protection in Historical Perspective.* Australia-Japan Research Center, Pacific Economic Paper no. 92. Canberra: Australian National University.

Schiff, Maurice. 1983. "Information, Expectations and Policies: A Study of the World Wheat Market." Ph.D. diss., University of Chicago.

Tangerman, Stefan, and Wolfgang Krositz. 1982. *Protectionism in the Livestock Sector with Particular Reference to the International Beef Trade.* Göttingen: Institut für Agrarökonomie der Universität Göttingen.

Trychniewicz, E. W., and G. E. Schuh. 1969. "Econometric Analysis of the Agricultural Labor Market." *American Journal of Agricultural Economics* 51 (November): 770–87.

Tyers, Rodney. 1982. "Effects on ASEAN of Food Trade Liberalization in Industrial Countries." Paper presented to the Second Western Pacific Food Trade Workshop, Jakarta, 22–23 August.

Tyers, Rodney, and Kym Anderson. 1984. *Price, Trade and Welfare Effects of Agricultural Protection: The Case of East Asia.* Australia-Japan Research Center, Pacific Economic Paper no. 109. Canberra: Australian National University.

United States. 1976. "Export Taxes." An interagency report prepared for submission to the GATT. Pt. 4, sec. G. Mimeographed. Washington, D.C.: Department of the Treasury.

World Bank. 1982. *World Development, 1982.* Washington, D.C.: World Bank.

———. 1985. *World Development, 1985.* Washington, D.C.: World Bank.

Yeats, A. J. 1976. "Effective Protection for Processed Agricultural Commodities: A Comparison of Industrial Countries." *Journal of Economics and Business* 29 (Fall): 31–39.

———. 1981. "Agricultural Protectionism: An Analysis of Its International Economic Effects and Options for Institutional Reform." *Trade and Development: An UNCTAD Review* 3 (Winter): 1–29.

NINE

Financial Repression
and Liberalization

Yung Chul Park

1. INTRODUCTION

During the past two decades, a growing number of developing countries have followed a strategy of export-led industrialization in preference to one of import substitution. In the process, they have made attempts to liberalize their economies by removing trade restrictions and exchange controls and by deregulating domestic financial, labor, and other markets. These liberalization efforts have been hailed as a sign that developing countries have come to accept the liberal economic policies advocated by many economists.

During the 1970s, however, many countries found it too difficult to carry out liberalization policies and gave up early on. Some countries in Latin America pushed on in their liberalization efforts, only to find a decade later that they could liberalize neither their trade nor the financial regime. These experiences have made other countries reluctant to embark on any move toward a liberal economy in recent years.

In many developing countries, liberalization of financial markets has turned out to be much more difficult than deregulation of the trade regime, as it has complicated macroeconomic control during the transition period by raising real interest rates. This chapter attempts to investigate why major financial deregulation efforts have all ended in failure, and why in general it has been so difficult to liberalize the financial systems in developing countries. At the outset, it should be emphasized that in many cases the failure may have been caused by external events and the

The author is indebted to Larry Krause for his many helpful discussions and detailed comments on the first draft of this essay.

implementation of inappropriate macroeconomic policies simultaneously with the liberalization attempt.

This chapter does not address these general issues. Instead, it focuses on whether some inherent characteristics of the financial sector are inconsistent, or interfere, with full-scale financial liberalization, and whether there are institutional and market arrangements inappropriate for deregulation. For this purpose, section 2 discusses the rationale behind public regulation, and more properly, repression, of the financial sector in developing countries. (The public-good characteristics of the financial system and the distrust of the market mechanism seem to be the major reasons for repression.) This section also explains the evolution of economists' thinking on the role of finance, and the differences in economic performance that led to the accommodation of liberal financial policies in developing countries in the 1970s.

Section 3 analyzes the consequences of monetary reform, which is a partial financial deregulation, and also the major attempts at full-scale financial liberalization in Latin America. This section provides some explanations of why a variety of monetary reforms were successful while full deregulation met with failure. Concluding remarks are found in a final section.

2. FINANCIAL REPRESSION IN DEVELOPING ECONOMIES

2.1. Public Regulation of the Financial System

The financial system is an economic sector that uses productive factors to produce the services of a payments system, financial intermediation, and access to securities markets. It also provides financial products that meet the diverse tastes, needs, and circumstances of lenders and borrowers. It has its own industries—such as commercial banking, investment banking, and insurance—and also a superstructure of regulatory authority. The monetary system is one of the financial industries.

In most developing countries, open markets for primary securities such as stocks, bonds, mortgages, and commercial bills are insignificant. As a result, for all practical purposes, the banking system (broadly defined to include a variety of depository institutions) governs the financial system and is usually the only capital market available.[1]

1. *Bank* is used throughout as a generic term for those financial institutions that accept deposits or issue liabilities that are close substitutes for deposits. In this sense banks include traditional nonbank financial intermediaries. See also Drake 1986 for the underdevelopment of equity and bond markets in the Pacific.

Financial intermediaries perform the two closely related functions of processing information and risk (Greenbaum and Higgins 1983). By centralizing the collection and processing of information, the intermediaries can minimize the resources used. This cost advantage allows them to provide information about borrowers for resale to their clients (depositors) at a profit. In this sense, the financial intermediary serves as a broker. Risk processing, the second function of the intermediation firm, relates to qualitative asset-transformation. The financial intermediary is able at low transaction cost to transform large denomination assets, such as bank loans and investments, into smaller and more liquid ones, such as bank deposits.

The intermediary firm can exploit opportunities for expected profit because it is able to pay interest rates on its liabilities (such as deposits) that are lower than the rates earned on loans and investments. This role of asset-transformer requires the intermediary firm to hold a mismatched balance sheet consisting of short-term liabilities and long-term assets. The mismatched balance sheet, in turn, requires that the financial intermediary deal with the risk of interest-rate changes (interest-rate risk), and the risk of borrower default (credit risk).

Unlike other economic sectors, the financial system has always been subject to substantial public regulation in both developed and developing countries. Entry into financial industries requires government charters. The capitalizations, ownership, types of assets and liabilities, deposit and lending rates, and other activities of the financial intermediary are governed by regulations and sometimes by law. A natural and important question arises as to what characteristics and roles of the financial system make it so unique and different from other sectors that it is the object of public regulation.

The basic rationale for the regulation of the financial sector rests on the argument that both the payments system and the public confidence in the financial institutions and instruments on which the financial system is built bear the qualities of a public good.[2] Financial intermediaries (in particular, depository institutions) supply part of the circulating exchange media and are the institutions through which central bank mon-

2. Almost thirty years ago, Milton Friedman (1959, 8) observed that the market by itself cannot provide the stable monetary framework that is an essential prerequisite for the effective operation of a private market economy and "hence the function of providing one is an essential government function on a par with the provision of a stable legal framework." In a recent study with Schwartz (1986), Friedman is no longer so positive on public regulation of financial institutions, though he believes that the forces that have prevented free banking will continue to prevent it in the future.

etary control operations are transmitted to the economy at large. There is a widely accepted view that the payments system is a public good. "The use of a common monetary unit of account and the adoption of generally acceptable media of exchange in this numeraire carry important positive externalities," observes Tobin (1985, 20). Since free market competition by itself cannot achieve and protect these social benefits,[3] the government should supply the store-of-value characteristics of a monetary unit of account such as currency and should allow the banking industry to supply inside money (deposits) as a convenient substitute for currency. Because unfettered competition among the intermediaries is likely to increase the probability of bank failure and hence the risks of default and breakdown of the payments system, banks, it is argued, should be regulated.

There are two reasons why laissez-faire finance may not achieve or protect the positive externalities the financial system generates. One is that financial industries, and fractional reserve banking in particular, are inherently unstable and therefore subject to interruptions and breakdowns. The other is that informational asymmetries among participants may also leave financial markets vulnerable to market failure.

There is a common belief that the financial system is inherently unstable. This instability, which could undermine the safety of the payments system and generate other negative externalities, may necessitate financial regulation. Two related reasons for the instability are suggested in the literature.

One reason is associated with the role of banks as asset-transformers. In a banking industry characterized by a fractional reserve system, liquidity creation through the transformation of illiquid assets into liquid liabilities gives rise to the possibility of multiple equilibria, one of which is a bank-run equilibrium (Diamond and Dybvig 1983). When (for whatever reason) depositor confidence in a bank that is solvent is lost, all depositors—including those who would prefer to leave their deposits in if they were not concerned about the bank failing—withdraw immediately, thereby precipitating a liquidity crisis. The bank must liquidate all assets, which are sold at a loss. News of withdrawals could trigger more withdrawals at other banks by contagion, and the run on one bank could

3. As an alternative to the government-regulated monetary arrangement, a radical new system has been proposed in which the unit of account does not coincide with the unit of the medium of exchange, and no homogeneous medium of exchange exists. See Yeager 1985.

lead to the failure of other healthy banks, ultimately causing the recall of loans and consequently the termination of productive investment.

Another reason for the inherent instability stems from the technology of intermediation, which requires little specific physical or financial capital. Natural barriers to entry into the banking industry are small, so adjustments in banking service output must occur through the entry and exit of banking firms.[4] This type of output adjustment generates undesirable externalities, as it involves breaches of contract and hence is considerably more disruptive than output changes by existing firms.

In an effort to protect the safety and soundness of the payments system, and to minimize the negative externalities, governments insure deposits, act as lenders of last resort, and impose other regulations on the banking system. The deposit insurance system and the lender-of-last-resort function may, however, encourage banks to assume more risk than they otherwise would. The moral hazard problem associated with these guarantees provides another justification for public regulation of banks.

The notion of asymmetric information (different information sets for different individuals) has also been suggested as providing a rationale for the regulation of financial systems. The asymmetrical information problem is thought to be particularly serious in rental markets, such as labor, and financial markets where heterogeneous services are exchanged. For example, buyers of health and other insurance know more about their health and propensity to be involved in an accident than does the firm that insures them against those risks. Borrowers usually know more about their capacity to repay and honesty than do the lenders who accommodate them.

The presence of asymmetric information could result in the failure of markets. According to Greenbaum and Higgins, the vulnerability of financial markets to failure owing to informational asymmetries may provide a signaling and screening role for government to reduce the problems of observability, breaches of contract, and moral hazard that are likely to be large in financial service markets (1983, 224–25). Because of informational asymmetries, it is often stressed that for efficiency, the financial system must be built on confidence in the integrity of both financial instruments and institutions and trust that financial contracts will be honored and that a legal framework exists for their enforcement. The

---

4. According to Greenbaum and Higgins, the ability to borrow is all that is required to enter the financial intermediation business (1983, 225).

confidence needed to resolve informational asymmetries is a public good, and the role of financial regulation is to provide that public good (B. M. Friedman 1985).

Deregulation of financial firms, so that they are free to pay whatever interest is required to obtain funds and to charge whatever interest is bearable to borrowers, is certainly desirable on grounds of market efficiency. However, as Milton Friedman and A. J. Schwartz (1986) point out, it is an open question whether complete deregulation, or free banking, is desirable or feasible without government restrictions on banking activities. It is not likely that the market itself will be able to provide a stable financial system.

What, then, is the solution to this dilemma? The answer seems to be appropriate prudent regulation of financial intermediaries by such methods as forcing the intermediaries to keep honest and open books, forcing them to diversify their lendable resources by limiting exposure to single borrowers, and prohibiting self-dealing.

2.2. Government Control of the Financial System in Developing Economies
The financial sectors in developing countries are not only regulated, but heavily "repressed," if one uses the terminology of McKinnon (1973) and Shaw (1973). In many developing economies, governments impose on depository institutions (which constitute the major component of the financial system) a maze of interest restrictions on both deposits and loans, reserve requirements, and guidelines for credit allocation. When inflation is taken into account, bank deposit rates can be highly negative, and hence provide little incentive for savers to hold their wealth in the form of bank deposits. The bulk of limited bank credit is rationed and channeled to preferred industries and large borrowers with real-asset collateral. In response to interest restrictions, both savers and investors leave the organized financial sector and carry out their financial transactions through informal unregulated money markets.

Why are the financial systems in developing countries so heavily repressed? The public-good nature of the system (as discussed above) explains the control—or prudent regulation—in part, but there are also several other reasons, unique to developing economies. Shaw (1973, 92) cites historical apathy to usury, lack of effective control over the growth in nominal money, and misinterpretation of the role of financial repression. He also points out that the claim that market forces do not work in developing countries has also contributed to repressive financial policies.

Indeed, it is the widely held belief that financial markets are so imperfect that they cannot be relied upon for an efficient allocation of resources. Usually, the fragmentation of financial markets between regions and among would-be borrowers and the oligopolistic financial market structure (characterized by the ownership of dominant financial institutions by a handful of large businesses) are cited as the principal factors causing the market imperfections. It is also argued that financial markets, even if they are competitive and efficient, may "fail" to finance those projects with the greatest social merits because their private returns are low.

Governments in developing countries intervene extensively in the allocation of credit, in the apparent belief that without such intervention, credit allocation would not reflect social and economic priorities, often set by the governments themselves. In general, when a government assumes the role of the leading sector in economic development, it is only natural that it should repress the financial system by controlling interest rates and management of financial intermediaries so as to dictate the allocation of financial resources in the desired direction.

Efficiency and equity are not the only considerations that lead to government intervention in credit allocation in developing countries. Markets for labor, foreign exchange, and commodities are also subject to a variety of imperfections, and are often as heavily regulated as financial markets. The imperfections in, and control of, other markets often mandate alternative allocations of resources, and consequently invite government intervention in credit allocation.

In the absence of markets for primary securities, banks are the only source of outside financing, and access to bank credit could mean not only expansion, but the very survival of private enterprises. In setting up an interventionist policy regime, therefore, government control over the allocation of credit becomes the critical tool for formal and informal coercion and compliance (Jones and Sakong 1980, chap. 4). Government authorities do not necessarily have to exercise their controlling power; a mere threat to cut off the supply of credit is often enough to make private corporations comply with government wishes. In countries with less than democratic governments, policymakers find it necessary to retain the credit supply control in order to rein in the large industrial conglomerates that they may have helped create by providing subsidized credit in the first place.

While one could make a strong argument that an allocatively neutral system is neither desirable nor optimal, the heavy emphasis on the use of finance as the instrument of government in promoting economic development may have compromised, or conflicted with, prudential regulation of financial institutions. Perhaps it is that the need for prudent regulation is not well understood in developing countries. In fact, developing countries may have more of a problem with banks failing to keep honest books, being involved in self-dealing, concentrating their lending among a limited number of borrowers, and committing other improprieties in part because they are regulated by development planners, not by independent and well-trained bank examiners. It should be pointed out that oversight of development efforts rests with the planning agency, not the banking supervisory authorities. Prudent regulation is even more necessary in developing countries, where government control of financial institutions often provides the breeding ground for corruption.

2.3. *From Financial Repression to Financial Liberalization*

During the 1950s and 1960s, there were two lines of thought in the literature on the relationship between financial variables and real economic activity in developing economies. The main stream of development economics, heavily influenced by Keynesian theory, very much ignored the role of finance. The prevailing view then was that interest rates should be kept at a relatively low level to stimulate capital formation. This view, therefore, implicitly advocated an expansionary monetary policy as a means of promoting economic growth in developing countries.

A similar message was carried through in the monetary-growth models that flourished in the 1960s. In these models, real cash balances were treated as a substitute for physical capital. Economic agents could therefore satisfy their savings objectives by accumulating either real cash balances or capital. Inflation, which is a tax on holding money, would discourage the holding of money and encourage the accumulation of capital. Given the propensity to save, inflation would then increase the rate of growth of GNP as it sped up capital formation. Long (1983) argues that the monetary-growth models provided a rationale for an inflationary policy and the theoretical underpinning to the aggressive, expansionary fiscal policy that allocated a large share of resources to development expenditures in the 1950s and 1960s.

In the 1960s, while various development strategies and models ignored the potential contributions of the financial sector in the development process, a group of economic historians was examining the historical experiences of financial development to search for clues that might shed light on how finance affects real economic activity (Cameron 1967; Cameron 1972). In a classic contribution, Goldsmith found that as real income and wealth increase, in the aggregate and per capita, the size and complexity of the financial superstructure grow. However, he could not determine the direction of the causal mechanism. The underlying causality is likely to differ from country to country, and within individual countries from stage to stage in industrialization (1969, 48).

The causality could, in theory, run in both directions. The growth and diversity of financial instruments, markets, and participants could stimulate savings and investment, and also improve the allocative efficiency of the economy. Through these channels, financial growth could contribute to economic development. On the other hand, financial development may simply reflect economic growth whose main causes must be sought elsewhere. Gerschenkron (1962) was one of the early writers to emphasize the major role of banking in the process of industrialization. Examining the historical experiences of Central Europe, Germany, and Russia, he argues that the banking system, or broadly the financial system, could play a key role at certain stages of economic development, as it serves as the prime source of both capital and entrepreneurship.

The leading role of financial intermediaries was further elaborated by Patrick (1966) who developed the hypotheses of supply-leading and demand-following finance. The demand-following phenomenon implies that as the economy grows, it generates additional and new demands for financial services, which bring about a supply response in the growth of the financial system. In opposition to this passive financial response, Patrick suggests, the creation of financial institutions and the supply of their financial assets, liabilities, and related financial services—in advance of demand for them—could not only accommodate but also induce growth by generating incentives to savers to increase their rate of savings and to entrepreneuers to invest more. Emphasizing the relevance of the supply-leading hypothesis in the earlier stage of economic development, Patrick advocates realistic interest policies and the promotion of the efficiency of financial intermediation through private market mechanisms in developing countries well before financial liberalization became a new orthodoxy.

Inflationary development policies did not help promote capital formation or economic growth in many developing countries in the 1960s. Nor did the inward-looking development strategy. In fact, many developing countries that adopted import-substitution strategies, in which trade flows were restricted and financial prices (including interest rates and exchange rates) were distorted, witnessed a marked slowdown in the real rate of growth and suffered from a high rate of inflation and balance-of-payments difficulties.

In sharp contrast, countries that undertook trade liberalization and monetary reform aimed at encouraging the holding of financial assets by paying positive real interest rates were successful in stabilizing their economies while sustaining rapid growth. Brazil, Taiwan, and Korea are examples of renewed growth by following an outward-looking development strategy. The experiences of these countries, together with historical case studies of financial development, led to a rethinking of finance and growth that by the mid 1970s culminated in a general acceptance of monetary reform and a move toward financial and overall economic liberalization in developing countries.

As Sjaastad (1983) and Edwards (1985) point out, the economic liberalization that swept the Southern Cone countries—Argentina, Chile, and Uruguay—during the 1970s was a clear reaction to the failures of the preceding economic philosophies, which had replaced the allocative function of the price system with that of redistribution. Pervasive government intervention, distorted relative prices, and restrictive trade and financial regimes were blamed for poor economic performances, which in turn set the stage for overall economic liberalization.[5]

Finally, there was the rapid pace of financial deregulation in advanced countries, which undoubtedly helped sustain the momentum for financial liberalization in developing countries. During the 1970s, the high and variable rate of inflation, coupled with financial and technological developments, provided strong incentives for financial innovation. This eventually led to a rapid pace of financial deregulation and dramatically changed the nature of the financial sector in advanced economies. The process of financial innovation and deregulation in the United States, the United Kingdom, and other developed countries appears to have strengthened the position of, and given more confidence to, the supporters of financial liberalization in developing countries.

5. It would indeed be difficult to determine the extent to which the macroeconomic problems in these three countries can be attributed to populist economic policies. Nevertheless, in all three countries economic liberalization was adopted as an alternative economic philosophy. In so doing, expectations were generated that economic liberalization would not only improve microeconomic efficiency but also solve macroeconomic difficulties. Nothing in theory, however, suggests that liberalizing the financial and trade regimes will stabilize the economy, reduce unemployment, and redress current account problems. These misguided expectations may explain why authoritarian military regimes in the Southern Cone, which traditionally subscribe to a more populist ideology, readily accepted liberal economic policy.

3. CONSEQUENCES OF MONETARY REFORM AND FINANCIAL LIBERALIZATION

3.1. Monetary Reform

McKinnon (1973) and Shaw (1973) were the two most influential economists in advancing the cause of financial liberalization in the early 1970s. They provided a theoretical basis for, as well as empirical evidence of, the benefits from a liberal financial regime in developing countries. Combining a number of national experiences, including those of Brazil, Korea, and Taiwan, McKinnon (1973) develops a framework in which a monetary reform—an exogeneous increase in bank deposit and lending rates close to an equilibrium level—is shown to be conducive to a high rate of capital accumulation and economic growth through financial deepening.[6]

In most developing countries the insignificance of institutionalized markets for primary securities implies that the financial instruments for saving in these countries are limited to currency, demand, and time and savings deposits, the sum of which is often defined as broad money or M_2. According to McKinnon (1973), an increase in the nominal interest rate on time and savings deposits controlled by the monetary authorities would induce savers to increase their rates of saving, because the increase means a higher rate of return on savings adjusted for the risk, convenience, and liquidity of savings instruments.

After interest-rate reform, more investment resources will be allocated through the banking system than before. This is because in response to the higher rate of return to savings, owners of wealth are likely to save more in terms of M_2 (a flow effect) and also move out of inventories, precious metals, foreign currencies, and lending to informal credit markets; the liquidity thus generated will flow into bank savings deposits, which become more attractive saving instruments than before (a portfolio shift effect). Assuming that banks have scale economies in collecting and processing information, they will be more efficient in seeking out borrowers with investment projects yielding high real returns. Since investment opportunities with high yields abound in developing countries, the high real cost of financing would not discourage, but

6. Shaw is equally convinced about the positive effects of financial liberalization. According to him, financial liberalization (which he does not define explicitly) could raise ratios of private domestic savings to income, open the way to superior allocations by widening and diversifying the financial markets on which investment opportunities compete for savings flow, and even tend to equalize the distribution of income (1973, 9–12).

rather stimulate, investment through a greater availability of credit. Interest-rate reform thus has the effect of enhancing growth both by increasing the savings ratio and by reducing the capital-output ratio (Long 1983).

The effect of an exogenous increase in the real interest rate on savings, which can be either positive or negative in theory, is essentially an empirical issue.[7] The economics literature abounds with empirical studies examining the relationship between saving and a variety of measures of the real rate of interest. Fry (1978, 1980) shows empirically that for a sample of developing countries, saving is positively affected by real deposit rates of interest, as is real M_2 demand. However, many other empirical studies find that the impact of real interest rates on saving is negligible, though all of these studies are subject to theoretical and estimation problems of one kind or another (Mikesell and Zinser 1972; Giovannini 1983).[8]

While the interest sensitivity of saving remains a controversial empirical question, others have emphasized the efficiency gains from the high interest rate policy (Patrick 1966; Galbis 1977). Improvements in the process of financial intermediation, such as those brought about by higher real interest rates, could result in a high rate of economic growth because they help shift resources from low-yielding investments to investments in the modern technological sectors. This efficiency improvement is claimed to be sizable in developing countries where disparities in the rates of return to capital are wide and indivisibilities of physical capital are substantial.

The validity of this argument rests, of course, on the assumption that banks have a comparative advantage in gathering and analyzing information on alternative investment projects. This may not always be true, however. As McKinnon himself points out, banks may have little

7. McKinnon argues that in an earlier stage of development in developing countries, money (M) and physical capital are likely to be complements rather than substitutes in savers' asset portfolios. If this hypothesis is valid, then an increase in the real interest rate on time and savings deposits will lead to an increase in the real demand for M, and a corresponding increase in real savings (1973, chap. 6). Fry (1978) shows in an empirical study that the hypothesis did not hold in a number of Asian developing countries he examined.

8. McKinnon cites the Korean monetary reform in 1964–66, in which real deposit and lending rates were raised in a remarkable policy shift that had the effect of sharply increasing saving, had a buoyant impact on investment and output, and altered the future course of the economy (1973, 105–11). Cole and Park argue that the effect of the financial reform was ambiguous because it was only one of many changes that contributed to an upward shift in the savings function (1983, 204–11).

experience in identifying borrowers who can pay high real interest rates on their loans (1981, 383).

There are also more serious problems than the lack of experience in credit allocation among bank officers. In the absence of asset portfolio regulations, banks could utilize the increased availability of credit to finance consumption rather than investment spending.[9]

In countries where informal credit markets are extensive and efficient, high deposit rates could result in an overall credit contraction. This is because high deposit rates induce a shift of resources out of informal financial markets with no lending restrictions and into the organized banking sector where reserve requirements and credit ceilings are strictly enforced (Taylor 1983, 197). Improvement in efficiency hinges critically on who controls the banking system. In many developing countries financial markets are dominated by a few oligopolistic commercial banks, which are often connected with large industrial groups through ownership or management. These commercial banks often channel a large share of their resources to the firms with which they are affiliated (Long 1983). Given these market distortions, high interest rate policies may not result in any improvement in the allocation of credit, because the banks could simply supply more credit, after a monetary reform, to large industrial groups that are favored clients at the banks but not necessarily efficient.

A monetary reform can invite greater direct government involvement in credit allocation, as it did in Korea, unless it is accompanied by a relaxation of other regulations governing bank-asset management. Insofar as the government has a strong inclination to intervene in resource allocation, the increased availability of credit, which means an allocation of more resources through the banking system than before, will persuade policymakers of a greater need to tighten their grip on the banking industry. The effects of a monetary reform on the autonomy of the financial system could be more negative than positive.

3.2. Financial Liberalization

According to Shaw (1973) and McKinnon (1973), monetary reform is a step toward a fully liberated financial sector and should be distinguished from full financial liberalization. No country, developed or developing, has ever attempted to establish laissez-faire finance. Beginning in the mid 1970s, however, the Southern Cone countries of Latin America

---

9. Patrick 1966 is concerned with this consequence of financial decontrol.

(Argentina, Chile, and Uruguay) embarked on a course of extensive and radical economic liberalization. The important element was financial deregulation in which state-owned financial intermediaries were privatized, interest rates were freed to be determined in financial markets, controls over banks' asset management were lifted, and foreign banks were allowed to operate in domestic financial markets.

As noted in the preceding section, a variety of monetary reforms are claimed to have succeeded in a number of developing countries in the 1960s. McKinnon and Shaw suggest that if a monetary reform (a partial liberalization) can mobilize domestic savings and allocate them to efficient uses, as has been claimed, full financial liberalization may produce the optimal result of maximizing investment and further raising the average efficiency of capital investment.[10] Contrary to this expectation, the financial liberalization efforts of the Southern Cone countries ended in renationalization of banks, reimposition of banking regulations, and chaotic financial markets. Because of their radical nature and traumatic results, the liberalization experiences of the Southern Cone countries have generated a great deal of research interest and subsequently produced a voluminous literature (which is still growing) on just what went wrong in these countries.[11] In this section an attempt will be made to identify some of the characteristics of, and institutional arrangements in, the financial sector that doomed the liberalization efforts. It will also be argued that the success of monetary reform does not necessarily imply a similar success of full-scale financial liberalization.

The economic liberalization in the three Southern Cone countries was undertaken from an exceedingly difficult situation, characterized by serious inflation, unemployment, and current account problems. Not surprisingly, economic liberalization was pursued simultaneously with a stabilization program. Consequently, it is difficult to determine the extent to which liberalization efforts should be held responsible for the failure. Sjaastad (1983) and Edwards (1985) argue that the economic crises all three countries encountered in the early 1980s did not arise from trade and financial liberalization, but from the implementation of stabilization programs. They are in a distinct minority. Most other observers claim that economic liberalization—in particular, misguided financial

10. McKinnon points out that the best policy, as against various second-best policies designed to eliminate financial repression, would be to move to a completely open capital market where borrowing and lending take place at high-equilibrium rates of interest (1982, 382).

11. For a listing of these studies, see Edwards 1985 and Corbo and de Melo 1985a.

deregulation in an undisciplined manner—played a major role in determining the magnitude of the crises in all three countries.

A careful reading of the available studies on the Southern Cone experiences of economic liberalization in the 1970s suggests that financial deregulation:

(1) complicated macroeconomic management, inasmuch as it created incentives for destabilizing behavior on the part of banking firms;
(2) did not help mobilize domestic savings despite a marked increase in real interest rates to over 3 percent per month and diversification of financial instruments;
(3) did not help establish competitive market structure in the financial sector, but instead resulted in the domination of financial intermediaries by large nonfinancial economic groups;
(4) did not produce efficiency gains, partly because of distortions in credit allocation associated with (3); and
(5) dried up long-term finance.

One lesson to be drawn from the Southern Cone experience is that banks and *financieras* (expanded finance companies) do not always intermediate between savers and investors as is widely perceived in the financial literature, but sometimes transfer net savings of one group to finance consumption of other groups. During the deregulation period, Chilean banks and *financieras* actively competed with retailers and department stores for customers seeking consumer loans. In Uruguay the increased availability of credit from financial intermediaries went to finance consumer credit, with the consequence that consumer credit as a percentage of commercial bank credit rose from 4 percent two years earlier to 12 percent in 1981 (Hanson and de Melo 1985).

In all three countries, it appears, the financial intermediaries were active in financing the purchases of imported consumer durables by making credit available for such purposes. Unregulated, financial intermediaries—knowingly or unknowingly—can easily be drawn into speculation in real estate, commodities, and stock. The subsequent increase in asset prices stimulated consumption spending in Chile, as it implied an increase in private wealth (Harberger 1984).

Financial deregulation produced an undesirable effect in that it dried up long-term finance in the three countries. Even at the height of the financial boom, maturities of both deposits and loans at the banks were less than six months (Diaz-Alejandro 1985). In the meantime, savers became increasingly sensitive to changes in interest rates, and more receptive to new kinds of instruments yielding higher rates of return than the existing ones. On the other hand, private firms were hardly in a position to finance their fixed investment at a real interest cost of over 3 percent per month. Simply to avoid bankruptcy and ride out the rough period in the hope that interest rates would eventually come down, they continued to borrow at the short end of the market and had their short-term loans rolled over. Given the high variable real interest rates, banks, in order to avoid the default and interest rate risk, did not want to make any long-term loans. Banks had the incentives to match the maturities of their assets and liabilities. In the process, they became less like financial intermediaries and more like finance companies and securities brokers.

While these undesirable consequences of financial deregulation were serious enough, most analysts of the Southern Cone experience point out that the undisciplined behavior of financial intermediaries was critical in bringing down the entire liberalization program (Diaz-Alejandro 1985; Harberger 1984; Corbo and de Melo 1985).

At the center of the controversy lie the moral-hazard consequences of financial deregulation, a universal problem inflicting the financial system with a deposit-insurance system. When deregulated, financial intermediaries did not behave in the prudent manner expected of them either in Argentina, which had a deposit-insurance system, or in Chile, which did not. The harshest indictment of the financial deregulation comes from Harberger (1984): "Chile could well have avoided the problem that started in mid-1981 had the banks been better regulated" (249). "I think that the biggest mistake of the policymakers ultimately lay in overlooking the need to keep the banking system under a strict discipline" (248).

During the liberalization period financial intermediaries in both Chile and Argentina took excessive risks and extended too many bad loans, and the insurance system, as the argument goes, was the major cause of their irresponsible behavior. Over time, these institutions accumulated a large stock of nonperforming loans. Instead of writing off these loans as bad debts, they rolled them over and let interest rates accumulate along the way, thereby increasing their bankruptcy probabilities (Harberger 1984).

With the rapid accumulation of nonperforming loans and the subsequent profit squeeze, some of the intermediaries experiencing financial difficulties began to offer higher interest rates to compete for new deposits, which were needed to make up the shortfall on interest payments to depositors. They were able to attract new deposits, because depositors were hardly concerned about the insolvency possibility of these institutions because payment of their deposits was guaranteed by the government (Fernandez 1985; Corbo 1985). The competition among intermediaries for deposits was in part responsible for a high real interest rate in excess of 3 percent per month during the latter part of the 1970s in Chile.[12]

Early in the deregulation process, some banks in Argentina and Chile ran into trouble and had to be liquidated. Practically all depositors were rescued in Argentina, and even though there was no institutionalized insurance system in Chile, the government was forced to bail out the insolvent banks by taking over their bad debts. The bailout sent out a clear signal to domestic residents as well as foreign banks that the government would in the end assume the nonperforming loans of financial intermediaries. With this implicit guarantee, foreign banks became more aggressive and at the same time less stringent in extending loans to these countries (Harberger 1984). Domestic firms took the government's bailout operation as a sign that the government would in the end socialize their debts and began distress borrowing (Fernandez 1985).

A disturbing question, then, is why the banking institutions did not write off the bad loans instead of accumulating them. The moral hazard is one reason, but there are other explanations. One, pertaining to the Chilean case, points out that writing off the loans would have meant a loss in banks' competitiveness. The reduction in capital and surplus that is inevitable with writing off bad loans automatically reduced the legal limits on lending, deposits, and borrowing from abroad, which were expressed as multiples of capital and competitiveness. These legal limits made banks extremely reluctant to dispose of their bad loans (Harberger 1984).

Another explanation finds fault with the pace of financial deregulation, which, in all three countries, may have been too rapid and abrupt for banking institutions to adjust to new market arrangements. Bank managers and officers under government ownership and control had seldom been guided by profit motive in their management, had had little

12. The high interest rate, combined with an exchange rate that was "preannounced" (pegged to the U.S. dollar) in an effort to stabilize domestic prices, brought about a huge inflow of foreign capital, which led to a sharp real exchange-rate appreciation and a subsequent current account deterioration. When the authorities could no longer manage the burgeoning current account deficit and consequently were forced to devalue, domestic firms heavily in dollar debt could not make the loan payments. Capital flight ensued, the availability of foreign loans dried up rather quickly, and banks became insolvent and had to be rescued by the government. See Dornbusch 1984 and Corbo 1985.

experience in, or for that matter reason to, seek out creditworthy borrowers, and had not established any efficient procedure for evaluating loan applications and supervising credit use. When they plunged into free competition, it was not altogether clear whether the officers of the newly liberated financial intermediaries were prepared or trained to withstand the rigors of the competitive market.

A third explanation focuses on the large share of nonperforming loans in the asset portfolios of many of the denationalized or decontrolled banks in both Chile and Argentina even before the liberalization began.[13] As Harberger (1984) notes, hundreds of Chilean corporations that had been in the hands of the government were generating substantial losses and were on the verge of technical bankruptcy around the mid 1970s when they were denationalized. At that point, the Chilean banks began to pile up a stock of bad loans. With this past legacy, Chilean banks were in a disadvantageous position to compete for deposits with the newly established intermediaries, such as *financieras,* after the relaxation of the entry barriers. These old banks were paying very high market rates on all deposits while incurring large losses on nonperforming loans. For the survival of these institutions, the government should have taken measures to relieve the banks of this bad debt burden before proceeding to a rapid liberalization.

Many corporations in government hands in both Argentina and Chile before the economic liberalization was set in motion were in a very weak financial position, and a reasonable assumption would be that the banks under government control were directed to support these unhealthy firms by making generous amounts of credit available at a subsidized interest rate. A large part of the loans extended to the troubled firms eventually became nonperforming. Consequently the governments in both countries bore some responsibility for the accumulation of bad debts. Financial deregulation did not absolve the economic authorities from their past mistakes.

Furthermore, it was not clear who should be held accountable if and when those loans made by the government became nonperforming. As long as this ambiguity remained, it appears, banking institutions were less inclined to dispose of the bad loans, since they could always blame the government for their problems with bad debts and ask for assistance. Thus the past legacy of government intervention in credit allocation

13. A large increase in the nonperforming loans of commercial banks in the late 1970s has been one of the major causes delaying financial deregulation in Korea (Park 1985).

was an important source of, and at least aggravated, the nonperforming loan problem that eventually led to banks' bankruptcy.[14]

A fourth explanation, which is the most important one from the perspective of this chapter, blames the close association of financial intermediaries with nonfinancial firms. In my view, the control of banks and *financieras* by a few industrial conglomerates was primarily responsible for the lack of discipline in the banking industry in the Southern Cone countries. To further substantiate this point, a typical case of the interpenetration of economic and financial power in developing countries, and how this acts as a constraint on financial liberalization, will be sketched.

The real sector of many developing economies is often dominated by a limited number of industrial groups and large public enterprises. Since they account for a large share of total output, a large part of bank credit is then allocated to these groups and enterprises. Because of the limited availability of equity financing and subsidized low interest rates, large corporations rely heavily on bank credit financing, and hence are highly leveraged.

As noted before, economic liberalization is usually undertaken in a crisis atmosphere, when the rate of inflation often exceeds several hundred percent a year, and industrial capacities are underutilized and layoffs are widespread. This means that the large industrial groups and public enterprises are also experiencing financial difficulties, so that the banks that extended credit to these corporations will also find themselves in a weak financial position. Most likely, the banks will start accumulating bad loans.

Suppose financial deregulation is undertaken under these difficult circumstances. As part of the deregulation, the ownership or management control of the banks is turned over to the private sector. An important question in this regard, then, is who, in the end, will control these banking firms? Private investors will find that bank shares are not a very attractive instrument for their savings because of the poor financial condition of the banks. On the other hand, large industrial groups and corporations will be very anxious to acquire a controlling interest of at least one bank, because they know that those who control the banks will also control themselves.

14. In view of the Latin American experience, it may be better for the government to take over outstanding bad loans and put them in a separate government fund for liquidation. This way the legacy from the past would not poison the future. The author owes this point to Larry Krause.

In denationalizing, governments in developing countries lay down a number of restrictions designed to prevent industrial groups from gaining control of the banks by limiting bank stock ownership. Despite all sorts of stringent ownership regulations, the large conglomerates find ways, mostly through cross ownership arrangements, in which they can control the management of the banks.[15] Once they take over the institutions, they start using the banks as a private means for mobilizing resources. It is therefore not surprising that as long as these groups are borrowing just to remain in business, the banks will be forced to support them at any cost.

The moral hazard associated with deposit insurance and bailout was certainly a factor contributing to the imprudent bank behavior during the deregulation transition period in Argentina and Chile. However, it is debatable whether better regulation of bank activities would have mitigated the problem as long as the banks were controlled by a few industrial groups and conglomerates, in particular when these groups believed that the government could not afford to let them go bankrupt.

Freer entry into financial industries is not necessarily a solution to the concentration problem. As noted in the preceding section, completely free entry may be undesirable for the stability and soundness of the financial system. Even when new banks and other intermediaries are chartered to promote competition in financial markets, the government must establish and enforce certain ownership regulations to ensure a wide dispersion of the stocks of the new institutions. Otherwise, it is likely that these new institutions will also be taken over by the industrial conglomerates that control the other banks and intermediaries.

An interesting question arises at this stage of discussion. Why did major financial liberalization efforts meet with failure, whereas partial deregulation—monetary reform—has succeeded, or at least has not resulted in a breakdown of the financial system?

In developing countries, money is the most attractive instrument of private wealth accumulation because, as McKinnon points out, it is a means of payment sanctioned by the state. McKinnon is also right in saying that financial instruments other than money cannot be easily

15. Although the Chilean authorities took a number of legal and regulatory precautions in denationalizing the banks so as not to allow industrial groups or conglomerates to take control of these institutions, in the end the large business groups found ways in which they could dominate the intermediation industry. Diaz-Alejandro (1985) argues that the close association of financial intermediaries with nonfinancial corporations led to the heavy use of debt by private firms, concentration of loans in banks' affiliates, and distortions in credit allocation.

marketed, because lenders know little or nothing about either the honesty or the repayment capability of potential borrowers in developing economies—a case of market failure owing to informational asymmetries (1973, 38). Money is a riskless asset because economic agents believe that their deposits are insured regardless of whether there is a formal insurance system or not, and that the government will bail out banks when they are in trouble. Perhaps, as Diaz-Alejandro (1985) notes, they may know that domestic political and judicial systems are not compatible with laissez-faire finance. More important, however, is the fact that government intervention in credit allocation carries with it an implicit promise that the government will protect depositors from the risk of bank default.

A liberal reform will not make marketing of nonmonetary financial assets any easier than before (remember that the problem is informational asymmetries and uncertainty), but it could impair the viability of the payments system and will reduce the value of deposits as an attractive financial instrument. That is, the efficiency gains from liberalization may be partially or fully offset by the loss of the value of deposits as an instrument of capital accumulation. If the government authorities retain the deposit-insurance system and lender-of-last-resort function, a full-scale financial liberalization will most likely produce serious moral hazards and other problems. This seemingly unavoidable trade-off between efficiency gains (if they could be realized, that is) and safety of the payments system associated with financial deregulation may explain why the success of monetary reforms does not ensure a similar success of full-scale liberalization efforts.

4. THE IMPORTANCE OF FINANCIAL MARKETS AND THE ORDER OF ECONOMIC LIBERALIZATION

In most developing countries, the financial system is hardly the only sector that is regulated. Virtually all markets—including the foreign exchange, labor, and commodity markets—are subject to a maze of controls that vary in the degree of severity and enforcement. If the policy objective is to liberate all of these controlled markets, one must ask whether all markets can, and should, be liberalized simultaneously and immediately, or whether individual markets should be decontrolled in a predetermined sequence gradually over a period of time. Because economic theory tells us very little about optimal transition paths, analyses of the order of liberalization have been empirical and unavoidably judgmental.

While one could make a strong case for an immediate and simultaneous liberalization on theoretical as well as practical grounds (Krueger 1983), it appears that an immediate full liberalization of all markets is neither feasible nor desirable because of the existence of externalities, market imperfections, adjustment costs, and other political constraints. If, indeed, total and simultaneous removal of all controls is not optimal, then questions arise as to the chronological order in which individual markets should be deregulated, the speed at which controls should be dismantled, and the welfare effects of partial liberalization.

Concerning the timing issue, many economists would agree that trade and financial liberalization should proceed in stages rather than all at once. The celebrated Chilean trade liberalization in the 1970s took almost six years to bring down the average tariff rate to 10 percent in 1979, from 94 percent in 1973. In order to minimize adjustment costs and certainly to placate domestic opposition, it would be desirable to preannounce and carry out on schedule a trade liberalization program so that exporters, importers, and producers of import-competing goods could restructure their investment and production.

As for financial deregulation, entry of new financial intermediaries should be gradual and deposit rates must be deregulated slowly, though lending rates could be freed immediately. If the financial system were deregulated suddenly and completely, new entrants into financial industries would offer rates of interest higher than those paid by existing institutions such as banks in order to compete for deposits. Consequently, they would force the existing banks to pay market rates on all deposits (old as well as new), notwithstanding that the existing banks earned market rates only on their new loans. As a result, the existing banks would incur substantial capital losses on existing assets, which would have to be borne by the owners of the banks. If the capital loss were large relative to the net worth of the banks, bankruptcy might result (Mathieson 1980). Meltzer (1985) therefore advocates gradual deregulation of the financial sector.

In general, given the existence of other controlled markets that are interrelated, it is impossible to determine whether removal of distortions in a single market will enhance welfare. However, Krueger (1983) argues that liberalization of any market is likely to be welfare-improving, except for liberalization of the capital account and agricultural prices when the exchange rate is overvalued in a country that has a comparative advantage in tree crops.

The sequencing of individual market liberalization for an optimal transition to a fully liberalized economy is also a complex issue, as it has welfare as well as macroeconomic implications. Although the sequencing issue has been raised only recently, there appears to be a consensus among economists that the capital account should not be opened up until current account transactions and domestic financial markets are deregulated. One of the main reasons for cautioning against opening the capital account has to do with the destabilizing capital flows triggered by the liberalization, which have in many countries led to a real exchange-rate appreciation or depreciation that complicates macroeconomic policy management. On the other hand, opening the capital account at the very end of a liberalization program can be justified on theoretical grounds. Krueger (1983) and Frenkel (1982) suggest that trade liberalization prior to the opening of the capital account is preferable on welfare grounds. That is, either sequence will entail welfare losses, but the loss associated with liberalizing the current account first is likely to be smaller.[16]

Another argument emphasizes the difference in the speed of adjustment in the asset and commodity markets. The speed of adjustment is much faster in financial markets than in commodity markets. Financial asset portfolios are flexible and portfolio decisions can be easily changed, whereas because of time lags, the structure of production, investment, and trade adjust slowly to new arrangements. Therefore, if the capital account is opened first, portfolio decisions are likely to be consistent with the undistorted condition in the long run, whereas because of trade restrictions, real investment decisions will be distorted. Once the trade account is liberalized, the real investment decisions will be reversed. Since the faster speed of adjustment in financial markets to new information means that the financial adjustment will have at most a temporary effect on the production and investment structure, it is easier and cheaper from a social point of view to reverse wrong portfolio decisions than real investment decisions. Thus, it follows that the real side of the economy should be liberalized first. Such an order of liberalization

16. Krueger (1983) points out that exchanges of financial assets are exchanges of the capitalized values of income streams, so that income streams generated by distorted prices are the inappropriate ones to trade. It follows that the trade regime should be decontrolled prior to capital account liberalization. Frenkel (1982) also argues that the cost of distortions associated with trade-first liberalization is likely to be small compared to the cost of the opposite liberalization sequence. Edwards (1984) argues that a trade-account-first ordering can also be justified by Johnson's (1967) theory of immiserizing capital accumulation.

also has the virtue of providing policymakers with the opportunity to observe the market's reaction and to correct policy mistakes that are bound to arise.

Both welfare considerations and the difference in the speed of adjustment suggest that the real and financial sectors of the economy should be separated in any market liberalization. Furthermore, they suggest that the real side of the economy should be decontrolled as quickly as is consistent with other major social objectives, and that the capital account should be opened up only after trade liberalization.

Analysts are almost unanimous on the trade–capital account ordering of liberalization, but little is known about the appropriate sequencing of the opening up of the trade account on the one hand and domestic financial deregulation on the other. McKinnon (1982) seems to argue that domestic financial deregulation should precede the liberalization of current account transactions. However, the arguments for decontrolling the capital account at the last stage of the liberalization process suggest that the desirable ordering may be the opposite.

In what follows, it is argued that both sequencing schemes are likely to produce adjustment problems with equally serious negative welfare implications. My conclusion is that it makes little difference a priori whether domestic financial deregulation is preceded or followed by trade liberalization, and therefore that developing countries should liberalize whichever sector they find more convenient to liberalize at the moment. However, it should also be noted that practical considerations related to macroeconomic policy management seem to suggest that trade-first liberalization may be safer, and hence preferable.

McKinnon's argument for domestic financial decontrol before trade liberalization appears to be based on the proposition that "the case for free trade is clear when the domestic capital market is working freely" (McKinnon 1973, 132).[17] That is, economic arguments for restricting foreign trade become superfluous and misleading once financial liberalization is under way. Under a liberalized financial regime, any firm

---

17. In all fairness, it should be pointed out that McKinnon's position on this issue is rather ambiguous. McKinnon 1982 clearly indicates that domestic financial markets should be deregulated before liberalization of current account transactions. In his reply to David Stockman's comment on his paper in the same publication, however, McKinnon states that "certain fiscal and foreign-trade conditions should be satisfied before the government moves to fully liberalize the domestic capital market . . . , and before it removes exchange controls on the capital account" (191). He also believes that the norm for economic liberalization is Chile, where major reforms for financial deregulation were completed by the end of 1975.

will be able to borrow more easily than before as long as it has good prospects and tariff revenues are not needed to subsidize new domestic producers. I shall show below, however, that McKinnon's ordering is not optimal.

Domestic financial markets will adjust promptly to new arrangements induced by domestic financial deregulation, but the commodity market will send out wrong relative price signals and will induce real investments in the wrong industries insofar as the current account remains regulated. In fact, a liberalized domestic financial market could exacerbate the wrong investment decisions, because now firms with artificially good prospects brought about by trade restrictions may be able to borrow more easily than before.

Furthermore, it is not altogether clear whether a liberalized domestic capital market would throw out correct interest-rate signals. To show this, let us assume that domestic factor markets are fully liberalized and competitive. In a small open economy with controlled capital account transactions, however, the existing wage-rental ratio is likely to differ rather substantially from the one that will be established after liberalization of the capital account. This is because controls on capital will continue to distort domestic portfolio decisions and restrict the inflow of foreign capital below the level that may be most efficient.

The future liberalization of both current account and capital account transactions will therefore lead to a reversal of investment decisions, inasmuch as liberalization will change domestic relative prices and interest rates. Once again, it is difficult to determine whether a domestic financial liberalization in the presence of trade restrictions and foreign-exchange controls would be welfare-improving.

The preceding argument, however, is not totally convincing. A fairly obvious point is that a liberalized current account will send out correct relative price signals—but a repressive financial regime could interfere with the expected movement of resources (triggered by trade liberalization) to the sectors with the highest rates of return to capital, thereby negating the benefits of freer trade. Financial market controls—credit rationing, interest-rate ceilings, and entry restrictions—not only result in an inefficient allocation of resources, but also interfere with mobility of capital between industries and sectors.

Financial intermediaries long entrenched in a regulatory environment and seldom guided by profit motives are often unable to respond to the new incentive structure produced by trade liberalization. Removal of trade restrictions generates incentives to shift resources out of import-competing industries and into the exportables sector if it is accompanied by a real depreciation of the exchange rate. However, export industries are new, investment in these industries is often perceived to be subject to high risks, and new exporters often do not have viable credit records or collateral. For these reasons, and because of simple inertia, the controlled financial intermediaries may be unable or unwilling to finance the new investment projects in the exportables sector, and as a consequence could not facilitate the sectoral resource shift expected of a trade liberalization. Furthermore, real wage rigidity often restricts labor mobility and results in massive unemployment when trade restrictions are quickly removed. A regulated financial system could thus compound a situation that is bad enough already.

Even when financial intermediaries' unresponsiveness to new arrangements and information is discounted, it is not clear if a trade liberalization will improve welfare and resource allocation. In developing economies, some industries are protected in domestic markets, others are given interest and tax subsidies, and still others are favored by financial institutions in credit allocation. In a financially repressed regime, where banks are often the major source of industrial financing, access to bank credit could be critical for both a firm's expansion and its survival.

Preferential treatment in credit allocation is an immeasurably valuable subsidy, which cannot easily be quantified. Elimination of some distortions through trade liberalization will therefore end up favoring some industries and discriminating against others more than before, and could conceivably increase the variations in the effective rates of protection across industries. Hence it does not necessarily lead to a more efficient allocation of resources.

On the appropriate order of liberalization of domestic financial markets and the trade account, I have presented a rather obvious argument, but it nevertheless points to the futility of the market-sequencing discussion. The rationale for liberalizing financial markets is to allow the allocation of resources taking place through financial markets to better respond to incentives created elsewhere in the economy.

To the extent that the incentives are wrong because relative prices are distorted by the trade restrictions, the advantage of financial liberalization, which aims at developing a more effective set of responses on the part of the financial system to new information, will be lost. Conversely, a trade liberalization may provide correct incentives as it removes distortions in the relative price structure. However, a controlled financial system is not able to better respond to the set of correct incentives, and thereby does not allow realization of the benefits of free trade.

What conclusions can one draw from the preceding discussion? One conclusion is that neither the trade nor the financial regime can be deregulated immediately. Economic and political constraints suggest that liberalization reform can only be carried out, if at all, in a piecemeal fashion over a period of time in both financial and commodity markets. Since neither sequencing (trade first and finance later, or the opposite order) is a priori desirable from the point of view of welfare improvement and the minimization of adjustment costs, trade and financial liberalization should begin at the same time, though conceivably allowance could be made for the difference in the speed of deregulation. If, for whatever reasons, it is not possible to liberate both regimes simultaneously, it does not in theory make much difference which regime is decontrolled first. The experiences of Korea and other countries that have followed an export-led industrialization strategy suggest, however, that trade-first liberalization is preferable—provided that the government intervenes in financial markets in such a way as to channel more financial resources to export-oriented industries, as Korea was able to do in the 1960s.

There are two other reasons why the trade-first sequencing may be desirable. One, economists do not know enough about how banks and other financial intermediaries would behave in a laissez-faire environment. In many cases, including the Southern Cone experiences, financial deregulation has invariably led to high real interest rates, often above the expected real rate of return to capital. The causes of such an increase in real interest rates are not fully known. Until we understand more about the full impact of financial deregulation, caution is in order in liberalizing financial markets.

Another reason for advocating trade liberalization prior to domestic financial deregulation is that with a more effective control over monetary aggregates, economic authorities will be better able to deal with some of the macroeconomic problems (such as current account deteriorations) that may be brought about by the trade liberalization. As Krueger (1983) points out, most of the trade liberalization efforts in developing countries have been undertaken in a crisis environment with a very high rate of inflation, and have been accompanied by stabilization policies designed to slow down inflation. The failure of the liberalization programs can largely be attributed to failure in stabilizing the economy. In view of this experience, the postponement of financial deregulation may be desirable in the sense that it provides the authorities with one more effective policy instrument to combat inflation, thereby increasing the probability of success of the trade liberalization program.

5. SUMMARY AND CONCLUDING REMARKS

There is considerable empirical evidence showing that developing countries following outward-looking development strategies and liberal economic policies have in general outperformed those pursuing restrictive trade and financial policies or attempting to develop their industries through import substitution. Despite this ample and clear evidence, a large number of developing countries are still trapped in a maze of controls over economic activity.

A number of developing countries that attempted to liberalize their economies in the 1970s had to give up the reform programs shortly after their inception for a number of economic and political reasons. Some countries managed to push through liberal reforms, but a decade later they were faced with economic crises of unprecedented proportions. Discouraged by these experiences, other developing countries have been extremely reluctant to undertake economic liberalization.

In comparison to trade liberalization, full deregulation of the financial system has been much more problematic than expected, as it hampers macroeconomic control during the transition period. The purpose of this essay has been to investigate why it has been difficult to liberalize financial markets in developing countries, and why some major liberalization efforts ended in failure. In particular, this essay focuses on whether there are inherent characteristics and institutional arrangements of the financial sector that interfere with or limit the scope of liberalization.

In developing countries the financial system is not only regulated, but heavily repressed. One frequent explanation for the repression is that financial markets are so imperfect that they do not mobilize resources as much as they should and therefore do not allocate in an efficient manner. Even when they are competitive, it is argued, allocations through the financial market conflict with equity considerations. Without government intervention some sectors receive more financial resources than socially and economically desirable, while others may be left out of the allocation process.

Unlike other sectors of the economy, the financial system—in particular, the payments system—has strong public-good characteristics and carries positive externalities. In general, free market competition may not be able to realize and protect the benefits of a stable financial system. In this regard, of particular importance to our analysis is that the banking industry, which constitutes the main component of the financial sector in developing countries, is inherently unstable. Without public regulation, the payments system could be subject to breakdowns and interruptions owing to bank failures.

Financial markets are, in general, vulnerable to failure owing to informational asymmetries, which again are likely to be more serious in developing economies. In the absence of state intervention, it is difficult to develop public confidence in financial institutions and instruments, a critical ingredient for building a stable financial system. In order to protect the safety and soundness of the payments system, governments institute deposit insurance systems and also act as lenders of last resort. These guarantees create moral hazards, thus providing further justification for regulating the financial system.

A third factor that interferes with financial liberalization is the high degree of business concentration (a limited number of affiliated enterprises accounting for a disproportionately large share of all markets), a feature many developing countries have in common. Eager to sustain rapid growth through the exploitation of such technological factors as increasing returns to scale, minimum efficient size of firm, and indivisibilities in production processes, policymakers of developing countries often allocate a large share of their limited resources to a handful of private enterprises, thereby allowing the formation of powerful industrial groups. Needless to say, they account for a large part of the domestic bank credit, and exercise dominant influence in practically all markets.

As long as these market imperfections in the real side exist, financial deregulation is not likely to develop a competitive market structure in the financial system—largely because industrial groups usually find ways in which they can control management and credit allocation of banking institutions even when bank ownership regulations are strictly enforced.

The concentration problems could easily frustrate financial deregulation when the deregulation is undertaken from a difficult macroeconomic situation, in which most business groups will also find themselves in precarious financial situations. When the banking industry is deregulated, the business groups will make certain that they secure a controlling interest in the banks, because the credit supply could easily determine their fate. Once they take control of banks, they will use these intermediaries as private means for mobilizing resources. As a result, when the large business groups are in trouble, so are the banks. When the groups are driven to distress financing just to remain in business, the connected banks will pay whatever interest rates markets will bear to attract depositors.

Relaxation of the barriers to entry into the banking industry is not an answer to the concentration problem. It has already been established that entry into the banking industry cannot be completely liberalized. Even when entry requirements are relaxed, the business groups can exercise their market power to block the establishment of, or to control, new entrants. Opening the bank intermediation market to foreign competition will not help mitigate the problem. Foreign bank branches could in fact add to the instability, since inasmuch as their actions are dictated solely by considerations of profit, they are freer to move in and out of the market, and could also serve as conduits for capital flight.

A fourth factor that often constrains financial liberalization is the use of discretionary credit allocation as a major tool for coercion and compliance. Because of the critical importance of access to bank credit, control of credit allocation has been shown to be the most effective means of ensuring the compliance of the private sector with government commands. In general, authoritarian regimes in developing countries will find the use of credit allocation as a major means of enforcing command irresistible. Many governments in developing countries have promoted business concentration to achieve rapid growth by their credit allocation policies. It is indeed an irony that they have to use credit policy to rein in the business groups they helped create in the first place.

If laissez-faire finance is indeed neither feasible nor desirable, is there an alternative system? What is needed is prudent regulation of banks on the part of government in order to strike a balance between competitive efficiency and safety of the banking system. However, policymakers, who in developing countries have a propensity to activist development policies, could easily succumb to the temptation of crossing the fine line of prudent regulation by intervening in credit allocations. In so doing, the government becomes a public monopoly in the only capital market available, that is, the bank credit market.

The public-good nature of the financial system may also explain why monetary reform—a partial liberalization—has been successful in mobilizing savings and in allocating them to efficient uses, whereas full-scale financial liberalization has not. Financial deregulation may succeed initially in inducing savers to save more and also in terms of financial assets. As the deregulation proceeds further, however, it is at some point bound to threaten the soundness and safety of the financial system—in particular, the payments system. Once public confidence in the system is eroded and the moral hazard begins to spread, financial liberalization efforts will in all likelihood come to an end. Especially when liberalization efforts are made in economically difficult situations, the moral hazards triggered by the accumulation of nonperforming loans virtually assure disaster.

In view of these potential problems with financial liberalization, what is the most effective way of liberalizing domestic financial markets without impairing the payments system? This chapter argues that there are certain institutional reforms developing countries should undertake before moving to full financial liberalization.

The first and most important reform is to institute safeguards to keep large business groups and banks at arm's length from each other, in order to prevent such groups from dominating the banking system. The second necessary reform is to separate the monetary and intermediation functions of banks, as Tobin (1985) suggests. This can be done by creating several categories of deposit liabilities backed by specific earmarked assets, one of which is 100 percent reserve deposits at the central bank. Deposit insurance is then limited to certain other liabilities.

The third reform is the development of nonbank financial intermediaries, such as mutual funds, trust, finance, and insurance companies, and pension funds, which could be subject to less government control.[18] Before embarking on full liberalization of a system dominated by the banking industry, it may be necessary to invest in developing nonbank financial intermediaries and markets for primary securities to increase the depth, breadth, and resilience of the system. Liberalization may begin with these institutions, so that they can compete in, and eventually integrate with, the organized financial system and informal credit markets. This will build up more pressure for further liberalization and eventually force deregulation of the banking sector.

This chapter has also examined whether there is any appropriate order in which domestic financial deregulation and trade liberalization should be carried out. While there is no doubt that capital account deregulation should be undertaken, if at all, at the very last stage of any liberalization program, little can be said about the desirability of liberalizing domestic financial markets prior to trade liberalization or vice

18. It should be noted that nonbank financial intermediaries also have attributes of a public good, and as such should be subject to prudent regulation.

versa. If, for whatever reason, it is not possible to liberalize both regimes simultaneously, developing countries are well advised to liberalize whichever is convenient, because in theory it does not make much difference which is deregulated first.

REFERENCES

Cameron, R. 1967. *Banking in the Early Stages of Industrialization.* New York: Oxford University Press.

————. 1972. *Banking and Economic Development.* New York: Oxford University Press.

Cole, D., and Yung Chul Park. 1983. *Financial Development in Korea, 1975–1978.* Studies in the Modernization of the Republic of Korea, 1945–1975. Cambridge, Mass.: Council on East Asian Studies, Harvard University.

Corbo, V. 1985. "Reforms and Macroeconomic Adjustments in Chile during 1974–84." In Corbo and de Melo 1985b, 893–916.

Corbo, V. and J. de Melo. 1985a. "Overview and Summary." In Corbo and de Melo 1985b, 863–66.

————, eds. 1985b. *Liberalization with Stabilization in the Southern Cone of Latin America.* Special issue of *World Development* 13 (August).

Diamond, D. W., and D. H. Dybvig. 1983. "Bank Runs, Deposit Insurance, and Liquidity." *Journal of Political Economy* 91 (June): 401–19.

Diaz-Alejandro, C. F. 1985. "Good-bye Financial Repression and Hello Financial Crash." *Journal of Development Economics* 19 (April): 1–24.

Dornbusch, Rüdiger. 1984. "External Debt, Budget Deficits, and Disequilibrium Exchange Rates." In G. W. Smith and J. T. Cuddington, eds., *International Debt and Developing Countries.* Washington, D.C.: World Bank, 1984.

Drake, Peter J. 1986. "The Development of Equity and Bond Markets in the Pacific Region." In Augustine H. H. Tan and Basant Kapur, ed., *Pacific Growth and Financial Interdependence.* Sydney: Allen & Unwin.

Edwards, Sebastian. 1984. *The Order of Liberalization of the External Sector in Developing Countries.* Essays in International Finance no. 156. Princeton: International Finance Section, Department of Economics, Princeton University.

————. 1985. "Stabilization with Liberalization: An Evaluation of Ten Years of Chile's Experiment with Free Market Policies, 1973–83." *Economic Development and Cultural Change* 33 (January): 223–54.

Fernandez, R. B. 1985. "The Expectations Management Approach to Stabilization in Argentina during 1976–82." In Corbo and de Melo 1985b, 871–92.

Frenkel, J. A. 1982. "The Order of Economic Liberalization: Lessons from Chile and Argentina—A Comment." In *Economic Policy in a World of Change,* 199–201. Carnegie-Rochester Conference Series on Public Policy 17.

Friedman, B. M. 1985. "Monetary and Regulatory Policies for Developing Financial Systems." In *Monetary Policy in a Changing Financial Environment.* Seoul: Bank of Korea.

Friedman, Milton. 1959. *A Program for Monetary Stability.* New York: Fordham University Press.

Friedman, Milton, and A. J. Schwartz. 1986. "Has Government Any Role in Money?" *Journal of Monetary Economics* 17 (January): 37–62.

Fry, M. J. 1978. "Money and Capital or Financial Deepening in Economic Development." *Journal of Money, Credit and Banking* 10 (November): 464–75.

————. 1980. "Saving, Investment, Growth and the Cost of Financial Repression." *World Development* 8 (April): 317–27.

Galbis, V. 1977. "Financial Intermediation and Economic Growth in Less Developed Countries: A Theoretical Approach." *Journal of Development Studies* 13 (January): 58–72.

Gerschenkron, A. 1962. *Economic Backwardness in Historical Perspective: A Book of Essays.* Cambridge, Mass: Harvard University Press.

Giovannini, A. 1983. "The Interest Elasticity of Savings in Developing Countries." *World Development* 11 (July): 601–7.

Goldsmith, R. W. 1969. *Financial Structure.* New Haven: Yale University Press.

Greenbaum, S. I., and B. Higgins. 1983. "Financial Innovation." In G. J. Benston, ed., *Financial Services: The Changing Institutions and Government Policy.* Englewood Cliffs, N.J.: Prentice-Hall.

Harberger, A. C. 1984. "Lessons for Debtor-Country Managers and Policymakers." In G. W. Smith and J. T. Cuddington, eds., *International Debt and Developing Countries.* Washington, D.C.: World Bank.

Hanson, J., and J. de Melo. 1985. "External Shocks, Financial Reforms, and Stabilization Attempts in Uruguay during 1974–83." In Corbo and de Melo 1985b, 917–39.

Johnson, H. G. 1967. "The Possibility of Income Losses from Increased Efficiency or Factor Accumulation in the Presence of Tariffs." *Economic Journal* 77 (March): 151–54.

Jones, Leroy P., and Il Sakong. 1980. *Government, Business, and Entrepreneurship in Economic Development: The Korean Case.* Studies in the Modernization of the Republic of Korea, 1945–1975. Cambridge, Mass.: Council on East Asian Studies, Harvard University.

Krueger, Anne O. 1983. "Problems of Liberalization." Paper presented at a conference on the world's economic growth problems, Mexico City, April.

Long, M. 1983 "Review of Financial Sector Work in the World Bank." Mimeographed.

McKinnon, Ronald. 1973. *Money and Capital in Economic Development.* Washington, D.C.: Brookings Institution.

————. 1981. "Financial Repression and the Liberalization Problems within Less Developed Countries." In S. Grassman and E. Lundberg, eds., *The Past and Prospects for the World Economic Order.* London: Macmillan & Co.

————. 1982. "The Order of Economic Liberalization: Lessons from Chile and Argentina." In *Economic Policy in a World of Change,* 159–86. Carnegie-Rochester Conference Series on Public Policy 17.

Mathieson, D. J. 1980. "Financial Reform and Stabilization Policy in a Developing Economy." *Journal of Development Economics* 7 (September): 359–95.

Meltzer, A. H. 1985. "Policies for Growth with Low Inflation and Increased Efficiency." In *Monetary Policy in a Changing Financial Environment.* Seoul: Bank of Korea.

Mikesell, R. F., and J. E. Zinser. 1973. "The Nature of the Savings Function in Developing Countries." *Journal of Economic Literature* 11 (March): 1–26.

Park, Y. D. 1985. "Economic Stabilization and Liberalization in Korea, 1980–84." In *Monetary Policy in a Changing Financial Environment*. Seoul: Bank of Korea.

Patrick, H. T. 1966. "Financial Development and Economic Growth in Underdeveloped Countries." *Economic Development and Cultural Change* 14 (January): 174–89.

Shaw, E. S. 1973. *Financial Deepening in Economic Development*. New York: Oxford University Press.

Sjaastad, Larry A. 1983. "Failure of Economic Liberalization in the Cone of Latin America." *World Economy* 6 (March): 5–26.

Taylor, L. 1983. *Structuralist Macroeconomics*. New York: Basic Books.

Tobin, J. 1985. *Financial Innovation and Deregulation in Perspective*. Bank of Japan Monetary and Economic Studies. Tokyo: Bank of Japan.

Yeager, L. B. 1985. "Deregulation and Monetary Reform." *American Economic Review* 75 (May): 103–7.

TEN

Monetary Stabilization in LDCs

Ronald I. McKinnon

Economic liberalization and monetary stabilization are complementary concepts. When inflation is high and uncertain, the full deregulation (liberalization) of markets in goods, financial capital, or labor services cannot work well.

Part 1 of this chapter analyzes the difficult problem of bringing domestic inflation under control in a liberalizing economy, with emphasis on interest-rate and foreign-exchange management. How can certain key prices—interest rates, exchange rates, and wage rates—be kept properly aligned during the process of disinflation?

Part 2 then examines the proper role of international capital flows in promoting this stabilization, with particular focus on the syndrome of LDC overborrowing when a liberalization program appears to be successful. However, overborrowing in Latin America and elsewhere in the Third World over the past two decades indicates something more than domestic financial mismanagement within LDCs. Institutional arrangements in the international capital market have proved defective: large commercial banks from the industrial countries have been implicitly subsidized to undertake unduly risky international lending. The possibilities for increasing the efficiency of the international capital market by restructuring the regulatory arrangements governing international banks and the Eurocurrency system are then discussed.

I would like to thank Lawrence Krause of the University of California, San Diego, and Vittorio Corbo of the World Bank for their helpful comments.

1. THE DOMESTIC INTEREST RATE
AND FOREIGN EXCHANGE MANAGEMENT:
LESSONS FROM CHILE AND KOREA

Why should price-level stabilization be the first order of business in promoting sustainable economic development?

In financial markets within inflationary economies, savers and investors must contract at real rates of interest, which are only known ex post. Thus, to minimize the price-level risk to both parties, free capital markets typically operate at very short term. But this short-term indebtedness, which could take the form of the intermediate-term loans with floating interest rates, leaves nonbank firms highly vulnerable to future fluctuations in their own effective real rate of interest. The financial positions of banks, which dominate "organized" lending in LDCs, become correspondingly precarious.

In other words, high and variable general price inflation is inevitably associated with high variability in relative prices. Individual firms find it more difficult to project the future course of their own real profits. Because borrowing and lending are short-term, the risk of default on fixed-interest loan contracts is correspondingly high. The economy's ability to allocate capital efficiently is severely impaired.

In foreign trade, the real exchange rate in inflationary economies is difficult to predict. As domestic price inflation fluctuates relative to the nominal exchange rate, the future profitability of exporting or importing becomes highly uncertain. Exporters, and businessmen whose products must compete with imports, find it more difficult to make sensible investment decisions. Exchange-rate uncertainty also makes import liberalization—particularly the elimination of nontariff barriers such as quotas and exchange controls—more difficult politically and also less desirable economically.

Because the government's own fiscal deficits and general lack of control over central-bank credit are usually responsible for this price-level uncertainty, a second-best case can be made for officially indexing a few key prices whose relative values are potentially sensitive to monetary disturbances: the exchange rate, some standard bank interest rates (including perhaps that on government bonds), and a basic standard wage. Without such indexing, exporters and importers, depositors and borrowers, workers and managers would face too much uncertainty for liberalized (unregulated) open markets to work well. Such indexing is commonplace in inflation-prone Latin America.

Difficulties in controlling government fiscal deficits are, of course, not peculiar to less developed countries. Lacking open markets in government bonds or other primary securities, however, LDCs are more likely to lose control over domestic money growth when fiscal deficits appear, because the government must sell the bulk of its own debt to the banking system—within which the central bank is often the principal buyer. Therefore, inflation in LDCs is best considered a form of taxation to cover uncontrollable gaps between government expenditures and traditional taxes. Indeed, when inflation accelerates in LDCs, traditional tax revenues may lag even further behind expenditures leaving the price level highly unstable (see Aghevli and Khan 1978; Tanzi 1977).

From this starting point of a (typical) inflationary and partially indexed less developed economy with uncontrolled government deficits, suppose that a major fiscal reform suddenly makes full monetary (price-level) stabilization feasible. Government expenditures, including credit subsidies financed by the central bank, are reduced and/or traditional tax revenues are increased. The otherwise quite different experiences with inflation and disinflation of Chile and Korea in the late 1970s and early 1980s are useful benchmarks. Both achieved sufficient internal fiscal control to eliminate the need for the inflation tax as a means of public finance. Thus both could embark on credible programs for stabilizing their domestic price levels.

Even as improved fiscal policy permits growth in domestic central bank credit to be reduced in the transition from very high to low inflation, there remain difficult problems of how to manipulate previously indexed wages, interest rates, and the exchange rate. As the economy evolves toward price-level stability, the government must consistently manage these key *nominal* prices in order to prevent serious *real* price misalignments. What are the basic issues?

— Should access to foreign capital be limited so as to secure control over the real exchange rate?
— Can "orthodox" tight money based on high real interest rates be effective in disinflating?
— Should monetary policy rely on fixing the nominal exchange rate and international commodity arbitrage to stabilize domestic prices?
— Is traditional backward-looking indexing of wages or exchange rates consistent with price-level stabilization in the future?

A historical case-study approach is used to analyze these fundamental problems of keeping exchange rates, interest rates, and wages

TABLE 10.1   Chilean Tariff Reform

		Average nominal tariff rate (%)	Maximum nominal tariff rate (%)[a]
1973	July–December	94	over 500
1974	January–June	80	160
	July–December	67	140
1975	January–June	52	120
	July–December	44	90
1976	January–June	38	70
	July–December	33	60
1977	January–June	24	50
	July–December	18	35
1978	January–June	15	20
	July–December	12	15
1979	June 30 onwards	10[b]	10
1980		10	10
1981		10	10
1982		10	10

SOURCE: Banco Central de Chile, mimeograph.

[a] With a few exceptions for some (but not all) automotive vehicles. Small cars may be imported at the standard tariff rates.

[b] Of the 4,301 commodities or tariff lines that are classified for customs purposes, only 12 are exempt from any duties.

"correctly" aligned during the transitional period of disinflation that is a precondition for full-scale economic liberalization. The failed Chilean stabilization attempt from 1978 to 1982 is treated first. Then some key differences with the more successful, but less demanding, Korean stabilization of 1979 to 1983 are pointed out.

Economic Repression and Liberalization in Chile

By the end of 1973, virtually every measure showed that the Chilean economy had become massively repressed. In foreign trade, extremely high tariffs—on the order of 100 percent (table 10.1)—significantly understated the actual degree of protection. Exchange controls, quotas, and outright prohibitions proliferated over the whole range of both imports and exports.

Table 10.2 shows the basic macroeconomic and financial statistics for the Chilean economy from 1970 to 1982. The government budget deficit was out of control and had become fully monetized, reaching almost

TABLE 10.2 Chile: Macroeconomic Overview, 1970–82

	1970	1973	1974	1975	1976	1977	1978	1979	1980	1981	1982
Production											
GDP (% real changes)	2.1	−5.6	1.0	−12.9	3.5	9.9	8.2	8.3	7.5	5.3	−14.5
Unemployment rate (%)	5.7	4.8	9.2	13.5	15.9	14.2	14.2	13.8	11.8	10.9	20.4
Gross domestic investment rate (% GDP)	16.7	7.9	21.2	13.1	12.8	14.4	17.8	17.8	21.0	20.7	9.9
Gross national savings rate (% GDP)	15.1	5.3	20.7	7.9	14.5	10.8	12.6	12.5	13.9	6.6	0.04
Balance of Payments[a]											
Exports	1,112	1,309	2,151	1,590	2,116	2,185	2,400	3,835	4,705	3,836	3,706
Imports	956	1,288	1,794	1,520	1,473	2,151	2,886	4,190	5,469	6,513	3,643
Current account balance	81	−294	−211	−491	148	−511	−1,088	−1,189	−1,971	−4,733	−2,304
Changes in reserves	114	−21	−55	−344	414	113	712	1,047	1,244	70	−1,165
Total foreign debt	3,123	4,048	4,744	4,854	4,720	5,201	6,664	8,484	11,084	15,542	17,153
Fiscal											
Public-sector expenditures (% GDP)	40.6	—	39.7	39.5	37.0	34.7	34.2	32.4	30.3	35.6	43.3
Fiscal deficit (% GDP)	2.7	24.7	10.5	2.6	2.3	1.8	0.8	−1.7	−3.1	−1.6	2.4
Total change in monetary base (% GDP)	2.9	22.2	7.5	7.2	8.0	5.3	3.4	2.5	2.3	0.0	−0.02
Money and Prices											
M/GDP (%)	11.0	22.3	11.1	11.2	11.7	13.0	16.0	17.4	19.3	23.4	24.7
Annual real lending interest rates (%)	−11.0	−76.1	−36.9	16.0	64.3	56.8	42.2	16.6	11.9	38.7	35.1
Annual change in CPI (%)	34.9	508.1	375.9	340.7	174.3	63.5	30.3	38.9	31.2	9.5	20.7

Annual change in WPI (%)	33.7	1,147.1	570.7	410.9	151.5	65.0	38.9	58.3	28.2	− 3.9	39.6
Real wage rate[c] index (1970 = 100)	100.0	60.8	60.2	63.9	82.9	86.2	85.9	87.2	96.5	110.6	107.1
Real exchange rate[c] index (1975 = 100)	102.6	99.5	88.9	100.0	86.6	83.6	91.0	79.9	69.4	69.7	87.9
Terms of trade[d] index (1960 = 100)	145.0	148.0	137.0	86.0	87.0	79.0	78.0	110.0	100.0	76.0	62.0

SOURCES: Luders 1985; World Bank 1984; *Economic and Social Indicators*, various issues; and Banco Central de Chile, *Boletín mensual*, various issues.

[a] In millions of U.S. dollars. Exports: f.o.b. millions of U.S. dollars. Imports: c.i.f. millions of U.S. dollars in 1970 and 1973; other years f.o.b.
[b] Nominal (30–89 days) peso loan rates, deflated by official CPI.
[c] Dollars/pesos.
[d] Export prices/import prices.

25 percent of GNP in 1973. Moreover, this understated the extent to which the central bank—either directly or indirectly—was forced to provide subsidized credit lines to a wide variety of enterprises and government agencies throughout the country.

Chile had a long history of using the central bank and a large state-owned commercial bank (the Bank of Chile) to provide credit subsidies for "development" purposes to enterprises throughout the country. But under Salvadore Allende's socialist government in 1970–73, worker collectives seized operational control of most industrial enterprises and some large farms. Because wages rose sharply, relative to (nominally frozen) output prices, these enterprises began to run with large negative cash flows—which were then covered by new and extended credit lines from the banking system.

The result was massive inflation in the mid 1970s, partially repressed in 1973 by price controls, but subsequently becoming open with their removal. Because of the inflation, interest-rate restrictions, and heavy reserve requirements (more than 80 percent) on deposit-collecting banks, the Chilean financial system operated with negative real rates of interest from 1973 into 1975. The domestic flow of loanable funds in any open, organized capital market was virtually nonexistent. In view of this economic chaos, as well as for political reasons, foreign capital (other than short-term trade credit) was completely unavailable to the Chilean economy.

In 1974, however, there began a remarkable series of liberalizing reforms and moves toward monetary and fiscal stabilization—the results from which are immediately evident by glancing at tables 10.1 and 10.2. Government expenditures were cut, income taxes were rationalized, and commodity taxes were consolidated through the imposition of a uniform 20 percent value-added tax. By 1978 the fiscal deficit was negligible, and surpluses developed over the next three years.

Equally importantly, the government undertook additional draconian measures to liberalize the domestic financial system. It phased out automatic official credit lines to prop up failing industrial and agricultural enterprises. Reserve requirements on deposit-taking banks were greatly reduced, and by 1976 formal interest ceilings on deposits and loans were eliminated. Commercial banks, the principal financial intermediaries, were sold back to the private sector, thus creating a vigorous competitive market for deposits and loans. Interest rates rose sharply from negative to very high positive levels, thus encouraging high real financial growth (table 10.2).

However, with the benefit of hindsight, we now know that interest rates became unduly high in real terms. This created severe adverse risk selection among nonbank borrowers and substantial moral hazard among the banks themselves. The failure to exercise proper supervisory control over the banking system was not, at the time, recognized as such, but became an important contributing factor to the ultimate breakdown of Chile's otherwise well-designed program of economic liberalization, as we shall see.

Reforms were equally remarkable in the foreign-trade sector. Nontariff barriers had been pretty well eliminated by 1977; table 10.1 shows how tariffs averaging over 90 percent in 1973 were scaled down to a flat 10 percent across all imported commodities by mid 1979, a reform that lasted through 1982.

Given the severe distortions that had developed in the Chilean economy by 1973, these new policies for freeing international trade and eliminating domestic financial repression seemed to be remarkably well ordered in a "textbook" sense. They were widely applauded by almost all economists who were then first-hand observers. Thus the numerous banking failures and severe downturn of the economy from late 1981 to 1984, leaving the economy with a huge dept-overhang relative to the size of its shrunken GNP, was distressing not only to Chileans but to the economics profession.

Granted, much of Chile's economic decline was owing to adverse world economic conditions in the early 1980s: the unexpected deterioration in the terms of trade of nonoil primary products, the sharp increase in international real interest rates, and unexpected appreciation of the dollar, which further contributed to the real cost of servicing Chile's external debt.

Nevertheless, a careful assessment of the monetary stabilization program, where price inflation was successfully reduced from several hundred percent per year in the mid 1970s to almost zero by late 1981 is in order. Did the authorities make any substantial technical errors in the administration of their foreign exchange and domestic financial policies? With the benefit of hindsight, what should they have done differently to support their general goal of liberalization?

Vittorio Corbo (1985, 1986) has developed the now generally accepted view of where Chilean financial policy went astray. In order to curb domestic price inflation, beginning in early 1978 the rate of depreciation in the nominal exchange rate was deliberately reduced below the differential between inflation in Chilean prices and that prevailing in the

international economy. The apparent real interest costs of foreign borrowing in dollars fell below those prevailing in domestic financial markets in pesos. The resulting huge inflow of foreign capital forced an undue appreciation in the real exchange rate. This caused a profit squeeze
in Chilean industry and agriculture, and defaults on domestic bank
loans. The subsequent banking collapses in 1982–83 were worsened by
previous regulatory lapses that had permitted the commercial banks to
accumulate too many bad loans.

However, what the Chilean financial authorities should have done
with respect to foreign-exchange and interest-rate policies in the late
1970s remains to be spelled out. Let us review their policy options.

The Monetary Stabilization Problem of February 1978.   What was the economic dilemma facing the Chilean authorities at the beginning of 1978,
prior to their fateful adoption of an "active" (my terminology: see
McKinnon 1981) downward crawl for the exchange rate?

While the government had virtually eliminated any need for the inflation tax as a means of public finance, in 1977 the rate of price inflation was still over 60 percent. Although it was substantially less than in
1975 and 1976, the authorities rightly thought this inflationary momentum to be unwarranted.

Prior to February 1978 the exchange rate had been "passively" (but
only partially) adjusted to compensate for internal price inflation and to
roughly balance international payments—with significant restrictions
on inflows and outflows of private capital. Even so, a very sharp real appreciation of the currency took place from 1975 to 1977 (see table 10.3).
And this increase in the real value of the peso was probably important
in reducing price inflation from more than 300 percent in 1975 to less
than 70 percent in 1977.

True, the peso was greatly undervalued in 1975, because capital flight
forced a rapid depreciation of the currency. Yet if the same ad hoc
exchange-rate adjustments had continued after 1977, the real value of
the peso could well have continued to increase. Few people now realize
that the exchange-rate policy the Chilean authorities were following
prior to February 1978 was not sustainable indefinitely.

What was needed was a "forward-looking" monetary policy that
would stabilize the domestic price level and price expectations while at
the same time preventing further appreciation in the real exchange
rate. At the beginning of 1978, *some* substantial change in monetary and
exchange-rate policies was warranted to break the economy's inflation-

ary momentum. The highly desirable fiscal reforms by themselves were not sufficient to establish monetary control.

The Domestic Monetarist Solution. One school of thought—actively advocated in Chile in 1977–78—was the standard Friedman-Meltzer approach of "domestic monetarism": secure control over the domestic monetary base, get rid of capital account restrictions, and float the exchange rate. Then, target some domestic monetary aggregate such as M_1 or M_2 to grow at a smooth rate consistent with future price-level stability and/or some deliberate pace of disinflation. A credible announcement effect would then directly reduce private inflationary expectations.

In my view, this strategy could well have proved more devastating to the Chilean economy than what actually happened. Because of the fast pace of financial transformation (the demand for real cash balances was rapidly increasing as inflation diminished), the authorities could not accurately estimate what the "correct" rate of growth in domestic nominal M_1 and M_2 should be. (And table 10.2 shows that the ratio of M_2 to GNP was indeed unstable.) This unpredictable growth in monetary aggregates is characteristic of any economy moving from a state of repression to a more liberalized financial system. Suppose they had directly tightened control over the monetary base and successfully reduced inflationary expectations. With an open capital account in the balance of payments, a massive shift in international portfolio preferences in favor of the Chilean peso would have occurred anyway—perhaps even earlier. The problem of excessive capital inflows would still remain.

Because asset markets adjust much faster than do goods markets, in 1978 a floating Chilean peso would have appreciated sharply—even in nominal terms. Although price inflation might then have come down more rapidly (despite the presence of backward-looking wage indexing), the gross overvaluation of the peso would have occurred much sooner, crushing the profitability of the Chilean export and import-competing sectors even before the tariff reductions were completed in mid 1979.

In summary, adopting a floating exchange rate in the 1970s would not have solved the fundamental problem of avoiding excessive capital inflows and real currency appreciation in the course of moving the increasingly open Chilean economy from very high inflation to a stable price level. Even the much milder U.S. price disinflation of 1980–82 led to a sharp appreciation of the floating dollar, along with a depression in American tradable goods industries.

TABLE 10.3   Chile: Measures of International Competitiveness
(1979 II = 1)

Year and Quarter		PM/PN	PX/PN	PT/PN	PT/W	PX/PM	Nominal Exchange Rate[a]
1975							
	I	1.640	1.663	1.652	2.168	1.014	2.57
	II	1.664	1.689	1.677	2.463	1.015	4.36
	III	1.703	1.707	1.705	2.205	1.002	6.03
	IV	1.752	1.777	1.765	2.208	1.014	7.80
1976							
	I	1.732	1.774	1.753	2.218	1.024	10.48
	II	1.529	1.522	1.526	1.923	0.995	12.43
	III	1.340	1.370	1.355	1.628	1.022	13.91
	IV	1.184	1.277	1.230	1.427	1.079	16.55
1977							
	I	1.096	1.151	1.123	1.251	1.050	18.43
	II	0.904	0.990	0.946	1.117	1.095	19.44
	III	0.910	0.940	0.925	1.059	1.033	22.26
	IV	0.954	0.968	0.961	1.171	1.015	25.99
1978							
	I	1.016	0.967	0.992	1.106	0.952	29.11
	II	1.016	0.907	0.960	1.078	0.893	31.25
	III	0.999	0.875	0.935	1.047	0.876	32.69
	IV	0.999	0.897	0.947	1.065	0.898	33.58
1979							
	I	0.987	0.924	0.955	1.003	0.936	34.72
	II	1.000	1.000	1.000	1.000	1.000	36.26
	III	1.082	1.185	1.132	1.051	1.095	39.00
	IV	0.984	1.103	1.042	1.032	1.121	39.00

The Exchange Rate as the Forward Signal.   In February 1978 a successful monetary stabilization clearly required some unambiguous signal(s)—around which private expectations could easily coalesce—indicating that price inflation would be reduced to the international level in the near future. Quite plausibly, the authorities decided to use the dollar exchange rate as the intermediate target for Chilean monetary policy: both as a signal for what they intended the rate of disinflation to be and, partly, as a forcing variable through international commodity arbitrage for achieving it.

The sweeping trade liberalization gave the authorities confidence (false, as it turned out) that domestic price inflation would quickly con-

TABLE 10.3   (*continued*)

Year and Quarter		PM/PN	PX/PN	PT/PN	PT/W	PX/PM	Nominal Exchange Rate[a]
1980							
	I	0.939	1.118	1.025	0.920	1.191	39.00
	II	0.925	1.092	1.004	0.864	1.178	39.00
	III	0.917	1.017	0.966	0.832	1.109	39.00
	IV	0.874	0.916	0.895	0.736	1.048	39.00
1981							
	I	0.846	0.844	0.845	0.687	0.998	39.00
	II	0.786	0.775	0.780	0.631	0.986	39.00
	III	0.744	0.709	0.726	0.579	0.953	39.00
	IV	0.723	0.681	0.702	0.569	0.942	39.00
1982							
	I	0.696	0.606	0.649	0.532	0.871	39.00
	II	0.713	0.611	0.660	0.549	0.857	40.34
	III	0.937	0.837	0.886	0.755	0.893	50.01
	IV	1.366	0.893	1.104	0.963	0.754	69.28

SOURCE: Corbo 1985, 895.

PN = Price index for nontradables obtained from the Cortazar Marshall CPI based on the equation estimated in Corbo 1982.

PM = Import price index in pesos, obtained as a Divisia index of the exchange-rate adjusted industrial components of the wholesale price index for Argentina, Brazil, Japan, Germany, and the United States, using the structure of imports from each of those countries as a weighting base. The index is also adjusted for average customs duties.

PX = Export price index in pesos, measured as a Divisia index of major Chilean exports, excluding copper.

W = Nominal manufacturing wage rate.

PT = Geometric average of PX and PM with weights of 0.50 for each.

[a] The nominal exchange rate is the number of units of domestic currency required to purchase one U.S. dollar.

verge to the international level if the exchange rate were fixed. Because fiscal policy was such that the central bank could subordinate monetary policy to achieve any reasonable target for the nominal exchange rate, such a policy was credible and seemed potentially effective in stabilizing the price level.

This was the rationale for announcing and widely publicizing an active forward downward crawl, or *tablita*, for adjusting the exchange rate on a daily or weekly basis by very small amounts. The numbers going into the preannounced *tablita* were inevitably somewhat arbitrary: 24 percent depreciation in 1978 and 14 percent in 1979, after which the nominal exchange rate would be fixed indefinitely. The announcement effect was designed to allow private contracts denominated in pesos to anticipate the cessation of inflation.

Table 10.3 shows these decelerating movements in the nominal exchange rate converging in mid 1979 to a fixed exchange rate, which was sustained through June 1982. This *tablita* system broke down with the exchange devaluations of 1982 amid general economic decline.

The Indexing Problem.   This movement to an active downward crawl—or "forward" stabilization—in the nominal exchange rate by the Chilean government was not itself a policy mistake, as is often suggested. Rather the absence of suitably supporting capital-market and labor-market policies—as well as external stress—eventually caused the stabilization policy to fail.

Consider the labor market first. Corbo (1985) correctly emphasizes the inconsistency between the forward-looking indexing of the nominal exchange rate and the backward-looking indexing of money wages, which is often found in high-inflation economies. Chilean wages were linked to the *past* rate of inflation, which was very high relative to that anticipated in the future. Thus, as international competition from newly liberalized foreign trade and the ever-slower downward crawl in the nominal exchange rate slowed price inflation in the tradables industries, growth in money wages continued at a much faster pace. Indeed, from early 1978 to early 1982, Corbo's data in table 10.3 show that the ratio of tradables prices to wages fell more than 50 percent.

In retrospect, it seems as if money wages in February 1978 should have been put on the same forward-looking *tablita* as the exchange rate. Similarly, all other prices indexed to ongoing inflation, such as charges for the use of public utilities, should have been put on the same *tablita*.

Putting wages under the same forward-looking indexing procedure would have fixed them in terms of the prices of tradable goods. The price of nontradables could, however, still have continued to edge upwards. However, because wages are a dominant factor in determining the cost of nontradable services, the sharp fall in the ratio of p_t / p_n between 1978–81, shown in column (3) of table 10.3 would not have occurred.

However, if the economy tended to absorb large amounts of foreign financial capital while the exchange rate was pegged by the *tablita* (as happened), the domestic money supply would expand unduly and this inflationary pressure would effect the prices of nontradables more than tradables. Therefore, in the presence of massive capital inflows, even "correct" wage indexation could not have fully resolved the problem of avoiding exchange overvaluation.

In summary, it is now commonly accepted that better synchronization of those indexation procedures under government control in February 1978 would surely have prevented much of the gross overvaluation of the peso that was later observed. But why the downward-crawling *tablita* rather than moving directly to a fixed exchange rate?

In the extreme case, where the government controls all nominal prices in the economy, inflation could be halted immediately by decree. The authorities could simply promulgate a fixed exchange rate—as well as fix all other nominal prices under their control. No forward-looking *tablita* would be necessary other than the announcement that the nominal exchange rate would remain fixed indefinitely. In effect, the *tablita* could be completely truncated with no continued inflationary momentum in domestic prices.[1]

In the newly liberalized Chilean economy of early 1978, however, the move to free trade was designed to restructure relative prices. Thus a general freeze of nominal prices of all goods and services would have been out of keeping with the very nature of the reforms (unlike one on wages, which were controlled by the government anyway). Without such a general freeze, therefore, one could expect some price inflation to continue even if wages were put on the same *tablita* as the exchange rate.

In general, the greater the forward contracting in pesos in private transactions, the stronger the case for stretching out the *tablita* for some months. Assuming the Chilean government was unwilling to undertake a general price freeze, the active forward crawl toward a fixed exchange rate within two years does not seem wrong—even with the benefit of

1. Are there other circumstances where a government could impose a fixed nominal exchange rate directly without fear of real overvaluation? Consider the last stages of extreme hyperinflation, such as occurred in Germany from 1921 to 1923. When the price level is increasing rapidly and erratically on a daily basis, hour-by-hour or even minute-by-minute exchange-rate quotations are the most efficient source of information telling people how fast inflation is actually proceeding. Everyone then keys on (indexes to) the exchange rate in determining domestic prices and wages. Significant backward-looking indexing tends to disappear, and virtually all forward contracting uses foreign exchange as the numeraire. (See Dornbusch 1985.) Consequently, a dramatic stabilization of the exchange rate will immediately stabilize domestic prices and wages, even if they are not directly controlled by the government. One must be cautious, however; a dramatic act such as the introduction of a new currency along with a new fiscal policy might be necessary to convince people that the exchange rate is likely to remain stable.

hindsight—provided that other controlled prices in the economy were also on the same *tablita*.

Monetary Stabilization before Full Financial Liberalization. How should domestic financial policy be implemented during the transaction from high to low inflation?

In Asian countries like Korea and Taiwan, regulatory authorities have been more consistently cautious than their Latin American counterparts about decontrolling (fully liberalizing) the activities of commercial banks—for which the state is necessarily the lender of last resort. Bank loan portfolios have been more carefully monitored (not always benevolently), and competition in the money markets has typically been limited by state-set standard deposit and loan rates. Indeed, until the early 1980s, Korean and Taiwanese commercial banks were state-owned. In both countries, open money-market competition has been pretty well confined to a fringe of nonbank trust and finance companies, as well as a vigorous informal credit market.

At the same time, however, these Asian economies have generally avoided substantial financial repression by having official bank deposit and loan rates set at levels that are moderately positive—say, 5 to 10 percent—in real terms. The Taiwanese government has consistently maintained positive real interest rates by keeping domestic prices stable, rather than allowing inflation to develop and having to use high nominal rates of interest to offset it (Cheng 1986), and real financial growth has been correspondingly higher in Taiwan, with virtually no dependence on foreign borrowing. Korea has been less consistent in following a non-repressive financial strategy, but has managed to avoid inflationary extremes, such as those found in Latin America.

Only in the mid 1980s, when domestic prices in both Korea and Taiwan had been stable for some time, such that flows of funds through nonbank intermediaries as well as primary securities markets at long term became more fully developed, were both governments willing to contemplate more complete decontrol and privatization of their commercial banks. In other words, *both Asian governments first sought monetary (price-level) stabilization together with some financial deepening, before fully liberalizing the capital-market activities of commercial banks.*

In contrast, the failed liberalizations during 1977–82 in the Southern Cone of Latin America—not only in Chile, but also in Uruguay and in Argentina—were all characterized by rather complete deregulation and privatization of the commercial banks while inflation remained high and unstable. Banks could pretty much charge what they wanted on loans, and bid freely for foreign funds in dollars as well as domestic funds in pesos, despite the fact that their deposit bases were either implicitly or explicitly insured by their home governments and the nonbank parts of their domestic capital markets remained undeveloped.

With the benefit of hindsight, we are beginning to understand that full liberalization of the banks in such inflationary circumstances was premature. Unduly high real interest rates will likely prevail in such circumstances, leading to adverse risk selection—both in the quality of the nonbank borrowers who come forward and in the banks' own behavior. And these problems with exercising prudent control over bank loan portfolios become magnified in stressful periods when the central bank is trying—one way or another—to impose "tight" money in order to disinflate successfully.

High Real Interest Rates and Adverse Risk Selection.   Again the Chilean experience with bank supervision and control is very useful for understanding how adverse risk selection works itself out in inflationary circumstances. Table 10.4 summarizes some extensive financial data provided by Rolf Luders (1985) on the extraordinary pattern of deposit and loan rates—both nominal and real—after most commercial banks had been returned to the private sector by 1976. Two characteristics stand out.

The first is the very high real interest rates, calculated ex post on the basis of experienced inflation rather than on ex ante expectations of it. For example, in 1978 the "real" lending rates on peso loans was 42.2 percent on an annualized basis—although lending was typically much less than a year in duration. The net annualized spread between peso deposits and loans was about 10.7 percentage points, after taking out the effects of reserve requirements. To achieve these real yields, the nominal peso loan rate was 85.3 percent, less than a third of what it had been in the more inflationary year 1976.

The second striking characteristic of table 10.4 is the large spread between the apparent interest costs of borrowing in pesos compared with borrowing from domestic banks in dollars, which, after the deregulations of the mid 1970s, accounted for almost half of total bank loans (Luders 1985). Adjusted downward for the experienced rate of peso devaluation, this spread was as high as 48.9 percentage points in 1976 and then fell to 8.6 percentage points (still high) in 1980 before increasing again to 24.3 percentage points in 1981. It then fell sharply with the

TABLE 10.4   Chile: Interest Rates on 30-Day Bank Deposits and Loans
(% per annum)

	1976	1977	1978	1979	1980	1981	1982
Peso deposits:							
Nominal	197.9	93.7	62.8	45.1	37.4	40.8	47.8
Real[a]	8.6	18.5	24.9	4.4	4.8	28.6	22.4
Peso loans:							
Nominal	350.7	156.4	85.3	62.0	47.0	51.9	63.1
Real[a]	64.3	56.8	42.2	16.6	11.9	38.7	35.1
Gross spread	57.2	33.7	14.5	12.1	7.1	12.3	10.7
Net spread[f]	8.1	17.4	10.7	7.4	5.2	6.3	9.5
Interest differential:[d]							
Peso/dollar deposits	2.9	7.8	0.0	8.7	14.0	19.5	− 1.2
Peso/dollar loans	48.9	36.4	8.6	14.1	17.1	24.3	5.6
Dollar deposits:							
Nominal[b]	8.9	8.9	11.1	13.5	15.1	17.8	14.6
Real[e]	− 18.1	7.9	4.6	− 5.8	12.3	7.6	40.0
Dollar loans:							
Nominal[c]	13.9	13.9	16.1	20.7	19.9	22.2	18.3
Real[e]	− 14.3	12.9	9.3	0.1	− 8.6	11.6	44.5
Change in consumer prices	174.3	63.5	30.3	38.9	31.2	9.5	20.7

SOURCE: Luders 1985, taken from Banco Central de Chile, *Síntesis monetaria y financiera*, various years.

[a] All real peso interest rates are calculated monthly, based on monthly changes in the Chilean consumer price index in pesos, before being annualized.

[b] Nominal dollar deposit rates are costs of borrowing abroad: LIBOR plus average spread charged to Chilean commercial banks.

[c] Nominal dollar loan rates are interest charged domestic customers by Chilean banks.

[d] To calculate interest differential, nominal interest rates in dollars are first adjusted upwards by the (experienced) rate of exchange devaluation.

[e] The "real" interest rate in dollars is:

$$\frac{(1 + \text{nominal rate})\,(1 + \text{devaluation rate})}{1 + \text{peso inflation rate}} - 1$$

[f] Net spread after effects of compulsory non-interest-bearing reserve requirements against peso deposits are taken out.

"surprise" devaluations of 1982. Indeed, often the "real" cost (adjusted for the domestic rate of price inflation less the rate of exchange devaluation) of borrowing in dollars was negative—even though real borrowing costs in pesos remained very high.

At the time, virtually everyone thought this difference was owing to imperfections in financial arbitrage because of the remaining restrictions on foreign capital inflows. Indeed, this belief prompted the authorities to loosen capital restrictions even further in 1980—thus worsening the overborrowing syndrome shown by the very rapid 1978–81 buildup of external debt (table 10.2).

Sadder but wiser, we now understand that these incredibly high interest rates on peso loans represented, in large part, the breakdown of proper financial supervision over the Chilean banking system. Neither officials in the commercial banks themselves nor government regulatory authorities adequately monitored the creditworthiness of a broad spectrum of industrial borrowers: "The internal source of difficulty in Chile was a proliferation of bad loans within the banking system. The rolling over of these loans, capitalizing interest along the way, created what I call a 'false' demand for credit, which, when added to the demand that would normally be viable, allowed real interest rates to reach unprecedented (and, to many, incredible) levels" (Harberger 1985, 237).

This form of Ponzi game, however, had a peculiarly international flavor. Chilean financial intermediaries—not only banks—incurred exchange risk as they extended loans. James Tybout (1986) and others have shown that the large economic groups, or *grupos*, used their control over domestic banks together with their overseas contacts to get dollar credits at relatively low interest rates in order to relend at the extremely high, but, as it turned out, false, interest rates denominated in pesos. (Because banks were officially restricted from directly assuming foreign-exchange exposure, they simply made dollar loans to the *grupos'* industrial companies, which then did most of the ongoing lending in pesos.) Thus these *grupos* continued to show increases in their nonoperating earning in 1980 and 1981, well after their operating earning had soured. Some were recording unrealized capital gains, from some very dubious assets, as earnings on their books.

Of course, it is a little unfair to imply, with the benefit of hindsight, that all these Chilean firms actually knew at the time that they were engaged in a Ponzi game. Many probably suffered from excessive optimism regarding future asset values and rates of return—hopes that were ultimately dashed by the real exchange-rate overvaluation and the downturn in the international economy, neither of which were easy to predict at the microeconomic level. Nevertheless, the extraordinary level of "real" interest rates from 1977 to 1981 should have alerted the authorities to the adverse risk selection.

Scaling Down Nominal Interest Rates in Line with the Tablita. Should more comprehensive financial measures in the capital markets have been taken in February 1978 to assist with the macroeconomic stabilization of Chilean price levels? Except to advocate more stringent (unspecified) controls on foreign capital inflows, authors writing on the experiences of the Southern Cone do not seem to have fully come to grips with this financial issue.

Clearly, everyone now agrees that money wages—along with other significant prices that the government controlled—should have been put on the same forward-looking *tablita* as the exchange rate. But did it then make sense to have left extremely high nominal interest rates (over 80 percent in 1978) on peso loans in place when the government was planning such a fast convergence to price stability? Politically, Chilean workers would be less likely to accept a scaledown of their nominal claims when nominal interest rates remained so high. Perhaps a standard nominal interest rate on peso loans, whose term structure was indexed to the *tablita*, should have been promulgated simultaneously with the new exchange-rate policy in February 1978. The authorities could have aimed at keeping the standard loan rate between 8 to 12 percent in real terms, with real deposit rates 2 to 3 percentage points below this level.

The Korean Experience, 1979–83

Are there precedents of other governments scaling down domestic nominal interest rates in the course of a major disinflation? The Korean government's successful price-level stabilization of 1979–83 provides one such example. The relevant interest-rate data are provided in table 10.5.

Although much less than Chile, Korea suffered from inflation averaging over 20 percent during 1979–81. In real terms, its standard nominal loan rate of 20 percent (made somewhat greater by the use of compensating won balances) was slightly negative.

Then, with a big fiscal improvement and monetary stringency, Korea's internal inflation rate was driven down to about 7 percent in 1982 and only 3 percent in 1983. The Korean authorities anticipated declining inflation by quickly reducing the standard loan rate in stages, to 10 percent by mid 1982. Nevertheless, the loan rate became positive in real terms (see the far-right-hand column of table 10.5). Over the same interval, the standard short-term interest rate on won deposits was reduced from 14.4 to 6 percent.

It should be noted, however, that the Bank of Korea did not attempt to use the exchange rate as the forcing variable for domestic price-level stabilization. Indeed, as table 10.6 shows, from 1980 to 1983 the won depreciated a bit faster than the reduction in the domestic inflation rate. In part because the Korean foreign-trade sector was not as fully liberalized as the Chilean, the Korean government did not believe that international commodity arbitrage could be used to stabilize the domestic price level. Instead, the nominal exchange rate was managed by an informal downward crawl to adjust passively to declining domestic inflation. Thus, as price-level stability was secured, the syndrome of exchange overvaluation was avoided.

This scaling down of domestic interest rates as inflation slowed, while maintaining the rate of downward crawl in the won against the dollar to reflect the inflation differential between Korea and the United States, prevented undue incentives for moving foreign capital into the Korean economy. Even so, the Korean government maintained substantial controls on the capital account to prevent a further untoward buildup of international indebtedness.

A Rationale for Interest-Rate Management.   Why should interest rates on bank assets and liabilities be reduced in the course of a major disinflation by deliberate public policy? Shouldn't nominal interest rates be bid down by the market, be allowed to fall naturally, as inflation recedes?

First, the question of correct macroeconomic signaling. If an individual sees very high nominal interest rates above recorded inflation, he could interpret this as a signal that most other people in the economy expect inflation to continue and the stabilization program to fail—even though the high nominal rates could be explained ex post on other grounds. Indeed, if enough firms borrow heavily at very high nominal rates of interest, it becomes more probable that the government will keep the inflation rate high in the future in order to bail them out. This reinforces private fears that inflation will not wind down.

Second, when inflationary expectations are still high and uncertain, the problem of adverse risk selection at the microeconomic level in the Stiglitz-Weiss sense is particularly acute (see Stiglitz and Weiss 1983, 913–27). In contracting at any nominal interest rate substantially above the "normal" 10 to 20 percent range approximating average real rates of return, the borrower must bet on what the future inflation rate will be—and also determine the riskiness of his own project. He will then accept a riskier project in the hopes of a favorable high yield in case inflation doesn't bail him out and he has to default anyway.

But the Stiglitz-Weiss model has a natural check on adverse risk selection. The financial institution will charge a less-than-market clearing rate of interest and simply ration equivalent borrowers observationally. Or, if more information becomes available, risk-averse lenders will gravitate toward those borrowers who appear to be safer, with more collateral or equity participation.

TABLE 10.5 Nominal and Real South Korean Interest Rates

	GNP Deflator (rate of change)	Curb Market Rate[a]		Yields on Corporate Bonds		Yields on Government Bonds		Bank Lending Rate[b]	
		Nominal	Real[c]	Nominal	Real	Nominal	Real	Nominal	Real
1979 1/4	20.1	44.0	23.9	26.1	5.9	23.4	3.3	19.1	−1.1
2/4	20.3	42.1	21.8	26.8	6.5	24.2	3.9	19.0	−1.3
3/4	21.4	40.7	10.3	26.9	5.5	25.5	4.1	19.0	−3.6
4/4	22.6	42.7	20.1	27.1	4.5	27.5	4.9	19.0	−3.6
Year average	21.2	42.4	21.2	26.7	5.5	25.2	4.0	19.0	−2.2
1980 1/4	25.5	50.8	25.3	30.5	5.0	30.3	4.8	24.3	−1.2
2/4	27.8	48.8	21.0	31.9	4.1	30.6	2.8	24.7	−3.1
3/4	23.7	42.5	18.8	29.7	6.0	27.9	4.2	23.7	—
4/4	25.9	37.7	11.8	28.1	2.2	26.2	0.3	20.8	−5.1
Year average	25.6	45.0	19.4	30.1	4.5	28.8	3.2	23.4	−2.2
1981 1/4	21.7	36.6	14.9	24.9	3.2	24.8	3.1	20.0	−1.7
2/4	17.0	35.2	18.2	22.8	5.8	22.2	5.2	20.0	3.0
3/4	17.1	33.8	16.7	22.9	5.8	21.8	5.7	20.0	2.9
4/4	10.5	35.4	24.9	27.0	16.5	25.5	15.0	19.0	8.5
Year average	15.9	35.3	19.4	24.4	8.5	23.6	7.7	19.8	3.9
1982 1/4	13.2	32.6	18.6	21.7	8.5	20.5	7.3	16.1	2.9
2/4	7.6	33.1	25.5	17.3	9.7	17.1	9.5	13.9	6.3
3/4	6.6	27.5	20.9	14.3	7.7	15.0	8.4	10.0	3.4
4/4	3.7	29.0	25.3	15.7	12.0	16.7	13.0	10.0	6.3
Year average	7.1	30.6	23.5	17.3	10.2	17.3	10.2	12.5	5.4

1983 1/4	4.8	24.1	19.3	14.9	10.1	14.4	9.6	10.0	5.2
2/4	2.2	27.5	25.3	14.0	11.8	13.5	11.3	10.0	7.8
3/4	2.2	26.8	24.6	14.0	11.8	13.4	11.2	10.0	7.8
4/4	2.9	24.7	21.8	14.2	11.2	13.8	10.9	10.0	7.1
Year average	3.0	25.8	22.8	14.2	11.2	13.8	10.8	10.0	7.0
1984 1/4	1.2	24.1	22.9	14.0	12.8	13.4	12.2	10.4	9.2
2/4	2.6	25.7	23.1	13.3	10.7	13.6	11.0	10.5	7.9
3/4	6.0	23.5	17.5	14.4	8.4	14.7	8.7	10.5	4.5
4/4	5.1	25.4	20.3	14.9	9.8	15.2	10.1	11.1	6.0
Year average	3.9	24.7	20.7	14.2	10.2	14.2	10.2	10.6	6.6

SOURCES: Cho 1985 and Bank of Korea, *Economic Statistics Yearbook*, various years.

[a] Bank of Korea survey data.

[b] Interest rate on bank loans up to one year.

[c] Real interest rate = nominal interest rate − the rate of change of the GNP deflator.

TABLE 10.6   South Korean Exchange Rates and International
Competitiveness, 1978–85
(indices 1980 = 100)[a]

Year and Quarter		U.S. Dollar per Won	Effective Exchange Rates[b]	
			Nominal	Real[c]
1978	IV	125.1	117.7	94.8
1979	I	125.1	120.2	99.6
	II	125.1	123.8	107.1
	III	125.1	123.4	107.2
	IV	125.1	127.5	112.2
1980	I	106.2	110.4	103.7
	II	102.0	102.8	100.6
	III	98.8	97.1	98.1
	IV	93.1	90.6	96.5
1981	I	93.1	88.3	96.0
	II	90.8	90.0	100.1
	III	89.0	92.2	105.8
	IV	88.3	89.9	102.3
1982	I	85.3	89.2	102.0
	II	83.2	88.9	101.9
	III	81.7	89.9	103.1
	IV	81.4	89.8	102.5
1983	I	80.4	85.5	99.4
	II	78.7	84.3	97.2
	III	77.2	83.8	96.1
	IV	76.2	81.9	93.0
1984	I	76.2	81.5	93.2
	II	75.9	81.3	92.5
	III	74.8	82.7	94.0
	IV	73.9	82.7	93.4
1985	I	72.2	83.2	94.2

SOURCES: Aghevli and Marquez-Ruarte 1985; Korean authorities and IMF
staff estimates.
[a] An increase indicates appreciation.
[b] Trade-weighted.
[c] Adjusted by relative movements in consumer prices.

However, this natural tendency to prudence among nonbank lenders
may be seriously undermined in the case of banks, custodians of the
money supply, who receive (de facto) deposit insurance from the government. This insurance leads to serious problems of moral hazard where,
unless closely supervised, private banks may well undertake very risky
and seemingly high-yield lending on the presumption that adverse outcomes leading to major losses will have to be covered by the monetary

authority—while net profits from favorable outcomes will still accrue to the owners (bank shareholders). Insured financial intermediaries will exhibit more risky behavior than the uninsured.[2] And, in the event, mass insolvencies in the Chilean banking system in 1982–83 led to a renationalization of the banks in order to protect domestic depositors as well as foreign creditors.

Even in the highly developed capital market of the United States, federal deposit insurance is creating severe problems for bank supervisors in curbing undue risktaking by commercial banks as well as savings and loan institutions (see Kane 1985). In a developing country without an equities market or well-developed accounting standards, and where private (but insured) banks are the principal lenders, the probability of a capital-market equilibrium with very high "real" (but phoney) interest rates and undue adverse risk selection is much greater (Cho, 1986).

Although government supervisory control over private banks can prevent undue risktaking at falsely high real rates of interest, this supervision does not guarantee that the government itself will not exert pressure to make bad loans! The Korean price-level stabilization of 1980–84 was very successful, but the government's pressure on the banks in the 1970s was less benign. Because of its determination to support the development of domestic heavy industry and Korean contractors undertaking major construction projects in the Middle East and elsewhere, the Korean government coerced the banks into making risky long-term loans, many of which became nonperforming. In the 1980s the Bank of Korea still provided subsidized credit lines (official discounting at below-market interest rates) to various commercial banks to enable them to avoid bankruptcy by keeping these old (1970s) loans on their books. This bad loan syndrome continues to hinder the full liberalization of the Korean financial system despite the successful monetary stabilization.

Implementing Tight Money in the Transition from High to Low Inflation.   In retrospect, it seems clear that Chile should have tightened up more on the domestic flow of bank credit (inclusive of that financed by foreign borrowing) and relied less on the exchange rate as a lever for securing

2. In Stiglitz and Weiss 1983, dealing with adverse risk selection, the lending "bank" was (implicitly) assumed to be risk neutral. However, one can show that when (1) there is deposit insurance, and (2) macroeconomic instability causes positive covariance in default probabilities among nonbank borrowers, the bank itself becomes a risktaker. Moral hazard exists that induces the bank to make unsafe loans at interest rates that are "too high." See McKinnon 1986.

the price level. However, because of acute potential problems with adverse risk selection, orthodox tight money relying on very high nominal (and real) interest rates could not work.

The Koreans implicitly recognized this in bringing about their successful price-level stabilization. Nominal interest rates were scaled down consistent with keeping real rates positive, albeit below market clearing levels. And although the Bank of Korea also reduced reserve requirements as fiscal policy improved, central bank credit was rationed to the commercial banks—and foreign capital inflows were limited—in order to secure the desired deflation without significant overvaluation of the exchange rate. That is, tight money was imposed while real rates of interest were kept positive and fairly constant by decree.[3] This meant that, in order to disinflate, the Korean banking system as a whole rationed credit to the private sector. However, because the Korean government's fiscal deficits were simultaneously reduced (as was also the case in Chile), the real flow of loanable funds to the private sector actually increased, thus relieving the supply constraint on domestic output. No net credit squeeze on the private sector was necessary once the Korean government and its various special agencies stopped directing the flow of bank credit to itself.

Given the equally good, and perhaps even more favorable, fiscal conditions existing in Chile, it seems—with the benefit of hindsight, of course—that in February 1978 the Chileans should have followed an internal interest-rate and bank-credit policy more like Korea's of 1981–83. Then some of the burden of bringing about disinflation could have been taken off nominal exchange-rate policy, which, as I have suggested, was not itself misguided.

2. CONTROLLING INTERNATIONAL CAPITAL FLOWS

Overborrowing in the course of an economic liberalization program is a problem of which our profession has become acutely aware owing to the recent experience of the Southern Cone countries.

In the particular case of Chile, analyzed above, a huge inflow of foreign capital from 1978 through early 1982 appreciated the real ex-

3. Most students of economic development no longer have to be persuaded of the importance of keeping positive real rates of interest at substantial levels in order to avoid the syndrome of "financial repression" (McKinnon 1973; Shaw 1973). More recently, there has been substantial empirical work showing that LDCs that maintain higher real interest rates, and high real financial growth, tend to be more successful (International Monetary Fund 1983; Fry 1978).

change rate and undermined the Chilean central bank's control over the money supply and domestic credit expansion. As suggested in part 1, this financial deluge from abroad could have been slowed if (1) the term structure of nominal interest rates had been scaled down in line with the slowing of the "active" downward crawl in the exchange rate, and (2) internal inflation itself had been moderated by putting wages and other key internal prices on the same forward-looking *tablita*.

That said, I very much doubt that, without a system of exchange controls in place for preventing borrowing from abroad, inflows of foreign capital would not still have been "excessive." If the Chilean monetary stabilization cum trade liberalization had continued to appear successful, or at least was not obviously on the brink of collapse, some unavoidable pressure to overborrow would still have been there.

The Korean Experience of the Mid 1960s

A neater capsule experience we could study, without being distracted by the widespread overborrowing by LDCs in the 1970s, whether or not they were liberalizing, is the Korean liberalization of the mid 1960s. Korea prior to that time had an export/GNP ratio of less than 3 percent—almost all foreign exchange earnings were U.S. military counterpart or funds from USAID (the U.S. Agency for International Development). Inflows of private foreign capital were negligible because foreign bankers considered the repressed Korean economy to be risky and unprofitable. Joan Robinson and the Cambridge group used to compare North Korea very favorably to South Korea as a successful model for economic development!

Under pressure from USAID in 1964, there were major trade reforms in Korea, a unification of the currency associated with a large exchange-rate devaluation, and some liberalization of imports. But then in 1965, under the influence of Edward Shaw, John Gurley, and Hugh Patrick, there was a major financial reform. The domestic capital market, which had been totally moribund, was suddenly brought back to life when interest rates were removed from very low pegs at negative real levels to high pegs at positive real levels. This was accompanied by a major fiscal reform: there was no change in the tax law, but a different director was put in charge of the tax-collection mechanism. Tax revenues doubled in the course of a year. These reforms laid the basis for the Korean economic success in subsequent years.

By the end of 1965, when these reforms had taken hold and exports had begun to grow rapidly, the domestic price level was actually stable.

Both the financial and foreign-trade reforms were very successful. By the end of 1965, however, international lenders had sharply changed their assessments of Korea's prospects. At the time of the major liberalization in foreign trade and finance, the profitability of the economy increased in the eyes of foreign lenders and domestic borrowers. Such sharp shifts in portfolio preferences are not smooth—apparently because of the great herd instinct among international bankers.

So beginning in mid 1966, a large inflow of short-term capital suddenly hit the astonished Koreans. An acute dilemma resulted for macroeconomic policy. If the Korean government simply let the exchange rate appreciate, that would, of course, hit Korea's nascent export industries very hard, something they found unacceptable. If the government just hung on with the fixed exchange rate while being inundated with finance capital, it would lose control over the money base and inflation would come back (which it did). In fact, the real exchange rate would still turn against exporters as the prices of nontradables were bid up; the change would just not be so precipitate (for a more complete analysis, see McKinnon 1973).

Moreover, scaling down the newly increased domestic interest rates conflicted with the pressing need to encourage real growth in domestic financial intermediation. Relative to GNP, the Korean banking system—and the flow of loanable funds—was much smaller in the early 1960s than in the early 1980s.

Once lost, price stability in Korea was not regained until the Kim Jae-Ik stabilization of 1981–83, discussed in part 1. After 1966 inflation and eventually devaluation proceeded, along with some degree of regression in financial liberalization. The burden of foreign indebtedness was troublesome in the 1970s, although manageable in the Korean case.

Market Failure in the Adjustment of International Asset Portfolios

The question is, what should the Koreans have done in 1965–66 and the Chileans have done in 1978–81 when confronted with large capital inflows? Why, in a sense, did the international capital market fail in each period?

Once a successful stabilization cum liberalization program, where the profitability of the economy suddenly rises, is undertaken, there is a once-and-for-all attempt by foreign lenders to get a piece of the action and increase their claims on the newly liberalized economy. This inundation with foreign capital is possible even in the case of a pure trade liberalization when there is not a major financial stabilization occurring at the same time. But if there is a major financial stabilization, with interest rates moved from low pegs to high pegs as in the Korean case, or interest ceilings removed altogether in the Chilean mode, then the inflow of capital is greatly exaggerated.

So what is the nature of the market failure here? Initial expectations of future profitability turn out to be wrong. People look at the real exchange rate and interest rates immediately after the reform and project them into the indefinite future. They look at profitability myopically as individuals and borrowers, not taking into account what will happen if they all transfer foreign capital simultaneously. What seems profitable for any one of them will become less profitable within a few years.

You might think this irrational. People should be able to grasp this system and see that the real exchange rate will turn against exporters once capital inflows increase at the macroeconomic level. But these were once-in-a-lifetime experiences for the Koreans in the 1960s and the Chileans in the 1970s, and for most of the international lenders in each episode. Individuals cannot easily anticipate what will happen to the general equilibrium of the economy in the future.

This problem is made more acute insofar as the financial flow into LDCs, even though it may be financing longer-term projects, is usually very short-term. And short-term finance might have to be repaid just at the juncture when the real exchange rate starts to turn adversely against exporters. So, if this myopia exists in the international capital market, there is a very good case for doing what the Chilean government tried to do: keep short-term funds out while allowing longer-term borrowing. By 1979, however, the Chilean government was not stringent enough in preventing the accumulation of short-run indebtedness by Chile's private sector.

In addition, we know that in any purely private capital market each individual borrower faces an upward-sloping supply curve for finance. That is not really a distortion. The more that is borrowed, the riskier the loan gets at the margin. The upward-sloping supply curve imposed by private lenders accurately reflects the increasing riskiness to the private borrower as he increases his exposure.

Consider instead the real world of the 1970s and 1980s, where governments guarantee all credit flows. The host government in the borrowing country guarantees private foreign credits, either officially or unofficially. In the lending countries, there are official export-import banks and deposit insurance for commercial banks. Consequently, the normally upward-sloping supply curve for finance did not face individual private borrowers in the Third World in the 1970s. Because of the government guarantees that were involved, they could borrow at a virtually flat rate of interest.

Combining this microeconomic distortion with macroeconomic myopia, capital inflows by private borrowers are further magnified at the time the liberalization occurs. Overborrowing in the Southern Cone in the 1970s was of an order of magnitude greater than what had occurred in Korea in the mid 1960s: an (impossible) attempt to absorb large amounts of foreign capital very quickly.

In the more recent Kim Jae-Ik stabilization of 1981–83, the Korean authorities—fearful of the existing high level of international indebtedness—more deliberately limited new inflows, in addition to scaling down domestic interest rates as described above. Also, perhaps fortunately, by the early 1980s international banks were so overcommitted in their LDC lending that they did not swamp the Korean economy a second time.

Encouraging Liberalization without Absorbing Foreign Capital
Where do we come out on this for policy? At the very minimum, official agencies such as the World Bank and the International Monetary Fund should not try to buy a trade or financial liberalization by giving aid. It is wrong to try to bribe someone into liberalizing, because by injecting capital at the time the liberalization occurs, the liberalization is made much harder to sustain. The abortive efforts to liberalize trade in Pakistan and India in the 1950s and 1960s, where aid was sometimes used as a lever to induce governments in the subcontinent to expand the flow of imports into their economies, may indeed have failed for this reason. If foreign capital is allowed to come in, the real exchange rate turns against exporters and firms competing with imports and makes it unduly hard for them to adjust to the removal of protection.

The temptation to bribe a country into opening its trade accounts often occurs because it has an uncovered fiscal deficit, which the international agency agrees to cover if it agrees to liberalize. This is a bad combination if any liberalization is to be sustained for more than a few months or a year. Fiscal policy should be brought under control before, or along with, the move to liberalize foreign trade and the domestic capital market. Liberalization of the capital account of the balance of payments then comes last (for more complete analysis, see McKinnon 1982, 159–86, and Edwards 1984).

I realize the Chilean experiment ultimately broke down (as all Latin American economies got themselves into trouble in the early 1980s), even though Chilean fiscal policy was sound. Nonetheless, there is still a strong case for not requiring a big fiscal prop from some outside lender. As far as possible, trade liberalization and financial stabilization should be a "bootstrap" operation that a country performs for itself—possibly with technical assistance from agencies such as the World Bank. Exports and imports should remain in normal balance. If a big injection of official capital finances an unusual bulge in imports during liberalization, the wrong price signals are thrown out in private markets. Then, too, private lenders often magnify any such official injection by following the lead of the World Bank or IMF. Clearly, free inflows of foreign financial capital should only be allowed at the tail end of an otherwise successful program of liberalization. During liberalization, stringent controls on suddenly increased inflows of short-term capital are warranted.[4]

Reforming the International Capital Market

Apart from these macroeconomic control problems within individual LDCs, there is the failure of the institutions in the international capital market per se. Government guarantees—both in the industrial economies that do the lending, and in the borrowing countries—have created massive incentives to misallocate capital. How can one succinctly characterize the distortions involved?

(1) Neither private lenders in industrial countries nor private borrowers in LDCs see normal commercial risks. Good and bad projects get the same government credit guarantees.

(2) Commercial banks in the industrial economies have been less regulated in their risktaking in international lending than in their domestic lending. This inadvertent regulatory loophole was, in part, associated with the development of the Eurocurrency market in the late 1960s. Moreover, public agencies in the industrial countries, such as the U.S. Federal Deposit Insurance Corporation, give commercial banks undue incentive to take risks in the unregulated part of their loan portfolios without worrying about a run on their deposits. Consequently, commercial banks have completely preempted the inherently risky lending to LDCs. The dominance of commercial banks in the international capital market is an artifact of unbalanced regulatory policies in the industrial countries.

4. Immodestly, I should note that this need for restraint on the absorption of foreign capital was all spelled out in McKinnon 1973, chap. 11, before the international debt crisis in its modern format had evolved.

(3) Mainly as a consequence of (1) and (2), there has been virtually no development of a "normal" long-term primary securities market where borrowers in LDCs sell bonds or equities to individual lenders in the wealthier economies.

Clearly, the private international capital market today looks very different from how it did prior to World War I. At that time, the building of American or Argentinian railways was financed largely by the issue of long-term sterling bonds in London. Tea or rubber plantations were financed by the flotation of equities. A major bankruptcy in, say, a railway project would put the bond holders out of pocket without jeopardizing the solvency of any major bank or the monetary system. Commercial banks were confined to discounting short-term trade bills associated with identifiable inventories or goods in transit. Merchant banks did the (risky) underwriting of bonds or equity flotations and on occasion provided risk capital directly to overseas investment projects.

Although it sounds anachronistic, I think that the international market in private financial capital in the 1980s should be encouraged to evolve back to something closer to its late-nineteenth-century format. This would happen naturally, of course, if official guarantees of private credits were phased out, deposit insurance were circumscribed, and the regulation of the commercial banks' international and domestic activities were brought into better balance with respect to loan-loss provisions, capital restraints on lending heavily to one borrower (or guarantor), and so on. Commercial banks, the custodians of the national money supply and the international payments mechanism, should not be in the business of highly risky long-term lending.

Unlike in the nineteenth century, however, official agencies such as the World Bank or IMF would still play an important role for those countries that remained poor credit risks if and when the private flows of international finance were so liberalized. The World Bank's technical assistance and long-term project support for poor countries would remain invaluable, as would IMF's role as an international crisis manager on a shorter-term basis. Both would nicely complement the evolution of an active long-term international market in bonds and equities from which deposit-taking commercial banks were largely absent, although they might play a limited "facilitating" role:

> Even in an international bond or equity market, there is room, indeed an essential role, for banks—even perhaps for deposit-taking commercial banks. We saw that in all the major pre-1914 capital markets, financial in-

termediaries played a vital part, in examining the creditworthiness of governments and others seeking to borrow in negotiating the terms and conditions of a loan with the borrowing government, in organising or undertaking underwriting, in placing issues, and in marketing bonds by stock exchange listing or direct sale to the public. In London the financial intermediaries involved were specialised institutions, merchant banks and others functioning as issue houses, and stockbrokers and others as underwriters.

In France, Germany and the USA, industrial and even commercial banks were actively involved in foreign lending, individually or in consortia. But—and this is the decisive difference between most pre-1914 and general post-1970 practice—the banks did not, except temporarily, lend their own funds. They acted strictly as short-term intermediaries, taking up foreign securities but then selling them to the public as rapidly as possible. Thus they did not, to anything like the extent prevalent in the 1970s, themselves assume the risks of long-term lending.[5]

Of course, getting commercial banks out of the long-term international capital market cannot be accomplished any time soon. The existing debt-overhang in less developed countries is so large that only the banks have the capability of—and a strong enough vested interest in—refinancing it. In 1987 and beyond, the commercial banks must keep on lending to prevent widespread defaults in LDCs and the breakdown of their foreign trade.

That said, one need not implicitly assume that the commercial banks should dominate the international market in the 1990s as they did in the 1970s. Major changes in bank regulations are long overdue to avoid recurrence of another cycle of overlending by banks similar to that of the 1970s.

CONCLUSIONS

What then have we learned about increasing the efficiency of the international capital market in serving less developed countries?

To improve the institutional format for the international *supply* of loanable funds to LDCs, part 2 of this chapter argues for

(1) restructuring the nature of banking regulations in the industrial countries—undue incentives for large commercial banks to act directly as international financial intermediaries, apart from short-term well-collateralized lending, should be eliminated; and

5. Arndt and Drake 1985, 387. Arndt and Drake provide a most incisive analysis of how the nineteenth-century international capital market compares favorably with its distorted modern counterpart.

(2) phasing out various government credit guarantee programs—whether in the form of officially insured trade credits from institutions such as the U.S. Import-Export Bank or payment guarantees by LDC governments for international borrowing by their own nationals.

The objective of both of these measures is to encourage the development of more appropriate financial instruments—bonds or stocks—as better vehicles for longer-term, and necessarily risky, international transfers of capital to (selected) viable projects within LDCs.

But in order for LDCs to have an effective international *demand* for such loanable funds (by being willing and able to sell attractively structured primary securities in the world capital market), domestic price-level and exchange-rate stabilization is essential. Indeed, such monetary stability was characteristic of the late-nineteenth-century gold standard, when large transfers from mature to developing countries did occur through direct sales of primary securities, and was true for Mexico from 1954 to 1971, when it sold bonds in the New York capital market.

Consequently, part 1 of this chapter used the Chilean and Korean experiences as case studies and deals at some length with how best to secure monetary stability in LDCs once the necessary fiscal preconditions are satisfied. Successful financial and trade liberalization would set the stage for individual enterprises within an LDC to attract longer-term capital in the future by direct sales of primary securities in, say, the Eurobond market.

Somewhat paradoxically, however, an LDC liberalization program, where price-level and exchange-rate stability are achieved, is likely to attract "too much" private capital from abroad at the time it appears to be successful. Thus, in the transitional short run during the liberalization process, inflows of foreign capital should be strictly limited.

REFERENCES

Aghevli, Bijan, and Jorge Marquez-Ruarte. 1985. *A Case of Successful Adjustment: Korea's Experience during 1980–84*. IMF Occasional Paper no. 39. Washington, D.C.: International Monetary Fund.

Aghevli, Bijan, and Moshin Khan. 1978. "Government Deficits and the Inflation Process in Less Developed Countries." *International Monetary Fund Staff Papers* 25 (September): 383–416.

Arndt, H. W., and P. J. Drake. 1985. "Bank Loans or Bonds: Some Lessons of Historical Experience." *Banca Nazionale del Lavoro Quarterly Review*, no. 155 (December): 373–92.

Banco Central de Chile. Various issues. *Boletín mensual*. Santiago: Banco Central de Chile.

————. Various years. *Síntesis monetaria y financiera*. Santiago: Banco Central de Chile.

Bank of Korea. 1986. *Economic Statistics Yearbook, 1986*. Seoul: Bank of Korea.

Cheng Hang-Sheng. 1986. "Financial Policy and Reform in Taiwan, China." In H.-S. Cheng, ed., *Financial Policy and Reform in Pacific Basin Countries*, 143–60. Lexington, Mass.: Lexington Books.

Cho Yoon Je. 1985. "Status of Financial Liberalization." Unpublished paper. International Economic Research Division, World Bank.

————. 1986. "Inefficiencies from Financial Liberalization in the Absence of Well Functioning Capital Markets." *Journal of Money, Credit and Banking* 18 (May): 191–99.

Corbo, Vittorio. 1982. "Inflacion en una economia abierta: El caso de Chile." *Cuadernos de Economia* (April): 5–15.

————. 1985. "Reforms and Macroeconomic Adjustments in Chile during 1974–84." *World Development* 13 (August): 893–916.

————. 1986. "The Role of the Real Exchange Rate in Macroeconomic Adjustment: The Case of Chile, 1973–82." Paper presented at the Central Bank of Ecuador conference "Trade Liberalization," Quito, January 24.

Dornbusch, Rüdiger. 1985. *Inflation, Exchange Rates, and Stabilization*. NBER Working Paper no. 1739. Cambridge, Mass.: National Bureau of Economic Research.

Economic and Social Indicators. 1953–87. Santiago: Various publishers.

Edwards, Sebastian. 1984. *The Order of Liberalization of the External Sector in Developing Countries*. Essays in International Finance no. 156. Princeton: International Finance Section, Department of Economics, Princeton University.

Fry, Maxwell. 1978. "Money and Capital or Financial Deepening in Economic Development." *Journal of Money, Credit and Banking* (November): 464–75.

Harberger, Arnold C. 1985. "Lessons for Debtor Country Managers and Policy Makers." In G. W. Smith and J. T. Cuddington, eds., *International Debts and the Developing Countries*, 236–57. Washington, D.C.: World Bank.

International Monetary Fund. 1983. *Interest Rate Policies in Developing Countries*. IMF Occasional Paper no. 22. Washington, D.C.: International Monetary Fund.

Kane, Edward J. 1985. *The Gathering Crisis in Federal Deposit Insurance*. Cambridge, Mass.: MIT Press.

Luders, Rolf. 1985. "Lessons from Two Financial Liberalization Episodes: Argentina and Chile." Unpublished paper.

McKinnon, Ronald. 1973. *Money and Capital in Economic Development*. Washington, D.C.: Brookings Institution.

————. 1981. "Monetary Control and the Crawling Peg." In John Williamson, ed., *Exchange Rate Rules*, 38–49. New York: Macmillan Co.

————. 1982. "The Order of Economic Liberalization: Lessons from Chile and Argentina." In *Economic Policy in a World of Change*, 159–86. Carnegie-Rochester Conference Series on Public Policy 17.

————. 1986. "Financial Liberalization in Retrospect: Interest Rate Policies in LDCs." Paper presented at conference on development economics, Yale University, April 11–13.

Shaw, Edward. 1973. *Financial Deepening in Economic Development*. New York: Oxford University Press.

Stiglitz, Joseph E., and Andrew Weiss. 1983. "Credit Rationing in Markets with Imperfect Information." *American Economic Review* 73 (December): 913–27.

Tanzi, Vito. 1977. "Inflation, Lags in Collection, and the Real Value of Tax Revenue." *International Monetary Fund Staff Papers* 24 (March): 154–67.

Tybout, James. 1986. "A Firm-Level Chronicle of Financial Crises in the Southern Cone." *Journal of Development Economics* 24 (December): 371–400.

World Bank. 1984. *Annual Report*. Washington, D.C.: World Bank.

NOTES ON CONTRIBUTORS

Lawrence B. Krause is professor of international relations and Pacific studies at the University of California, San Diego.

Kim Kihwan is the former president of the Sejong Institute and Korea Development Institute in Seoul.

Anne O. Krueger is professor of economics at Duke University.

Gustav Ranis is director of the Economic Growth Center at Yale University.

Assar Lindbeck is director of the Institute for International Economic Studies at the University of Stockholm.

Chen Sun is president of the National Taiwan University.

Parvez Hasan is the chief economist of the Asian Division of the World Bank.

Juergen B. Donges and *Ulrich Hiemenz* are senior staff members of the Kiel Institute of World Economy in West Germany.

Wontack Hong is professor and chairman of the Department of Economics of Seoul National University.

D. Gale Johnson is provost and director of the Office of Economic Analysis of the University of Chicago.

Yung Chul Park is professor of economics at Korea University.

Ronald I. McKinnon is professor of economics at Stanford University.

INDEX

Africa, 105, 114, 229; agriculture in, 303, 327

Agricultural liberalization: difficulty of, 312–16; effect of, 17–18, 316–29; and prices, 283–84, 286

Agricultural products: as exports, 41–42, 68, 72, 285, 290; import controls on: *see* Agricultural protection; as imports, 74–75, 77; income spent on, 285–86; processing of, 304–7

Agricultural protection, 274, 279, 288, 301, 304–6; costs of, 287–89, 295, 298, 308; history of, 17, 289–98; international price effects of, 319–25; negative, 290, 298; politics of, 244, 300–304; in South Korea, 262, 268

Agriculture: discrimination against, 6, 37, 42, 69, 76, 83, 88–89, 104, 108, 114, 116, 132; and economic growth, 41–42, 52–53, 88, 158, 301–2; government intervention in, 40–45, 114–15, 287–89, 303 (*see also* Agricultural protection); labor force in, 284–86, 301, 316–20 (*see also* Farm incomes); political influence of, 14, 228, 302–4, 312; price support for, 88, 289, 290, 294–95, 298–99, 329; prices, 6, 17, 39, 42, 51, 283–88, 309, 324–25; productivity of, 28n.1, 29, 73, 75, 132, 285–86, 319; self-sufficiency in, xiv, 18, 206, 301, 307–12; technology for, 75, 112–13

Allen, Roy, 324

Anderson, Kym, 321

Argentina, 31; debt in, 177, 218, 392–94; exports from, 230–32, 234; inflation in, 223; liberalization attempts in, 138–39, 226–27, 237–38, 341, 345–51, 380

Australia, 325–26

Austria, 226n.5, 292

Balance of payments: and external shocks, 183–84; 237–38; and import controls, 13, 36, 215, 217, 255–56; and liberalization, 136, 227; and planning, 8, 149

Balassa, Bela, 134–35, 180, 237

Bangladesh: and agricultural liberalization, 325, 327; trade to, 172–73

Banks, 18–21; denationalization of, 195–96, 372; deregulation of, 20, 97; in developing countries, 94, 333; government guarantees for: *see* Deposit insurance; industrial control of, 344, 350–51, 360, 362; instability of, 335–36, 360, 362; international investment by, 22, 177, 179, 366, 392–93; nationalization of, 218, 345; regulation of, 19–21, 35, 224, 335–36, 361, 380–81, 389, 397; risktaking by, 20, 22, 24, 373–74, 385, 388–90, 395; role of, in industrialization, 340. *See also* Financial liberalization; Financial markets

Bates, Robert H., 303

Beef, 315, 323–45

403

Compositor: BookMasters, Inc.
Text: 10/12 Baskerville
Display: Baskerville
Printer: Braun-Brumfield, Inc.
Binder: Braun-Brumfield, Inc.